Fearless
Baking

OTHER BOOKS BY ELINOR KLIVANS

BAKE AND FREEZE DESSERTS

BAKE AND FREEZE CHOCOLATE DESSERTS

125 COOKIES TO BAKE, NIBBLE, AND SAVOR

Fearless Baking

OVER 100 RECIPES
THAT ANYONE CAN MAKE

Elinor Klivans

SIMON & SCHUSTER
NEW YORK LONDON
TORONTO SYDNEY SINGAPORE

SIMON & SCHUSTER
Rockefeller Center
1230 Avenue of the Americas
New York, New York 10020

DESIGNED BY DEBORAH KERNER

Manufactured in the United States of America

10 9 8 7 6 5 4 3 2 1

Library of Congress Cataloging-in-Publication Data
Klivans, Elinor.
Fearless baking : over 100 recipes that anyone can make / Elinor Klivans.
p.   cm.
Includes bibliographical references and index.
1. Baking. I. Title.

TX761 .K55 2001
641.8'15—dc21

2001031103

ISBN 0-684-87259-5

Acknowledgments

Judith Weber, my agent, who always knows the right road to send me down.

Janice Easton, my editor, whose passion for this book launched it on its great beginning.

Sydny Miner, my editor, whose expertise brought this book to its glorious finish.

Estelle Lawrence, my copyeditor, who checked each recipe so thoroughly and in such an encouraging manner.

Cole Riggs, Linda Osborne, and David Massucci, the photography team, who took such care with every photo and understood the concept of this book so well.

Roberta Rall and Sara Culmer, the food stylist and "sous" food stylist, who baked everything so perfectly and to look exactly the way it does when I make it.

An exceedingly big thank-you to the brilliant publishing group at Simon & Schuster; especially Toni Rachiele for so carefully supervising the in-house copyediting and Michael Accordino for his excellent cover design.

My husband, Jeff, who has the most amazing palate and tasted every single item in this book, some many times over, until we made everything better.

My daughter, Laura, who proofread every recipe, then sent back her encouraging notes, and my son-in-law, Michael, who is always ready to listen and try to help me.

My son, Peter, whose proofreading never lagged even though he lived thirteen time zones away and ended up correcting many a recipe late into the night.

My parents, Selma and Lester Wishnatzki, who gave me my start and filled my childhood with goodness and home baking.

A big thank-you to the Fearless Testers who bravely tested many of the recipes in this book: Carole Emanuel, Abby Fitzgerald, Karen Good, Howard Grossman, Helen Hall, Rosie Levitan, John Quattlebaum, Dawn Ryan, Allyson Shames, Louise Shames, Joe Siewers, Dana Strickland, Lisa Ward with Tucker's help, and Michael Williams.

A big thank-you to my circle of supporters and encouragers: Melanie Barnard, Flo Braker, Sue Chase, Susan Derecskey, Susan Dunning, Natalie and Harvey Dworken,

Lisa Ekus, Carole and Woody Emanuel, Barbara Fairchild, Betty and Joe Fleming, Mutzi Frankel, Karen and Michael Good, Kat and Howard Grossman, Helen and Reg Hall, Carolyn and Ted Hoffman, Pam Jensen and Stephen Ross, Kristine Kidd, Alice and Norman Klivans, Dad Klivans, Susan Lasky, Robert Laurence, Rosie and Larry Levitan, Jeanne McManus, Gordon Paine, Mary Jane Quattlebaum, Joan and Graham Phaup, Janet and Alan Roberts, Louise and Erv Shames, Gail Venuto, Elaine and Wil Wolfson, Jeffrey Young, and the family, friends, and Monday club members who shared their baking triumphs with me.

To Jeffrey, Laura, and Peter,
who make my journey
a continuous blaze of glory

To the memory of Selma Klivans,
who thought everything I baked was "divine,"
especially the brownies

Contents

Perfectly Easy Chocolate Chip Butterscotch Blondies ▪ Peanut Butter and Milk Chocolate Brownies ▪ Banana Butterscotch Blondie Sundae ▪ Any-Season Fruit Crumble ▪ Toasted Hazelnut Peach Crisp ▪ Apple Crumble Bars ▪ Deep-Dish Apple Strudel Pie ▪ Big-Top Corn Muffins ▪ Maple Muffins with Carrots, Pineapple, and Pecans ▪ Big, Easy Popovers ▪ Green Tomato and Cornmeal Pecan Crisp ▪ Baked Blintz ▪ Layered Cheddar, Vegetable, and Cashew Nut Pie ▪ Zucchini Bread Pudding

Contents
12

Introduction

Baking can result in a grand success or a total disaster. *Fearless Baking* is a recipe-by-recipe course in baking that will guarantee you success cookie by cookie and cake by cake. Even first-time bakers will be surprised at the ease and speed with which they'll turn out the same kinds of quality homemade treats they've envied in others' homes. Experienced bakers will find focused instruction on each aspect of baking, and original fail-safe recipes that can broaden your repertoire.

Several years ago my husband and I visited our son Peter, who was living in Japan. Since Peter was busy at work all day and we were unfamiliar with the territory, each night he would write out specific directions for the next day's sightseeing. Aside from names and locations, he also wrote helpful hints and little warnings to us. He would caution us to check that we took the up stairs rather than the down stairs in a train station, or note to watch out for different train lines coming in on the same track. Appreciative of the careful directions, I suddenly had a realization and asked him, "Peter, you've made all of these mistakes already, haven't you? That's how you know where to tell us to be so careful!"

I was right, and it inspired me to provide the same sort of detailed instruction for bakers. Whenever I try a recipe for the first time, I often either have a question or make a mistake. With that in mind, I have included a "baking answers" section at the beginning of every recipe to anticipate questions or problems, and explain the baking ideas that the recipe introduces or emphasizes. In a recipe for a butter cake, for example, the "baking answers" section explains the specific cake-mixing process; in a recipe for an angel food cake, it gives a detailed description of how to whip egg whites. In addition, the directions in each recipe not only include visual measurements, but also often provide descriptive instructions for recognizing when a batter is properly mixed or an item is done. We never got on the wrong train in Japan, and I believe that my directions will help you take the right turns with your baking, developing the confidence to make baking natural, comfortable, and a whole lot of fun.

The early chapters of *Fearless Baking* lay out and explain the basic baking terms and methods, and the equipment and ingredients that you should have on hand. Then, beginning with recipes that require nothing more difficult than stirring ingredients together, the chapters follow a natural order of slowly adding new skills and ingredients and building on what has been previously explained. I was surprised at how many recipes required nothing but stirring, and you'll be amazed at your scrumptious results on the first try. Muffins, crumbles, and brownies are just a few examples. Because I wanted *Fearless Baking* to be accessible to all, the rest of the chapters require no equipment more expensive than a handheld electric mixer—a $20 to $25 investment.

As you bake your way through, you'll notice that the simplest recipes are at the beginning of each chapter. As the chapter progresses, techniques or variations on techniques and new ways of using ingredients are added. I haven't isolated every possible idea in the baking world, but the ten I have covered provide a broad range of recipes to get you started and keep you baking for years to come. Bakers at all levels can choose recipes that they are comfortable making, while bakers with some experience can skip around and choose a new technique to try or a recipe that appeals to them.

One reason I know this book works is that many brave and "fearless testers" tested the techniques in each recipe. Whenever friends or family mentioned that they were afraid of a particular baking task, I asked them to test a recipe that used it. When my son-in-law, Michael, mentioned that he had never baked a cake, I whizzed the Lemon-Glazed Lemon Pound Cake off for him to try. My nonbaking friends and my daughter's young-baker friends all joined the group of brave testers as well. In fact, I have yet to meet some of my testers. When an amazing cookie baker from North Carolina sent me a letter about her love of cookie baking, she promptly became one of the cake testers. Clearly, the only reason I still have any friends left is that the recipes resulted in delicious treats and lots of fun for all. Of course, I learned a lot in the process. I now try not to assume anything about what I think people know. I also realize that a pastry brush or a wire rack is not necessarily found in everyone's kitchen, or that telling people to line a tube pan with paper could stop them in their tracks if I don't explain how to cut the paper. Surprisingly, I discovered that many people do not read a recipe through before beginning to bake, and I cannot encourage you strongly enough to read and shop before starting to bake.

Friends and family taste-tested many of the recipes, but I must thank my husband Jeff for faithfully tasting every version of every single recipe in this book. Finally, my daughter Laura and my son Peter earn my gratitude for reading every recipe for clarity, even though they loved finding my errors and delighted in telling stories about my recipe titled "currant scones" that had no currants, or my misplaced modifiers that implied I had married my friend Sue Chase.

But even with all that support, what really kept me going was the thought of helping others bake. Whenever I mentioned to a friend or relative that I was writing a book called *Fearless Baking,* they all had the same response—it was uncanny. "You must have been inspired by me," or "That is the book that I need!" I hope that I have written the book you need. I know that this is the baking book that I wish I had had to help me learn to bake.

Baking Language from "A" to Zest

The first thing you will notice when reading a recipe is that baking words often have their own unique meaning. In baking language, "fold" has nothing to do with paper, "flute" does not refer to music, and "score" is not a touchdown. Below is a brief description of words often used in baking directions.

Bake blind ⤙ To bake or partially bake a pastry crust before adding the filling.

Batter ⤙ An uncooked mixture of dry and wet ingredients that is pourable. Batters are made into cakes, brownies, muffins, and all manner of baked goods. They can vary in thickness from thin to thick, but all are liquid enough to pour.

Beat ⤙ To mix vigorously in a circular motion with a mixing spoon or an electric mixer.

Blanch ⤙ To loosen the skin of a nut or fruit by briefly cooking it in boiling water for about 1 minute. The boiling is followed by a plunge in cold water, and the skins slip off easily. Unblanched nuts refer to nuts that have skins. Almonds and peaches are common examples of fruit and nuts that are blanched to remove their skins.

Blend ⤙ To combine 2 or more ingredients into a smooth mixture. Blending is usually achieved by stirring or beating.

Cream ⤙ To beat a solid fat, such as butter or shortening, with sugar to form a smooth-looking creamy mass. Creaming creates a lighter mixture because air is incorporated during the beating process.

Crimp ⤙ To press 2 layers of pastry together to seal them. A fork or fingers can be used to crimp and form a decorative edge.

Cut in ⤙ To mix a cold solid fat into dry ingredients, such as flour or sugar, to achieve a crumbly mixture. Cutting in can be done with fingertips, a fork, 2 knives working together, a countertop electric mixer on low speed, or a pastry blender. A pastry blender has several U-shaped wires attached to a handle and is a tool for cutting fat into dry ingredients.

Dot ~ To scatter small pieces of an ingredient, usually butter, over the top of dough or pie filling.

Dough ~ An uncooked mixture of dry and liquid ingredients that is thicker and stiffer than a batter. Although dough is soft, the mass is firm enough to roll or knead. Some cookie doughs are soft enough to drop from a spoon onto a baking sheet.

Drizzle ~ Using a spoon or the tines of a fork to drop a thin stream of liquid frosting, glaze, or melted chocolate in a random pattern over the top of a baked item.

Dust ~ To sprinkle cornmeal or flour over a work surface to prevent sticking, or to sift powdered sugar or cocoa powder over a baked item. Dusting produces a light coating.

Flute ~ To form a decorative, fluted, grooved edge like the sides of a Greek column on an unbaked piecrust by pressing the dough between your thumb and forefinger.

Fold ~ A method used to gently combine a light mixture with a heavier one. Whipped egg whites and melted chocolate are examples of light and heavy mixtures best combined by folding. Folding is accomplished by using a rubber spatula to dig down to the bottom of a bowl that is holding the 2 mixtures and bringing the 2 mixtures up and over each other until they are combined.

Glaze ~ Glazing adds a light coating to unbaked or baked items. Unbaked items can be glazed by brushing them with beaten egg, cream, melted butter, or jam to color or flavor them. Baked items can be glazed with a thin coating or drizzle of frosting, flavored syrups, melted jam, or jelly to produce a sweet coating or shiny finish.

Knead ~ To press, fold, and stretch a ball of dough to achieve a smooth mixture. Kneading is done by pushing the dough down and forward against a firm surface then folding it in half and repeating the process until the dough is smooth.

Mix ~ A general term for combining 2 or more ingredients to incorporate them together or distribute them throughout a mixture. Mixing does not always produce a smooth mixture; blending does.

Ribbon ~ Used to describe a desired consistency for a thick batter that often consists of eggs and sugar. When the beater is lifted from a batter at the ribbon stage, the batter that drips back into the bowl forms a ribbonlike pattern.

Score ~ To make shallow cuts in dough either to make a decorative pattern or to mark it for cutting into pieces after baking.

Sift ~ To put dry ingredients through a flour sifter or wire mesh strainer to aerate them, break up lumps, or blend ingredients.

Stir ❧ To mix ingredients in a circular motion with a large spoon or an electric mixer on low or medium speed. Stirring is a slower action than beating.

Strain ❧ To pour or press ingredients through a wire mesh strainer or cheesecloth. Straining removes unwanted particles or produces a smooth puree or sauce.

Unmold ❧ To remove a baked item from its baking pan or container.

Whip ❧ To beat rapidly with an electric mixer or wire whisk to incorporate air into a liquid. This addition of bubbles of air to mixtures lightens them and increases their volume. Eggs, egg whites, and whipping cream are commonly whipped.

Whisk ❧ To use a multiwired whisk rather than an electric mixer to either whip air into a mixture or to smooth out a mixture. A whisk has a group of U-shaped wires joined to a handle.

Zest ❧ To remove the colored rind from citrus fruit. Zest also refers to the rind that is removed.

Ingredients to Have on Hand in Your Pantry

The first step in preparing to bake is to gather your ingredients to be sure you have what you need. The ingredients for all the recipes in this book, with the exception of some particular brands of chocolate and peeled hazelnuts (unpeeled hazelnuts are available), were all found at my local supermarket. Since I live in a small town in Maine, I figure that if I can get them here, you can get them anywhere.

Think of the ingredient list for a recipe as your shopping list. Before making a trip to the market, always check recipes that you plan to make so you can buy any missing items. It is also a good idea to make a note ahead of time if your flour, sugar, or any other basic ingredient runs low, so you can replace it on your next trip to the market. Once you start baking, you'll be hooked, and you never know when you'll want to whip something up at the last minute.

But remember that although many ingredients have a long shelf life, some should be checked for freshness before you go shopping. For example, baking powder has an expiration date, brown sugar should be soft, and nuts should be tasted to note a fresh rather than a rancid taste. I bake often, yet I sometimes discover that my dark brown sugar is rock solid or that my can of baking powder has expired. And even though there are many methods for softening hard brown sugar, I find that unless the brown sugar will be melted with liquid ingredients, it is best to discard it and buy a new box.

Below is a list of the ingredients used in many of the recipes, including a brief description of each and what to look for when buying them. There is also a list of mail-order sources at the end of the book for any ingredients that you may wish to order.

Butter, Shortening, and Oils ❧ All butter and margarine is the full-fat type. Low-fat margarine or low-fat butter products have water added and do not work in these recipes. When butter is used, it is unsalted. With unsalted butter, the amount of salt added to a recipe is controlled by you, not hidden in a stick of butter. However, the margarine I use is corn oil margarine and it does include salt.

I store unsalted butter and margarine in my freezer to keep them fresh. For vegetable shortening, I use Crisco shortening and buy it in the easy-to-measure stick form—do not use the butter-flavored shortening. When a recipe calls for vegetable oil, I use corn or canola oil and for olive oil I use extra-virgin olive oil from the first pressing of olives. Occasionally taste or smell all your oils to check that they have a fresh smell and taste and have not turned rancid. Baking with rancid oil isn't bad for your health, but it will take the pleasant flavor out of whatever you bake with it.

Chocolate ❧ The recipes call for unsweetened chocolate, semisweet chocolate, milk chocolate, white chocolate, or Dutch process unsweetened cocoa powder. Unsweetened chocolate is pure chocolate liquor with no added sugar, semisweet chocolate has sugar added to the chocolate liquor, and milk chocolate has sugar and milk solids added to the chocolate liquor. White chocolate does not contain chocolate liquor; it contains cocoa butter, sugar, and milk solids. Unsweetened cocoa powder is chocolate liquor with some of the cocoa butter pressed out. Dutch process cocoa powder is treated with an alkaline solution, which slightly sweetens its flavor and darkens its color.

Unsweetened and semisweet chocolate can be wrapped and stored in a cool, dark place for up to one year. Since milk and white chocolate contain milk solids that could turn rancid, I store them wrapped in the freezer until I am ready to use them. Defrost frozen chocolate with its wrapping on so any condensation occurs on the wrapper. It takes a few hours to defrost, but overnight is also fine. If you want to use part of a large piece of chocolate, the frozen chocolate breaks easily into pieces. Rewrap and return any remaining frozen chocolate to the freezer.

Use the type of chocolate specified in the recipes, as any substitutions will change the sugar, fat, and chocolate content and can ruin the result. White chocolate is not regulated as strictly as dark chocolate, so check the label to see that the white chocolate contains cocoa butter. Buying a good brand of chocolate or tasting it is a good idea. Lindt is a good-quality brand of chocolate easily found in supermarkets. Below are some brands of chocolate that I prefer to use.

unsweetened chocolate—Baker's, Nestlé, and Guittard

semisweet chocolate—Baker's, Lindt, and Callebaut

semisweet chocolate chips—Nestlé and Guittard

white chocolate chips—Ghirardelli Classic White Chips and Guittard Vanilla Milk Chips

milk chocolate—Lindt and Callebaut

white chocolate—Lindt and Callebaut

unsweetened cocoa powder—Droste or Hershey's European; both are Dutch process

Citrus Zest ❧ Citrus zest is the outside colored part of the rind of lemons, limes, oranges, and grapefruit. It is usually used after being grated into tiny shreds. Grate only the colored part of citrus rind; the white pith under the rind is bitter. Wash and dry the fruit before using it.

Cream and Milk ⤳ The cream in cartons labeled light whipping cream or whipping cream has from 30 to 36 percent butterfat. Note, though, that cartons labeled light cream that do not have the word whipping are not the same and will not whip. For my recipes, I use the term whipping cream and this is the cream that I use most often. Heavy whipping cream contains 36 to 40 percent butterfat; carton labels include the word "heavy" and should be labeled "heavy whipping cream" or "heavy cream." In recipes that use it, I use the term heavy whipping cream

Half-and-half contains at least 10.5 percent butterfat and is used when you want something that is somewhere between milk and cream in richness.

Whole milk contains 4 percent butterfat, low-fat contains 1 to 2 percent butterfat, and skim milk is considered fat-free. If the milk in a recipe should have a particular fat content, I have noted it. Otherwise, use any fat-content milk.

An 8-ounce (half-pint) container of cream, milk, half-and-half, or sour cream measures 1 cup, and a 16-ounce (pint) container measures 2 cups.

Eggs ⤳ For consistency, I always use large eggs in my recipes. I do have access to eggs from local farms and use them because I know that they are fresh and have nice bright yellow yolks. Many farm stands, farmers' markets, and upscale markets offer fresh local eggs. Eggs should be stored in the refrigerator.

I use room-temperature eggs for cheesecakes and let eggs sit at room temperature for 1 hour for pound cakes. When they are not cold, eggs combine smoothly with the other ingredients and won't cause the cream cheese in cheesecake batters or the large quantity of butter in pound cakes to firm up and become lumpy.

There is an ongoing debate about whether or not to bring egg whites to room temperature before whipping them firm. Tradition says yes, but I must admit that most of the time I forget to bring egg whites to room temperature before I use them. To clarify the matter for myself, I decided to do an experiment with cold egg whites and some room-temperature ones. After whipping them, I measured the volume results carefully, but noticed no significant difference. Beating sugar into the whipped egg whites did not seem to make any difference either. I have noticed that people in various parts of the country seem to have different results, so maybe there is some difference in other climates or with different egg producers. My choice is that it is not necessary to bring all egg whites to room temperature before whipping them, but it is fine to do so if you prefer.

Egg whites that are left over from a recipe can be frozen for up to 3 months. Put them in a clean, grease-free plastic freezer container, leaving at least an inch of air space, press plastic wrap onto the surface of the egg whites, and cover the container tightly. Label the container with the date and the number of egg whites in the container. Defrost the covered egg whites overnight in the refrigerator. I do not freeze or store leftover egg yolks. I use egg yolks immediately, or I discard them.

Since salmonella has been found in a small percentage of the millions of eggs sold in our country, I take precautions with eggs. Salmonella is killed at 160°F. I cook all custards to at least this temperature and use an instant-read food thermometer to check that this temperature is reached. The pastry cream on page 106 is brought to a boil that is well over 160°F., so there is no worry about cooking the eggs to a specific temperature.

Flavorings and Spices ❧ "Pure" is the word to look for with vanilla extract and almond extract. I use the McCormick brand, which is readily available in supermarkets. Instant coffee, liquor, and liqueurs should be used sparingly. They are flavorings rather than main ingredients, and too large a quantity can add bitterness.

Use fresh spices and fresh dried herbs and store them tightly covered. Storage times and conditions for different herbs and spices vary, and a simple way to check to see if they are fresh is to put a dab on your finger and taste it. If the spice or herb is no longer fresh, it will have little or no taste. Ground nutmeg loses its flavor quite quickly, so I buy whole nutmeg and use a nutmeg grater to grate fresh nutmeg whenever I need it. Although I usually use supermarket cinnamon to test my recipes, extra-fancy Vietnamese cassia cinnamon from Penzeys Spices (see Mail-Order Sources, page 384) is a full-flavored strong, sweet cinnamon that is worth trying. Penzeys has opened retail stores in Wisconsin, Minnesota, and Connecticut to sell their fresh spices and herbs.

Ground black pepper becomes dry and flavorless quickly, so I keep a pepper grinder filled with whole fresh peppercorns and grind fresh pepper as I need it. I use kosher salt, which is free of preservatives and has a clear, fresh salt taste. This slightly coarse salt does pass through my flour sifter and strainer. I do not use sea salt for baking, as it usually has a stronger salt flavor than kosher salt and recipes would have to be adjusted.

Flour ❧ I use unbleached all-purpose flour and cake flour in the recipes. I prefer unbleached all-purpose flour because it has not been treated with chemicals to whiten it. Fine-textured cake flour produces light and tender cakes and can be used in combination with unbleached all-purpose flour to produce tender pie pastry and cookies. Cake flour is commonly sold in 2-pound boxes that are usually found on a supermarket shelf near, and often above, the bags of flour. I do not use self-rising flour.

Fruit, Vegetables, and Fresh Herbs ❧ I have given information about specific fruits and vegetables in the recipes where they are used, but there are some general points to note when choosing fruit and vegetables. Buy fruit and vegetables in their season. They will be at their prime and will be at their lowest price. Look for fruit and vegetables that are free of bruises, look bright rather than dull, and have a fresh look about them. Pass by anything that looks shriveled or moldy. Summer peaches and strawberries will smell sweet and of the fruit if they have begun to ripen. Take a whiff and buy the ones that have the strongest peach or strawberry aroma.

Garlic and Fresh Herbs ❧ Look for bulbs of garlic that are plump, not shriveled or dried out, and are free of mold. Spring, summer, and fall is when you will find the plumpest, freshest garlic bulbs. I try to buy a few months' supply of garlic at our local farmers' market. The cloves of young, fresh garlic will not have a bitter small green strip in the center, but if you do find this green center, use a small knife to remove it and discard it.

Fresh herbs, such as basil or chives, should look bright green and not wilted.

Leavening Agents ❧ Baking soda, or sodium bicarbonate, is an alkaline leavening that is combined with an acid ingredient such as sour cream, molasses, or buttermilk to activate it. Once it is mixed into a moist batter, the baking soda activates and the batter should be baked. If kept dry, baking soda can be stored indefinitely.

I use double-acting baking powder. Double-acting baking powder contains baking soda (alkaline) and two acid ingredients. One of the acid ingredients is activated by liquid and the other is activated by heat. Batters that include double-acting baking powder do not have to be baked immediately, although this is usually a good plan to follow. Store baking powder tightly covered, and do not use it past the expiration date that is usually printed on the bottom of the can.

Nuts ❧ I use blanched almonds (without skins), unblanched almonds (with skins), pecans, walnuts, and peeled hazelnuts in the recipes. Since new crops of nuts appear in supermarkets from October to December, this is a good time to buy a year's supply. If the nuts are stored in the freezer in a tightly sealed heavy-duty freezer bag or plastic freezer container, they can be kept in good condition for up to one year. Defrost the nuts before using them in recipes, so they do not turn a batter cold and thick. Fresh nuts can be stored for a month in the refrigerator, but the freezer is best for longer storage. If any nuts are black or wrinkled, discard them. Pecan halves sometimes have small pieces of a bitter shell-like piece attached to the center that should be removed and discarded.

Sugars and Sweeteners ❧ Granulated sugar, light brown sugar, dark brown sugar, and powdered sugar are used in these recipes. All sugars should be stored tightly covered and in a clean, dry place. If granulated sugar becomes wet, it dries to a hard rocklike substance and cannot be used. Brown sugar contains molasses, and light brown sugar has less molasses than dark brown sugar. I do not use the granulated brown sugar. I store brown sugar in a sealed plastic bag that is rolled tightly against the sugar to keep it moist and to keep the air out. Powdered sugar, or confectioners' sugar, is granulated sugar that has been ground to a powder. Cornstarch is added to powdered sugar to prevent caking, but in some recipes powdered sugar is sifted before it is used in the recipe to remove possible lumps.

Light and dark corn syrup, molasses, and maple syrup are liquid sweeteners that are stored in the refrigerator to prevent any mold from forming. I use unsulfured molasses, which has a milder flavor than sulfured molasses and has not been processed with sulfur. Blackstrap molasses is too strong and bitter to use for baking.

Basic Baking Utensils— What You Need and What Is Nice to Have

Using the right utensils makes baking go smoothly. Measuring will be accurate, mixtures will blend the way you want them to, and baking will become comfortable. With the two groups of utensils listed here, you can prepare any recipe in this book. The first group of items is a list of general baking utensils to have on hand. This group is further divided into smaller and larger utensils. The second, smaller group lists items that are used occasionally in several of the recipes and can be bought as needed. I have tried to keep the number of baking-pan sizes to a minimum, and the short list of pans includes pans for making every recipe in this book. Although it would be fun to try to bake every recipe in the book, I imagine that even the most enthusiastic baker will not attempt this, so I suggest choosing some recipes to try, reading through the recipe, and acquiring pans and utensils as you need them. Another way to start out slowly is to borrow some baking utensils—mothers are often a good source for this.

These are the basic utensils that are used repeatedly.

Baking Pans ❧ Good-quality pans are worth buying. In the long run they will cost less and produce successful results that you will enjoy baking. A heavyweight baking sheet will turn out great cookies for years, while a flimsy one warps and bends easily and often produces burned cookie bottoms. As a new bride, I bought the least-expensive baking pans that I could find. When I began to replace them with sturdy, heavyweight pans, the difference it made in my baking was a revelation.

It is important to use the pan sizes specified in a recipe. Changing the size of a particular pan alters baking times and can cause some very odd changes in the texture and baked result. I once received an angry letter from a professional chef who was having trouble with a cake from one of my recipes overflowing out of the pan during baking. After some detective work, it turned out that he was using a pan with the correct dimensions, but the depth was 1 inch rather than 2 inches. The "Measure, Mix, and Bake!" chapter explains baking techniques and describes my method, on page 38, for figuring out if it is acceptable to substitute another size pan for the one called for in a recipe.

Type of Baking Pan	Pan Size
Baking sheets for cookies	17 x 14 inches to 15 x 12 inches
Jelly roll pans with 1-inch rim	15½ x 10½ x 1 inches
Loaf pans	9 x 5 x 3 inches or 6- to 8-cup capacity
Muffin tin or tins	to hold 12 muffins
Muffin tin with large openings (Texas size)	to hold 4 large popovers
Pie pan or pie dish, ovenproof glass	9-inch diameter, about 2 inches deep
Pie pans or shiny metal or ceramic pie dishes	9-inch round about 1½ inches deep
Round cake pans	2 pans—9 x 2 inches
Rectangular or square baking pans	9 x 9 x 2 or 11 x 7 x 2 inches
Rectangular baking pans, large	13 x 9 x 2 inches
Springform pans	9 x 3 inches
Tart pans with removable bottoms	9-inch round, 1-inch-high sides
Tube pans with fixed bottoms	9½ or 10 inches round, at least 3¾ inches high

Above is a list of all the pans used in this book. The jelly roll pan, loaf pan, and 13 x 9 x 2-inch rectangular pan are used in a small number of recipes in the book. Below is a brief description of the pans followed by the basic utensils to have on hand.

Baking sheets for cookies • These usually have open sides so that cookies can slide easily off the pan. The best baking sheets have a rim at one or both ends to grasp when removing the hot pans from the oven. Baking sheets come in different sizes and it is not crucial to have a specific size, but I prefer a larger baking sheet that holds more cookies. Heavyweight shiny metal, rather than dark metal, baking sheets are your best bet for producing evenly browned baked goods.

Jelly roll pans • These are baking sheets with 1-inch sides all around for baking thin cakes or for some bars. The chocolate cake for the Texas Chocolate Sheet Cake (page 175) and the ice cream cake roll (page 290) use a jelly roll pan.

Loaf pans • The most common loaf pan measures 9 x 5 x 3 inches, but loaf pans come in many sizes. I often use a capacity measurement. If the loaf pan holds 6 to 8 cups, it works fine for my recipes. If the Deep South Pound Cake (page 157) is baked in a loaf pan, you will need two of them. Aluminum foil loaf pans from the supermarket can be used. The Zuccotto—Italian

Chocolate and Vanilla Cream Cake (page 341) and the Deep-Dish Strawberry Whipped Cream Cake (page 312) each call for 1 loaf of this pound-cake recipe.

Muffin tins • Muffin tins come in pans that hold 6 or 12 muffins. I find 2 tins that hold 6 muffins each more versatile to own. Muffins, cupcakes, and the Fifty-Fifty Crumb Buns (page 148) all bake in muffin tins. The large popovers call for a muffin tin (Texas size) with openings that have a 1-cup capacity. I bought my pan in the supermarket. Large-size individual ovenproof baking cups with at least a ¾-cup capacity will work for the popovers.

Pie pans • I prefer shiny metal or ovenproof ceramic or glass pie pans. Dark metal pans hold the heat and can cause overbrowning. Glass pie pans, also called pie dishes, have the added advantage of allowing you to see what the crust looks like on the bottom of the pan as it bakes. The Chile, Cheese, and Chorizo Quiche (page 226) and Mom's Lemon Meringue Pie (page 270) are best baked in a fairly deep glass pie dish. I use a 9-inch-diameter Pyrex pie dish that is just under 2 inches deep as an all-purpose pie pan.

Round cake pans • These are used for baking any round cake, including the layers for frosted cakes. I use either heavy aluminum or All-Clad stainless steel–covered cake pans. The All-Clad pans have nice ear handles to hold when removing cakes from the oven and produce evenly baked cakes. I was given these deluxe baking pans to use for testing my recipes, and the only drawback that I see to them is their price, which is expensive.

Springform pans • I use a springform pan whenever I can. The sides release so there is never a problem about removing a cake or frozen dessert from its pan. Springform pans can actually serve as a mold for assembling a dessert. For an ice cream pie, you can bake the crust in the pan, put the layers together in the pan, and produce a perfectly straight-sided and evenly layered ice cream pie once the sides of the pan are removed.

Square or rectangular baking pans • These come in metal or ovenproof glass and I use either. Although it is sometimes recommended, I do not find that I have to adjust the oven to a lower temperature when using ovenproof glass pans.

Tart pans with removable bottoms • Tart pans have ridged 1-inch-high sides that produce a neat scalloped edge on baked tart crusts. Using a pan with a removable bottom makes it easy to remove the tart from its pan. The flat removable bottom of a tart pan is useful for moving cake layers around or sliding a cake or a cheesecake onto a platter. It works as a large, round spatula.

Tube pans with fixed bottoms • Tall tube pans with fixed bottoms and a center tube are used for baking large, thick cakes. When the center tube heats in the oven, cakes bake evenly by baking outward from the center tube and inward from the sides. Some angel food cake tube pans come with a removable bottom, but the batter for such cakes as a marble cake or pecan cinnamon coffee cake would leak out of a removable-bottom pan, so I recommend buying a tube pan with a fixed bottom that will work for all tube cakes. Chiffon and angel food cakes bake in ungreased pans, so choose a tube pan that does not have a nonstick lining. By taking into account the above notes, you can use 1 tube pan for baking many types of large cakes.

Electric Mixers ✶ I used a handheld mixer to test all of the recipes in this book. These mixers are less expensive than a standing countertop mixer and can do any job for any recipe included here. I used 3 different types of hand mixers: a Hamilton Beach mixer that I acquired with Green Stamps at least 25 years ago, a 2-year-old KitchenAid professional 9-speed mixer, and a Braun Multimix that I bought for under $20 at our local discount store. All 3 mixers performed the job (although the motor on the older Hamilton Beach mixer became pretty hot when mixing a stiff cookie dough), but each had its specialty. Hand mixers now come with beaters that have flat metal spokes or rigid wire spokes. I would opt for a hand mixer with the new wire spokes, so cookie dough does not get caught in the beaters. The flat metal beaters of the Hamilton Beach required quite a bit of scraping when I was mixing a firm dough. The wire spoke beaters did a fine job of whipping egg whites and whipped cream to a firm stage. The only advantage to my ancient Hamilton Beach over the new models is that this less powerful mixer is lighter in weight than my new ones. The KitchenAid mixer is my first choice because it has the wire beaters, and the speeds can be regulated from very slow to fast. The Braun mixer is the best for the price. It has the wire beaters, but it cannot be set to a very slow speed.

Of course, a standing countertop mixer works for any of the recipes.

Food Processors ✶ Several recipes in the book are mixed quickly and smoothly in a food processor. The food processor is the easiest way to grate the frozen shortening for the Fearless Piecrust (page 199). If given a choice, choose a large-capacity food processor with a powerful motor. An 11-cup capacity is a good general size. My current food processor is over 20 years old and proof that quality is a good investment.

Frying Pans, Saucepans, and Double Boilers ✶ Frying pans with sloping sides or straight-sided sauté pans are useful for browning onions and vegetables or cooking them to evaporate moisture. A frying pan with a 2-quart capacity is useful. Choose a pan with a heavy bottom. I prefer a pan with a nonstick finish that cleans easily.

I use saucepans with stainless-steel interiors, which will not react with acidic foods or discolor white chocolate. These saucepans have either a copper- or aluminum-clad bottom or inner lining to help the pans conduct heat evenly. Nonstick or ceramic pans are also nonreactive, but unlined aluminum, unlined copper, or cast-iron pans are reactive and can react with such acidic foods as buttermilk or tomatoes. A good range of sizes to own is a small 1-quart, a medium 2-quart, and large 3- and 4-quart saucepans.

My 2-quart saucepan has a stainless-steel insert to convert it into a double boiler and this is what I use for the 7-minute frosting (pages 263–66). If you don't have a double boiler, heat a small amount of water in a 4-quart saucepan and place a 2-quart nonreactive saucepan filled with whatever needs to be cooked or melted over the 4-quart saucepan. The rim of the smaller saucepan must rest on the rim of the larger saucepan. A copper- or aluminum-clad bottom on the saucepan diffuses the heat evenly and reduces the chance of overheating the ingredients.

Ovens ❧ Oven temperatures will vary about 10 degrees within the oven, with the upper third and rear of the oven usually being the warmest. It is a good idea to have your oven checked periodically by a service person or with an oven thermometer to see if the oven temperature that it is set at is accurate. A clue that there might be a problem is when your baked goods suddenly begin burning or underbaking during a normal baking period. I give visual tests for doneness in the recipes, which is a reliable way to check for doneness.

I baked all of these recipes in a standard oven, but a convection oven that has a fan to circulate air during baking produces an even heat all over the oven, so baked goods seldom need to be rearranged during baking for even cooking. If you bake with a convection oven, reduce the oven temperature by 25° to 50°F. My new convection oven needs a reduction of 25°F, but my older model (18 years) requires a 50°F temperature reduction. A good way to test what temperature reduction is best for your convection oven is to bake something that you are familiar with baking, bake it at either 25° or 50°F. lower than you would in a standard oven, and note what happens.

The utensils listed below are the inexpensive smaller items to have on hand that I use repeatedly.

Cooling Racks ❧ I use a rectangular cooling rack with thin cross-woven wires, which support a cake without digging into it. Rectangular racks hold almost any size cake or a large number of cookies. Owning 2 wire racks is useful.

Graters and Peelers ❧ I use the new microplane graters, patterned after a woodworker's rasp, to grate citrus rind, and I strongly recommend that you buy one of these great tools, which make grating citrus rind fun. For grating larger shreds of cheese, I use a 4-sided box grater.

A stainless-steel vegetable peeler with a 2½-inch vertical blade that is an extension of the handle is an inexpensive multitask tool. It is used for peeling vegetables, grating chocolate curls, and removing large strips of rind from citrus fruit.

Knives ❧ A small, sharp paring knife with a 4½-inch blade is useful for loosening desserts from their pans. A large chef's knife with an 8-inch blade is good for chopping and for cutting large cakes and firm desserts like ice cream pies. A serrated bread knife with an 8-inch blade splits cake layers evenly.

Measuring Spoons and Cups ❧ One set of 4 metal measuring spoons is all you need. It is important to use dry measuring cups for easy and accurate measuring of dry ingredients and a liquid measuring cup for measuring liquid ingredients. The dry measuring cups come in sets of 4 gradations and I recommend buying the stronger metal ones over the plastic ones. Measure dry ingredients by filling the cup and leveling the top with a thin metal spatula. For liquids, use cups with clear markings and place the measuring cup on a flat surface when measuring. A 2-cup liquid measuring cup is a good general size to have on hand.

Metal Tins or Rigid Plastic Containers ❧ These are useful for storing and freezing cookies, bars, and sauces. Square containers take up less room in a freezer. I prefer metal tins for storing or freezing cookies and bars. They do a good job of keeping moisture from food. I find cookies remain crisper longer at room temperature if stored in a metal tin. Check plastic containers to make sure that they are free of odors before storing anything in them.

Mixing Bowls ❧ I state the size of a mixing bowl in the recipes, so that you can choose a bowl that is large enough to hold the ingredients. A small mixing bowl refers to a 2- to 3-cup capacity, a medium bowl about a 6-cup capacity, and a large bowl a 2- to 5-quart capacity. It is fine to choose a mixing bowl that is larger than the one called for in a recipe. Several recipes call for using 2 large mixing bowls. Pyrex bowls are heatproof, inexpensive, and chip resistant, and I have been using the same set for over 30 years. Stainless-steel bowls are another inexpensive option and are easy to clean, will not react with ingredients, and are virtually unbreakable. I do not recommend plastic mixing bowls because they can absorb odors and fat.

Mixing Spoons ❧ Have at least 1 wooden spoon to use when cooking sugar to a high temperature. Since wood is a poor conductor of heat, a wooden spoon will not draw heat from a mixture, nor will it melt. For general mixing, I have several heatproof plastic mixing spoons, which do not absorb odors as wooden spoons might.

Paper, Nonstick, and Aluminum Foil Liners ❧ Parchment paper, which usually comes in rolls, is the most practical liner for baking pans and for lining baking sheets. Wax paper can be used to line cake pans since the paper is covered by the cake batter, but it is not suitable for lining cookie sheets since it will smoke and burn where it is not covered by the cookies. In most cases, I find parchment paper easier to handle, but heavy aluminum foil can be used in its place.

Another baking liner now available is a nonstick liner. I use them for lining baking sheets and they work especially well when used for lace cookies. There are two types of nonstick liners available. Thin nonstick liners can be cut to fit baking sheets, or more expensive, thick Silpat nonstick liners can be bought finished in 2 sizes to fit most baking sheets. Both of them can be wiped clean and used repeatedly. Both liners are available from King Arthur Flour's Baker's Catalogue, and Silpat liners are available from Bridge Kitchenware, listed in Mail-Order Sources on page 384.

Pastry Brush ❧ This is really handy to have for brushing an egg wash or melted butter over a dough or for brushing a liquid glaze onto a cake. Buy a good-quality pastry brush that will not drop its bristles into your desserts. A 1-inch-wide brush with 2-inch-long bristles is a useful size. I clean mine in the dishwasher.

Rolling Pins and Where to Roll Dough ❧ Choose a rolling pin that is comfortable for you to handle. I prefer wood, but there are marble and stainless-steel rolling pins available. These do remain cooler than a wooden rolling pin, but I find wooden rolling pins work fine, and marble ones are quite heavy.

For a rolling surface, I use a freestanding white ceramic cutting board that has hard rubber feet. The surface remains cool; it measures a substantial 16 x 18 inches; it is lightweight; and it can be washed in the kitchen sink. When I'm not using it for rolling, it doubles as an extra cutting surface. I bought it at a local kitchen design center, but kitchen shops and department stores are another source. A clean, smooth kitchen countertop or a clean canvas pastry cloth also work well. Some sticky doughs are rolled between pieces of wax paper and these are best rolled on the flat countertop.

Spatulas ❧ A rubber spatula is used to scrape every bit of batter from a bowl. A thin metal spatula is used for frosting cakes, smoothing glazes, and smoothing the top of a batter in its pan before it is baked.

An wide offset metal spatula, which looks like a pancake turner with a long blade, is useful for sliding desserts onto a platter and sliding bars off a baking liner, or cookies off a baking sheet.

Strainers and Sifters ❧ I have a flour sifter with a rotary handle that I use for sifting flour with most other ingredients. If I use the flour sifter to sift cocoa, it must be cleaned, which is difficult, so I use a mesh strainer to sift cocoa powder by itself or with other ingredients.

A mesh strainer can substitute for a flour sifter. I use a strainer or a flour sifter to sift dry ingredients onto a large piece of wax paper and save cleaning an additional bowl. Strainers can strain lumps from dry ingredients, remove lumps from batters, remove overcooked bits from custards, and remove small seeds from fruit. My strainer holds about 4 cups of dry ingredients and is a good size for general use. Strainers can be washed in the dishwasher for easy cleaning.

Whisks ⌁ A stainless-steel sauce whisk is an inexpensive but valuable utensil for mixing a mixture smooth, whisking lumps out of mixtures, or for adding melted chocolate smoothly to cold whipped cream. I prefer to beat egg whites and whipped cream with an electric mixer rather than a whisk, so I seldom use a balloon whisk, which has a round bottom and more wires than a sauce whisk does.

The list below describes utensils that are used occasionally in some of the recipes or are nice to have:

Cardboard Cake Circles ⌁ Cookshops sell these corrugated paper circles in several sizes. They provide a good flat surface for holding a cake and are useful for transporting or freezing a cake so that a favorite platter doesn't have to sit in the freezer for several months. I cover cardboard cake circles with a doily when carrying a cake to a friend, so there is no platter to break or return. If a dessert has a high butter content that might be absorbed by the cardboard circle, wrap the circle with aluminum foil. The circles can also be cut from clean cardboard and wrapped with aluminum foil. Stack 2 pieces of cardboard together so they do not bend under the weight of a cake.

Instant-Read Thermometer ⌁ I use an instant-read food thermometer that measures from 0° to 220°F. Instant-read food thermometers make an accurate check for testing the temperature of custard mixtures or ingredients, such as soft butter, hot milk, or cream.

Pastry Bags and Pastry Tips ⌁ A 16-inch pastry bag is a good all-purpose size. Wash pastry bags after each use with soap and water and dry them on a sunny windowsill to prevent them from developing a musty odor. There are also strong plastic disposable pastry bags available that I recommend highly. A writing tip with a small hole for drawing thin lines, dots, or letters, and a large star tip such as an Ateco #5 for piping swirls are the 2 pastry tips that I use in this book. A round tip with a ½-inch opening is another useful size for piping out a meringue mixture into a circle or other shape. I prefer 2-inch-long pastry tips to the 1-inch-long size.

Measure, Mix, and Bake! Explaining Baking Techniques

Baking techniques have descriptive names, but these are the briefest of descriptions. We know what blend or whip means, but when these words refer to mixing ingredients, a more detailed description is desirable for understanding the process. The baking techniques that are used in this book are described below. I have divided them into the 3 groups of measuring, mixing, and baking, which is in the order that they are normally performed in a recipe. Since chocolate decorations and freezing baked goods come under the heading of finishing or storage, I have listed those at the end.

What can you expect to find in a recipe? ⤴ Recipes are reassuring. There is no flying by the seat of your pants when using recipes, because you are working from a complete list of supplies and detailed instructions that explain how to make a dish. But understanding how to read recipes and knowing what information they offer is the best way to become comfortable with baking.

My recipes begin with an introductory paragraph that describes the dish and may tell about its heritage or what inspired it. This introduction leads you into the recipe and helps you to decide whether or not to try it. It is followed by a "Baking Answers" section that has helpful hints for following the specific directions in a particular recipe and anticipates questions that might arise while making it. If some or all of the recipe can be prepared ahead of time, there is "A Step Ahead" section with storage directions included when needed.

The details of the recipe follow, and it's always a good idea to read them through well beforehand so you can plan for any advance steps such as softening butter or cream cheese, chilling a mixture or dough, and preheating the oven. Above the ingredient list is a short line that tells the number of servings or number of pieces the recipe makes. A pie often has 8 servings, but brownie or cookie recipes usually give the number of pieces.

The ingredient list tells what to have on hand and how much is required for the recipe.

Even if I bake something often, I still check the ingredient list against my pantry supplies before shopping. It's an easy way to avoid discovering an item is missing as you start to bake. Ingredients are listed in the order that they are added, so I measure each ingredient and set it out on the counter in the order that it will be used. When all of the items have been mixed in, I know that everything has been included.

Multipart recipes separate the ingredients and directions into groups. A cake with a frosting has one ingredient list for the cake and one for the frosting. Directions for making the cake and those for making the frosting are also grouped separately.

Directions for mixing, baking, and serving the recipe follow the list of ingredients. First, preheat the oven and prepare baking pans by lining or buttering them, if needed. Readying ingredients that require some sort of combining or preparation beforehand comes next. Sifting dry ingredients or preparing fruit are examples. Then the mixing of individual ingredients begins. As each group of ingredients is mixed together, there is a visual clue and often a numerical mixing time given. For example, flour may be mixed just until it is incorporated. Or an instance of a visual and a time clue is when eggs might be blended into a mixture until the mixture is smooth or for about 2 minutes. Complete detailed explanations of such techniques as whipping cream or beating egg whites are listed for easy access in this technique chapter, but the process is described in each recipe.

Once ingredients are mixed and doughs are formed into desired shapes, it's time to bake. Now the oven does all of the work. All that's necessary is to decide when something is done. As in mixing, having both a visual and a time test is helpful, especially since individual ovens differ in how they cook food. Timed tests are approximate and such visual tests as checking a cake with a toothpick or checking the color of a meringue should be followed. When baking is completed, the recipe tells how to cool the item, remove it from the pan, serve it, and store it. Any variations on the recipe appear at the end.

Measure

MEASURING INGREDIENTS

Measuring accurately is an easy way to make sure that your baking succeeds. Measure dry ingredients by filling dry measuring cups to the top and leveling the top evenly. A thin metal spatula works well for scraping excess off the top of the cup. I also use a clean finger, which is always handy, to gently level the top, while carefully making sure that I do it evenly. Liquid measuring cups should be placed on a flat surface and filled to the desired level. Holding a liquid measuring cup in the air can cause a false measurement if the cup tilts. Use standard measuring spoons to measure tablespoons, teaspoons, and fractions of teaspoons. Fill the measuring spoon to the top and level off the top smoothly. It is useful to know that 3 teaspoons equals 1 tablespoon and 4 tablespoons is the same as ¼ cup.

The word order of ingredients signals different ways to measure. One cup of chopped nuts is different from one cup of nuts, chopped. If "chopped" appears before the word "nuts," measure chopped nuts. If chopped appears after the word nuts, measure the nuts and then chop them. I measure flour before I sift it. Sifting flour adds about 2 tablespoons of volume per cup, so it would make a big difference in a recipe if flour was sifted and then measured. To accurately measure brown sugar, pack it firmly into a dry measuring cup. Brown sugar is moist and does not spread evenly in a measuring cup if it is gently spooned into it.

Some ingredients are measured by weight but include volume measurements for clarity. For example, 1 stick of butter weighs ¼ pound. To avoid confusion, I give the weight, but also state the quantity in sticks of butter—6 ounces of butter would also be listed as 1½ sticks. But an odd-numbered amount, such as 5 tablespoons, would be listed in tablespoons. Note that butter wrappers have tablespoon markings on them. It's easy to cut through the wrapper and cut butter evenly when the butter is cold. Chocolate is another ingredient that is often measured by weight. Baking chocolate comes in boxes of 1-ounce pieces, and large chocolate bars are sold by weight—6 ounces of chocolate chips equals 1 cup, so 3 ounces equals ½ cup and 2 ounces is ⅓ cup.

When measuring sticky ingredients such as corn syrup or molasses, rub the measuring cup or measuring spoon lightly with vegetable oil and the sticky syrups pour out easily.

Some useful measurements to know are:

3 teaspoons = 1 tablespoon

16 tablespoons = 1 cup or 8 fluid ounces (4 tablespoons = ¼ cup or 2 fluid ounces)

⅓ cup = 5 tablespoons + 1 teaspoon

2 cups = 1 pint

2 pints = 1 quart

4 cups = 1 quart

4 quarts = 1 gallon = 16 cups

4 ounces butter = 8 tablespoons = 1 stick

1 cup chocolate chips = 6 ounces

1 cup nuts = about 4 ounces (varies slightly with type of nut and whether chopped or not)

PAN MEASUREMENTS

The baking pan measurements given are the inside measurements of the pan. The pan measurements given in a recipe should be followed, and only pans of similar size substituted. Using a larger pan for a cake could cause the thinner cake to dry out and burn. On the other hand, using too small a pan could cause the batter to rise and spill over the sides of the pan while certainly affecting the baking time. Some pans of similar size that can substitute for each other are 9-inch round pans for 8-inch square pans and 10-inch round pans for 9-inch square pans, as long as the depth of both pans is equal.

I do have a method for determining if it is possible to substitute another size pan than the one called for in a recipe. First, check that both pans have the same depth, then find the area of each pan. If one pan is round and another square or rectangular, you must figure out the area of a circle for the round pan. If you find that the area of each pan is within 8 inches of the other and the depth is the same, there should be no problem using either pan. For example, many of my recipes call for a 9 x 9 x 2-inch square pan or an 11 x 7 x 2-inch rectangular pan. The area of the square pan is 81 inches, the area of the rectangular pan is 77 inches, and the depth of each is the same 2 inches. Since the difference in area is only 4 inches, either pan works. Baking sheets for cookies can be various sizes, but using smaller sheets requires baking more batches.

READYING INGREDIENTS TO MEASURE AND PREPARING PANS FOR BAKING

Sometimes an item on an ingredient list calls for a preliminary preparation such as peeled peaches or grated citrus zest. Similarly, before you mix ingredients, the directions tell you how to prepare the pan for that recipe. This may include buttering a pan or lining it with parchment paper or aluminum foil.

BLANCHING TO PEEL PEACHES AND TOMATOES ▪ After a quick plunge in hot water and a quick cooling in cold water, peach or tomato skins can be removed easily. To peel peaches or tomatoes, fill a large bowl with ice cubes and water and have ready a saucepan of boiling water large enough to cover 4 or 5 peaches or tomatoes. Put the peaches or tomatoes in the boiling water. Boil them for about 30 seconds, then use a slotted spoon to transfer them to the ice water. If you have more peaches or tomatoes to peel, add them to the boiling water and repeat the process. Leave the peaches or tomatoes in the ice water for about 5 minutes or just until they are cool enough to handle. Pierce the skin with the tip of a sharp knife, and the skin slips off easily.

GRATING CITRUS ZEST ▪ The colored part of the rind of lemons, limes, and oranges produces citrus zest. Grate and use only the colored part of the rind. It has a good, strong citrus flavor, while the white pith under the rind is bitter. Recently, an excellent grater for grating citrus zest has appeared on the market. Inspired by a woodworker's rasp, it is a long thin rectangular piece of metal with tiny holes that is sometimes marketed as a microplane grater. Sweep the fruit against the holes and clouds of finely shredded zest will roll right off the grater. A 4-sided box grater that has a side with small teardrop-shaped holes also works. Less desirable and more time consuming is to peel the colored rind from the fruit and chop it very finely. Lemon zester tools remove the zest, but they produce strips that still need to be finely chopped. When a recipe calls for zest and juice, it is easier to grate the zest before squeezing the juice.

Citrus zest often clings to the beaters of an electric mixer during mixing. Scrape the zest off the beaters and stir it back into the mixture.

INGREDIENT TEMPERATURE: COLD, SOFT, OR MELTED ▪ Cutting cold butter or shortening for pastry and crumb mixtures into small pieces simplifies and speeds up the mixing process. On the other hand, when butter is going to be blended smoothly into a batter or dough, it must be softened. Let butter sit at room temperature to soften. To check to see if the butter is properly softened, press it with your finger; it should be easy to make an indentation. If the recipe calls for butter to be melted, measure it before melting it, and heat it over low heat to prevent the butter from popping and bubbling up or burning.

In order for whipping cream to whip properly, it must be cold. Cream or milk that is going to be incorporated into a mixture such as a cake batter will probably be cold. When cold cream or milk is added to a creamed butter and sugar mixture, it chills the mixture slightly, hardens tiny pieces of butter, and causes a curdled look. This is not a problem because the mixture smooths out when flour is added. Adding the flour and liquid to a batter in alternate portions prevents excessive curdling. Begin and end the additions with the flour mixture to further reduce curdling and assure a smooth result at the end. When a recipe requires milk or cream to be heated, it is done over a low heat and explained in the recipe directions.

Ingredient lists sometimes specify that eggs should be at room temperature or cold or that yolks and whites should be separated. It is easier to separate eggs when they are cold and then bring them to room temperature. Some cookie dough recipes call for cold eggs in order to produce a slightly firmer dough than room temperature eggs would.

CRACKING AND SEPARATING EGGS ▪ To crack whole eggs, rap the eggshell crosswise along the middle of one side of the egg on the thin edge of a bowl to make an even break on the eggshell about halfway around. Hold the egg over a bowl to catch drips and use your thumbs to pull the 2 halves of the shell apart, dropping the whole egg into the bowl. Egg whites are usually separated from the yolks so that they can be whipped and the yolks and whites added separately to a recipe. To separate egg yolks from egg whites, have ready a small bowl for the yolks, a small bowl to break 1 white at a time into, and a large bowl to hold all of the egg whites that will be used. It is a good idea to break egg whites into a small bowl then transfer them one at a time to a large bowl, so if the yolk breaks and mixes into the white, you will have lost only 1 egg white. Make the same crosswise break as when cracking a whole egg, but as you pull the halves of the eggshell apart keep the yolk in one half of the shell (the yolk clings to the shell) and let the egg white drip into a small bowl. Carefully pour the remaining egg yolk from 1 half-shell to the other until all of the white has dripped into the small bowl. Put the egg yolk in another small bowl. Transfer the white to the large bowl and continuing separating as many eggs as needed.

NUTS AND COCONUT: TOASTING, PEELING, CHOPPING, AND GRINDING ■
Toasting nuts intensifies their flavor and, in some cases, actually changes the taste. Walnuts and pecans can be toasted to deepen their flavor, but almonds and hazelnuts are toasted to a golden color that changes their flavor. Both toasted and untoasted almonds are used in these recipes, but hazelnuts are always toasted in my recipes before they are used. If nuts are frozen, thaw them before toasting or allow additional baking time. I toast all nuts by spreading them in a single layer on a baking sheet and baking them in a preheated oven. Walnuts and pecans bake at 325°F. for about 8 minutes. Blanched sliced or slivered almonds bake at 350°F. for 12 to 15 minutes until they become evenly golden, and blanched whole almonds and hazelnuts bake at 350°F. for about 15 minutes until they become golden. Shake the baking pan once during the baking to redistribute the nuts and ensure that they toast evenly. Just before the nuts are ready, you should smell a pleasant aroma of toasting nuts. Hazelnuts acquire a sheen as some of their oil rises to the surface during baking. Watch nuts carefully during baking to prevent them from burning.

Hazelnuts must have their bitter peel removed before they are used. The easiest method is to buy previously peeled hazelnuts. These are usually available in specialty markets, but they can be ordered through the mail from King Arthur Flour Company (see page 384). Otherwise, I find blanching is the easiest way to remove the peel from hazelnuts. To blanch them, fill a saucepan with enough water to cover the hazelnuts and bring the water to a boil. Add the hazelnuts and boil them, uncovered, for 5 minutes. Drain the hazelnuts in a strainer, immerse them in cold water for several minutes to cool, drain again, and peel the nuts with a small sharp knife. The skin will come off easily, and they will dry out in the oven when they toast. If the hazelnuts are not toasted immediately, dry them with a clean dish towel and refrigerate or freeze them.

Nuts can be chopped in a food processor, but I prefer to chop them with a large sharp knife, which allows more control over the size of the chopped nut. A food processor invariably grinds some of the nuts rather than chopping them, which won't ruin a recipe but might change the result slightly. When I list nuts as finely chopped, they are about ⅛ inch in size, while coarsely chopped nuts are between ¼ inch and ⅜ inch in size. To grind rather than chop nuts, a food processor fitted with the steel blade works well. For finely ground nuts, process the nuts with some of the sugar, powdered sugar, or flour from the recipe, which allows the nuts to become finely ground without forming a paste.

To toast coconut, position a rack in the middle of the oven and preheat the oven to 300°F. Spread the coconut in a thin, even layer on a baking sheet. One baking sheet holds up to about 4 cups. Bake for about 15 minutes until the coconut becomes evenly golden, stirring twice during the baking. Watch the coconut carefully toward the end of the baking time to prevent burning. Cool the coconut before using it, about 30 minutes.

PANS: GREASING AND LINING ▪ Greasing pans, usually with butter, helps baked goods release easily from the pan. When I soften butter for a recipe, I remove the butter and rub the butter wrapper, which has some butter clinging to it, over the inside of the pan that I want to grease, and then rub the pan with additional soft butter (not using the measured butter for the recipe), if necessary. Paper liners ensure that a baked good will not stick to the pan or that cookies will not stick to a baking sheet. Lining baking pans also makes cleanup easy. Parchment or wax paper can be used to line cake pans, but baking sheets must be lined with parchment paper as wax paper burns where it is exposed. Aluminum foil, preferably heavyweight foil, can be used to line baking sheets and makes a good heavy liner for baking pans that hold bars that have a tendency to stick to the pan. The heavy aluminum foil is less likely to tear than regular weight. Leave some ends of foil overhanging the edge of the pan so that the baked bars and foil lift out easily.

To cut liners for any pan bottom use the bottom of the pan for a guide. To cut a liner for a tube pan turn the pan upside down. Place a piece of wax or parchment paper on top of the bottom of the pan and use the bottom of the pan as a guide to cut a paper circle the same size as the bottom. Use the tip of the scissors to draw an outline in the middle of the paper circle for the hole in the bottom of the pan. Set the pan aside. Fold the marked paper circle in half and cut along the outline of the hole. Open the circle and fit it inside the bottom of the pan. To cut a paper liner that fits inside a round or square baking pan, turn the pan upside down and use the bottom of the pan as a guide. Place a piece of wax or parchment paper on top of the bottom of the pan and use the bottom of the pan as a guide to cut a circle or square the same size as the bottom. I usually cut 2 or 3 paper liners at a time. After washing and drying the baking pan, I put a clean liner in the bottom of the pan, so it is ready for baking another cake.

I grease pans with the same type of shortening that is used in the recipe I am baking. For example if I use oil in a cake, I rub the inside of the cake pan with oil. Grease the bottom and sides of a baking pan carefully so that there are no bare spots. Occasionally a recipe directs to grease the bottom only of a pan. When adding a liner to the bottom of a baking pan, butter the pan bottom, then add the liner and butter it. The butter on the pan holds the liner in place, and a buttered liner releases easily from a cake.

SIFTING DRY INGREDIENTS ▪ Sifting dry ingredients removes lumps and aerates them slightly. One cup of flour becomes about one cup plus 2 tablespoons after sifting. Sifting also distributes small quantities of ingredients like baking powder throughout a mixture. Sifting the dry ingredients changes the final result, so sift where directed but sift only when the recipe calls for sifting. Occasionally the directions call for stirring the ingredients together but not sifting them. This is to blend the ingredients but not aerate them.

To sift dry ingredients, put all of them in a dry strainer or flour sifter and strain or sift them into a bowl or onto a piece of wax paper. It is a good habit to sift ingredients when you are ready to use them, since dry ingredients that are sifted ahead on a humid day can absorb moisture if left to sit.

Mix

When you have everything ready to prepare a recipe, it is time to mix it together. Ingredients can be mixed to many stages. They might be mixed smooth or into crumbs, beaten vigorously, or simply blended together. Such ingredients as whipping cream or egg whites have basic methods for mixing them to a desired stage. The list below, which is in alphabetical order, includes the baking terms that you might encounter when mixing a recipe. No recipe uses all of them, but this is the place to check for any unfamiliar terms.

BEATING EGGS ▪ The word "beating" is a signal that mixing will be vigorous. Use a large bowl for beating eggs to allow for expansion as the eggs or egg whites take in air. Whole eggs and egg yolks are beaten until their color lightens and they thicken. When sugar is beaten with eggs, egg yolks, or egg whites, the mixture becomes more dense and the foam more stable.

When egg whites are beaten, their foamy mixture is more delicate than that of egg yolks. Because acid helps to stabilize egg white foams, cream of tartar, an acid, is often beaten with them. As a general rule, I add 1/16 of a teaspoon of cream of tartar for each egg white. Egg whites will not whip properly if they come in contact with fat, so remove every speck of egg yolk that might have fallen into egg whites. An eggshell half works well for removing egg yolk from egg whites. If a yolk breaks and distributes itself throughout an egg white, it is a good idea to discard that egg white or use it for something else. As long as the egg whites do not contain any egg yolk, and the mixing bowl and utensils are clean and absolutely free of fat, there will be no problem.

Properly beaten egg whites are shiny and will form a soft point or peak if you dip a spoon in the egg white and lift it out. At the soft-peak stage, the moving beaters form smooth curving lines in the egg whites. Egg whites at the soft-peak stage look creamy; they combine smoothly and easily with other mixtures. It is preferable to underbeat egg whites slightly than to overbeat them. Overbeaten egg whites look lumpy and dull and form big, white clumps if you try to fold them into another mixture.

I beat egg whites with an electric mixer on low speed until the cream of tartar is dissolved. Then I increase the speed to medium and beat until the soft peaks form. It is easier to check the egg whites and control the results on medium speed rather than on high speed.

Adding sugar to beaten egg whites stabilizes the foam just as it stabilizes an egg yolk foam. After sugar is added to egg whites, the mixture thickens. When adding sugar, begin adding it just as the egg whites reach the soft-peak stage. Again, add it sooner rather than later if you are unsure. Add sugar slowly so the egg whites have time to absorb it. Adding 1 tablespoon of sugar every 15 to 30 seconds is a good interval. Egg whites beaten with sugar form firm peaks if you dip a spoon in the egg whites and lift it out.

BLENDING ▪ Blending mixes ingredients to the point that ingredients no longer have a separate identity but are incorporated completely into a mixture. The 2 ways to incorporate ingredients smoothly are to stir them to make a mixture smooth or to beat them to make a mixture smooth. Beating also incorporates air into the mixture. "Beating" refers to a more vigorous action than stirring.

CREAMING SOLID FATS WITH SUGAR ▪ Creaming fat and sugar together beats air into the fat-sugar mixture and forms a smooth mixture that combines easily with other ingredients in a recipe. The fluffy, light-colored mixture that results from thorough creaming is full of air cells, which expand and lighten cakes and cookies. Most of the sugar crystals do not dissolve during creaming, and their rough texture helps to hold the air in the creamed mixture. Softening butter, margarine, or vegetable shortening to room temperature, considered as 65° to 75°F., produces a smooth fluffy mixture that is easy to blend other ingredients into. The fat is softened so that it produces a creamy mixture that is able to take in air.

CUTTING IN INGREDIENTS ▪ Fingertips, a pastry blender, a fork, or 2 dull knives can be used to mix firm, cold pieces of shortening or butter into a crumb mixture, usually for a crumb topping or a pastry crust. The final size of the crumbs varies depending on the recipe.

FOLDING ▪ Folding is done with a rubber spatula and is a gentle mixing method used to combine a light mixture with a heavy mixture without deflating the lighter mixture. I use a whisk or the rubber spatula to first lighten the heavier mixture by stirring a small amount of the lighter mixture into the heavier one. Then I use the rubber spatula to fold the remaining light mixture into the heavier one. The motion of the spatula is to dig down to the bottom of the mixture and bring the 2 mixtures up and over each other. Use a large bowl and turn the bowl as you fold so that the mixtures blend quickly.

KITCHEN TEMPERATURES ▪ One doesn't always think about the temperature in the kitchen, but if you have ever watched ice cream melt quickly in a hot kitchen or cream cheese take hours to soften in a cold kitchen, the effect it can have on mixing becomes clear. Even batters may bake for a longer or shorter time if they are mixed in a cold or warm kitchen, since what is going into the oven might be a colder or a warmer mixture. In a warm summer kitchen, chocolate melts fast, butter softens quickly, and whipping cream should not sit around in its bowl waiting to be whipped. In the summer, it is a good idea to chill the beaters and bowl before whipping the cream, and chill the flour for a piecrust so it doesn't melt the cold shortening during mixing. One of the best things about a warm kitchen is that chocolate softens slightly and chocolate curls (especially white and milk chocolate) roll off a vegetable peeler easily if they are in a warm environment.

KNEADING DOUGH ■ In this book "kneading" refers to the few strokes needed to smooth out a ragged dough such as a biscuit or cobbler dough. The kneading motion is to push and fold. Push the dough down and forward with the heel of your hand against the rolling surface, then fold the dough in half and repeat the process until the dough looks smooth. Usually, about 10 strokes do the job.

MELTING CHOCOLATE ■ If you think about a piece of chocolate melting smoothly in your mouth, it is melting at your body temperature of 98.6°F. You could hold it in your mouth for a long time (if you had that much willpower) and it would never burn or turn grainy. That is because it is melting slowly at the consistent low temperature it prefers. When melting chocolate for baking, think of that example and melt it slowly, over gentle heat, and do not subject it to sudden temperature changes. Exposure to high heat or a burst of steam from boiling water burns chocolate just as it would burn your hand. For a temperature range that could be checked with an instant-read thermometer, chocolate begins to melt at 92°F. and should be completely melted by the time it reaches 113°F. If exposed to higher temperatures, it can become lumpy and grainy. This doesn't mean that you have to stand over melting chocolate with a thermometer, but that as chocolate melts, it shouldn't be exposed to boiling water, high cooking temperatures, steam, or prolonged heat. Just remember low and slow.

I use one of two methods to melt chocolate. Both use pieces of chopped chocolate so the chocolate melts evenly. The first is to put chopped chocolate or the chocolate plus other ingredients that must melt with it in a heatproof container and let it sit on top of a pan of hot, but not boiling, water, until it melts. Stir the chocolate or mixture so it melts evenly. Putting the pan of water on a low heat keeps the water in the pan hot. If the water begins to boil and steam is escaping, turn off the heat. As soon as the chocolate melts, remove it from over the hot water. The second method is to put chopped chocolate in a heatproof container and melt it in an oven that has been heated to a low 175°F. Although the oven is at 175°F., the chocolate is not being heated to this temperature. It is surrounded by the low, dry heat. As soon as the chocolate melts, remove it from the oven. This is long before it can overheat. I use this method when I am melting chocolate by itself, so I do not have to stir it. It would be awkward to try to stir the chocolate in the oven. I find the oven method such an easy, reliable melting method that leaving the chocolate in the oven for a couple of additional minutes is not a problem.

For even melting, chop chocolate into small pieces that are about ½ inch in size. If the chocolate is left in large pieces, the outside could become too warm before the inside has a chance to melt. Since I use the pan-over-hot-water method when I'm melting chocolate with other ingredients such as butter, I can easily stir the mixture to encourage even melting, blend the ingredients as they melt, and even speed up the melting process. I use the oven method when I'm melting chocolate by itself and there is no need to stir it. Microwave ovens are another option for melting chocolate, but I don't own one. Follow the manufacturer's directions for melting chocolate in a microwave.

TEMPERATURE OF INGREDIENTS ▪ The temperature of ingredients is important for mixing properly. Butter might be cold, soft, or melted, and each produces various results. For example, cold butter produces soft crumbs for a topping, while melted butter makes the crumbs crisp.

Although the temperature of ingredients determines how batter looks during the mixing process, it doesn't always affect the end result. When mixing a cake batter, a cold liquid is often added to a beaten mixture that contains butter, and the mixture might look curdled after the cold liquid is added. Once the flour is incorporated, the finished batter becomes smooth again.

USING A PASTRY BAG ▪ Pastry bags are handy for filling items quickly and neatly or for decorating. I often fit a pastry bag with a star tip to add a simple decorative touch to a dessert. For example, piping casual swirls of frosting on top of the Dark Chocolate Cupcakes with Fudge Frosting (page 296) makes a luscious-looking finish. To fill a pastry bag, press a pastry tip, pointed side down, into the hole in the bottom of the bag and prop the bag inside a deep measuring cup or glass to hold it steady while filling it. Fill the bag about half full, then twist the bag firmly closed against the filling so the air is pushed out and the contents are pressed firmly down into the bag. Hold the bag with one hand (I'm right-handed so I hold the bag with my right hand; left-handed persons would reverse the process). Squeeze the bag with one hand, using just enough pressure to force the contents through the pastry tip, and use your other hand to guide the tip. Do a practice swirl or two on a piece of paper to get the feel of using the pastry bag and tip and to push out any air bubbles from the mixture in the bag. Squeeze with a steady pressure to push out the contents in a steady stream. Stop the pressure and lift the bag to stop the process.

WHIPPING CREAM ▪ Cream whips best if it is cold and can remain cold during the whipping, so on a warm day it is a good idea to chill the bowl and beaters in the refrigerator or freezer. Cream whips in less time on a cold day in a cold kitchen than in a warm kitchen.

Use an electric mixer on medium speed to beat the cream either to a softly whipped or firmly whipped stage. At the softly whipped stage, the movement of the beaters will form smooth lines in the cream, and if you dip a spoon in the cream and lift it out, the cream will form a point that falls over at its tip. Softly whipped cream forms a soft mound on a spoon that falls off the spoon. The texture of the whipped cream is like a thick, fluffy sauce. At the firmly whipped stage, the movement of the beaters of a hand mixer will form wrinkled lines in the cream, and if you dip a spoon in the cream and lift it out, the cream will form a point that stands straight up and remains that way. Firmly whipped cream forms a firm mound on a spoon that holds its shape. The movement of the beaters of a standing countertop mixer is different, and the mixer forms a small teardrop shape when cream is firmly whipped.

Bake

BAKING CRUSTS BLIND ▪ When a crust is baked blind, it is baked without its filling. Usually this is done to keep a bottom crust somewhat crisp when it is baked with a liquid filling. For example, the liquid custard filling of a quiche could make a crust soggy, and baking it blind prevents this. A soggy crust is one that falls apart or loses its crust identity, but is not the normal texture of a bottom crust, which is soft.

To bake a crust without its filling, have the cold unbaked pastry in its pan ready to bake. Preheat the oven to 375F°. Line the prepared crust with aluminum foil, preferably heavy foil, and fill the aluminum foil with dried beans or metal pie weights, spreading them evenly over the bottom of the crust. They do not have to come to the top of the pan. A crust in a 9-inch pie pan holds about 2½ cups of beans. Fold the foil lightly over the edges of the crust. Bake the crust for 10 minutes, or as directed in the recipe. Protect your hands with potholders and carefully remove the aluminum foil by lifting it and the pie weights carefully from the crust. Set the weights aside to cool and store for another use. Prick the crust in about 6 places with a fork to prevent the crust from bubbling up. If a filling, such as for a quiche, is especially liquid, the crust might be brushed with egg white after the foil and weights are removed. The combination of brushing with egg white and baking it blind seals the crust more strongly than just baking it blind would. Baking this unfilled crust uncovered for about 5 more minutes partially bakes it, while baking it for about 12 more minutes bakes it completely and to an appealing golden color.

WHEN IS IT DONE? ▪ Individual ovens vary in how they bake, so baking times are always approximate guidelines and visual clues are necessary. Once you bake a recipe, you will become familiar with when it is done to your satisfaction. When 2 cake pans are in the oven, the one in the rear usually cooks faster and recipes often direct to reverse the pans front to back in the oven about halfway through the baking time. If there are pans baking on both racks, the pans are often reversed top to bottom to ensure even baking.

Many recipes are ready when they reach a certain color. If your chocolate chip cookies are crisper than you would prefer, next time bake them for less time and to a lighter color. A visual clue for checking to see that cookies are done might be to look at the color of the cookie bottom or to see that the edges are browned and the center remains light golden. Lace cookies become flat and bubble gently when done. A visual clue for a cheesecake or a walnut pie that has a soft filling is to bake it until you can give it a gentle shake and it looks set, but an apple pie bakes until the crust is an appealing golden brown and the apples test tender if a toothpick is inserted into the pie. Cakes and bars are usually tested with a toothpick, and, depending on the recipe, are done either when the toothpick comes out with a few moist crumbs clinging to it or when the toothpick comes out clean. Touching the top of a cake to check to see if it feels firm is another test, but this is then verified with the toothpick test that actually penetrates the cake. If you insert a toothpick into the edge of a cake and then insert it into the center of a cake, you will actually be able to feel the difference between a still liquid center and a baked edge. A soft meringue topping is done when lightly browned, and crisp meringues are done when they feel crisp on the outside. Caramelized sugar turns a rich dark golden color when perfectly cooked.

Cake layers and cookies usually cool on a wire rack. This allows air to circulate, so that steam does not form around the warm cake or cookie and make it soggy. Cake layers are often cooled top side down, as the top is firmer.

Freezing Baked Goods and Chocolate Decorations

Cookies, bars, biscuits, muffins, cakes without frosting, cakes with rich chocolate or cream cheese frostings and fillings, or chocolate glazes all freeze well. The general guidelines are to cool everything thoroughly before wrapping it for the freezer, wrap it carefully while covering it completely, label it with the date and contents, and thaw it wrapped so the condensation that forms during defrosting forms on the wrapper rather than on a cake or cookie. I wrap cookies, bars, biscuits, and muffins with plastic wrap, seal them in rigid plastic freezer containers or metal tins, and freeze them. Whole cakes without frosting should be wrapped in plastic wrap, then heavy aluminum foil. If the cake is frosted, put it in the freezer without a wrapping to firm the frosting or glaze, then wrap it with plastic wrap and heavy aluminum foil. Unbaked piecrusts can be put into their pie pan and wrapped with plastic wrap and heavy aluminum foil and frozen. It is not necessary to defrost the piecrust before baking it, but remember that your pie pan will be tied up with this piecrust while it is in the freezer, so you may want to own several pie pans. I have often searched for a specific pan that I needed for a recipe only to find it holding something in my freezer.

To freeze chocolate decorations, line a rigid plastic freezer container or a tin with plastic wrap or waxed paper and gently spoon or lift the chocolate decorations into the container. Gently press plastic wrap onto the chocolate. Seal the container tightly, label with the date and contents, and freeze up to 3 months. Do not defrost the chocolate decorations before using them, so they are less likely to melt.

Making Decorative Chocolate Shapes and Chocolate Curls

Many chocolate decorations are simple and fun to make, yet they add an impressive finish to a dessert. The chocolate lace that tops the Chocolate Icebox Pie (page 321) is made from melted chocolate that is drizzled in a random, lacy pattern while a vegetable peeler is the only tool needed to make the white chocolate curls that cover the Deluxe Coconut Cream Pie (page 324).

Chocolate decorations can be made from bittersweet, semisweet, milk, or white chocolate. Unsweetened chocolate tastes too bitter to use for the decorations. Chocolate decorations melt easily when handled with warm hands so they are less likely to break if they are used cold. Chill or freeze the chocolate shapes or curls before using them, or better yet, make them ahead and store them in the freezer for up to 3 months. I have listed directions below for making chocolate lace, chocolate shapes and cutouts, chocolate flames, and chocolate curls, which can be used to embellish desserts.

To melt the chocolate for any of these decorations, preheat the oven to 175°F. Use about 6 ounces of chocolate so there is a good quantity of chocolate to work with. It is wise to make extras to allow for breakage, and any leftover shapes or curls can be frozen for later use. Place dark chopped chocolate in an ovenproof container and any white or milk chopped chocolate in separate nonreactive ovenproof containers. Leave the chocolate in the oven until it melts, about 12 minutes. Remove the chocolate from the oven and stir it until it is smooth and ready to use.

MAKING CHOCOLATE LACE

For chocolate lace, line a baking sheet with parchment paper. Use a teaspoon to drizzle thin lines of dark, milk, or white chocolate over the parchment. Drizzle the chocolate in a circular motion to make a lace pattern or in crisscrossing lines to form a crosshatch pattern. Check to see that the lines connect so the lace has a sturdy structure. Three ounces of chocolate will cover an area about 12 x 10 inches. If desired, drizzle lines of white chocolate over dark chocolate or dark over white. Put the baking sheet in the freezer for about 30 minutes to firm the chocolate. Carefully turn the chocolate, paper side up, on the baking sheet. Peel the paper from the chocolate. Break or cut the chocolate lace into random pieces about 3 to 4 inches in size or into a larger 5-inch piece to decorate a whipped-cream-topped dessert such as the Chocolate Icebox Pie on page 321. Turn the chocolate lace top side up to use it.

MAKING CHOCOLATE SHAPES AND CUTOUTS

Chocolate triangles, strips, squares, and flames are cut with a knife, and circles, hearts, half-moons, and stars are best cut with metal cutters. Use cutters in different sizes to produce multiple sizes of any shape. A metal biscuit cutter does double duty as a chocolate cutter. Cut out half-moons by using only half of a round cutter or a half-moon-shaped cutter.

To make the shapes, turn a baking sheet bottom side up, cover it with parchment paper, and tape the paper to the baking sheet with masking tape. The baking sheet smoothly supports the paper and chocolate, and the tape keeps the paper from sliding around when you spread the melted chocolate. Use a thin metal spatula to spread 6 ounces of melted chocolate evenly over the parchment paper into a rectangle about 13 x 10 inches. The chocolate should be thick enough so that the paper does not show through the chocolate. At this stage the chocolate looks shiny and wet. Put the chocolate-covered baking sheet in the refrigerator and chill it just until the chocolate looks dull and dry and is still soft but no longer melted. This will take about 5 minutes for white chocolate and about 3 minutes for dark chocolate. Do not let the chocolate harden, as it tends to shatter when cut or pressed with a metal cutter. The chocolate can also sit at room temperature until it looks dull and dry and is firm enough so the edges do not run together when the chocolate is cut. Depending on the room temperature, this can take from 10 minutes to 1 hour.

For triangles, strips, squares, and cutouts, use a large, sharp knife to trim the edges of each slightly firmed chocolate sheet into a 12 x 9-inch rectangle. Use a small smooth-bladed knife (not serrated edge) to mark twelve 3-inch squares on each sheet of chocolate. Cut each square diagonally into triangles or strips, if desired. Do not draw the knife across the chocolate, but press down on the chocolate to make sharp edges. The knife should cut cleanly and completely through the chocolate, and the chocolate should be firm enough so that it does not cling to the knife. If the chocolate is too soft and runs together, chill it for a minute or two, watching it carefully, or let it sit until it is firm enough to hold the cut marks. If the chocolate hardens and then cracks when it is cut, warm the chocolate sheet in a low, about 200°F., oven for a few seconds. It is preferable not to chill or rewarm the chocolate repeatedly so the chocolate keeps its even chocolate color. For cutouts, do not trim the edges of the chocolate into a rectangle but use a heart, star, round, or half-moon-shaped metal cutter to cut out chocolate shapes. Depending on the size of the cutter used, you will have about 12 to 24 chocolate shapes. Return the cut chocolate to the refrigerator to firm completely, about 30 minutes.

MAKING CHOCOLATE FLAMES

For the flames for the Blaze of Glory Chocolate Cake on page 376, spread the melted chocolate into about a 12 x 9-inch rectangle on the parchment paper as for triangles and strips. Then sweep the tip of the thin metal spatula across the edges on the long sides of the chocolate rectangle to form random-shaped ragged and pointed edges that resemble the top of a flame. The ragged edges should be thick enough so the paper does not show through the chocolate. This makes them less likely to break, but a break or two is no problem as you want a ragged edge. Let the chocolate firm until it doesn't run together when it is cut. Cut lengthwise down the middle to divide the chocolate into two 4-inch-high strips that are about 12 inches long. Then cut the long strips into pieces that are 1½ to 2 inches wide. Refrigerate the chocolate strips until they are firm.

Remove the baking sheet from the refrigerator. Carefully turn the chocolate paper side up on the baking sheet. Peel the paper from the chocolate, and the chocolate flames separate easily. Use a small sharp knife to separate any flames that stick together or break them apart; irregular-shaped flames look good. Turn the chocolate flames smooth bottom side up to use them.

MAKING CHOCOLATE CURLS

A vegetable peeler is a good tool to use to make chocolate curls. The only trick to making chocolate curls is to use a large, thick piece of chocolate (about 8 ounces is a good size) and to have the chocolate in a very slightly softened state so that it forms curls when you pull the peeler over it. To check to see if the chocolate is at a good temperature for peeling into curls try making a few chocolate curls. If the chocolate is too firm, flakes form and if the chocolate is too soft, it forms soft lumps that clog the vegetable peeler. When the chocolate is at the right temperature, chocolate curls roll easily off the vegetable peeler. White and milk chocolate are softer than dark chocolate, and on a warm day they may be ready to form curls without any preparation.

Have ready a baking sheet lined with wax paper and a stainless-steel vegetable peeler with a 2½-inch-long swivel blade. Hold the chocolate between the palms of your hands and warm it with your hands for about 2 minutes. White and milk chocolate take less time to soften, while any chocolate takes longer to warm if the room is cold. If you are holding chocolate in your hands to warm it and your hands are cold, run them under warm water to warm them slightly and dry them. When the chocolate is ready, it feels slightly sticky in your hand. Dark chocolate loses some of its shine. Another method to warm chocolate slightly is to put it in a sunny window for about 5 minutes, watching it closely so it doesn't actually melt.

To shave the chocolate into curls, hold the chocolate in one hand and use the vegetable peeler to scrape curls from the block of chocolate in a single layer onto the baking sheet. Scrape the peeler away from you. Scrape in 1½- to 2-inch-long strokes along the chocolate and try to make the curls about 1 inch wide. Scrape along all sides of the chocolate. The curls will vary in shape and size. Longer shavings form curls that roll over each other, and shorter shavings form more of a curved shape. As the piece of chocolate becomes too small to form curls, stop the shaving and save the small piece of chocolate for another use. You can make about 4 cups of chocolate curls from an 8-ounce piece of chocolate. If the chocolate begins to flake and break rather than form curls, it is too hard and should be held between your hands again or put in the sun until it softens. If the chocolate is too soft and begins to clog the vegetable peeler, let it sit at room temperature or chill it briefly until it is firm enough to shave into curls. Put the baking sheet in the freezer for about 30 minutes to firm the curls, then spoon them carefully over the soft top of a dessert, press them gently onto the sides of a frosted cake, or freeze them. If the chocolate curls are frozen, carefully spoon the frozen curls directly onto the cake or dessert. Seal the container and return any remaining chocolate curls to the freezer. Chocolate curls look best on a dessert when there is a thick, generous layer of them. A mound of chocolate curls on the center of a frosted cake looks inviting.

Frequently Asked
Baking Questions Answered

1. What if I don't have the same size pan that is called for in the recipe?
It is important to use the same size pan, including the depth, called for in a recipe. Some dimensions and pans that are interchangeable with each other are 9-inch round pans with 8-inch square pans and 10-inch round pans with 9-inch square pans, as long as the depth of both pans is equal. Also, if you calculate the area of the pan called for in a recipe and the area of the pan that you want to use and they are within 8 inches of each other and have the same depth, there should be no problem using either pan. This formula is explained on page 38 (Measure, Mix, and Bake! Explaining Baking Techniques).

2. Can I substitute?
margarine for butter—Yes, in most cases, but it must be a full-fat margarine. Low-fat margarine has added water. It changes the baked result, and not for the better. If you have a recipe that depends on the good flavor of butter, such as a pound cake or butter cookies, then butter is the one to choose.
unsweetened chocolate for semisweet or bittersweet chocolate—No on this one; unsweetened chocolate has no sugar, and the recipe would come out bitter unless the sugar was adjusted. Once sugar quantities are changed it leads to other changes, so it is not a good idea to just add more sugar. It is better to take a quick trip to the market and buy the correct chocolate. Generally, semisweet chocolate and bittersweet chocolate can be used interchangeably.
fresh, frozen, or canned fruits for each other?—In my recipes, I specify when frozen fruit can be substituted for fresh fruit. When using frozen fruits, I usually call for unsweetened frozen fruit, which is individually quick frozen and is most like fresh fruit. However, freezing changes the texture of fruit and causes it to give off juices when it defrosts, so the best use for frozen fruit is often when it is baked in a cake, but not as a topping added after baking or as the filling for a fruit pie. I use canned fruit only in specific cases that are noted in those recipes. Canned pineapple packed in its own juice, such as the crushed pineapple used in the Crushed Pineapple Upside-Down Cake (page 163), is a good choice when a recipe calls for pineapple.

3.   When is it done?

For cookies the best test is a visual test, and they are usually done when their edges and bottoms are lightly browned. Break a cookie in half to see if it looks done. It is better to lose one cookie than to ruin a whole batch. Most brownies, bars, and muffins can be tested by inserting a toothpick into their center. Test the center rather than the edge as this is the last part to become done. If the toothpick comes out dry or with moist crumbs clinging to it (usually for dense, moist brownies and bars), they are done. For cakes, first touch the top gently to check to see if it feels firm, then insert a toothpick in the center. When the toothpick comes out dry, the cake is done. Check cakes often toward the end of their baking time. A toothpick comes out clean from a dry, overbaked cake too. Crumb-topped cakes always feel firm on top, so use only the toothpick test. The jiggle test is the one to use for cheesecakes, bread puddings, and soft, custard-type pies and tarts. When you give these baked items a gentle shake, if the center looks set and does not jiggle around, they are done. Fruit pies should have a lightly browned crust. Firm fruits can be tested with a toothpick for tenderness. Look for some bubbling of the liquid in fruit pies that include soft fruits such as peaches and blueberries, but they should be done by the time the topping looks done. Meringues are ready when their outside is crisp and they are lightly colored.

4.   Why do my cookies and cakes burn on the bottom?

Most cookies contain a large amount of sugar in proportion to the other ingredients, which can cause cookies to burn easily, especially on the bottom, if they bake for too long. Prevent any burned bottoms by checking cookies often at the end of their baking time, checking the cookie bottoms by using a metal spatula to lift a cookie, placing baking sheets on racks set in the middle or upper third of the oven, and reversing baking sheets on the racks halfway through their baking. It is a good idea to check the temperature of your oven with an oven thermometer for accuracy. I bake most cookies in an oven set at a moderate 350°F. or at a lower temperature to discourage overbrowning.

Cakes are less likely to burn on the bottom than cookies, but they should bake on a rack set on the middle or upper third of the oven. I bake thick cakes in an oven set at a low 325°F. so the bottom of the cake does not burn before the center is done. An accurate oven temperature and frequent testing are important.

5.   My dark chocolate has a white coating. Can I use it?

This white coating is called bloom. Fat bloom forms a whitish film on the outside of chocolate when the cocoa butter in chocolate melts slightly, then firms again. Aside from appearance, fat bloom doesn't harm the chocolate, but it does indicate chocolate has been exposed to warm temperatures and has not been shipped or stored under the best conditions. Sugar bloom is a different story. If moisture condenses or forms on chocolate, some of the sugar in the chocolate can dissolve and produce an undesirable crusty or grainy surface on the outside of the chocolate. The chocolate should not be used, as it will not melt smoothly and would taste gritty.

6. **Can I freeze it?**

Many baked goods can be frozen. As a general rule of thumb, you can freeze everything except custard-type items, baked fruit pies, soft meringue pies, whipped cream desserts, and cakes covered with a no-fat whipped egg white–type frosting, such as a 7-minute frosting. Wrap baked goods carefully for freezer storage, and remember: what you put into the freezer is what you will take out of it. If a cake has been around for several days and is stale, freezing it does not miraculously make it fresh. But freezing your freshly baked goods is a great way to bake ahead and prolong the quality of baked goods. Cool everything completely before wrapping and freezing, wrap tightly and carefully, label with the date and contents, and defrost with the wrapping on. Individual cookies, brownies, and muffins should be wrapped in plastic wrap and sealed tightly in metal or plastic containers. Pies and cakes should be wrapped with plastic wrap then heavy aluminum foil. If there is a soft or sticky topping or frosting, let the item sit in the freezer without its wrapping until the topping is firm, then wrap it. Defrost at room temperature items that will be served at room temperature; defrost items that will be served cold in the refrigerator. Leave the wrapping on during defrosting to prevent condensation from forming on the dessert itself.

7. **How many does it serve?**

Serving sizes are quite variable, and the richer the dessert, the smaller the portion. Usually a cheesecake is cut into a smaller-size serving than a piece of apple pie. The inch measurements below are of the diameter of the dessert.

Some good general guidelines are:

a 9-inch pie serves 8

a 9-inch cheesecake or ice cream pie in a springform pan serves 12 to 16

a 9-inch 2-layer cake serves 12 to 16

a 9-inch tart serves 8

large cakes baked in a tube pan serve 12 to 16

8. **Why does my dough stick and tear when I roll it?**

Dough seldom sticks or tears if it is cold when it is rolled out. For an especially moist, sticky dough, I recommend rolling the dough between 2 pieces of wax paper. Remember that a tear in a piecrust dough can be patched with scraps of dough.

Most frequently admitted cause of baking goof-ups ◦ I was in a hurry, and I forgot to read through the recipe before I began to make it and didn't have all of the ingredients or the right baking pans available.

Just Stir
and Bake

I F EVER A GROUP OF RECIPES WAS DESIGNED TO ENCOURAGE BAKING, IT'S THIS ASSORTMENT OF BROWNIES, BARS, MUFFINS, SWEET AND SAVORY CRUMB-TOPPED CRISPS, AND EVEN AN EASY APPLE PIE. SUCCESSFULLY BAKING A MOIST BUTTERSCOTCH AND CHOCOLATE CHIP brownie or a big, puffy popover is a mouthwatering way to gain baking confidence and skills—and have a good time doing it.

As the first chapter of *Fearless Baking,* these recipes are the easiest to make. They also call for a minimum of equipment—no electric mixer, just a bowl and spoon. When I call for a specific utensil when mixing, though, please follow my directions. Spoons, whisks, forks, or fingertips are used to produce different results. For example, to mix a smooth brownie batter you can use a large spoon to stir wet ingredients (like soft or melted butter or eggs) with the sugar, then use the same spoon for mixing the dry ingredients into the liquid batter. A large spoon may also be used in making muffins to stir the liquid ingredients into the dry ingredients, since muffin batters benefit from a minimum of stirring. But with crumb toppings that combine butter pieces with sugar and flour to form a crumbly mixture it's easier to use your fingertips—in fact, I've actually found that a handheld electric mixer doesn't do a good job of this. Or, when making a popover batter that combines a large proportion of liquid to flour, a multiwired whisk is a useful tool. Finally, an ordinary fork works best for lightly mixing whole eggs together.

There aren't any difficult techniques here either. The only thing to master is softening butter, which isn't much harder than leaving it out on the counter for a while. When recipes call for chocolate, it is only for pieces of chopped chocolate or chocolate chips that don't have to be melted. Although melting chocolate is easy, there are some specific guidelines to follow that are better tried after a few baking successes, so I've saved that for the chapter on chocolate.

The main difference among these recipes is that brownies, muffins, crumb-topped desserts, and puddings use different methods to check to see if they are done. When checking a smooth-topped brownie or muffin, gently touch the top, and if it feels firm, insert a toothpick in the center. When the toothpick comes out dry, or in some cases with a few moist crumbs clinging to it, it is done. Crumb toppings are baked to the point that a desired color such as golden or light brown is reached. Apple, pear, and green tomato fillings should be baked until they feel tender when tested with a toothpick, but softer fruits such as blueberries or peaches should be ready by the time the topping looks done. Finally, with a moist bread pudding just bake it until it looks firm and set when you give it a gentle shake.

Perfectly Easy Chocolate Chip Butterscotch Blondies

If you've never heard the word "blondie" in reference to dessert before, these will be a great introduction. They are moist and chewy as a brownie should be, but the brown sugar and butter produce a blond butterscotch-flavored brownie. Chocolate chips add plenty of chocolate to the fudgy texture in the simplest of ways—no melting or chopping of chocolate. Mixing them is as simple as stirring ingredients together, making them a good idea for a first baking attempt. After all, there is nothing like a big baking success to build confidence and fill you with pride.

Baking Answers ❧ Melting the butter on a low heat prevents it from browning or burning. Cutting the stick of butter in several pieces helps it melt quickly and evenly. Measure the butter before melting it. One stick of solid butter, which is 8 tablespoons, measures more than 10 tablespoons after melting.

If you're undecided as to whether the brownies are done, it's better to bake them for less time. Slightly underbaked brownies will be extremely soft and moist, while overbaked ones could be dry and hard. Check for doneness every 2 or 3 minutes as the end of the baking time nears. As soon as a toothpick no longer comes out wet, the brownies are done. Warm chocolate chips will always wet a toothpick, so if a toothpick penetrates a chocolate chip, test another spot.

MAKES 12 TO 16 BLONDIES

Necessities ❧ *One 9-inch square baking pan or one 11 x 7-inch baking pan, both with 2-inch-high sides, and a wire rack*

1¾ cups unbleached all-purpose flour	1½ cups packed light brown sugar
1 teaspoon baking powder	2 large eggs
½ teaspoon salt	2 teaspoons vanilla extract
¼ pound (1 stick) unsalted butter, melted	1½ cups (9 ounces) semisweet chocolate chips

Mix the Batter

↝ Position a rack in the middle of the oven. Preheat the oven to 325°F. Butter the bottom and sides of a 9 x 9 x 2-inch or 11 x 7 x 2-inch pan.

Sift the flour, baking powder, and salt into a medium bowl and set aside.

Put the melted butter and brown sugar in a large bowl, and stir with a mixing spoon until the brown sugar is evenly moistened with the butter. The mixture will be thick. Add the eggs and vanilla and stir until the eggs are completely blended and the mixture looks smooth. Add the flour mixture and stir just until it is incorporated and there is no loose flour. The batter will be thick. Stir in the chocolate chips. Scrape the batter into the pan, spreading it evenly. Use a rubber spatula to scrape all of the batter from the bowl and spread the batter evenly in the pan.

Bake and Serve the Blondies

↝ Bake for about 35 minutes just until a toothpick inserted into the center comes out dry or only slightly moist. The toothpick should not have liquid clinging to it. If the toothpick penetrates a chocolate chip, test another spot. Cool the blondies thoroughly in the pan on a wire rack, about 1 hour. Cut the blondies into 12 to 16 pieces and use a thin metal spatula to remove the blondies from the pan. Wrap individual blondies in plastic wrap and store at room temperature up to 3 days. The wrapped blondies can be sealed tightly in a clean plastic container or metal tin and frozen up to 3 months. Defrost as many wrapped blondies as needed at room temperature.

Peanut Butter and Milk Chocolate Brownies

These brownies are like inside-out peanut butter cups: peanut butter brownies enclose a milk chocolate center. The generous quantity of peanut butter in these bars makes them especially dense and fudgey.

Baking Answers ⌦ Using chopped milk chocolate rather than milk chocolate chips produces the middle layer of milk chocolate in these brownies. Milk chocolate chips hold their shape when baked, but chopped milk chocolate melts and forms the desirable unbroken milk chocolate layer throughout the middle of the brownies. Milk chocolate chips wouldn't ruin the brownies, but chopped chocolate is preferable here.

Use a clean meat pounder or hammer to break large bars of milk chocolate into small pieces. Leave the chocolate in its wrapper to prevent flying chocolate pieces. Six ounces of milk chocolate pieces measure about 1 cup.

Soft peanut butter blends easily with soft butter. If the peanut butter has been refrigerated, soften it to room temperature. I use the regular or the low-sodium, but not the low-fat peanut butter. Use a rubber spatula to scrape peanut butter out of a jar or measuring cup easily.

These are rich brownies so I cut them into 16 pieces rather than the usual 12.

MAKES 16 BROWNIES

Necessities ⌦ *One 9-inch square baking pan or one 11 x 7-inch baking pan, both with 2-inch-high sides*

1 cup unbleached all-purpose flour	¾ cup granulated sugar
½ teaspoon baking powder	2 large eggs
¼ teaspoon salt	1 teaspoon vanilla extract
¼ pound (1 stick) soft unsalted butter	6 ounces milk chocolate, such as Lindt
1 cup smooth peanut butter, room	or Dove Bar, broken into about
temperature	½-inch pieces
½ cup packed light brown sugar	

Mix the Batter

Position a rack in the middle of the oven. Preheat the oven to 325°F. Butter the bottom and sides of a 9 x 9 x 2-inch or 11 x 7 x 2-inch baking pan.

Sift the flour, baking powder, and salt onto a piece of wax paper or into a small bowl and set aside.

Put the butter and peanut butter in a large bowl and stir with a large spoon until they are blended together. You may see a few specks of butter. Stir in the brown sugar and granulated sugar, mixing until they are incorporated and there is no loose sugar. Stirring vigorously, beat in the eggs and vanilla until the mixture looks smooth. Add the flour mixture and stir just until it is incorporated and there is no loose flour. Spread about two thirds of the batter into the pan, spreading it evenly with a thin metal spatula or a nonsharp table knife. Scatter the milk chocolate pieces evenly over the batter. Drop spoonfuls of the remaining batter over the milk chocolate, using a rubber spatula to scrape all of the batter from the bowl. Use a thin metal spatula or the table knife to spread the batter evenly over the chocolate. The chocolate will be covered, but may show through the batter.

Bake and Serve the Brownies

Bake for about 35 minutes until the top feels firm when gently touched and the edges are light brown. Inserting a toothpick as a test doesn't work because the warm milk chocolate clings to the toothpick. Cool the brownies thoroughly in the pan for about 1 hour. Cut the brownies into 16 pieces and use a thin metal spatula to remove them from the pan. Wrap individual brownies in plastic wrap and store at room temperature up to 3 days. Wrapped brownies are ready to pack in lunch boxes or picnic baskets. These brownies can be served with a scoop of chocolate or peanut butter fudge ice cream.

Individual brownies can be wrapped in plastic wrap then heavy aluminum foil and stored in the freezer for up to 3 months. Defrost the wrapped brownies as needed.

Banana Butterscotch Blondie Sundae

Brownies and blondies are natural partners with ice cream and warm sticky sauces. The classic example is a fudge brownie topped with ice cream and hot fudge sauce. Try these not-too-sweet banana blondies topped with vanilla ice cream, banana slices, and dark butterscotch sauce and make room for a new classic.

Baking Answers ✦ Individual blondies can be served by themselves or packed into lunch boxes and picnic baskets. The butterscotch sauce can be used without the blondies as a sundae sauce.

When cooking the ingredients for the butterscotch sauce, let the sugars dissolve before bringing the mixture to a boil. This prevents them from turning grainy and sticking to the bottom of the pan. The sugars dissolve easily if they are cooked over low heat and stirred constantly. Once the sugars dissolve, increase the heat and boil the mixture to thicken it. When the cream is added to the hot butterscotch sauce, the mixture will bubble up, so be careful not to burn yourself. Use a medium saucepan so the mixture does not overflow. For butterscotch sundaes, pour the warm sauce over coffee, butter pecan, or vanilla ice cream.

A Step Ahead ✦ Individual blondies can be wrapped in plastic wrap then heavy aluminum foil and stored in the freezer for up to 3 months. Defrost the wrapped blondies as needed. The butterscotch sauce can be cooled and stored in the refrigerator for up to 10 days. Put cold sauce in a medium saucepan and warm it over low heat.

MAKES 12 BLONDIES

Necessities ✦ *One 9-inch square baking pan or one 11 x 7-inch baking pan, both with 2-inch-high sides, and a wire rack*

BANANA BLONDIES	4 medium bananas, sliced
1⅓ cups unbleached all-purpose flour	¼ pound (1 stick) soft unsalted butter
1 teaspoon baking powder	1⅓ cups packed dark brown sugar
¼ teaspoon salt	2 teaspoons vanilla extract
1 teaspoon ground cinnamon	2 large eggs

BUTTERSCOTCH SAUCE— MAKES 1½ CUPS	¼ teaspoon salt
	½ cup light corn syrup
6 tablespoons (¾ stick) unsalted butter	½ cup whipping cream
¾ cup packed dark brown sugar	1 teaspoon vanilla extract
¼ cup granulated sugar	

3 pints vanilla or banana walnut ice cream for serving with the sundaes	3 medium bananas, sliced, for serving with the sundaes

Make the Blondies

↝ Position a rack in the middle of the oven. Preheat the oven to 325°F. Butter a 9 x 9 x 2-inch or 11 x 7 x 2-inch baking pan.

Sift the flour, baking powder, salt, and cinnamon together and set aside.

Put the 4 sliced bananas in a medium bowl and mash them with a fork into small pieces, about ½ inch in size. Some of the bananas will be mashed almost smooth.

Put the butter and brown sugar in a large bowl and stir them with a mixing spoon until they are blended together and there is no loose sugar. Stir in the mashed bananas and vanilla to combine them with the other ingredients. You will see small pieces of banana. Stir in the eggs until they are incorporated. The mixture will look curdled. Mix in the flour mixture just until it is incorporated and the mixture looks smooth. Use a rubber spatula to scrape the batter into the prepared pan and spread it evenly.

Bake the Blondies

↝ Bake for about 35 minutes, just until a toothpick inserted in the center comes out looking slightly moist. There will be some moist bits of banana in the blondies. Cool the blondies thoroughly in the pan on a wire rack, about 1 hour. Cut the blondies into 12 pieces and use a thin metal spatula to remove the blondies from the pan. The blondies can be wrapped and stored at room temperature up to 3 days.

Make the Butterscotch Sauce

↝ Put the butter, brown sugar, granulated sugar, salt, and corn syrup in a medium saucepan and cook over low heat until the sugar dissolves, stirring constantly. Increase the heat to medium-high and bring the mixture to a boil. Boil for 2 minutes, stirring often. Remove from the heat and stir in the cream and vanilla until they are blended into the mixture. Be careful, the mixture may bubble up. Serve warm. The sauce can be covered with plastic wrap and refrigerated up to 10 days. Put the cold sauce in a saucepan and warm it over low heat.

◦ For each serving place a blondie in an individual shallow bowl. Top each blondie with ice cream then banana slices. Spoon the warm butterscotch sauce over the top.

Any-Season Fruit Crumble

L ong ago on our honeymoon, we stayed at the Connaught Hotel in London, a bastion of comfortable English tradition. They served what I considered then, and still do, the finest of fruit crumbles. It was served very hot and had a thick golden crumb topping that was baked on top of perfectly cooked and sweetened fruit. Although the crumb topping was crisp on top, it remained pleasantly soft in the middle. At that time, rooms at the hotel cost £12 per night, but current rates are quoted in hundreds of pounds—a big change there. We skip sleeping there now but still dine in the restaurant, where I have had the crumble made with rhubarb in the spring, apples in the fall, or blueberries on a warm summer night. Happily, some things never change.

Since the same crumb topping works with many fruits, I've given a basic recipe that uses chopped apples and a chart for substituting other fruits.

Baking Answers ◦ Cutting the cold butter into small pieces puts you well on the way to making the crumbs. Although you can mix the crumb mixture with a pastry blender, fork, or 2 knives, I find it easiest and quickest to mix it with my fingertips. I rub the pieces of butter and dry ingredients between my thumb and fingertips until the crumbs of butter blend with the dry ingredients. It's easy to pick out any large stray pieces of butter and break them into the desired small pieces for the crumbs.

I find apple coring tools difficult to push through apples and pears and inevitably leave some of the core and seeds with the fruit. My method slices the peeled apple or pear away from its core. First, peel the fruit and place it with the stem end up (it's the narrow end of a pear) upright on a cutting surface. Then, place the knife blade about ½ inch out from the center of the stem. Cutting downward, cut off a section of the apple or pear. Turn the fruit a quarter turn and cut another section. After cutting away about 4 large pieces of apple or pear, the fruit will be cut from the core.

Since the acid in some fruits discolors aluminum pans, bake the crumble in an ovenproof glass or ceramic baking dish. Pyrex glass baking dishes, in square or deep pie dish shapes, work well. These dishes can go from oven to table.

When changing the variety of fruit for a crumble, the amount of sugar added to the fruit and the baking times may change. Some fruits benefit from the addition of lemon juice, cinnamon, or flour. Since fruit varies in sweetness, mix in the least amount of sugar suggested, then taste the sweetened fruit and add more sugar if it seems needed. Adding too much sugar masks the good fruit taste.

A Step Ahead ⚬ The crumble can be baked a day ahead, covered, and stored at room temperature. Uncover the crumble and warm it in a 250°F. oven for 15 minutes.

The chart below gives guidelines at a glance for a variety of fruit crumbles. Measure the fruit after any peeling and cutting.

AMOUNT OF FRUIT	SUGAR AND FLAVORINGS	BAKING TIME AT 350°F.
6 cups peeled, cored, and chopped or sliced apples or pears	2 tablespoons sugar, 1 tablespoon fresh lemon juice, ½ teaspoon ground cinnamon	about 40 minutes, until the fruit is tender
5 cups blueberries (6 cups if using small wild blueberries)	2 to 4 tablespoons sugar ½ teaspoon ground cinnamon (if using frozen blueberries, mix in 2 tablespoons flour)	about 35 minutes, just until the fruit begins to bubble
6 cups peeled (page 38), pitted, and sliced peaches	2 to 3 tablespoons sugar	about 30 minutes, until the crumb topping is golden
5 cups peeled (page 38), pitted, and sliced peaches and 1 cup fresh raspberries	3 to 4 tablespoons sugar	about 30 minutes, until the crumb topping is golden
6 cups cut-up rhubarb (cut in ½-inch pieces)	about ½ cup sugar ½ teaspoon ground cinnamon	about 40 minutes, until the rhubarb is tender

SERVES 6

Necessities ⚬ *A baking container with a 2½-quart capacity, such as an 8- or 9-inch square baking dish or a 9½- to 10-inch-diameter round pie dish, both with 1¾- to 2-inch-high sides*

FRUIT FILLING	2 tablespoons sugar
6 cups peeled and cored apples chopped into ½- to ¾-inch pieces (about 6 large apples)	½ teaspoon ground cinnamon
	2 teaspoons fresh lemon juice

CRUMBLE TOPPING—	½ teaspoon salt
MAKES ABOUT 3 CUPS CRUMBS	¼ pound (1 stick) cold unsalted butter,
¾ cup unbleached all-purpose flour	cut into ¾-inch pieces
½ cup sugar	

Prepare the Filling

~ Position a rack in the middle of the oven. Preheat the oven to 350°F. Put the apples in a glass or ceramic baking container with about a 2½-quart capacity. Either an 8- or 9-inch square baking dish or a 9½- to 10-inch-diameter round pie dish, both with 1¾- to 2-inch-high sides, works well. Mix the sugar and cinnamon together in a small bowl. Sprinkle the sugar mixture and lemon juice over the apples. Stir the mixture to combine the ingredients, spreading them in an even layer in the baking dish. Set aside.

Mix the Topping

~ Put the flour, sugar, and salt in a large bowl and use a large spoon to stir them together. Add the butter pieces, stirring to coat them with the flour. Rub the butter pieces and flour between your thumb and fingertips or cut them together with a pastry blender until coarse crumbs form that are about ½ to ¾ inch in size, there is no loose flour, and the mixture looks pale yellow rather than white. Sprinkle the crumbs evenly over the apple mixture.

Bake and Serve the Crumble

~ Bake about 40 minutes until the crumb topping is golden but with a few spots of light brown, and the apples are tender when tested with a toothpick. Let the crumble cool about 15 minutes before serving. Spoon the warm crumble onto individual plates and serve with a scoop of vanilla ice cream, if desired. The crumble can be baked a day ahead, cooled, covered, and stored at room temperature. Warm it, uncovered, in a preheated 250°F. oven for 15 minutes.

Toasted Hazelnut Peach Crisp

Toasted hazelnuts and melted butter team up to make a crumb topping that truly deserves to be called "crisp." The hazelnuts enrich this crumb topping with their unique nut flavor while making a nice contrast to the juicy peach filling.

Baking Answers ⤙ Using melted butter produces a crisper crumb topping and requires less butter than using cold butter. Melt the butter slowly over low heat.

Peaches cook and soften quickly. When the crumb topping is crisp and golden, the peaches will be done.

Try to buy peeled (blanched) hazelnuts, or see page 40 for directions for peeling them. King Arthur Flour Company (see page 384) ships peeled hazelnuts. Pecans, walnuts, or chopped, sliced, or slivered toasted almonds can substitute in the same proportions for the hazelnuts. Any of the fruits listed in the chart on page 64 can be used with this crumb topping; use the listed flavor additions and suggested baking times.

SERVES 6

Necessities ⤙ *A baking container with a 2½-quart capacity, such as an 8- or 9-inch square baking dish or a 9½- to 10-inch-diameter round glass pie pan, both with 1¾- to 2-high-inch sides*

PEACH FILLING
6 cups peeled (page 38), pitted, and sliced ripe peaches (about 6 medium peaches)

2 to 3 tablespoons sugar
1 tablespoon fresh lemon juice

HAZELNUT CRUMB TOPPING
¾ cup unbleached all-purpose flour
⅓ cup granulated sugar
⅓ cup packed light brown sugar
½ teaspoon ground cinnamon

¼ pound (1 stick) unsalted butter, melted
¾ cup peeled, toasted hazelnuts (page 40), chopped coarsely

Prepare the Filling

⤷ Position a rack in the middle of the oven. Preheat the oven to 350°F.

Put the peaches in a glass or ceramic baking container with about a 2½-quart capacity. Either an 8- or 9-inch square baking dish or a 9½- to 10-inch-diameter round glass pie pan or ceramic baking dish, both with 1¾- to 2-inch-high sides, works well. Sprinkle the sugar and lemon juice over the peaches. Stir the mixture to combine the ingredients, spreading them in an even layer in the baking dish. Set aside.

Mix the Topping

⤷ Put the flour, granulated sugar, brown sugar, and cinnamon in a large bowl and use a large spoon to stir them together. Stir in the melted butter until crumbs form and the mixture looks evenly moist. Stir in the hazelnuts. Sprinkle the crumbs evenly over the peach mixture.

Bake and Serve the Crisp

⤷ Bake about 35 minutes until the crumb topping is golden brown and the peach filling just begins to bubble at the edges. Let the crisp cool for about 15 minutes before serving. Spoon the warm crisp onto individual plates and serve with a scoop of vanilla ice cream, if desired. The crisp can be baked a day ahead, cooled, covered, and stored at room temperature. Warm it, uncovered, in a 250°F. oven for 15 minutes and serve warm.

Apple Crumble Bars

With a press-in butter crust and a thin layer of apples in the filling, these bars create a portable version of apple crisp. The same crumb mixture forms both the crust and crumb topping. You can transform the bars from snack fare to party dessert by serving them warm and topped with vanilla ice cream.

Baking Answers ⟿ Chop the apples into small, fairly even pieces so they cook evenly. Golden-colored raisins have a slightly milder taste than the dark ones and blend nicely with apples, but dark raisins can be substituted.

Lining the pan with aluminum foil allows you to remove warm bars from the pan easily without breaking them. Let the foil lining extend over the edges of the pan so it is easy to lift the foil and warm bars from the pan.

MAKES 12 TO 16 BARS

Necessities ⟿ *One 9-inch square baking pan or one 11 x 7-inch baking pan, both with 2-inch-high sides*

CRUST AND TOPPING	
2 cups unbleached all-purpose flour	¾ cup packed light brown sugar
¼ cup powdered sugar	6 ounces (1½ sticks) cold unsalted butter, cut into ½-inch pieces

APPLE FILLING	
3 cups peeled and cored apples chopped into ½-inch pieces (about 3 large apples)	1 tablespoon granulated sugar
	1 tablespoon fresh lemon juice
	1 cup golden raisins

Powdered sugar for dusting, optional	Vanilla ice cream for serving, optional

Mix the Crust and Topping

⟿ Preheat the oven to 325°F. Line a 9 x 9 x 2-inch or 11 x 7 x 2-inch baking pan with heavy aluminum foil that extends over 2 ends of the pan. Butter the foil that will touch the bars.

Put the flour, powdered sugar, and brown sugar in a large bowl and use a large spoon to stir them together. Add the butter pieces, stirring to coat them with flour. Rub the butter pieces and flour mixture between your thumb and fingertips or use a pastry blender to cut the butter into the flour until fine crumbs form that are about ½ inch in size and there is no loose flour. Remove 2 cups of the mixture and set aside. Transfer the remaining mixture to the prepared pan and press it evenly over the bottom.

Mix the Filling

↝ Stir the apples, sugar, and lemon juice together in a large bowl. Stir in the raisins. Spoon the filling over the prepared crust, distributing it evenly. Sprinkle the reserved crumbs evenly over the apple filling.

Bake and Serve the Bars

↝ Bake until the crumb topping is golden and the apples are soft when tested with a toothpick, about 55 minutes. Carefully lift the aluminum foil and bars from the baking pan. Loosen the foil from the sides of the bars. Cut into 12 to 16 pieces. Use a wide spatula to slide the bars off the foil. Serve warm, with vanilla ice cream, if desired. Or, cool the bars thoroughly in the baking pan at room temperature. The bars firm as they cool. Cut into 12 to 16 pieces. Use a thin metal spatula to remove the bars from the pan. Dust the bars with powdered sugar, if desired. Serve at room temperature.

Deep-Dish Apple Strudel Pie

Once you peel and slice the apples, this is an almost instant apple pie. Store-bought phyllo pastry is the secret to the crisp top crust.

Baking Answers ❧ For a crisp crust, serve the pie warm. If the pie has cooled, you can restore its crisp topping by warming it in a 250°F. oven for about 15 minutes or until it is warmed thoroughly. Boxes of paper-thin sheets of phyllo pastry can be found in supermarkets in the freezer or refrigerated sections. Phyllo pastry is soft and pliable but must be kept covered with a clean, damp dish towel to prevent it from drying out when you are working with it. Wet the dish towel, then wring it out well before placing on the phyllo pastry. Since phyllo pastry has little flavor, it is usually spread with melted butter and sometimes sugar and spices before baking. Leftover pastry can be rolled up tightly in plastic wrap and stored in the refrigerator for up to 1 week.

I partially bake the apples before adding the pastry topping. Since the pastry bakes so quickly, raw apples wouldn't have time to bake tender.

A Step Ahead ❧ Assemble the pie, cover with plastic wrap, and refrigerate overnight. The cold pie takes about 35 minutes to bake.

SERVES 6

Necessities ❧ *A baking container with a 2- to 2½-quart capacity and at least 2-inch-high sides*

APPLE FILLING	
8 cups peeled and cored apples sliced about ½ inch thick (about 8 large apples)	3 tablespoons sugar
	1 tablespoon unsalted butter, melted
	1 teaspoon fresh lemon juice
	½ teaspoon ground cinnamon

PASTRY TOPPING	
¼ cup sugar	6 phyllo pastry sheets, defrosted if frozen
1 teaspoon ground cinnamon	3 tablespoons unsalted butter, melted

Mix the Filling

❧ Position an oven rack in the middle of the oven. Preheat the oven to 325°F. Put the apples in a baking container with a 2- to 2½-quart capacity. Either an 8- or 9-inch square baking dish or a 9½- to 10-inch-diameter round pie dish, both with at least 2-inch-high sides, works well. Mix in the sugar, melted butter, and lemon juice. Bake, uncovered, for 20 minutes, stirring once. Remove the pan from the oven and stir in the cinnamon. Set aside to cool to lukewarm for about 30 minutes before topping with phyllo pastry.

Increase the oven temperature to 375°F.

Add the Topping

❧ Stir the sugar and cinnamon together in a small bowl. Stack the phyllo sheets and, using the rim of the baking container as a cutting guide, with a sharp knife or scissors cut 6 circles the same size as the diameter of the baking container. Discard the scraps. Cover the stack of phyllo circles with a clean damp dish towel. Press 1 circle of phyllo pastry gently over the apples. Brush lightly with melted butter and sprinkle about 2 teaspoons of the sugar mixture over it evenly. Repeat the layering with the remaining sheets of phyllo pastry, ending with the melted butter and a sprinkling of the sugar mixture.

Bake and Serve the Pie

❧ Bake about 30 minutes until the pastry topping is light brown. Cut through the pastry topping with a knife, then use a large spoon to serve the warm pie. Shallow bowls make nice serving dishes, and vanilla ice cream is a good accompaniment. This pie is best served warm the day it is baked.

Big-Top Corn Muffins

White, yellow, or blue, sweet or savory, stone-ground or not—making corn muffins can involve a lot of choices. I've made my choice with these moist, somewhat sweet, deep yellow corn muffins. They are large muffins that form wide, crisp tops as they rise just over the top of the muffin tin openings during baking. Supermarket cornmeal produces the fine light-textured muffin that I prefer; stone-ground cornmeal produces a more intense corn flavor, but the texture becomes heavier and more dense. Since these muffins take only minutes to mix, try them either way and choose your own favorite.

Baking Answers ❧ These corn muffins use the basic simple and fast method for mixing muffins. Stir the liquid ingredients together in a mixing bowl and sift the dry ingredients into another bowl. Then combine the two mixtures, stirring just enough to moisten the dry ingredients. Vigorous or prolonged stirring develops the gluten in the flour, which can toughen the texture and coarsen the grain. To combine the ingredients quickly and with a minimum of stirring, I pour the dry ingredients over the liquid ones. When the batter is mixed properly, you will see small lumps but no big white globs of flour.

I use muffin tins that hold a full ½ cup of liquid and measure 2¾ inches across the top. If the muffin tins are slightly smaller, you will need to fill more openings, will have a smaller muffin, and will probably need to shorten the baking time by several minutes. For large muffins, pour muffin batter to ⅛ inch from the top of the opening, so the baked muffins rise over the edge of each opening. Butter the openings and the top of the pan generously to prevent the tops from sticking to the pan. The tops and the sides of the baked muffins will be light brown and slightly crisp and will release easily. Paper muffin liners do not produce crisp sides to the muffins, so I rely on buttering the tin thoroughly. This recipe makes 8 large muffins, leaving 4 empty openings in the muffin tins. The empty openings allow space for the muffin tops to spread over the top of the pan. Rather than protecting the empty openings in the pan by the usual method of filling them with water, I fill empty muffin tin openings with paper muffin liners during baking. This protects the pan and allows me to turn the tins upside down to release the muffins from the pan.

These muffins have a large proportion of cornmeal and need a generous amount of leavening in the form of baking powder and baking soda in order to rise properly. Baking soda is included because it reacts with the acid buttermilk that is used for the liquid.

A Step Ahead ✺ The muffins can be baked a day ahead, cooled, covered, and stored at room temperature. Warm them, covered with aluminum foil, in a preheated 275°F. oven for 15 minutes.

Necessities ✺ *2 muffin tins that hold 6 muffins each, or 1 muffin tin that holds 12 muffins, and 1 wire rack for cooling the muffins*

1 tablespoon (or more) soft butter for greasing the pan	1 teaspoon baking soda
1 cup unbleached all-purpose flour	½ teaspoon salt
1¼ cups yellow cornmeal	1¼ cups buttermilk (nonfat is fine)
½ cup sugar	1 large egg
2 teaspoons baking powder	2 ounces (½ stick) butter, melted

Mix the Batter

✺ Position a rack in the middle of the oven. Preheat the oven to 400°F. Generously rub soft butter, using about 1 tablespoon, around the inside and top rims of 8 openings in a muffin tin. Use either 2 tins with 6 openings or 1 tin with 12 openings. Alternate the filled muffin openings with the empty ones as much as possible to allow space for the tops of the muffins to spread.

Sift the flour, cornmeal, sugar, baking powder, baking soda, and salt into a medium bowl and set aside. Put the buttermilk, egg, and melted butter in a large bowl and use a fork to stir them together until the egg is blended into the mixture. Pour the flour mixture over the buttermilk mixture and stir slowly with a large spoon for about 20 strokes just to combine the ingredients until there is no loose flour. There will be small lumps, about ⅛ inch in size, but no large lumps of batter-coated flour. Pour a scant ½ cup batter into the buttered pan openings, filling them to ⅛ inch from the top.

Bake and Serve the Muffins

✺ Bake about 17 minutes until the tops are light brown and a toothpick inserted in the center comes out dry. Use a small knife to gently loosen the tops of the muffins from the top of the pan. Cool 5 minutes in the pan. Using potholders to protect your hands, invert the muffin pan onto a wire rack and tap the bottom of the tin to release the muffins. If all of the muffins do not release when the tin is lifted, lift the tin and tap the edge on the side of the wire rack or use the small knife to loosen the sides of the muffins from the pan. Serve the muffins warm with butter and jam if desired. Strawberry jam makes a good jam choice. The cooled muffins can be wrapped in plastic wrap and stored at room temperature for 1 day. Warm them, covered with aluminum foil, in a preheated 275°F. oven for about 15 minutes before serving them.

Maple Muffins with Carrots, Pineapple, and Pecans

If one thing is abundant on my sister Susan's farm, it is food. So it was no surprise to me that her special muffin recipe has more fruit and nuts than batter. "It's the pieces of dried pineapple that make my muffins so good," she wrote on the recipe. I think the pure maple syrup and all of the carrots, pineapple, raisins, and pecans have a lot to do with it too.

Baking Answers ❧ I found cut-up pieces of dried sweetened pineapple in my local natural foods store. It is easier to use than cutting up the slices of dried pineapple, and the ⅜-inch pieces are the perfect size. If whole slices of sweetened dried pineapple are used, it takes about 3 slices to make 1 cup of chopped pineapple.

Grate the peeled carrots on the large teardrop-shaped holes of a four-sided grater or in a food processor using the grating blade. If using the food processor, cut the carrots into 1-inch pieces to produce short shreds of grated carrot.

These muffins use only maple syrup as the sweetener. The liquid ingredients and carrots are stirred together, the dry ingredients are mixed into them, then the pineapple, raisins, and pecans are stirred just to distribute them.

I use paper muffin liners to line muffin tins, so these extremely moist muffins remove easily from the pan. The muffins rise only slightly, so the paper liners in the muffin tins can be filled almost to the top with batter.

MAKES 12 MUFFINS

Necessities ❧ *2 muffin tins that hold 6 muffins each, or 1 muffin tin that holds 12 muffins, and paper muffin liners*

1 cup unbleached all-purpose flour	1 teaspoon vanilla extract
1 teaspoon baking powder	2 cups packed peeled and grated carrots
1 teaspoon baking soda	(about 5 medium carrots)
¼ teaspoon salt	1 cup (about 3 slices) dried sweetened
1 teaspoon ground cinnamon	pineapple cut into about ⅜-inch
⅔ cup pure maple syrup	pieces
2 large eggs	½ cup raisins
3 ounces (¾ stick) unsalted butter, melted	¾ cup coarsely chopped pecans

Mix the Batter

◆ Position a rack in the middle of the oven. Preheat the oven to 400°F. Line 12 muffin tin openings with paper muffin liners.

Sift the flour, baking powder, baking soda, salt, and cinnamon together onto a piece of wax paper or into a medium bowl. Set aside.

Put the maple syrup, eggs, melted butter, vanilla, and grated carrots in a large bowl and stir vigorously with a large spoon, about 30 strokes, to blend the ingredients thoroughly. Add the flour mixture to the maple syrup mixture and stir them together, just until they are blended and there is no loose flour. Add the pineapple, raisins, and pecans to the mixture, stirring just to distribute them evenly throughout the batter.

Use a tablespoon to scoop the batter into the muffin liners, dividing the batter evenly among the 12 muffin liners in the tin and filling each liner just to the top.

Bake and Serve the Muffins

◆ Bake about 20 minutes until the tops look dry and a toothpick inserted in the center comes out clean. Cool the muffins in their pan. Using a dull knife as an aid, lift the muffins in their liners out of the muffin tin. Serve the muffins warm or at room temperature. They can be served plain or with butter. The cooled muffins can be wrapped in plastic wrap and stored at room temperature for up to 2 days. Warm them, covered with aluminum foil, in a preheated 275°F. oven for about 15 minutes before serving them.

Big, Easy Popovers

Large, billowy popovers that are crisp on the outside, moist and almost hollow on the inside, and dripping with melted butter and jam, make a most indulgent quick bread. This popover recipe was one of the nicest birthday presents that I ever received. My mother-in-law, Selma Klivans, gave me this foolproof version along with some large ceramic baking cups to use for baking them. They take minutes to stir together and consistently "pop" into large puffy popovers. Although they look fragile once baked, these popovers are quite stable, so they can be held in a turned-off oven for up to 30 minutes.

Baking Answers ✥ To produce large popovers, bake them in large tins, ovenproof glass dishes, or ceramic cups. I found a Texas muffin tin in my supermarket that works well. The "Texas size" openings have a 1-cup capacity (8 ounces). They measure 3⅜ inches in diameter and are 1⅝ inches deep. The openings are not filled to the top, but are large enough to allow the batter to expand. I have also used 6-ounce Pyrex glass custard cups with good results. These should be placed on a baking sheet for easy handling. There are special popover pans with tapered openings with spaces between them, but it is not necessary to buy a special pan. Ordinary muffin tins with a 4-ounce capacity produce 6 smaller popovers that bake in about 40 minutes rather than 45 minutes.

Use cooking oil spray to grease the pan openings. Rubbing the pan with butter or oil does not keep the popovers from sticking as well as the cooking spray does.

I prefer to add some salt for the flavor it produces, but it won't affect the rise if you leave it out. It's the steam created by the liquid batter that makes popovers puff up.

To measure the capacity of the ungreased baking cups, measure a cup full of water, pour it into the opening, and note the quantity that the baking cup holds.

A liquid measuring cup or small pitcher with a lip works well for pouring the batter into the baking cups.

Note that the oven is not preheated. It is turned on when the popovers go into the oven.

Double the ingredients to make 8 popovers and have enough baking pans on hand. A combination of muffin tins and baking cups is fine.

MAKES 4 LARGE POPOVERS

Necessities ✥ *1 muffin tin with large openings (Texas size) or 4 ovenproof individual baking cups with a capacity of ¾ cup to 1 cup each, a can of unflavored cooking oil spray, and a baking sheet*

2 large eggs	*½ teaspoon salt*
1 cup milk (any fat content is okay)	*1 cup unbleached all-purpose flour*

❧ Position a rack in the middle of the oven. Have a baking sheet ready. Generously coat cooking oil spray over the bottom and sides of 4 openings in a muffin tin or 4 ovenproof individual baking cups with a capacity of ¾ cup to 1 cup each. Put muffin paper liners or ¼ cup of water in any openings that will remain empty. Alternate the filled openings of a muffin tin with the empty ones as much as possible to allow space for the popovers to spread. Or, use glass or ceramic baking cups with at least a 6-ounce capacity.

Mix the Batter

❧ Put the eggs, milk, and salt in a medium bowl and stir them with a fork to break up the egg yolks and combine the milk with the eggs. Pour the flour over the milk mixture and use a whisk to stir in the flour to incorporate it into the mixture. Whisk slowly rather than vigorously. The batter will have small lumps, but no large globs of flour on the bottom of the bowl, and will look like pancake batter. Cover and refrigerate the mixture for 30 minutes or up to 2 hours.

Bake and Serve the Popovers

❧ Pour the batter into a pitcher. Using a scant ½ cup (7 tablespoons) of batter for each popover, pour the batter into the prepared pan or baking cups. The batter should be at least ½ inch from the top of each opening. Put the muffin tin or baking cups on the baking sheet and put it in the oven. Turn the oven on to 425°F. Bake about 45 minutes until the tops and exposed edges are brown. Turn the oven off, puncture the sides of each popover in 3 places with a toothpick, and let them sit in the turned-off oven for 10 minutes. Remove as many popovers as needed for a first serving and leave the remaining ones in the oven for up to 30 minutes. Serve with butter and jam. Strawberry or raspberry jam makes a good choice. I eat popovers by breaking a small opening in the hot popover and dropping in a generous lump of butter, which melts inside the hot popover, then I spread on jam as I break off each "dripping with butter" piece.

Green Tomato and Cornmeal Pecan Crisp

Move over, fried green tomatoes—make way for a savory vegetable adaptation of a sweet fruit crisp! A green tomato and onion filling has a crunchy cornmeal and pecan topping and makes good use of that inevitable end-of-the-season surplus of not-quite-ripe tomatoes.

Baking Answers ⌁ Choose green tomatoes that have no soft spots or bruises and feel evenly firm. During the winter months, I have substituted those hard pink tomatoes that never seem to ripen—I call them bullet tomatoes—for the green tomatoes. They work well and I've finally found a use for winter tomatoes.

Either ordinary cornmeal or stone-ground cornmeal can be used for the crumb topping.

Using melted butter for the crumb topping, rather than cold butter pieces, adds to the crisp texture of the topping. When it is mixed, this crumb mixture forms fine or very small crumbs.

A Step Ahead ⌁ The crisp can be prepared in the morning, then set aside and loosely covered, to be baked later in the day.

SERVES 6

Necessities ⌁ *A glass or ceramic baking container with about a 2-quart capacity, such as an 8- or 9-inch square baking dish or a 9½- to 10-inch-diameter round pie dish, both with 1¾- to 2-inch-high sides*

GREEN TOMATO FILLING	
4 cups chopped green tomatoes cut into ½- to ¾-inch pieces (4 medium tomatoes)	2 tablespoons finely chopped parsley
	¼ cup chicken broth, low-sodium if using canned
½ cup (1 small) finely chopped onion	½ teaspoon salt
	¼ teaspoon freshly ground black pepper

CORNMEAL TOPPING	
¾ cup unbleached all-purpose flour	½ teaspoon salt
½ cup yellow cornmeal	¼ teaspoon freshly ground black pepper
1 tablespoon sugar	3 ounces (¾ stick) butter, melted
	½ cup coarsely chopped pecans

Make the Filling

🌭 Position a rack in the middle of the oven. Preheat the oven to 350°F. Butter a glass or ceramic baking container with about a 2-quart capacity. Either an 8- or 9-inch square baking dish or a 9½- to 10-inch–diameter round pie dish, both with 1¾- to 2-inch–high sides, works well. Put the green tomatoes, onion, parsley, chicken broth, salt, and pepper in a large bowl and stir them together. Transfer the mixture to the baking dish, spreading it evenly. Set aside.

Mix the Topping

🌭 Put the flour, cornmeal, sugar, salt, and pepper in a medium bowl and use a fork to stir them together. Stir in the melted butter, stirring until crumbs form and the mixture looks evenly moist. You will have a mixture of fine crumbs and small crumbs. Stir in the pecans. Sprinkle the crumbs evenly over the tomato mixture.

Bake and Serve the Crisp

🌭 Bake until the tomatoes are tender when tested with a toothpick and the mixture begins to bubble at the edges, about 45 minutes. If using pink winter tomatoes, bake about 40 minutes. Serve warm as a hearty vegetable side dish.

Baked Blintz

The usual blintz consists of a slightly sweetened cottage cheese mixture wrapped in a thin crêpe. Once filled, the blintzes are sautéed in butter and often served with sour cream. As much as I enjoy blintzes, the memory of my mother spending hours on their time-consuming preparation kept me from making them at home. That is, until my friend Rosie Levitan sent me this recipe that bakes a traditional filling between 2 layers of a batter that becomes soft, crisp, and somewhat crêpelike when baked. It takes only about 10 minutes to put together. It was the main dish at our daughter's wedding brunch—need I say more?

Baking Answers ◈ Using a combination of ricotta cheese and cottage cheese rather than cottage cheese alone produces an exceptionally smooth mixture for the filling.

Use a baking dish that measures 10 inches square; one that is 11 x 9 inches can also be used as long as it is 2 inches deep. I bake the blintz in an attractive baking dish that I can take to the table for serving.

When the blintz is done, the top forms a golden crisp crust with brown edges. The blintz can be served as a breakfast, brunch, or light dinner main dish. Fresh berries or a fruit salad and bacon, sausage, or smoked fish make good side dish accompaniments.

A Step Ahead ◈ Partially bake the blintz for 1 hour at 300°F. Let the blintz cool, wrap the dish in plastic wrap and heavy aluminum foil, label with the date and contents, and freeze it in its baking dish for up to 1 month. Defrost the wrapped blintz overnight in the refrigerator. Unwrap it and bake the cold blintz for about 40 minutes at 300°F. until the blintz is hot and the top is golden and crisp.

SERVES 10 TO 12

Necessities ◈ One 11 x 9 x 2-inch or 10 x 10 x 2-inch baking pan or ovenproof glass dish

FOR THE BATTER	
1 cup unbleached all-purpose flour	6 ounces (1½ sticks) unsalted butter, melted
1 tablespoon baking powder	2 large eggs
⅛ teaspoon salt	¼ cup milk (whole, low-fat, or nonfat)
½ cup sugar	1 teaspoon vanilla extract

FOR THE FILLING
2 pounds ricotta cheese
½ pound small-curd cottage cheese
2 large eggs

¼ cup sugar
¼ teaspoon salt
2 teaspoons fresh lemon juice

Mix the Batter

❧ Position a rack in the middle of the oven. Preheat the oven to 300°F. Butter the bottom and sides of an 11 x 9 x 2-inch or 10 x 10 x 2-inch baking pan or an ovenproof glass dish.

Put the flour, baking powder, salt, and sugar in a large bowl and stir them together. Add the melted butter, eggs, milk, and vanilla to the flour mixture. Use a large spoon to stir the mixture until the ingredients are combined and the mixture is smooth. Pour 1¼ cups of the batter in the bottom of the prepared pan, tilting the pan to spread it evenly. Set the remainder aside while you prepare the filling.

Mix the Filling

❧ Put the ricotta cheese, cottage cheese, eggs, sugar, salt, and lemon juice in a large bowl. Stir the mixture until the ingredients are combined. Spread the filling evenly over the batter in the pan. A thin metal spatula works well for spreading. Pour the remaining batter evenly over the ricotta cheese mixture.

Bake and Serve the Blintz

❧ Bake the blintz for about 1½ hours until the edges look brown and crisp. The top will be golden. Use a large serving spoon to serve the hot blintz. Serve with fresh strawberries, raspberries, or blueberries, or pass blueberry jam, if desired.

Layered Cheddar, Vegetable, and Cashew Nut Pie

This crunchy vegetable and nut pie evolved from a daily special that I tasted at a pub in Dedham, England. When I asked for the recipe, I was told the chef used whatever ingredients he had on hand that day. I jotted down the ingredients of that day and worked out this duplicate of the original pub version.

Rather than piecrust, it has a sprinkling of bread crumbs for its crisp bottom; otherwise, it's all filling. The lightly cooked vegetable and nut mixture is layered with cheese and tomatoes and has a golden brown cheese, bread crumb, and cashew nut topping.

Baking Answers
Any unseasoned type of bread crumb works for this pie, but the coarser texture of homemade bread crumbs is preferable. When I have stale, but not moldy, oatmeal, french, or whole wheat bread, I tear it into 1-inch pieces and process the stale bread in a food processor into uniformly sized crumbs. I seal the crumbs tightly in a heavyweight plastic freezer bag and freeze them for up to 3 months. The bread crumbs can be used directly from the freezer. Spoon out the amount needed and return any remaining crumbs to the freezer.

The vegetables have a preliminary cooking before the pie is baked. Stir them often so the vegetables cook evenly and small pieces don't burn.

Roasted unsalted cashew nuts can usually be found in the supermarket, but natural foods stores are another good source.

Freshly ground pepper delivers the best flavor. The flavor of black pepper comes from its natural oils. Once black pepper is ground, the oils begin to dry out and the pepper begins to lose its flavor.

Cool any leftover pie before refrigerating it to prevent the moisture that would form when a wrapped hot pie is put in the cold refrigerator.

A Step Ahead
The unbaked pie can be assembled in the morning, then covered and refrigerated for baking later in the day. Let the cold pie come to room temperature before baking it.

SERVES 6

Necessities
A 9-inch-diameter pie dish or round baking dish that has 1½- to 2-inch-high sides

1¾ cups unseasoned bread crumbs, fresh coarsely ground white, oatmeal, or whole wheat crumbs preferred

4 tablespoons olive oil

½ cup (1 small) thinly sliced carrot

1 cup (1 medium) thinly sliced onion

½ cup (½ stalk) thinly sliced celery

1 clove garlic, finely chopped

2 cups (about ½ pound) broccoli pieces (½- to ¾-inch pieces)

1 cup roasted unsalted cashew nut halves or pieces

⅛ teaspoon salt

⅛ teaspoon freshly ground black pepper

2 cups (about 8 ounces) grated mild Cheddar cheese

2 medium tomatoes, sliced ½ inch thick

Prepare the Pie

☞ Position a rack in the middle of the oven. Preheat the oven to 325°F. Brush olive oil over the bottom and sides of a 9-inch-diameter pie dish, such as Pyrex, or a ceramic baking dish that has 1½- to 2-inch-high sides. Press ½ cup of the bread crumbs evenly over the bottom of the dish. They will not form a solid layer.

Heat 3 tablespoons of the olive oil over low-medium heat in a large frying pan. Add the carrot, onion, and celery and cook until the onion softens, about 5 minutes. Add the garlic and broccoli and cook another 10 minutes. Remove the pan from the heat and stir in ¾ cup of the cashews. Add the salt and pepper and taste the mixture for seasoning.

Spread half the vegetable mixture evenly in the prepared baking pan. Sprinkle ¾ cup of the cheese evenly over the vegetables. Arrange half the tomato slices over the cheese. Sprinkle with ½ cup bread crumbs. Spread the remaining vegetable mixture over the bread crumbs. Sprinkle ¾ cup of cheese evenly over the vegetables and arrange the remaining tomato slices over the cheese. Put the remaining ¾ cup bread crumbs, ¼ cup cashew nuts, and ½ cup cheese in a small bowl and stir them together. Sprinkle the bread crumb mixture evenly over the tomatoes. Drizzle the remaining 1 tablespoon of olive oil evenly over the bread crumb topping.

Bake and Serve the Pie

☞ Bake, uncovered, for 1 hour and 15 minutes. The top will look light brown and crisp. Let the pie sit for 5 minutes to firm slightly, then cut it into slices and serve hot. Serve the pie with french bread for a one-dish meal. Leftover pie can be cooled, covered, and stored in the refrigerator overnight. To reheat it, cover the pie with aluminum foil and warm it in a preheated 300°F. oven until it is warm to the touch, about 20 minutes. The warm pie can be wrapped in clean dish towels, taken along on a picnic, and served at room (or outdoor) temperature.

Zucchini Bread Pudding

With its 2 pounds of zucchini, this savory brioche bread and vegetable cheese pudding goes a long way toward devouring the predictable summertime zucchini glut. However, it also makes a cozy, light winter supper. Two pounds of summer squash or any combination of 2 pounds total of summer squash and zucchini can be substituted.

Baking Answers ❧ When choosing zucchini, smaller is better. Choose ones that are no larger than 2 inches in diameter. Those giant county fair–prize zucchini are quite watery and can have thick skins.

Cook the onion and zucchini in butter just to soften but not to brown them.

Egg-enriched breads such as challah for brioche add flavor to the pudding.

A Step Ahead ❧ The steps of prebaking the bread cubes and sautéing the zucchini and onion can be done in the morning for when the dish is baked later in the day. After cooling and covering them with plastic wrap, let both sit at room temperature until the dish is ready to assemble.

The entire pudding can be baked the day before, and then cooled, covered with plastic wrap, and refrigerated. Uncover the cold pudding and heat it in a 325°F. oven for about 15 minutes until it is warmed thoroughly.

SERVES 8

Necessities ❧ *A shallow baking dish with a 2- to 2½-quart capacity*

3 cups of 1-inch cubes of brioche or other egg-enriched bread such as challah	2 large eggs
	½ teaspoon salt
	½ teaspoon freshly ground black pepper
6 tablespoons unsalted butter, melted	1 cup grated Jack or mild Cheddar cheese
1 cup (1 medium) chopped onion	
2 pounds (about 6 medium) coarsely chopped zucchini, cut into about ½-inch chunks	

Prepare the Pudding

⭗ Position a rack in the middle of the oven. Preheat the oven to 375°F. Butter the bottom and sides of a shallow baking dish with a 2- to 2½-quart capacity.

Put the bread cubes in the baking dish and drizzle 4 tablespoons of melted butter over them. Bake about 15 minutes, just until the edges of the bread cubes begin to brown lightly, stirring once to help them bake evenly. Set aside while you prepare the filling.

Heat 1 tablespoon of the melted butter over low-medium heat in a medium frying pan. Add the onion and cook until the onion softens but does not brown, about 5 minutes, stirring occasionally. Add the zucchini and cook just until it softens, about 8 minutes. Set the mixture aside to cool slightly.

Put the eggs, the remaining 1 tablespoon of melted butter, salt, and pepper in a large bowl and use a whisk to blend the ingredients thoroughly. Stir in the cooled zucchini mixture, including any juices that have formed. Pour the mixture evenly over the bread cubes in the baking dish. Sprinkle the grated cheese evenly over the top.

Bake and Serve

⭗ Bake until you can give the pudding a gentle shake and it looks firm and set, about 45 minutes. Serve hot as a combination of both bread and vegetable side dish or with a salad for a light supper.

No-Roll Crusts
with
Simple Fillings

FROM A CHEWY WALNUT BAR WITH A PRESS-IN CRUST, TO A FANCY FRENCH TART THAT HAS A CRUST MIXTURE SOFT ENOUGH TO BE SPREADABLE, TO A SAVORY HAM AND CHEESE PIE ENCLOSED IN A CRUST OF CRISP POTATOES, NO-ROLL CRUSTS COME IN MANY forms. Whether you are baking your first pie or cheesecake, or your fiftieth, you'll be pleased with the results from any of these foolproof crusts.

Crumb crusts are usually made from store-bought cookies or crackers. Graham crackers and sometimes chocolate cookies can be bought already ground into crumbs. Other cookies such as chocolate wafers or gingersnaps or crackers such as Ritz or saltines can be crushed with a rolling pin or processed in a food processor into crumbs. I often walk up and down the cookie and cracker aisle in my grocery to find new ideas for a no-roll crumb crust. Plain crisp cookies work well, but such sandwich cookies as Oreos can also be crushed into crumbs. Since the filling also moistens the crumbs, crumb crusts made from cookies with filling need less butter. To mix crumb crusts, stir the crumbs together with any included flavorings or sugar and enough melted butter to moisten them. Chopped or ground nuts, spices, citrus zest, or chocolate chips add variety to these crusts. To form the crust, press the crumb mixture evenly inside a buttered pan. A short baking crisps and firms these crusts while freshening their taste.

Press-in crusts are made from a crumbly butter and flour mixture that is usually sweetened. If cold butter is used, mix press-in crusts with your fingertips or a pastry blender. If soft butter is used, use an electric mixer to mix these crusts. The crumb mixture is spread evenly in the baking pan and pressed firmly into the pan. Although the unbaked mixture may barely hold together, baking melts the butter in the mixture and a tender, solid crust forms. These crusts usually have at least a partial baking before fillings are added. This prebaking before filling a crust produces a crisper crust that remains separate from the filling.

The pouring crust for the cherry custard tart (page 105) is a soft flour, egg, and butter mixture that is soft enough to spread. It bakes into a crust that is somewhere between a soft cookie and a crisp cake.

Finally, the Ham and Swiss Potato Pie (page 108) bakes in a nontraditional-type crust of prebaked thin, buttered potato slices.

Most of these fillings need only to be stirred together by hand or with an electric mixer. The cherry custard tart has a filling of vanilla pastry cream that is prepared by whisking hot milk into a mixture of egg yolks, flour, and sugar and cooking it to a thick pudding. Cheesecake fillings require only that the cream cheese be soft and the eggs at room temperature, so the ingredients combine to form a smooth mixture. The Orange Cream Cheese Pie with Shiny Strawberries (page 94) and the Savory Lemon, Sage, Parsley, and Thyme Cheesecake (page 110) have ultra-smooth cream cheese fillings that are processed in a food processor.

Lemon Chess Bars

These bars evolved from classic chess pie. They have a translucent silky-smooth lemon filling that is thickened with a small amount of cornmeal. The cornmeal dissolves in the filling and does its job "secretly." This no-roll crust is a butter-crumb mixture that is pressed into the pan. Partially baking the crust before adding the filling produces a soft but firm crust. I usually cut these into small bars, but large squares can be served for a dessert.

There are many explanations for the origin of chess pie. My favorite is the one about the Southern cook who, when asked the name of the pie she was serving, answered, "It's jess pie."

Baking Answers ❧ Remember to grate the lemon zest from the lemon before squeezing the juice. For the zest, grate only the yellow skin of the lemon. The white pith is bitter and has no lemon flavor.

The lemon filling is sticky and tends to stick to the sides of the pan. Lining the pan with buttered aluminum foil or parchment paper that overhangs all sides of the pan allows you to lift the cooled bars from the pan for easy cutting and prevents sticking.

A Step Ahead ❧ The crust can be mixed and prebaked a day ahead. Cover the cooled crust with plastic wrap and store at room temperature.

The bars can be frozen for up to 1 month. Place the bars side by side in groups of two or three and wrap them in plastic wrap. Place in a metal or plastic freezer container and cover tightly. Label with the date and contents. Defrost the wrapped bars in the refrigerator.

MAKES 25 BARS

Necessities ❧ *A 9-inch square baking pan or an 11 x 7-inch baking pan, both with 2-inch-high sides, and a grater for the lemon zest*

CRUST	¼ teaspoon salt
1 cup unbleached all-purpose flour	¼ pound (1 stick) cold unsalted butter,
¼ cup powdered sugar	cut into ½-inch pieces

FILLING	3 tablespoons cornmeal
3 large eggs	2 ounces (½ stick) unsalted butter,
1 large egg yolk	melted
¼ teaspoon salt	2 teaspoons grated lemon zest
1½ cups granulated sugar	¼ cup fresh lemon juice
¼ cup buttermilk	1 teaspoon vanilla extract

Powdered sugar for dusting the bars

Prepare and Bake the Crust

⌁ Position a rack in the middle of the oven. Preheat the oven to 350°F. Line a 9 x 9 x 2 or an 11 x 7 x 2-inch pan with 2 pieces of parchment paper or aluminum foil that extend over the 4 sides of the pan. Butter the bottom of the paper or foil.

Put the flour, powdered sugar, salt, and butter pieces in a large bowl. Rub the butter pieces and flour mixture between your thumb and fingertips or use a pastry blender to cut the butter into the flour until fine crumbs form that are about ¼ inch in size. A few odd larger crumbs will remain. Transfer the mixture to the prepared pan and press it evenly over the bottom.

Bake the crust for 15 minutes. The edges should be light brown. Reduce the oven temperature to 325°F.

Prepare the Filling

⌁ Mix the filling while the crust bakes. Put the eggs, egg yolk, salt, and granulated sugar in a large bowl and beat with an electric mixer on medium speed for about 2 minutes until the mixture looks fluffy, thickens, and lightens to a cream color. If using a handheld electric mixer, move the beaters around in the bowl. Mix in the buttermilk, cornmeal, melted butter, lemon zest, lemon juice, and vanilla until they are blended into the mixture. Pour the filling into the partially baked crust.

Bake and Serve the Bars

⌁ Bake about 40 minutes, until the top looks golden and is firm and set when you give the pan a gentle shake. Cool the bars at room temperature. Cover and refrigerate the cooled bars until well chilled, about 3 hours. The filling becomes firm when cold. Carefully lift the paper or foil liner with the bars from the baking pan. Use a small knife to loosen the liner from the sides of the bars.

Cut into 25 pieces, cutting 5 rows across and 5 rows down. Or, cut the bars into larger pieces, if desired. Use a wide metal spatula to slide the bars off the baking liner. Dust the bars with powdered sugar. Serve cold. Leftover bars can be covered and refrigerated for up to 3 days.

Three-Layer Walnut Bars

W hen I first tasted these bars at a party, I couldn't figure out what was in them. They were so moist that I was sure they included dates or some sort of fruit, but they didn't. Luckily, Barbara Moses shared her recipe, because I never would have guessed how simple the ingredients were. The filling bakes on top of a thin press-in crust and turned out to include walnuts, brown sugar, and coconut. After baking, the bars are topped off with a fresh orange and lemon–flavored powdered sugar frosting. Although you'll need to prepare 3 layers for these bars, they all assemble in minutes.

Baking Answers ⤙ For the crust, butter and flour are mixed to fine crumbs and pressed into the bottom of the pan. This crust uses soft rather than cold butter, so it can be prepared with an electric mixer. For the filling and frosting, the ingredients need only to be stirred together.

Remember to grate the orange zest from the orange before squeezing the juice. For the zest, grate only the orange skin of the orange. The white pith is bitter and has no orange flavor.

Refrigerate the frosted bars for easy cutting. When cold, the bars can be cut into neat pieces and the frosting won't crack or crumble. Since the bars are rich, I cut them into 36 pieces. I prefer the firm, almost fudgelike consistency that the cold bars have, but they may be served at room temperature as well.

A Step Ahead ⤙ Once the frosting is firm, the bars can be frozen. Place the bars side by side in groups of two or three and wrap them in plastic wrap. Place in a metal or plastic freezer container and cover tightly. Label with the date and contents. Freeze up to 1 month. Defrost the wrapped bars in the refrigerator.

MAKES 36 SMALL BARS

Necessities ⤙ *A 9-inch square pan or an 11 x 7-inch baking pan, both with 2-inch-high sides, and a grater for the orange zest*

CRUST	¼ pound (1 stick) unsalted butter
1 cup unbleached all-purpose flour	slightly softened for about 1 hour, cut into 6 pieces

FILLING	½ teaspoon salt
2 large eggs	1 teaspoon vanilla extract
1½ cups packed dark brown sugar	1 cup coarsely chopped walnuts
¼ teaspoon baking powder	½ cup shredded sweetened coconut

FROSTING	1 tablespoon fresh lemon juice
1½ cups powdered sugar, sifted	2 tablespoons fresh orange juice
2 tablespoons unsalted butter, melted	1 teaspoon grated orange zest

Prepare and Bake the Crust

∽ Position a rack in the middle of the oven. Preheat the oven to 350°F. Butter a 9 x 9 x 2-inch or an 11 x 7 x 2-inch baking pan.

Put the flour and butter pieces in a large bowl. Mix with an electric mixer on medium speed until fine butter-coated crumbs form, about 2 minutes. A few odd, large crumbs, about ¼ inch in size, remain. The mixture becomes a creamy color and there is no loose flour. Move the beaters around in the bowl if using a handheld electric mixer. Stop the mixer and scrape any mixture that becomes caught in the beaters as needed. If you press a clump of the mixture, it should hold together. Transfer the mixture to the prepared pan and use your fingertips to press it evenly over the bottom.

Bake the crust for 15 minutes. The edges should be light brown. Leave the oven on.

Mix the Filling

∽ Mix the filling while the crust bakes. Put the eggs in a large bowl and whisk to blend the whites and yolks thoroughly. Use a large spoon to stir in the brown sugar, pressing out any lumps of brown sugar. Stir in the baking powder, salt, and vanilla to incorporate them. Stir in the walnuts and coconut to distribute them evenly. Pour the filling over the partially baked crust. The crust will still be warm. Spread the mixture evenly over the crust, being careful not to disturb the crust.

Bake the Filling

∽ Bake about 30 minutes, until the filling looks set if you give it a gentle shake. Cool the bars for 30 minutes in the pan.

Mix the Frosting and Frost the Bars

꙰ Put the powdered sugar, melted butter, lemon juice, orange juice, and orange zest in a medium bowl and stir them together until a smooth frosting forms. The frosting has a syrupy consistency. Pour the frosting over the partially cooled bars, spreading it evenly with a thin metal spatula. Refrigerate the bars, uncovered, until the frosting is firm, about 30 minutes. Use a sharp knife to cut the bars into 36 pieces, cutting 6 rows in one direction, then 6 rows across.

Serve the Bars

꙰ Loosen the bars from the sides of the pan. Remove the bars from the pan; a thin metal spatula works well for this. Serve cold or at room temperature. The bars can be covered and refrigerated for up to 5 days.

Lemon Icebox Pie

Refreshing Lemon Icebox Pie makes a sweet way to cool off on a hot day. With only 4 ingredients and a cookie crumb crust, it's just what you might feel like making on a lazy summer day. As with all lemon desserts, I prefer to serve this pie cold, but this particular pie has a special feature if it's frozen. Since the pie never freezes rock hard, it can be prepared ahead of time, frozen, and served icy cold after only a few minutes of softening.

Baking Answers ꙰ Graham cracker crumbs can be found in the baking section of supermarkets, but whole graham crackers can be used. Put graham crackers between 2 sheets of wax paper and use a rolling pin to crush them into fine crumbs, or process the cookies in a food processor until crumbs form. This graham cracker crumb crust is slightly thicker than the one for the Glazed Fresh Raspberry Pie (page 97).

Sweetened condensed milk is found in the canned milk section of supermarkets, near the evaporated milk.

Remember to grate the lemon zest from the lemon before squeezing the juice. For the zest, grate only the yellow skin of the lemon. The white pith is bitter and has no lemon flavor.

To prevent a plastic wrap covering from sticking to the top of the pie, chill the pie until the top is firm, then cover it.

A Step Ahead ⤏ The pie can be frozen for up to 1 month. After refrigerating the pie until the top is firm, wrap the pie tightly with plastic wrap then heavy aluminum foil. Label with the date and contents. Let the wrapped frozen pie sit at room temperature for 15 minutes, then serve it.

SERVES 8

Necessities ⤏ *One 9-inch shiny metal or ovenproof glass pie pan and a grater for the lemon zest*

GRAHAM CRACKER CRUMB CRUST	½ teaspoon ground cinnamon
1½ cups graham cracker crumbs	5 tablespoons unsalted butter, melted
1 tablespoon sugar	

FILLING	1 cup fresh lemon juice
Two 14-ounce cans sweetened condensed milk	5 large egg yolks
	2 teaspoons grated fresh lemon zest

Prepare the Crust

⤏ Position an oven rack in the middle of the oven. Preheat the oven to 350°F. Butter the inside of a 9-inch pie pan.

Put the graham cracker crumbs, sugar, and cinnamon in a medium bowl and stir them together. Add the melted butter, stirring until the crumbs are evenly moistened with the butter. Put the crumb mixture in the prepared pan and use the back of your fingers or the back of a spoon to press the crumb mixture evenly over the bottom and sides of the pie pan. Bake for 6 minutes. Set aside. Leave the oven on.

Mix the Filling

⤏ Put the condensed milk and lemon juice in a large bowl. Use a large spoon or rubber spatula to blend them thoroughly. Add the egg yolks and lemon zest and stir until the yolks are incorporated and you see no yellow yolk. Pour the mixture into the prepared crust.

↬ Bake for 30 minutes. The top looks firm and set when you give the pan a gentle shake. Let the pie cool at room temperature for 1 hour. Refrigerate, uncovered, until the top is firm if you touch it gently, about 1½ hours. Cover the pie with plastic wrap and chill it thoroughly in the refrigerator for at least 5 hours or overnight. Store the pie in the refrigerator up to 3 days. Or, wrap the pie with plastic wrap and heavy aluminum foil and freeze it for up to 1 month.

Variation ↬ *Serve the pie with sweetened fresh strawberries. Slice 1 pint of cleaned strawberries. Put them in a small bowl and stir in 1 tablespoon sugar. Cover and refrigerate for 1 hour or up to 6 hours. Serve slices of the pie with spoonfuls of the strawberries and their juice.*

Orange Cream Cheese Pie with Shiny Strawberries

Several years ago I read a survey that named cheesecake topped with fresh strawberries as the most popular dessert in the United States. Whether or not the survey was accurate, the combination of creamy cheesecake covered with brightly glazed strawberries deserves to be at the top of any dessert list. This smaller version of the cheesecake classic conveniently bakes in a pie pan. Orange juice and orange zest flavor the cream cheese filling, and the top of the pie is covered with overlapping rows of halved strawberries.

Baking Answers ↬ Graham cracker crumbs can be found in the baking section of supermarkets, but whole graham crackers can be used. Put graham crackers between 2 sheets of wax paper and use a rolling pin to crush them into fine crumbs, or process the cookies in a food processor until crumbs form.

    Mixing the cream cheese filling in a food processor consistently produces an ultra-smooth pie filling, but the batter can be mixed with an electric mixer as directed on page 96. It is especially important to soften the cream cheese thoroughly if an electric mixer is used, so the cream cheese blends smoothly into the mixture.

    Bottles labeled pure almond extract are made with oil of bitter almond and are preferable to bottles labeled almond extract. The pure version is now available in supermarkets.

Remember to grate the orange zest from the orange before squeezing the juice. For the zest, grate only the orange skin of the orange. The white pith is bitter and has no orange flavor.

The number and size of strawberries that are in a pint vary, so you might not use all of the 2 pints for the topping.

When brushing melted jelly over the strawberry topping, use warm jelly that is syrupy and easy to spread. Brush the jelly gently and generously to coat the strawberries. If any bristles should fall off the brush, remove and discard them.

A Step Ahead ❧ The crumb crust can be mixed and prebaked a day ahead. Cover the cooled crust with plastic wrap and store at room temperature.

SERVES 8 TO 10

Necessities ❧ *One 9-inch shiny metal or ovenproof glass pie pan, a pastry brush, and a grater for the orange zest*

ORANGE GRAHAM CRACKER CRUMB CRUST	1⅓ cups graham cracker crumbs
	2 tablespoons sugar
5 tablespoons unsalted butter, melted	½ teaspoon grated orange zest
1 tablespoon fresh orange juice	
FILLING AND TOPPING	½ cup sour cream
2 large eggs	1 teaspoon vanilla extract
⅔ cup sugar	½ teaspoon pure almond extract
12 ounces cream cheese, softened 3 to 4 hours at room temperature	½ teaspoon grated orange zest
	3 tablespoons fresh orange juice
2 tablespoons unbleached all-purpose flour	
TOPPING	2 pints strawberries, cleaned, stemmed, and halved lengthwise
¼ cup red currant or strawberry jelly	

Prepare the Crust

❧ Position an oven rack in the middle of the oven. Preheat the oven to 325°F. Butter a 9-inch pie pan.

Put the melted butter and orange juice in a medium bowl and stir them together. Add the crumbs, sugar, and orange zest, stirring to blend them well. Put the crumb mixture in the prepared pan and use the back of your fingers or the back of a spoon to press the crumb mixture evenly over the bottom and sides of the pie pan. Bake for 6 minutes. Set aside. Leave the oven on.

Mix the Filling

~ In a food processor, process the eggs and sugar until they are smooth, about 1 minute. Add the cream cheese and process it with a few short bursts to break up the cream cheese, then process until the mixture is smooth, about 15 seconds. Stop the food processor and add the flour, sour cream, vanilla, almond extract, orange zest, and orange juice. Process just until the mixture is smooth, about 20 seconds. Pour the batter into the prepared crust.

Bake the Pie

~ Bake about 35 minutes, until the top looks firm and set when you give the pan a gentle shake. Cover the baked pie loosely with paper towels and cool for about 2 hours, until it is cool to the touch. Cover the pie with plastic wrap and chill it thoroughly in the refrigerator for at least 5 hours or overnight. Store the pie in the refrigerator for up to 4 days, but add the strawberry topping on the day you serve the pie.

Make the Topping and Serve the Pie

~ Heat the jelly in a small pan over low heat just until it melts. Remove the pan from the heat. Arrange a circular row of overlapping strawberry halves, cut side down, around the outer edge of the pie. For the most attractive result, let each strawberry half overlap slightly the one in front of it. Try to use strawberries of equal size. Continue filling in the top of the pie with circles of overlapping rows of strawberries to cover the top of the pie. Use a pastry brush to gently brush the melted jelly over the strawberries. Refrigerate the pie until serving time and serve cold.

Variation ~ *To mix the filling with an electric mixer, beat the softened cream cheese and sugar until smooth, then mix in the flour to incorporate it. Add the eggs, mixing until smooth. Scrape the sides of the bowl during the mixing and any batter that becomes caught in the beaters as needed. Mix in the vanilla, almond extract, orange zest, and orange juice. Mix in the sour cream until no white streaks remain and pour the batter into the prepared crumb crust.*

Glazed Fresh Raspberry Pie

If you're looking for the most luxurious pie that takes the least amount of work to put together, this raspberry pie is for you. With their intense flavor, fresh raspberries need little adornment, so my raspberry pie has only a graham cracker crumb crust heaped with fresh raspberries tossed with just enough glaze to sweeten it and hold the raspberries together. The finished pie looks as if it's filled with shimmering red rubies.

Baking Answers ❧ Graham cracker crumbs can be found in the baking section of supermarkets, but whole graham crackers can be used. Put graham crackers between 2 sheets of wax paper and use a rolling pin to crush them into fine crumbs or process the cookies in a food processor until crumbs form.

To prevent any lumps forming when cooking the glaze, stir the cornstarch and water together until the mixture is smooth and the cornstarch is dissolved. When the glaze mixture boils, it is the cornstarch mixture that causes it to thicken.

Mix the raspberries and glaze together gently, so as not to crush the berries.

Since this pie calls for almost 3 pints of raspberries, I usually make it in the summer when local raspberries are in season and the price is more reasonable. When choosing raspberries, look at the containers carefully and choose berries that are free of mold and don't look crushed. Raspberries are delicate and have a short shelf life, so the fresher the better. When buying local raspberries, it's best to buy ones that have been picked after a spell of several days of dry, sunny weather. Rain and fog cause raspberries to soften and mold quickly.

A Step Ahead ❧ The crumb crust can be mixed and prebaked a day ahead. Cover the cooled crust with plastic wrap and store at room temperature.

SERVES 8

Necessities ❧ *A 9-inch shiny metal or ovenproof glass pie pan*

GRAHAM CRACKER CRUMB CRUST	½ teaspoon ground cinnamon
1⅓ cups graham cracker crumbs	4 tablespoons (½ stick) unsalted butter, melted

GLAZE AND FILLING

1 tablespoon cornstarch

¾ cup water

5 cups (about 2½ pints) fresh raspberries

⅓ cup sugar

3 tablespoons seedless raspberry jam

Prepare the Crust

❧ Position an oven rack in the middle of the oven. Preheat the oven to 325°F. Butter a 9-inch pie pan.

Stir the crumbs and cinnamon together in a medium bowl. Add the melted butter and stir the mixture until the crumbs are evenly moistened with the butter. Put the crumb mixture in the prepared pan and use the back of your fingers or the back of a spoon to press the crumb mixture evenly over the bottom and sides of the pie pan. Bake for 8 minutes. Set aside to cool.

Make the Glaze and Fill the Pie

❧ Stir the cornstarch and water together in a small bowl to dissolve the cornstarch.

Heat 1 cup of the raspberries, sugar, jam, and the cornstarch mixture in a medium saucepan over medium heat, stirring constantly until the jam and sugar dissolve, about 4 minutes. Increase the heat to medium-high and bring the mixture to a boil, stirring constantly but slowly. Boil just until the glaze thickens and becomes clear. The glaze thickens soon after it boils. Put a strainer over a medium bowl and pour the warm mixture into the strainer. Press gently on the strainer to push through the liquid glaze, but not the seeds. Cool the glaze to room temperature, about 1 hour. Discard the seeds and any fruit pulp left in the strainer.

Put the remaining raspberries in a large bowl and gently mix in the cooled glaze to coat the raspberries evenly. I use my clean fingers to mix them together. It's messy, but gentle on the raspberries. Spoon the raspberry mixture evenly into the prepared crust.

Serve the Pie

❧ Cover and refrigerate the pie for at least 2 hours. Serve the pie cold on the day it is prepared.

Variation ❧ *For glazed strawberry pie, use 4 pints of cleaned strawberries and ¼ cup of sugar. Chop 1 cup of the strawberries to cook in the glaze, and halve the remaining strawberries for the filling. Spread the glaze-coated strawberry halves in the prepared crust, turning the top layer of strawberries so the cut sides face down.*

Vanilla Cheesecake

Toffee, lemon, and chocolate are all popular cheesecakes, but plain vanilla remains the classic favorite. Not that there is anything basic or plain about this silken-textured cheesecake that somehow achieves a dense, light, soft, and creamy combination in every slice.

Although cheesecakes have a fancy reputation that might make you think they are difficult to put together, they are one of the easiest desserts you'll ever bake. It does take time to soften the cream cheese for cheesecakes and bake and cool them, but that is time when you can be doing other things. The actual time spent mixing the batter is short, the process is straightforward, and it is time well spent for such a spectacular result.

Baking Answers ⋄ Graham cracker crumbs can be found in the baking section of supermarkets, but whole graham crackers can be used. Put graham crackers between 2 sheets of wax paper and use a rolling pin to crush them into fine crumbs, or process the cookies in a food processor until crumbs form.

Soften the cream cheese thoroughly so the cream cheese mixes easily into a smooth batter. If the cream cheese is cold, no matter how long you beat it, little white specks will remain in the batter. A quick method for softening cream cheese is to let the wrapped packages sit in a sunny window, just until the cream cheese feels soft if pressed with a finger. Having the eggs and cream at room temperature also helps to achieve a smooth batter. Let the eggs come to room temperature in their shells, then crack them open when you're ready to use them. Once eggs are cracked, the egg yolks can form a skin over the yolks if left too long at room temperature

Mixing a cheesecake batter is just a matter of combining ingredients rather than trying to beat air into the mixture. Cheesecake batters should be mixed on low speed and just to the point that each ingredient blends smoothly into the batter.

Baking cheesecakes in the warm, moist environment of a water bath suits them perfectly. To prepare a springform pan for baking in a water bath, wrap the unfilled pan with a large piece of heavy aluminum foil around the outside to make it watertight. The 18-inch-wide packages of foil allow you to wrap the pan using 1 large piece of foil. Fill the pan with the cheesecake batter, put the filled pan in a large baking pan, and place both in a preheated oven. Pour hot water into the large baking pan and bake the cheesecake in its steamy water bath. The foil covering the bottom protects the cheesecake from getting wet. A watering can with a long narrow spout is useful for adding water to the pan in the oven.

Cheesecakes like to cool slowly and to be protected from drafts. A good way to cool them is to leave the baked cheesecake in its water bath at room temperature, loosely covered with paper towels, for the first hour. The paper towels allow steam to escape, preventing any moisture from forming on the cheesecake. After 1 hour, the cheesecake is firmly set and can be removed from its water bath and uncovered for thorough cooling.

Store cheesecakes in the refrigerator, but let them sit at room temperature for about 1 hour before serving, to bring out the most flavor. If fresh fruit toppings are used, they will be at their best if added when the cheesecake is served.

A Step Ahead ❧ The cooled cheesecake can be covered and stored in the refrigerator for up to 1 week.

SERVES 12 TO 16

Necessities ❧ *One 9-inch springform pan with sides at least 2¾ inches high, a baking pan with at least 2-inch-high sides large enough to hold the foil-wrapped springform pan, and heavy aluminum foil for wrapping the pan*

GRAHAM CRACKER CRUMB CRUST	
1¾ cups graham cracker crumbs	1 tablespoon sugar
	¾ teaspoon ground cinnamon
	7 tablespoons unsalted butter, melted

VANILLA FILLING	
1½ pounds cream cheese, softened 3 to 4 hours at room temperature	1 tablespoon plus 1 teaspoon unbleached all-purpose flour
1 cup sugar	3 large eggs, room temperature
2 tablespoons fresh lemon juice	1 large egg yolk, room temperature
2 teaspoons vanilla extract	6 tablespoons whipping cream, room temperature

Prepare the Crust

❧ Position an oven rack in the middle of the oven. Preheat the oven to 325°F. Butter a 9-inch springform pan with sides at least 2¾ inches high. Wrap the outside of the pan with a large piece of heavy aluminum foil. Have ready a large baking pan with at least 2-inch-high sides that is large enough to hold the foil-wrapped pan.

Stir the graham cracker crumbs, sugar, and cinnamon together in a medium bowl. Add the melted butter, stirring until the crumbs are evenly moistened with the butter. Put the crumb mixture in the prepared pan and use the back of your fingers or the back of a spoon to press the crumb mixture evenly over the bottom and 1 inch up the sides of the pan. Be careful not to make the crust too thick at the bottom of the pan where the sides and the edges of the pan meet at an angle. Bake for 8 minutes. Set aside.

Prepare the Filling

✑ Put the cream cheese, sugar, lemon juice, and vanilla in a large bowl and beat with an electric mixer on low speed until the mixture looks smooth. If using a handheld electric mixer, move the beaters around in the bowl. Stop the mixer and scrape the mixture from the sides of the bowl and any that becomes caught in the beaters as needed throughout the mixing process. Mix in the flour to incorporate it. Put the eggs and egg yolk in a small bowl and use a fork to stir them vigorously to blend the yolks and whites. Add the eggs in 2 additions, mixing just to blend them into the mixture. Stop the mixer and scrape any thick batter from the sides of the bowl and or any batter that becomes caught in the beaters as needed. Mix in the cream, just until it is incorporated. Pour the batter into the baked crust in the springform pan.

Bake and Cool the Cheesecake

✑ Put the cheesecake in its wrapped pan in a large baking pan with at least 2-inch-high sides and place in the preheated oven. Pour hot water in the large pan to reach 1 inch up the sides of the springform pan.

Bake about 1 hour or until you give the cheesecake a gentle shake and the top looks firm. When done, the cheesecake looks set and may have a few tiny cracks around the edge. These cracks close up as the cheesecake cools.

Cool the cheesecake, covered loosely with paper towels, in the water bath for 1 hour. Carefully remove the cheesecake from the water bath. Remove the paper towels and foil wrapping and cool 1 hour more. The cheesecake should feel cool to the touch. Cover with plastic wrap and chill thoroughly in the refrigerator for at least 6 hours or overnight. The cheesecake becomes firm when cool.

Serve the Cheesecake

✑ Use a small knife to loosen the cheesecake from the sides of the pan, and remove the sides. Let the cheesecake sit at room temperature for 1 hour before serving. Use a large sharp knife to cut the cheesecake, wiping the knife clean after cutting each slice. A clean knife makes a neat slice. Leftover cheesecake can be covered with plastic wrap and stored in the refrigerator for up to 1 week.

Variations ✑ *This cheesecake can also be made with a chocolate crumb crust (page 103).*

Fresh berries or strawberry sauce (page 339) make good accompaniments to this cheesecake.

Strawberry Vanilla Cheesecake

Two layers of filling, one a soft pink strawberry and one a creamy white vanilla, bake in the dark chocolate crumb crust of this stunning cheesecake. The two flavors are made from one batter that is divided and flavored differently. Since the strawberries for the filling are pureed, frozen and defrosted unsweetened strawberries work fine. They add a consistently good strawberry flavor in any season when fresh, but out-of-season strawberries might not.

Baking Answers ⌀ I use a 9-ounce box of Famous Chocolate Wafers for the chocolate crumb crust. To make the crumbs, put about 8 cookies at a time between 2 pieces of wax paper and crush them with a rolling pin into fine crumbs, or process the cookies in 2 batches in a food processor until crumbs form.

Soften the cream cheese thoroughly so the cream cheese mixes easily into a smooth batter. A quick method for softening cream cheese is to let the wrapped packages sit in a sunny window, just until the cream cheese feels soft if pressed with a finger. Having the eggs at room temperature also helps to achieve a smooth batter. Let the eggs come to room temperature in their shells, then crack them when you're ready to use them. Once eggs are cracked the egg yolks can form a skin over the yolks if left too long at room temperature

Baking cheesecakes in the warm moist environment of a water bath suits them perfectly. To prepare a springform pan for baking in a water bath, wrap the unfilled pan with a large piece of heavy aluminum foil around the outside to make it watertight. The 18-inch-wide packages of foil allow you to wrap the pan using 1 large piece of foil. Fill the pan with the cheesecake batter, put the filled pan in a large baking pan, and place both in a preheated oven. Pour hot water into the large baking pan and bake the cheesecake in its steamy water bath. The foil covering the bottom protects the cheesecake from getting wet. A watering can with a long narrow spout is useful for adding water to the pan in the oven.

The only trick to baking a multilayered cheesecake is to bake the bottom layer until it is firm enough to have another layer of batter poured over it without collapsing. I add the top layer of batter by carefully pouring the batter slowly around the inside edge of the pan. The batter will flow evenly toward the center, gently covering the top of the cheesecake.

Necessities ❧ *One 9-inch springform pan with sides at least 2¾ inches high,*
a baking pan with at least 2-inch-high sides large enough to hold the foil-wrapped pan, and
heavy aluminum foil for wrapping the pan

CHOCOLATE CRUMB CRUST *2 cups chocolate wafer cookie crumbs*	*6 tablespoons (¾ stick) unsalted butter,* *melted*
STRAWBERRY AND VANILLA FILLING *12 ounces frozen and defrosted unsweet-* *ened strawberries or 2 cups fresh* *strawberries, cleaned and stemmed* *2 pounds cream cheese, softened 3 to 4* *hours at room temperature*	*1⅓ cups sugar* *2 tablespoons unbleached all-purpose* *flour* *4 large eggs, room temperature* *2 teaspoons vanilla extract* *2 teaspoons fresh lemon juice*

Prepare the Crust

❧ Position an oven rack in the middle of the oven. Preheat the oven to 325°F. Butter a 9-inch springform pan with sides at least 2¾ inches high. Wrap the outside of the pan with a large piece of heavy aluminum foil. Have ready a baking pan with at least 2-inch-high sides that is large enough to hold the foil-wrapped pan.

Put the crumbs and melted butter in a medium bowl, and stir them together until the crumbs are evenly moistened with the butter. Put the crumb mixture in the prepared pan and use the back of your fingers or the back of a spoon to press the crumb mixture evenly over the bottom and 1 inch up the sides of the pan. Be careful not to make the crust too thick at the bottom of the pan where the sides and the edges of the pan meet at an angle. Bake for 8 minutes. Set aside. Leave the oven on.

Prepare the Filling

❧ Put the strawberries in the work bowl of a food processor and process them to a puree. Strain the pureed strawberries into a small bowl, discarding any seeds or pulp in the strainer. Measure ¾ cup of the puree and set aside. Cover and refrigerate any remaining puree for another use, storing up to 3 days.

Put the cream cheese and sugar in a large bowl and beat with an electric mixer on low speed until the mixture looks smooth. If using a handheld electric mixer, move the beaters around in the bowl. Stop the mixer and scrape the mixture from the sides of the bowl and any that becomes caught in the beaters as needed throughout the mixing process. Mix in the flour to incorporate it. Put the eggs in a small bowl and use a fork to stir them vigorously to blend the yolks and whites. Add the eggs in 2 additions, mixing just to blend them into the mixture. Stop the mixer and scrape any thick batter from the sides of the bowl or any batter that becomes caught in the beaters as needed. Mix in 1 teaspoon of the vanilla. Put 2 cups of the batter in a medium bowl. Stir the remaining 1 teaspoon vanilla and lemon juice into the batter in the medium bowl and set aside. This will be for the vanilla layer. Mix the reserved strawberry puree into the batter in the large bowl, stirring just until the mixture is evenly pink. Pour the strawberry batter into the prepared crust in the pan.

Bake and Cool the Cheesecake

↬ Put the cheesecake in its wrapped pan in a large baking pan with at least 2-inch-high sides and place in the preheated oven. Pour hot water into the large pan to reach 1 inch up the sides of the springform pan.

Bake 45 minutes. Protecting your hands with pot holders, carefully slide the oven rack out several inches. Pour the reserved vanilla batter all around the inside edge of the pan. The batter will flow evenly to cover the top of the cheesecake. Bake an additional 20 minutes. When done, the cheesecake looks set and may have a few tiny cracks around the edge. These cracks close up as the cheesecake cools.

Cool the cheesecake, covered loosely with paper towels, in the water bath for 1 hour. Carefully remove the cheesecake from the water bath. Remove the paper towels and foil wrapping and cool 1 hour more. The cheesecake should feel cool to the touch. Cover with plastic wrap and chill thoroughly in the refrigerator for at least 6 hours or overnight. The cheesecake firms when cool, but this cheesecake will remain especially soft and creamy.

Serve the Cheesecake

↬ Use a small knife to loosen the cheesecake from the sides of the pan and remove the sides. Let the cheesecake sit at room temperature for 1 hour before serving. Use a large sharp knife to cut the cheesecake, wiping the knife clean after cutting each slice. A clean knife makes a neat slice. Leftover cheesecake can be covered with plastic wrap and stored in the refrigerator for up to 1 week.

S everal years ago I took a pastry course at the Lenôtre school outside of Paris. We made forty fancy cakes in one week, so there was no way that I could begin to remember everything we baked. All of their cookbooks were in French, but I brought several home to help steer me in the right direction. One of the books, *Desserts Traditionnels de France,* had an appealing photo of a tart that caught my eye at once. The tart had a crisp brown-edged crust and a soft vanilla pastry cream filling dotted with cherries, which were peeking through the golden crusty top. With the help of my French teacher, I translated the recipe. That was the hardest part of this tart, which is as easy as *un, deux, trois.*

The mixture for the bottom and top crust needs only to be stirred together and is soft enough to be spread in the bottom of the pan and piped over the pastry cream filling. There is no guesswork as to how much liquid to add and no rolling of dough. Normally, it would be difficult to spread the soft top crust mixture evenly over the soft pastry cream, but Lenôtre's idea of pressing it out of a pastry bag or plastic bag makes the process a cinch. When baked, the outside of the crust becomes crisp and the interior is soft and almost cakelike.

Baking Answers ⟋ I use dried cherries, which are sweet and in season anytime. They become soft and plump after sitting in hot water flavored with amaretto for 30 minutes. Raisins, dried apricots, or most dried fruits can be reconstituted this way. Adding an appropriate liqueur, brandy, or rum to the water adds to the flavor, but reconstituting them in hot water alone is fine.

Vanilla pastry cream is homemade vanilla pudding. It's a versatile, quick-cooking mixture that can fill a fresh berry tart or a Deluxe Coconut Cream Pie (page 324) and can even bake in a crust as in this recipe. Some other flavors to add to pastry cream could be various liqueurs, citrus zest, coffee, or chocolate. To make pastry cream, whisk hot milk into a lightly beaten but smooth mixture of egg yolks, sugar, and flour. The hot milk gently tempers the egg yolks so the mixture remains smooth. This mixture then cooks together until it boils and thickens. Since the mixture includes starch in the form of flour or cornstarch (I use flour), it boils without curdling. Straining the cooked pastry cream removes any stray lumps that might form. Be sure to store pastry cream in the refrigerator and use freshly made pastry cream within 3 days to prevent spoilage.

It's not necessary to own a pastry bag to pipe the top crust over the pastry cream. I use a one-gallon-size freezer-weight self-sealing plastic bag with a small hole cut in 1 corner to press the crust mixture through.

The almonds can be ground in a food processor.

A Step Ahead ⟿ Make the pastry cream a day ahead and refrigerate the covered pastry cream overnight.

Necessities ⟿ *One 9-inch springform pan and a 1-gallon-size freezer-weight self-sealing plastic bag*

PASTRY CREAM—
   MAKES ABOUT 1¾ CUPS

1½ cups whole milk
½ cup sugar
4 large egg yolks
3 tablespoons unbleached all-purpose flour

1 teaspoon vanilla extract

1 cup dried pitted cherries
1 tablespoon amaretto or almond-
   flavored liqueur, optional

CRUST
1 cup unbleached all-purpose flour
½ cup ground unblanched almonds
1 teaspoon baking powder
2 large eggs
¾ cup sugar
1 teaspoon vanilla extract

1 tablespoon amaretto
¼ pound (1 stick) unsalted butter,
   melted and cooled slightly

Powdered sugar for dusting the top of
   the tart

Cook the Pastry Cream

⟿ Put the milk in a medium, heavy saucepan and heat it over medium heat until it is hot and a few bubbles just begin to form around the edge. This is about 150°F. if measured with a food thermometer.

Put the sugar and egg yolks in a medium bowl and whisk until smooth. Add the flour and whisk it smooth. Whisking constantly, slowly pour the hot milk into the yolk mixture. Return the mixture to the saucepan and, stirring constantly with a large spoon, cook over medium heat until the mixture thickens and just comes to a boil. If you stop stirring for a few seconds, you will see 3 to 4 large bubbles. Stir the pastry cream often where the bottom and sides of the pan meet to prevent burning. Reduce the heat to low and cook, stirring constantly, for 1 minute. Remove from the heat and pour the pastry cream through a strainer into a medium bowl. Discard any bits in the strainer. Stir in the vanilla. Press a piece of plastic wrap onto the pastry cream and poke a few holes in the plastic wrap with the tip of a knife to let steam escape. Refrigerate the custard for a least 1 hour or overnight, until it is at least cool to the touch and slightly thickened.

Reconstitute the Dried Cherries

⟿ Put the dried cherries in a small bowl and sprinkle them with the amaretto, if used. Pour boiling water over the cherries, just to cover them. You will need about ½ cup of boiling water. Let the cherries sit in the hot water for 30 minutes. Drain the cherries and pat them dry with a paper towel.

Mix the Crust

↪ Position an oven rack in the middle of the oven. Preheat the oven to 400°F. Butter the inside of a 9-inch springform pan.

Stir the flour, almonds, and baking powder together in a small bowl. Set aside.

Put the eggs, sugar, vanilla, and amaretto in a large bowl. Stir with a large spoon until the mixture is smooth and the eggs incorporated. Stir in the melted butter. Stir in the flour mixture until it is incorporated. Let the mixture rest for 15 minutes. The mixture thickens as it sits but remains soft and spreadable. You will have 2 cups of crust mixture.

Assemble the Tart

↪ Use a metal spatula to spread 1 cup of the crust mixture evenly over the bottom of the prepared pan.

Leaving a 1-inch plain edge, spread the cooled pastry cream over the crust. Place the cherries evenly over the pastry cream. Use a one-gallon-size freezer-weight self-sealing plastic bag or a pastry bag fitted with a ½-inch plain tip to add the remaining crust mixture. If using a plastic bag, spoon the crust mixture into the plastic bag, pushing it down into a corner of the bag. Press out the air and seal the bag. Cut a hole about ½ inch across in the same corner. Or, if using a pastry bag, put a ½-inch round tip in the bottom of the pastry bag, fold about half of the top back, and spoon in the crust mixture. Unfold the top of the bag and close it by twisting it firmly against the crust mixture. Beginning at the outside edge and working toward the center, pipe rings of dough over the pastry cream by squeezing the bag and forcing the crust mixture through the hole in the bag. The dough circles will not touch each other. Use a metal spatula to gently spread the dough more evenly over the pastry cream. Some cherries and a few bits of pastry cream will show through the dough.

Bake and Serve the Tart

↪ Put the tart on a baking sheet so it's easier to move around. Bake for about 25 minutes, until the top is golden brown and looks set if you give it a gentle shake. Cool the tart at room temperature. Use a small knife to loosen the tart from the sides of the pan and remove the sides. Strain powdered sugar lightly over the top of the cooled tart.

Cover the tart and refrigerate it until cold, at least 5 hours or overnight. Serve cold within 3 days.

Variation ↪ *Various dried reconstituted fruits can be used in the filling. One cup of raisins, chopped dried apricots, or chopped dried pears all work well. Try adding 1 tablespoon of rum to the hot water for raisins or apricots, or 1 tablespoon of brandy for pears.*

Ham and Swiss Potato Pie

Rather than a sandwich of ham and Swiss on rye, this ham and Swiss pie sandwiches the filling between "crusts" of crisp potato slices. The bottom layer of sliced potatoes bakes without the filling into a crisp base that is then slathered with mustard, filled with ham and cheese, and topped with a crust of additional sliced potatoes. The pie bakes until the topping is crisp and the ham and cheese melt together. The neatly arranged bottom layer of potato slices makes a beautiful pattern when the pie is unmolded from the pan.

Baking Answers ⌁ Clarified butter has the good property of burning at a higher temperature than regular butter. It is used here to produce an evenly browned potato crust. To make clarified butter, melt the butter slowly, then remove the foam and milky residue. The clear butter that remains is clarified.

Slice the potatoes into even slices so they cook evenly. Partially cooking the potatoes used for the top layer of the tart assures that they will be cooked thoroughly when the pie is done. These half-cooked potatoes also slice easily into neat slices. Note that the potatoes for the top and bottom layers are listed as separate ingredients and are prepared and used differently.

Since the pie is served upside down with the crusty side up, only the very bottom layer of potatoes will show, and it needs to be carefully placed.

MAKES A 9-INCH PIE AND SERVES 6

Necessities ⌁ *One 9-inch round ceramic or ovenproof glass pie pan or a baking dish that has 1½- to 2-inch-high sides*

2 ounces (½ stick) unsalted butter

½ pound raw potatoes (2 medium-small or 1 large), not peeled, for the top layer of the tart

1¼ pounds raw potatoes (2 medium), peeled, sliced ⅛ inch thick, for the bottom layer of the tart

¼ teaspoon salt

⅛ teaspoon freshly ground black pepper

2 tablespoons Dijon-style mustard, or additional if desired

8 ounces Gruyère cheese (about 2¼ cups), grated

6 ounces thinly sliced baked ham, cut into 1-inch pieces

Prepare and Bake the Crust

⌁ To clarify the butter, melt it slowly over low heat in a small frying pan. Use a spoon to skim any foam off the top and discard the foam. Slowly pour the melted butter into a small bowl, leaving the milky residue that remains in the bottom of the pan. Discard the residue in the pan. You should have about 3 tablespoons of clear butter.

Simmer the unpeeled potatoes for the top layer in a medium saucepan for 20 minutes, just until they begin to feel tender when tested with a two-pronged fork. The center will still feel firm. Keep the potatoes covered with simmering water as they cook. Drain the potatoes and peel them when they are cool enough to handle. Set aside.

Position a rack in the bottom third of the oven. Preheat the oven to 400°F. Brush the bottom and sides of a 9-inch round ceramic or ovenproof glass pie pan or baking dish that has 1½- to 2-inch-high sides with 1 tablespoon of the clarified butter.

Soak the raw, sliced potatoes for the bottom layer for 15 minutes in cold water. Drain the potatoes and pat dry with paper towels. Arrange a layer of overlapping raw potato slices neatly in the bottom of the pan. Arrange the slices in concentric circles over the bottom for a neat pattern when the pie is unmolded. Arrange a double layer of potato slices standing up around the edge of the pan and use a knife to trim them even with the top of the pan. Sprinkle the potatoes with the salt and pepper. Arrange a second layer of overlapping potato slices over the bottom. These will not show when the pie is unmolded and do not have to be arranged perfectly. This bottom layer of potatoes helps support the potato slices standing up around the edge. You will have double-thick rows of potatoes over the bottom and sides. Brush the potatoes with 1 tablespoon of the clarified butter. Bake for 30 minutes. Cover the dish of potatoes tightly with aluminum foil and bake another 30 minutes. Remove the dish from the oven and remove the aluminum foil.

Add the Filling and Top Potato Layer

⌁ Spread the mustard evenly over the cooked potatoes in the baking dish. Sprinkle half of the Gruyère cheese evenly over the mustard. Cover the cheese evenly with the ham pieces. Sprinkle the remaining cheese evenly over the ham. Slice the reserved partially cooked potatoes for the top layer into ⅛-inch slices and arrange them to cover the cheese. Brush the top with the remaining clarified butter.

Bake and Serve the Pie

⌁ Bake the pie for 15 minutes; the potatoes on top will be soft and lightly colored. Remove the pie from the oven and let it rest for 2 to 3 minutes. Loosen the edges of the pie from the sides of the pan. Place a platter on top of the pie and invert the pie onto it. Replace any potatoes that stick to the pan. Leave the pie upside down with the browned crusty side up. Use a sharp knife to cut slices. Serve immediately while warm. Served with a salad, this pie makes a nice informal supper.

Savory Lemon, Sage, Parsley, and Thyme Cheesecake

Savory cheesecakes seasoned with herbs can be creative appetizers or sophisticated luncheon dishes. This fresh herb version has a cracker crumb crust and a unique, attractive parsley leaf decoration that bakes with the cheesecake. Although the ingredient list for the filling looks long, the ingredients are mostly common pantry items. Since the filling is made in a food processor, it goes together quickly and you're assured of a smooth result. When freshly baked, the cracker crumb crust is slightly crumbly, but it firms up overnight. Summer is a nice time to make this cheesecake, when the fresh herbs might be conveniently growing in your garden.

Baking Answers ⋅ To make the cracker crumbs, put about 10 crackers at a time between 2 sheets of wax paper and use a rolling pin to crush them into crumbs, or process the crackers in a food processor just until crumbs form.

Since this cheesecake is made in a food processor, the cream cheese becomes smooth during processing and doesn't have to be thoroughly softened as cream cheese must be when cheesecake batters are mixed with an electric mixer.

Let the eggs come to room temperature in their shells, then crack them when you're ready to use them. Once cracked, egg yolks can form a skin over the yolks if left too long at room temperature

Fresh herbs rather than dried make a big and better difference when used in this cheesecake. Flat-leaf Italian parsley has a good, fresh parsley flavor and works well for the decoration baked on top of the cheesecake. I plant a few seedlings every summer and am able to cut stalks as I need them until Thanksgiving; it's also available year round, along with other fresh herbs, in my supermarket.

Remember to grate the lemon zest from the lemon before squeezing the juice. For the zest, grate only the yellow skin of the lemon. The white pith is bitter and has no lemon flavor.

The baked cheesecake is about 1 inch high. This thin and savory cheesecake does not need to bake in a water bath.

A Step Ahead ⋅ The cooled cheesecake can be covered and stored in the refrigerator for up to 5 days.

MAKES 12 TO 16 SLICES AS AN APPETIZER OR SIDE DISH

Necessities ⋅ *A 9-inch springform pan*

CRACKER CRUMB CRUST

1½ cups cracker crumbs such as Ritz
(about 40 Ritz crackers)

3 ounces (¾ stick) unsalted butter,
melted

FRESH HERB FILLING

1 tablespoon extra-virgin olive oil

2 peeled garlic cloves, halved and any
green center removed

¼ cup fresh lemon juice

2 teaspoons grated lemon zest

1 large egg, room temperature

1 large egg yolk, room temperature

1 tablespoon all-purpose flour

1 tablespoon sugar

½ teaspoon ground hot Hungarian
paprika or cayenne pepper

½ teaspoon salt

¼ teaspoon freshly ground black pepper

12 ounces cream cheese, softened

1 cup sour cream

½ cup finely chopped green onions,
white and green parts (about 4
green onions)

2 tablespoons finely chopped flat-leaf
Italian parsley

1 tablespoon finely chopped fresh
thyme

1 teaspoon finely chopped fresh sage

24 whole leaves flat-leaf Italian
parsley for decorating the top of the
cheesecake

Prepare the Crust

☙ Position a rack in the middle of the oven. Preheat the oven to 350°F. Butter a 9-inch-diameter springform pan.

Put the cracker crumbs and melted butter in a large bowl and stir them together until the crumbs are evenly moistened with the butter. Press the crumb mixture evenly over the bottom and a scant ½ inch up the sides of the pan. Bake for 10 minutes. Set aside.

Prepare the Filling

☙ Put the olive oil, garlic, lemon juice, and lemon zest in the work bowl of a food processor and process until the garlic is finely chopped, about 30 seconds. Add the egg, egg yolk, flour, sugar, paprika, salt, and pepper and process just until the eggs are blended into the mixture. Add the cream cheese and process just until the mixture is smooth, about 1 minute. Add the sour cream and process just until it is incorporated and no white streaks remain. Pour the batter into a large bowl and stir in the green onions, chopped parsley, thyme, and sage. Pour the batter over the baked crust. Smooth the top. Gently place a border of whole parsley leaves on top of the cheesecake around the edge of the batter. Place the leaves flat, and they will float on top of the batter.

Bake and Serve the Cheesecake

Bake until the filling is set, about 25 minutes. Cool the cheesecake, covered loosely with paper towels, for 30 minutes. Remove the paper towels and cool 30 minutes more. This thin cheesecake cools quickly and should feel cool to the touch after 1 hour. Cover with plastic wrap and chill thoroughly in the refrigerator, for at least 3 hours or overnight. The cheesecake firms as it cools.

Use a small knife to loosen the cheesecake from the sides of the pan, and remove the sides. Cut into 12 to 16 slices to serve individual portions. Use a large sharp knife to cut the cheesecake and wipe the knife clean if any filling sticks to it. A clean knife makes a neat slice. Or, cut the cheesecake into bite-size pieces, put them in paper mini-muffin liners, and serve as appetizers. Serve cold or at room temperature. The covered cheesecake can be refrigerated for up to 5 days.

Mixing
a Smooth Dough

MY FAVORITE GIANT CHOCOLATE CHIP COOKIES, BUTTERY BISCUITS, AND JUICY PEACH COBBLERS HAVE A NICE THING IN COMMON. THEY ARE ALL MADE FROM COOKIE DOUGHS OR BISCUIT DOUGHS THAT HAVE AN EASYGOING NATURE. It is a simple process of blending ingredients together to make soft, smooth doughs. You can see when the ingredients are blended, so there is no guesswork involved. If you notice a lot of unincorporated flour, just continue mixing. And if cookie dough is mixed a bit longer than needed, there's no harm done.

Most cookie doughs begin by creaming soft butter and sugar together. This process beats the butter and sugar to a creamy-looking mass. There won't be loose sugar visible, but the sugar isn't dissolved until it melts during baking, so you would feel sugar granules if you touched the creamed mixture. These rough crystals of sugar actually help to separate the fat crystals and lighten cookies. In the recipes that follow, I've given the time that it took me to cream the butter and sugar, but a minute more or a few seconds less makes little difference. Any eggs and flavorings are then beaten into the creamed mixture. Cold eggs can cause bits of butter to harden and make the mixture look slightly curdled. However, this is not a problem because the flour mixture that is added next returns the dough to a smooth consistency. It's a good idea to add flour on low speed so it doesn't splash out of the bowl. Add any nuts or chocolate chips at the end. The dough for the summer peach tart is mixed by this same cookie dough method.

I line baking sheets with parchment paper. This paper seldom needs to be buttered, and cleanup is easy. Lining baking sheets with aluminum foil is another option, but I prefer the parchment paper, which is easy to cut and fit onto baking sheets. If you are not using parchment paper, butter the baking sheets for the Jumbo Chocolate Chip Cookies (page 115). The other cookies in this chapter are quite buttery and it is not necessary to butter the baking sheets. Once they go into the oven, watch the cookies carefully. Since cookies bake quickly, you want to stop baking them as soon as they are done.

I used a handheld electric mixer to mix these cookie doughs. Since cookie dough is usually thick, it's important to stop the mixer often to scrape the mixture from the sides of the bowl and any caught between the beaters. I noticed that the mixture seldom got caught between the thin wire beaters of my KitchenAid or Braun mixers and I recommend looking for that type of handheld mixer. The motors also have sufficient power to mix cookie dough. Clumps of butter and dough often became caught in the thicker metal of the conventional beaters of my older handheld mixer.

These cookies and bars can all be wrapped in plastic, sealed in a tin or plastic container, and frozen for future use. Wrapping cookies and bars in plastic wrap before freezing keeps them in good condition while they are frozen. Defrost them wrapped or in their freezing container so the moisture forms on the outside of the wrapper rather than on the cookie.

The method for mixing both the Flying Cloud Biscuits (page 137) and the Orange Spice Scones (page 139) is to stir liquid ingredients, which include the melted butter, with dry ingredients until a soft dough forms. To form a smooth dough, knead the soft dough for about 12 strokes by pushing the dough down and forward with the heel of your hand against the rolling surface and then folding it in half and repeating the process.

Cold shortening is used for the peach cobbler (page 134), so the mixing process is different. Mix small pieces of cold shortening with the dry ingredients to form crumbs. Stirring the liquid ingredients into this crumb mixture produces a soft but ragged dough. Several strokes of kneading make the dough smooth.

Jumbo Chocolate Chip Cookies

What are the greatest discoveries that have changed our world? Some claim it was the invention of the wheel, while others argue for the harnessing of electricity, but in the cookie lover's world there is no debate. It would have to be the chocolate chip cookie. Although it seems as if chocolate chip cookies have been around forever, it wasn't until 1930 that Ruth Wakefield, the owner of the Toll House Inn in Whitman, Massachusetts, created them. She cut up a chocolate bar, added it to her Butter-Drop Do cookies, and the rest is cookie history.

Measuring in at a hefty 4½ inches across, these chocolate chip cookies are big enough to satisfy even my monumental chocolate chip cookie craving. And as with all good chocolate chip cookies, these are crisp on the outside, soft and chewy on the inside, and loaded with chocolate chips. Ruth would love them.

Baking Answers ❧ Both butter and margarine are used in these cookies. The butter adds great flavor, while the margarine adds to the crisp exterior. Since margarine does not become hard when chilled, it doesn't need to be softened, but it is important to soften the butter so the dough is smooth and creamy.

I use a ¼-cup dry measuring cup to portion out the dough for each cookie.

With their high sugar content, chocolate chip cookies can burn easily, especially on the bottom. As they reach the end of their baking time, check the cookies often; opening the oven to have a look will not harm them.

When I was baking these cookies, I noted an interesting result. If they baked on a parchment-lined baking sheet, the cookies spread less and more uniformly than if they baked on a buttered baking sheet that had no paper. The cookies that baked on the buttered sheet formed a thin, crisp edge and were ½ inch larger than the ones baked on the paper. I think the direct heat of the baking sheet made the difference. Although I preferred the cookies from the buttered sheet, my husband Jeff felt both were equally good.

A Step Ahead ⬦ The cookies can be wrapped and frozen as directed below for up to 3 months.

MAKES FOURTEEN 4- TO 5-INCH COOKIES

Necessities ⬦ *2 heavyweight baking sheets and 2 wire racks for cooling the cookies*

1⅓ cups unbleached all-purpose flour	¼ cup granulated sugar
1 teaspoon baking soda	1 large egg
½ teaspoon salt	1 teaspoon vanilla extract
¼ pound (1 stick) soft unsalted butter	1½ cups (9 ounces) semisweet chocolate
2 ounces (½ stick) cold margarine	chips
¾ cup packed light brown sugar	

Mix the Dough

⬦ Position 2 oven racks in the lower middle and upper middle of the oven. Preheat the oven to 350°F. Butter 2 baking sheets or line 2 baking sheets with parchment paper.

Sift the flour, baking soda, and salt together onto a piece of wax paper or into a medium bowl and set aside.

Put the butter, margarine, brown sugar, and granulated sugar in a large bowl and beat with an electric mixer on medium speed until the mixture looks smooth and creamy, about 1 minute. Move the beaters around in the bowl if using a handheld electric mixer. Stop the mixer and scrape the mixture from the sides of the bowl and any that becomes caught in the beaters as needed throughout the mixing process. Mix in the egg and vanilla until they are blended in thoroughly. Decrease the speed to low and add the flour mixture, mixing just until it is incorporated and there is no loose flour. Use a large spoon to stir in the chocolate chips. Using ¼ cup of dough for each cookie, drop rounded mounds of dough 3 inches apart on the prepared baking sheets.

✦ Bake the cookies for about 12 minutes until the centers are golden and the edges are light brown, reversing the baking sheets after 7 minutes front to back and top to bottom to ensure even browning. Watch the cookies carefully as they near the end of their baking time. Remove the cookies from the oven as soon as the center is golden and the edges are light brown. Cool the cookies on the baking sheet for 10 minutes. Use an offset metal spatula or wide spatula to transfer the cookies to a wire rack to cool completely. As the cookies cool, they deflate slightly and the tops become wrinkled. Wrinkled tops indicate a very good chocolate chip cookie. The cookies can be stored tightly covered in a tin for up to 3 days. For longer storage, wrap the cookies in plastic wrap and seal them tightly in a clean plastic container or metal tin, label with the date and contents, and freeze them for up to 3 months. Defrost as many wrapped cookies as needed at room temperature. To refresh day-old cookies, or if you prefer cookies with warm, soft chocolate chips, spread the cookies in a single layer on a baking sheet, and warm them in a preheated 200°F. oven for about 5 minutes.

Buttery Brown Sugar and Oatmeal Shortbread

In case you need any proof of how good the combination of brown sugar and butter is, try whipping up a batch of this shortbread and take a whiff of it baking. You'll be convinced.

Shortbread is known for its full-flavored buttery taste and melting soft texture. Going one step further, this golden brown version combines the rich flavor of brown sugar with the butter while adding oatmeal for a bit of crunch.

Baking Answers ✦ Replacing some of the flour with cornstarch makes this shortbread especially tender. The term "short" refers to a dough that has a large proportion of fat to flour, fat in this case being synonymous with butter.

Use boxes of oatmeal that are labeled "old-fashioned" rather than quick-cooking. The quick-cooking oats have been cut into smaller pieces and provide little crunch.

Cut the baked shortbread into squares in the pan when it is warm and soft, but remove the squares from the pan after they cool so they don't break.

A Step Ahead ✦ The cooled shortbread can be frozen for up to 3 months. Wrap the pieces of shortbread in plastic wrap and seal them tightly in a clean metal or plastic freezer container. Label with the date and contents. Defrost as many wrapped pieces as needed at room temperature.

MAKES 24 RECTANGULAR COOKIES

Necessities ✦ *One 9-inch square pan or an 11 x 7-inch baking pan, both with 2-inch-high sides*

1 cup unbleached all-purpose flour	6 ounces (1½ sticks) soft unsalted butter
3 tablespoons cornstarch	½ cup plus 2 tablespoons packed light
½ teaspoon salt	brown sugar
1 teaspoon ground cinnamon	¾ cup oatmeal, not quick-cooking

Mix the Dough

✦ Position a rack in the middle of the oven. Preheat the oven to 350°F. Butter a 9 x 9 x 2-inch or 11 x 7 x 2-inch pan.

Sift the flour, cornstarch, salt, and cinnamon together onto a piece of wax paper or into a medium bowl and set aside.

Put the butter and brown sugar in a large bowl and beat with an electric mixer on medium speed for about 1 minute until the mixture looks smooth. Move the beaters around in the bowl if using a handheld electric mixer. Stop the mixer and scrape the mixture from the sides of the bowl and any that becomes caught in the beaters as needed throughout the mixing process. Decrease the speed to low and mix in the flour mixture, mixing just until the dough holds together and forms big clumps. Add the oatmeal, mixing just to distribute it evenly. Press the dough evenly into the prepared pan.

Bake and Serve the Shortbread

✦ Bake for about 25 minutes, until the top is lightly browned. Remove from the oven and immediately use a small sharp knife to cut 6 rows lengthwise and 4 rows across, cutting through to the bottom. Cool thoroughly. The shortbread will become crisp on the outside and remain slightly soft on the inside when cool. Use a thin spatula to lift the shortbread pieces from the pan.

The shortbread can be stored tightly covered in a tin for up to 4 days.

My Best Butter Buttons

I'm trying to bake the best butter cookies in the world," I told my daughter when she called during one of my many experiments for these cookies. Whether or not cookie world opinion calls these the best, there is no question that these are outstanding butter cookies. These cookies have a crisp yet soft, crumbly texture and a golden brown bottom, rich with the taste of browned butter. The tiny balls of dough bake into rounded disks of one-bite-sized cookies that would melt in your mouth if you could ever hold them there long enough.

Baking Answers ❧ If the dough is sticky and too soft to form into smooth balls, which can happen on a warm day, refrigerate it for 30 minutes to firm it.

Bottles labeled pure almond extract are made with oil of bitter almond and are preferable to bottles labeled almond extract. The pure version is now available in supermarkets.

Baking Experiments ❧ I tested these cookies many times, and all of them were good, but this version was my favorite. It also taught me a lot about butter cookie dough. If I added two more tablespoons of butter to the dough, the cookies spread quite thin and tasted too buttery—hard to believe but they did. When powdered sugar is substituted for the granulated sugar, the cookies lose their round puffy shape and bake into flat disks with a pebbly texture on top. I thought I had a brilliant idea when I stirred some mini-chocolate chips into the dough, but they were not as good as a chocolate chip cookie and no longer tasted like butter cookies. Substituting all-purpose flour for the cake flour made the cookies less tender. Finally, when I decided to include an egg yolk in the dough, I created the tenderest cookies of the lot.

A Step Ahead ❧ These cookies freeze easily and take up little space in the freezer. Line a metal or plastic freezer container with plastic wrap. A 2-quart container or the equivalent will hold all of the cookies. Fill the container with the cooled cookies, press plastic wrap onto them, and cover tightly. Label with the date and contents and freeze for up to 3 months. Defrost the wrapped cookies at room temperature.

MAKES ABOUT FIFTY-EIGHT 1½-INCH COOKIES

Necessities ❧ *2 heavyweight baking sheets and 2 wire racks for cooling the cookies*

1¼ cups cake flour	⅓ cup sugar
½ teaspoon baking powder	1 large egg yolk
¼ teaspoon salt	1 teaspoon vanilla extract
¼ pound plus 2 tablespoons (1¼ sticks) soft unsalted butter	¼ teaspoon pure almond extract

Mix the Dough

∽ Position 2 oven racks in the middle and upper third of the oven. Preheat the oven to 325°F. Line 2 baking sheets with parchment paper. It is not necessary to butter the paper.

Sift the flour, baking powder, and salt together onto a piece of wax paper or into a medium bowl and set aside.

Put the butter and sugar in a large bowl and beat with an electric mixer on medium speed until the mixture looks smooth and creamy and the color lightens, about 2 minutes. This thorough beating helps lighten the texture of the cookies. Move the beaters around in the bowl if using a handheld electric mixer. Stop the mixer and scrape the mixture from the sides of the bowl and any dough that becomes caught in the beaters as needed. Mix in the egg yolk, vanilla, and almond extract until they are blended into the mixture. Decrease the speed to low and add the flour mixture, mixing just until it is incorporated and a smooth dough forms. At first, the dough forms large crumbs, then it forms a smooth dough that pulls away from the side of the bowl.

Roll 1 level teaspoon of dough between the palms of your hands into ¾-inch balls. Place the cookie balls 1½ inches apart on the prepared baking sheets.

Bake and Serve the Cookies

∽ Bake the cookies for about 20 minutes, reversing the baking sheets after 11 minutes front to back and top to bottom to ensure that the cookies bake evenly. The cookie bottoms and edges will be evenly light brown. Cool the cookies on the baking sheet for 1 minute. Use a metal spatula to transfer the cookies to a wire rack to cool completely. Butter buttons can be stored at room temperature tightly covered in a tin for up to 5 days.

Variation ∽ *Press a small piece of a walnut or a pecan gently into the unbaked cookie ball and bake as directed.*

Double Walnut Meltaways

Baking these powdered sugar–coated walnut and butter cookies is an any-holiday-that-comes-along tradition at our house. No holiday in the offing? We make them anyway. I've tasted many versions of these cookies, but never ones like these that include both ground and chopped walnuts. The ground walnuts create the melting texture, while the chopped walnuts supply the distinct walnut flavor. You're probably familiar with these sugar-dusted cookies as the ones that disappear first from any cookie table.

Baking Answers ⤙ A food processor works well for preparing the ground walnuts, but it's easiest to control the size of the chopped walnuts by using a knife to cut them.

In addition to cookie balls, these cookies can be formed into crescent or ring shapes. For crescents, roll a rounded teaspoon of dough between the palms of your hands into a cylinder with tapered ends and curve it to form a crescent. For rings, roll the rounded teaspoon of dough between the palms of your hands into a rope about 4 inches long and press the ends together to form a circle. The baking time remains the same.

A Step Ahead ⤙ The cooled cookies can be frozen for up to 2 months. Place the bottoms of 2 cookies together and wrap them carefully in plastic wrap. Put the wrapped cookies in a metal or plastic freezer container and cover tightly. Label with the date and contents. Defrost the wrapped cookies at room temperature.

MAKES ABOUT 31 COOKIES

Necessities ⤙ *1 heavyweight baking sheet and 1 wire rack for cooling the cookies*

1 cup unbleached all-purpose flour	1 teaspoon vanilla extract
¼ teaspoon baking powder	½ cup ground walnuts
¼ teaspoon salt	¼ cup coarsely chopped walnuts
½ teaspoon ground cinnamon	1 cup powdered sugar, sifted, for coat-
¼ pound (1 stick) soft unsalted butter	ing the cookies
¼ cup powdered sugar	

Mix the Dough

✏ Position an oven rack in the middle of the oven. Preheat the oven to 300°F. Line a baking sheet with parchment paper. It is not necessary to butter the paper.

Stir the flour, baking powder, salt, and cinnamon together in a small bowl and set aside.

Put the butter, powdered sugar, and vanilla in a large bowl and beat with an electric mixer on medium speed until the mixture looks smooth and creamy, about 1 minute. Move the beaters around in the bowl if using a handheld electric mixer. Stop the mixer and scrape the mixture from the sides of the bowl and any that becomes caught in the beaters as needed throughout the mixing process. Decrease the speed to low and add the flour mixture, mixing just until it is incorporated and a smooth dough forms. Add the ground and chopped walnuts, mixing just to distribute them evenly.

Roll a rounded teaspoon of dough between the palms of your hands into 1-inch balls. Place them about 1½ inches apart on the baking sheet. Or, roll the dough into a cylinder with tapered ends and curve each cookie into a crescent. The cookies do not spread a lot during baking.

Bake and Serve the Cookies

✏ Bake until the bottoms are light brown, about 30 minutes. Cool the cookies on the baking sheet for 5 minutes. Use a thin metal spatula to transfer the cookies to a wire rack to cool completely. Put the sifted powdered sugar in a shallow dish or pie tin and roll each cookie in it until evenly coated. The cookies can be stored at room temperature, tightly sealed in a metal tin, for up to 5 days.

Maple Butter Pecan Wafers

Dorothy Conover is a woman after my own heart: she likes to make baking easy. To eliminate the rather time-consuming process of rolling and cutting out the dough for her thin, buttery, pecan cookies, she came up with a better idea. Dorothy forms the dough into smooth logs, chills it firm, then cuts the cold dough into thin, round wafers. It's a quick slice-and-bake method for making perfectly shaped cookies.

Baking Answers ◆ A large sharp knife cuts easily through the pecans in the dough and makes smooth, even cookie slices. Since warm, soft dough has a tendency to squash and flatten when you cut it, chill the dough logs thoroughly. When cold, dough logs cut into neat even slices. It's best to chill the dough in the refrigerator rather than the freezer, since frozen or partially frozen dough is difficult to cut and could even break apart.

Use pure maple syrup, which adds great flavor to these cookies.

A Step Ahead ◆ This recipe makes 2 logs of dough. They can be refrigerated overnight or frozen. I often slice and bake 1 log, then wrap the second one tightly in plastic wrap and heavy aluminum foil, and label it with the date and contents. The log of dough can be frozen for up to 2 months. Defrost the wrapped log in the refrigerator overnight, then slice and bake the cookies. Of course, both logs could also be frozen for later baking.

To freeze baked cookies, put the bottoms of 2 cookies together, wrap them in plastic wrap, then seal them tightly in a clean metal or plastic freezer container. Label with the date and contents and freeze for up to 3 months. Defrost as many wrapped cookies as needed at room temperature.

MAKES ABOUT 60 COOKIES

Necessities ◆ *2 heavyweight baking sheets and 2 wire racks for cooling the cookies*

½ pound (2 sticks) soft unsalted butter
½ cup granulated sugar
½ teaspoon salt
1 large egg yolk
2 tablespoons pure maple syrup

1 teaspoon vanilla extract
2 cups unbleached all-purpose flour
1¼ cups finely chopped pecans
¼ cup powdered sugar for dusting over
    the cookies

Mix the Dough

❧ Put the butter, granulated sugar, and salt in a large bowl and beat with an electric mixer on medium speed until the mixture looks smooth and creamy, about 2 minutes. Move the beaters around in the bowl if using a handheld electric mixer. Stop the mixer and scrape the mixture from the sides of the bowl and any dough that becomes caught in the beaters as needed. Put the egg yolk, maple syrup, and vanilla in a small bowl and stir them vigorously with a fork to blend them together. Add the egg mixture to the butter mixture, continuing to mix on medium speed until it is blended into the mixture. Decrease the speed to low and add the flour, mixing just until it is incorporated and a smooth dough forms. Use a large spoon to stir in the pecans and distribute them evenly.

Form the Cookie Log

❧ Divide the dough into 2 pieces and put each on a piece of plastic wrap. Form each into a log that is 8 inches long and 1½ inches in diameter. Roll up each log in the plastic wrap and roll them back and forth on the counter until smooth. Chill the logs of dough until firm, about 4 hours or overnight.

Bake and Serve the Cookies

❧ Position 2 oven racks in the middle and upper third of the oven. Preheat the oven to 325°F. Line 2 baking sheets with parchment paper.

Unwrap the cold dough logs and use a large sharp knife to cut them into ¼-inch-thick round slices. Place the cookies ¾ inch apart on the prepared baking sheets. The cookies do not spread much during baking. Bake about 18 minutes, just until the edges and bottoms are light brown. Cool the cookies on the baking sheet for 5 minutes. Use a thin metal spatula to transfer them to a wire rack to cool thoroughly.

Put about ¼ cup of powdered sugar in a strainer and sift it over the cooled cookies to coat them lightly. Use additional powdered sugar if necessary. The cookies can be stored at room temperature, tightly sealed in a metal tin, for up to 5 days.

Chocolate Hazelnut Snowballs

As popular as nutty powdered-sugar-covered cookies are, I've never seen a chocolate version. Chocolate and hazelnuts have such an affinity for each other that I was sure the combination would be a good choice. Using a small amount of sugar and a generous measure of cocoa powder gives the cookies a dark color and bittersweet chocolate flavor that contrasts nicely with the sweet powdered-sugar coating. The cake flour and ground toasted hazelnuts create the melting texture that makes these cookies dissolve in your mouth just like a tiny snowball.

Baking Answers ❧ Hazelnuts should have their bitter peel removed before they are used, and I always use them toasted. There are directions for peeling and toasting hazelnuts on page 40, but I try to buy peeled hazelnuts whenever possible. Peeled hazelnuts are usually found in cooking shops or are available from King Arthur Flour's Baker's Catalogue, listed in Mail-Order Sources on page 384.

Grinding the hazelnuts with some sugar in a food processor allows them to reach the desired finely ground stage without forming a paste.

A Step Ahead ❧ The cooled cookies can be frozen for up to 2 months. Place the bottoms of 2 cookies together and wrap them carefully in plastic wrap. Put the wrapped cookies in a metal or plastic freezer container and cover tightly. Label with the date and contents. Defrost the wrapped cookies at room temperature.

MAKES ABOUT 24 COOKIES

Necessities ❧ *1 heavyweight baking sheet and 1 wire rack for cooling the cookies*

¾ cup plus 24 peeled hazelnuts, toasted
   (page 40)
7 tablespoons granulated sugar
¾ cup cake flour
¼ cup unsweetened Dutch process
   cocoa powder, such as Droste or
   Hershey's European

¼ pound (1 stick) soft unsalted butter
1 teaspoon vanilla extract
¾ cup powdered sugar, sifted, for
   coating the cookies

Mix the Dough

ᴗ Position an oven rack in the middle of the oven. Preheat the oven to 300°F. Line a baking sheet with parchment paper.

Put the ¾ cup hazelnuts and 1 tablespoon of the granulated sugar in the work bowl of a food processor fitted with the steel blade. Process with a few short bursts to combine the ingredients. Process about 1 minute until the hazelnuts are finely ground. Set aside.

Sift the flour and cocoa powder together onto a piece of wax paper or into a medium bowl and set aside. Put the butter in a large mixing bowl and mix with an electric mixer on low speed for 15 seconds. Add the remaining 6 tablespoons granulated sugar and beat on medium speed for 1 minute until the mixture looks smooth. Mix in the vanilla. Move the beaters around in the bowl if using a handheld electric mixer. Stop the mixer and scrape the mixture from the sides of the bowl and any that becomes caught in the beaters as needed throughout the mixing process. Decrease the speed to low and mix in the nut mixture. Add the flour mixture, mixing just until it is incorporated and a soft dough forms. Roll rounded teaspoons of dough between the palms of your hands into 1-inch balls. Place them about 1½ inches apart on the baking sheet. Press a whole hazelnut gently into the center of each cookie so that half of the hazelnut is buried in the cookie dough. These cookies do not spread a lot during baking.

Bake and Serve the Cookies

ᴗ Bake for about 30 minutes. The cookies will flatten slightly, and the tops will have tiny cracks and feel firm to the touch. Cool the cookies on the baking sheet for 5 minutes. Use a thin metal spatula to transfer the cookies to a wire rack to cool completely. The cookies become crisp as they cool. Put the sifted powdered sugar in a shallow dish or pie tin and roll each cookie in it until evenly coated. Store the cookies tightly sealed in a metal tin for up to 5 days.

Lemon Cream Cookie Sandwiches

If you're looking for a cookie for a fancy tea party or to pair with ice cream for a special occasion dessert, look no further. You'll find it in these butter cookie coins filled with a simple lemon butter frosting that only look as if they take a lot of time to make. The perfectly shaped cookie disks are sliced from a cold log of dough, so there is no need to roll out the dough, while the lemon filling needs only a quick stir to blend it smooth.

Baking Answers

Remember to grate the lemon zest from the lemon before squeezing the juice. For the zest, grate only the yellow skin of the lemon. The white pith is bitter and has no lemon flavor.

Roll the log of dough back and forth until it is smooth and has an even thickness so the cookies form even circles that are the same size. If the log of dough is cold, it cuts easily into neat, even slices. Warm dough would flatten when sliced.

Bottles labeled pure almond extract are made with the oil of bitter almond and are preferable to bottles labeled almond extract. The pure version is now available in supermarkets.

The lemon butter cookies can also be served as single cookies.

A Step Ahead

The log of dough can be wrapped in plastic wrap and aluminum foil, labeled with the date and contents, and frozen for up to 3 months. Defrost the frozen log overnight in the refrigerator. It's not a good idea to try to cut the frozen log into cookies. Besides being difficult to cut, cookies cut from frozen logs of dough can break apart when the dough is sliced.

To freeze baked cookies, wrap pairs of cookie sandwiches in plastic wrap and seal them tightly in a clean metal or plastic freezer container. Label with the date and contents and freeze for up to 3 months. Defrost as many wrapped cookie sandwiches as needed at room temperature.

MAKES 20 COOKIE SANDWICHES OR 40 PLAIN COOKIES

Necessities ⤙ *2 heavyweight baking sheets and 1 wire rack for cooling the cookies*

LEMON BUTTER COOKIES	1 teaspoon grated lemon zest
¼ pound (1 stick) soft unsalted butter	½ teaspoon vanilla extract
⅓ cup granulated sugar	¼ teaspoon pure almond extract
⅛ teaspoon salt	1 cup plus 2 tablespoons unbleached
1 large egg yolk	all-purpose flour
2 teaspoons fresh lemon juice	

LEMON BUTTER CREAM FROSTING	½ teaspoon grated lemon zest
3 tablespoons soft unsalted butter	
½ cup powdered sugar, sifted	Ice cream for serving with the cookies,
¼ teaspoon vanilla extract	optional
½ teaspoon fresh lemon juice	

Mix the Dough

✎ Position 2 oven racks in the middle and upper third of the oven. Preheat the oven to 350°F. Line 2 baking sheets with parchment paper.

Put the butter, granulated sugar, and salt in a large bowl and beat with an electric mixer on medium speed until the mixture looks smooth and blended together, about 1 minute. Move the beaters around in the bowl if using a handheld electric mixer. Stop the mixer and scrape the mixture from the sides of the bowl and any that becomes caught in the beaters as needed throughout the mixing process. Mix in the egg yolk, lemon juice, lemon zest, vanilla, and almond extract until they are blended into the mixture. Decrease the speed to low and add the flour, mixing just until it is incorporated and a smooth dough forms. The dough forms large smooth clumps.

Form the Cookie Log

✎ Put the dough on a piece of plastic wrap and form it into a log about 10 inches long with flat rather than tapered ends. Roll up the dough in the plastic wrap and roll it back and forth on the counter until the log is smooth and about 1¼ inches in diameter. Chill the log of dough until firm, about 2 hours or overnight.

Bake the Cookies

✎ Unwrap the cold dough log and use a large knife to cut it into ¼-inch-thick rounds. Place the cookies 1 inch apart on the prepared baking sheets. Bake about 15 minutes just until the edges are light brown. Cool the cookies on the baking sheet for 5 minutes, then use a thin metal spatula to transfer them to a wire rack to cool.

Make the Frosting and Fill the Cookies

↶ Put the butter, powdered sugar, vanilla, lemon juice, and lemon zest in a small bowl and stir with a large spoon until smooth.

Turn half of the cooled cookies bottom side up. Spread a thin layer of frosting on the bottom of these cookies. Press a plain cookie, bottom side down, onto each frosted cookie.

Serve the Cookies

↶ Serve at room temperature. The cookie sandwiches can be wrapped in plastic and stored in the refrigerator up to 3 days. Let the cookies sit at room temperature for about 15 minutes before serving.

These cookies look nice arranged on a pretty glass plate. Use several small plates rather than a large platter that begins to look picked over when half of the cookies are gone. Dishes of ice cream holding scoops of raspberry or black raspberry and vanilla ice cream make a good and colorful accompaniment to the cookies. If you can find lemon ice cream, that's also a good choice. I find that creamy ice cream rather than sorbet goes better with these cookies.

Soft and Crunchy Golden Raisin and Apricot Oatmeal Bars

These are bars to satisfy both the chewy and the crisp oatmeal cookie lover. They have a soft oatmeal cookie bottom, a chewy fruit and nut filling, and a crunchy oatmeal crumb topping. Although the ingredient list looks long, once you have the dried apricots, apricot preserves, and golden raisins, the other items are ones that are usually on hand.

Baking Answers ↶ The oatmeal cookie dough that is used for the crust is partially baked, then cooled for 15 minutes to firm slightly. This prevents the fruit and nuts from sinking into the oatmeal crust, so the layers remain separated. This wouldn't be a disaster, but the well-defined layers would be lost.

Do not use quick-cooking oatmeal for these bars. Such finely cut oatmeal doesn't produce a crisp topping or add much flavor to the crust. In the filling, dark raisins can be substituted for the golden ones. I prefer the appearance of the golden raisin and apricot combination, but the final taste of either is similar.

A Step Ahead ⇝ The cookie crust can be partially baked, cooled, covered, and left at room temperature overnight. The crumb topping can be prepared ahead, covered, and refrigerated overnight.

These bars freeze well. Wrap individual bars in plastic wrap, then heavy aluminum foil, and store in the freezer for up to 3 months. Defrost the wrapped bars as needed.

MAKES 12 TO 16 BARS

Necessities ⇝ *One 9-inch square or one 11 x 7-inch baking pan, both with 2-inch-high sides*

OATMEAL RAISIN COOKIE CRUST	
¾ cup unbleached all-purpose flour	⅓ cup granulated sugar
½ teaspoon baking powder	⅓ cup packed brown sugar
¼ teaspoon salt	1 large egg
¾ teaspoon ground cinnamon	1 teaspoon vanilla extract
6 tablespoons (¾ stick) soft unsalted butter	¾ cup oatmeal, not quick-cooking
	½ cup raisins

APRICOT RAISIN FILLING	
½ cup apricot preserves or apricot fruit spread, such as Smucker's Simply Fruit	½ cup golden raisins
	½ cup (about 12) dried apricots cut in ½-inch pieces
	1 cup coarsely chopped walnuts

OATMEAL CRUNCH TOPPING	
¾ cup unbleached all-purpose flour	1 teaspoon ground cinnamon
½ cup oatmeal, not quick-cooking	¼ pound (1 stick) cold unsalted butter, cut into ½-inch pieces
1 cup packed brown sugar	

Make the Crust

⇝ Position a rack in the middle of the oven. Preheat the oven to 325°F. Butter a 9 x 9 x 2-inch or 11 x 7 x 2-inch pan.

Sift the flour, baking powder, salt, and cinnamon into a small bowl and set aside.

Put the butter, granulated sugar, and brown sugar in a large bowl and beat with an electric mixer on medium speed until the mixture looks smooth, about 1 minute. Move the beaters around in the bowl if using a handheld electric mixer. Stop the mixer and scrape the mixture from the sides of the bowl and any that becomes caught in the beaters as needed throughout the mixing process. Mix in the egg and vanilla until they are blended in thoroughly. Reduce the speed to low and add the flour mixture, mixing just until it is incorporated. Stir in the oatmeal and raisins, just to blend them evenly into the mixture. Use a rubber spatula to scrape the dough into the prepared pan. Use a thin metal spatula to spread the dough evenly over the bottom of the pan. Bake 15 minutes. The edges will be brown and the center soft. Leave the oven at 325°F. Cool about 15 minutes.

Add the Filling

↝ Spread a thin layer of apricot preserves over the slightly cooled and partially baked oatmeal crust. Sprinkle the raisins, apricots, and walnuts evenly over the jam.

Make the Topping

↝ Put the flour, oatmeal, brown sugar, and cinnamon in a large bowl and use a large spoon to stir them together. Add the butter pieces, stirring to coat them with flour. Rub the butter pieces and flour mixture between your thumb and fingertips or cut them together with a pastry blender until fine crumbs form that are about ½ inch in size and there is no loose flour. Sprinkle the crumbs evenly over the filling.

Bake and Serve the Bars

↝ Bake about 35 minutes until the crumb topping feels firm and looks golden. Cool the bars in the baking pan at room temperature. Cut into 12 to 16 pieces. Use a thin metal spatula to remove the bars from the pan. Serve at room temperature. The bars can be wrapped in plastic wrap and stored at room temperature up to 3 days.

Open-Face Summer Peach Tart

Although I grew up in a small Florida town, we spent our summers at my grandfather's house in Brooklyn. It was quite a contrast to move from my small Southern town, which had one doughnut bakery, to Brooklyn where you could find bakeries that specialized in the pastry of any European country. But there was only one bakery that reigned supreme in every category—Ebinger's. For years, I thought "dessert" was another word for chocolate, except when it came to Ebinger's blueberry crumb pies, lemon meringue tarts, orange-glazed cake, or open-face peach tarts. The peach tart was different from any I have ever tasted. It had neat rows of sliced peaches that covered the thick, yet soft, subtly almond-flavored crust. The peaches were baked with their skins, so they held their shape during baking and their edges turned an appealing brown that was slightly crisp. I'm still a chocolate lover, but I would never pass up this version of my all-time favorite peach tart.

The tart has the extra bonus of having an easy-to-mix crust that will not toughen from additional mixing and peaches that don't need to be peeled.

Baking Answers ⟿ Flour contains gluten, which adds structure to a crust. Replacing part of the flour with cornstarch, which has no gluten, produces a more tender crust than using more flour would. The crust is similar to a shortbread cookie, and the dough is mixed by the same method. The sugar and butter are beaten well, flavorings are added, and the dry ingredients are stirred in to make a soft, smooth dough.

Peaches vary in size and variety throughout the summer. Small peaches taste as good as large ones, and the first peaches are usually the smaller ones. Look for peaches that are not bruised. Bruised spots cause peaches to rot rather than ripen. I find smelling fruit a good way to judge it. If you can find peaches that have begun to ripen and are beginning to smell like a peach, snap them up. Pick out the ripest-looking peaches that have a creamy to deep yellow undercolor, rather than immature green ones. Try to choose the freshest varieties as they appear throughout the season. If a peach is mealy and dry on the inside, the peach variety was picked too late in its season or was stored too long.

Bottles labeled pure almond extract are made with oil of bitter almond and are preferable to bottles labeled almond extract. The pure version is now available in supermarkets.

During baking, the crust rises up around the peaches. Wherever peaches cover the crust, it remains very soft from the juices, but the bottom and edges of the crust become dark golden and crisp.

Baking the tart in a springform pan makes it easy to remove from the pan and produces the smooth-sided crust that I remember.

A Step Ahead ⤙ This tart is even better the day after it is baked. The crust softens and the almond flavor intensifies. If your kitchen is especially warm, keep the fruit in good condition by refrigerating the baked tart overnight, then bringing it to room temperature before serving it.

SERVES 8

Necessities ⤙ *One 9-inch springform pan with sides at least 2¾ inches high*

BUTTER CRUST	½ cup sugar
1 cup unbleached all-purpose flour	5 ounces (1 stick plus 2 tablespoons)
½ cup cornstarch	soft unsalted butter
½ teaspoon baking powder	1 teaspoon vanilla extract
⅛ teaspoon salt	¾ teaspoon pure almond extract

PEACHES	2 teaspoons fresh lemon juice
4 medium-large ripe peaches, rinsed	1 tablespoon sugar

Prepare the Crust

⤙ Position a rack in the middle of the oven. Preheat the oven to 425°F. Butter the inside of a 9-inch-diameter springform pan.

Sift the flour, cornstarch, baking powder, and salt together onto a piece of wax paper or into a medium bowl and set aside. Put the ½ cup sugar and the butter in a large bowl and beat with an electric mixer on medium speed until the mixture looks smooth, about 2 minutes. Move the beaters around in the bowl if using a handheld electric mixer. Stop the mixer and scrape the mixture from the sides of the bowl and any that becomes caught in the beaters as needed throughout the mixing process. Add the vanilla and almond extract, beating just to blend them into the mixture. Decrease the speed to low and slowly add the flour mixture, beating just to incorporate the flour and form a smooth dough. Press the dough evenly over the bottom of the prepared pan.

Add the Peaches

⤙ Cut each peach in half, remove the pit, and cut each half into 4 sections, slicing in a downward direction. You will have 32 peach slices. If the pit doesn't slip out easily, cut the slices inward toward the pit and remove them. Arrange a circular row of peach slices upright on the crust, skin side down. A pointed end of each slice should be touching the inside rim of the pan and the slices should touch each other. They look like little boats sitting on the dough. Press the peach slices gently into the dough. Fill in the center of the crust with a second circle of upright peach slices. Use a small spoon to sprinkle the lemon juice and sugar evenly over the peaches.

Bake and Serve the Tart

↝ Bake about 45 minutes until the edges of most of the peaches are browned and the edges of the crust are dark golden. Cool thoroughly at room temperature. Run a small knife around the sides of the pan to loosen the tart. Release the sides of the springform pan. Use a sharp knife to loosen the tart from the bottom of the pan and a metal spatula to slide the tart onto a serving plate. The tart can be covered and stored at room temperature for up to 3 days. In hot weather refrigerate the tart to preserve the fruit, but bring it to room temperature for serving.

All-American Peach Cobbler

Look for the meaning of "cobbler" in three different cookbooks and you will find three different explanations. Some bake the fruit with a cake batter, some use a pastry crust, and many bake biscuits on top of the fruit. The only consensus that I found is that cobblers are truly American desserts that include a simple fresh fruit filling baked together with some type of batter or dough in a deep dish. My peach cobbler is made with a soft biscuit dough that is rolled to match the size of the baking pan. I roll the dough for the bottom layer thicker than the top layer. Since the bottom layer of dough absorbs the fruit juices during baking, it has a nice soft, moist consistency, while the thin top layer of dough bakes crisp. Fruits that give off a generous quantity of juice for the dough to take in during baking make a good choice for cobblers. Ripe summer peaches fit the bill perfectly.

Baking Answers ↝ Peaches vary in size and variety throughout the summer. Small peaches taste as good as large ones, and the first peaches are usually the smaller ones. Look for peaches that are not bruised. Bruised spots cause peaches to rot rather than ripen. I find smelling fruit a good way to judge it. If you can find peaches that have begun to ripen and are beginning to smell like a peach, snap them up. Pick out the ripest-looking peaches that have a creamy to deep yellow undercolor, rather than immature green ones. Try to choose the freshest varieties as they appear throughout the season. If a peach is mealy and dry on the inside, the peach variety was picked too late in its season or was stored too long. When using peaches for baking, I buy more than I think I need, to allow for ones that don't ripen properly. You can always eat any that are left over.

This biscuit dough is made with vegetable shortening, which tenderizes the dough more than butter would. The biscuit mixing process is the same as for biscuits made with cold butter. Small pieces of cold shortening are mixed to a crumbly stage with the dry ingredients. When the liquid ingredients are stirred into the dry ingredients, a soft but ragged dough forms. It's the few strokes of kneading (page 44) that make the dough smooth.

Since the biscuit dough is not sweet, the fruit filling should contrast it by being generously sweetened.

A Step Ahead ❧ The peaches can be blanched, peeled, pitted, and cut up, then covered and refrigerated overnight.

The cobbler can be baked a day ahead, then warmed when served.

SERVES 8

Necessities ❧ *One 9- to 9½-inch round or one 8-inch square glass or ceramic baking container, both with 1¾- to 2-inch-high sides, a rolling pin, and a pastry brush*

PEACH FILLING	
5 cups peeled (see page 38) and pitted medium-large peaches cut in 1-inch pieces (about 2½ pounds)	3 tablespoons sugar
	1 tablespoon fresh lemon juice

COBBLER DOUGH	
2 cups unbleached all-purpose flour	1 large egg
2 teaspoons baking powder	
½ teaspoon salt	1 tablespoon unsalted butter, melted
2 tablespoons sugar	2 teaspoons sugar
4 tablespoons (¼ cup) cold vegetable shortening (such as Crisco), cut into ½-inch pieces	Vanilla ice cream to serve with the cobbler or cold whipping cream to pour over the cobbler, optional
½ cup milk (whole or low-fat)	

Mix the Filling

❧ Position a rack in the middle of the oven. Preheat the oven to 400°F. Grease with shortening or butter a 9- to 9½-inch round or an 8-inch square glass or ceramic baking container, both with 1¾- to 2-inch-high sides.

Put the peaches in a medium bowl. Sprinkle the sugar and lemon juice over the peaches and stir them together. Set aside or cover and refrigerate overnight.

Mix the Dough

↪ Sift the flour, baking powder, and salt into a large bowl. Stir in the 2 tablespoons of sugar. Add the shortening pieces, stirring to coat them with flour. Rub the shortening and flour mixture between your thumb and fingertips until coarse crumbs form that are about ½ to ¾ inch in size and the shortening pieces are coated with the flour. There will be loose flour. Put the milk and egg in a small bowl and stir it with a fork to break up the egg yolk. Pour the milk mixture over the flour mixture and stir with a large spoon until a soft dough that holds together forms. The dough looks ragged, not smooth. Turn the dough out onto a lightly floured board and knead it for about 10 strokes by pushing the dough down and forward with the heel of your hand against the rolling surface then folding it in half and repeating the process until the dough looks smooth. Divide the dough into 2 unequal pieces—1 piece that uses about two thirds of the dough for the bottom layer and 1 piece that uses the remaining third of the dough for the topping. Pat each piece of dough into a ball. On a lightly floured surface with a floured rolling pin, roll out the larger piece of dough to fit the bottom of the baking dish, about ⅜ inch thick. Hold the bottom of the baking dish over the dough to measure that the size is the same. Loosen the dough from the rolling surface with a knife if necessary. Drape the dough over the rolling pin and transfer it to the prepared baking dish, pressing the dough gently to fit the dish. Spoon the peach filling and any accumulated juices evenly over the dough. On a lightly floured surface with a floured rolling pin, roll out the remaining piece of dough to fit the top of the baking container. It will be about ⅛ inch thick. Loosen the dough from the rolling surface with a knife if necessary. Drape the dough over the rolling pin and place it over the peaches. Press the edges of the dough against the sides of the baking container to seal it to the container. The bottom and top doughs are not sealed together. Repair any holes in the top of the dough by pinching the dough together. Use a pastry brush to brush the top with the melted butter. Sprinkle the 2 teaspoons of sugar over the top. Use a sharp knife to cut 4 slits, about 1 inch long, in the top layer of dough to let steam escape.

Bake and Serve the Cobbler

↪ Bake for about 25 minutes, until the top is golden and the fruit is bubbling gently. The top crust will bubble up slightly in appealing waves and may pull away slightly from the edges. This is fine. Let the cobbler cool about 15 minutes before serving. Spoon the warm cobbler onto individual plates, and serve with a scoop of vanilla ice cream or a pitcher of cold whipping cream to pour over, if desired. The cobbler can be baked a day ahead, cooled, covered, and stored at room temperature. Warm it, uncovered, in a preheated 250°F. oven for 15 minutes.

Variations ↦ *One cup of blueberries or raspberries can be mixed into the peach filling. Or, for a cool season choice, use a mixture of cranberries and peeled, cored, and chopped apples or pears. Omit the lemon juice and use 1½ cups of fresh or unsweetened frozen and defrosted cranberries and 4 cups of chopped apples or pears mixed with ⅓ cup sugar and ½ teaspoon ground cinnamon. Bake the cobbler at 375°F. for about 35 minutes until the apples or pears are tender.*

Flying Cloud Biscuits

The ideal biscuit is tender, light, and easy to mix. That sounds simple, but as my husband noted as he bit into my umpteenth biscuit attempt, creating the simple recipes seems to challenge me the most. These biscuits welcome any challenge. The crisp, crusty exterior encloses a supersoft and light biscuit. Rather than the classic method of cutting in cold shortening with the flour, these biscuits use melted butter for the shortening. Mixing the dough becomes a comfortable process of stirring wet and dry ingredients together. Sour cream is the "secret" ingredient that makes these biscuits so tender.

Baking Answers ↦ Many biscuit recipes include several tablespoons of baking powder, which can give the biscuits a metallic aftertaste. I experimented with various quantities of leavening and found that 1 teaspoon of baking powder used with ½ teaspoon baking soda achieved this high-rising, light result and eliminated any metallic taste. Using a combination of all-purpose flour and cake flour and sifting the dry ingredients also produces lighter biscuits.

Butter the baking sheet or baking liner generously for crisp and browned biscuit bottoms.

Use a metal biscuit cutter to cut out biscuits. By cutting the dough cleanly and sharply, the biscuit cutter produces straight-sided biscuits that rise nicely. Any size round metal cutter works fine, but different sizes yield different numbers of biscuits.

A Step Ahead ↦ The biscuits can be baked a day ahead, cooled, covered, and stored at room temperature. To warm the biscuits, wrap them in aluminum foil and warm in a preheated 275°F. oven for about 15 minutes.

Necessities ✤ *1 heavyweight baking sheet, a rolling pin, a 2¾-inch round metal cutter, and a pastry brush*

1½ cups unbleached all-purpose flour	6 tablespoons (¾ stick) unsalted butter,
½ cup cake flour	melted
2 tablespoons sugar	1 cup sour cream (use full-fat)
1 teaspoon baking powder	¼ cup buttermilk (nonfat is fine)
½ teaspoon baking soda	1 tablespoon whole milk
¾ teaspoon salt	

Mix the Dough

✦ Position a rack in the middle of the oven. Preheat the oven to 375°F. Butter a baking sheet, or line a baking sheet with parchment paper and butter the paper.

Sift both flours, sugar, baking powder, baking soda, and salt into a medium bowl or onto a piece of wax paper.

Put half the flour mixture in a large bowl. Use a large spoon to stir in the melted butter, sour cream, and buttermilk to blend the 2 mixtures. Add the remaining flour mixture, stirring until a soft, ragged dough forms and most of the flour is incorporated.

Gather the dough into a ball and put it on a lightly floured rolling surface. Knead the dough about 12 times by pushing the dough down and forward with the heel of your hand against the rolling surface then folding it in half and repeating the process until the dough looks fairly smooth and there is no loose flour. Lightly flour the rolling surface and a rolling pin. Roll the dough into a ½-inch-thick circle and use a 2¾-inch round metal cutter to cut the dough into circles. Gather the dough scraps together, roll the dough out to ½-inch thickness, and cut the remaining biscuits. You can make a final biscuit with any remaining dough by rolling it between the palms of your hands into a ball and patting it into a ½-inch-thick disk. This not-quite-perfect biscuit can be for "tasting." Place the biscuits on the baking sheet about 2 inches apart. Use a pastry brush to brush the top of each biscuit with some of the milk.

Bake and Serve the Biscuits

✦ Bake about 15 minutes until the bottoms are golden brown and the tops are lightly colored. Cool the biscuits on the baking sheet for about 5 minutes. Serve warm with lots of soft butter, jam, and marmalade. The cooled biscuits can be wrapped in plastic wrap and stored at room temperature for up to 1 day. Warm them wrapped in aluminum foil in a preheated 275°F. oven for about 15 minutes before serving them.

Orange Spice Scones

Scones are similar to biscuits but are usually sweeter and are often served split and spread with butter and jam with a cup of tea. Although some scones are made with cream, which makes them quite rich, these spicy scones have all of the expected rich taste but are made with nonfat buttermilk. Scones can become shortcakes when split and heaped with summer fruit and whipped cream. These cinnamon- and ginger-flavored scones make a good shortcake matched with sliced peaches and sweetened whipped cream (see Strawberry Shortcake, page 318).

Baking Answers ⚬ When using ground spices, put a dab on your finger and taste the spice to be sure it is fresh. When ground ginger is not fresh, it will have no taste at all. I speak from the experience of having left a bottle of ground ginger in my pantry too long.

For the zest, grate only the orange skin of the orange. The white pith is bitter and has no orange flavor.

The mixing process for scones is similar to biscuits. Small pieces of cold butter or shortening are mixed to a crumbly stage with the dry ingredients. When the liquid is stirred into the dry mixture, a soft dough forms. The soft dough can be gathered into a ball, patted into a circle, and cut into wedges. There is no need to roll it.

To produce a slightly crisper bottom, I prefer to bake these scones directly on the baking sheet, without any paper liner.

A Step Ahead ⚬ The scones can be baked up to 2 days ahead, cooled, wrapped in plastic wrap, and stored at room temperature. Warm them, uncovered, in a preheated 250°F. oven for about 10 minutes before serving them.

MAKES 8 SCONES

Necessities ⚬ *1 heavyweight baking sheet and a pastry brush*

2 cups unbleached all-purpose flour	2 teaspoons grated orange zest
½ cup sugar	¼ pound (1 stick) cold unsalted butter,
1 teaspoon baking powder	cut into pieces
1 teaspoon baking soda	¾ cup cold buttermilk (nonfat pre-
½ teaspoon salt	ferred)
1 teaspoon ground cinnamon	1 large egg, lightly beaten with a fork
½ teaspoon ground ginger	2 teaspoons sugar

Mix the Dough

❧ Position a rack in the middle of the oven. Preheat the oven to 400°F. Have ready an ungreased baking sheet.

Stir the flour, ½ cup of the sugar, baking powder, baking soda, salt, cinnamon, ginger, and orange zest together in a large bowl. Put the butter pieces in the bowl and rub the butter and flour mixture between your thumb and fingertips until coarse crumbs form that are about ½ to ¾ inch in size and the butter pieces are coated with the flour. Or, use a fork or pastry blender to cut in the butter until pea-sized pieces form. Use a large spoon to stir in the buttermilk to form a soft dough. Gather the dough into a soft ball. Lightly flour a smooth, clean surface and pat the dough into an 8-inch-diameter circle. Cut the circle into 8 wedges. Place the wedges 2 inches apart on the baking sheet. Use a pastry brush to brush the top of each scone lightly with some of the beaten egg. Sprinkle the remaining 2 teaspoons of sugar evenly over the top.

Bake and Serve the Scones

❧ Bake about 15 minutes until the tops color slightly and the bottoms become light brown. Cool the scones on the baking sheet for about 5 minutes then serve them warm with plenty of soft butter and a choice of several jams or marmalades.

Variation ❧ *Cool the scones and split them horizontally. Spoon sliced peaches or strawberries and whipped cream (page 319) generously over each half.*

Butter Shortbread Cutouts

This cookie is exactly what you want a holiday cookie to be. The dough is easy to roll and produces cookies that taste even better than they look. Butter is responsible for most of the great flavor, and the flour and cornstarch combination produces a tender cookie. This dough is so easy to work with that it doesn't mind being rolled out several times or if little fingers give it some extra handling. Cookie cutters make a neat job of cutting out the designs, and the dough holds its shape during baking.

Baking Answers ✤ Refrigerating the dough firms it so that it is easy to roll out and doesn't stick to the rolling surface. But if the dough is refrigerated overnight, the butter firms the dough so much that the dough becomes too hard to roll. Letting the dough sit at room temperature softens it so it rolls easily. Depending on the temperature in your kitchen, the cold dough takes from 30 minutes to 1 hour to soften.

You can roll dough out on a freestanding ceramic cutting board, a piece of marble (I've used them in classes but never owned one), or right on a Formica or smooth countertop. A plastic cutting board will work also. Check to see that whatever surface you roll the dough out on is clean and free of odors.

Sprinkling a light dusting of flour on the rolling pin and rolling surface makes the cutout shapes easy to lift and transfer to the baking sheet. I slide a thin flat metal spatula or pancake turner under the dough to loosen it from the rolling surface and move it over to the baking sheet.

Seven inexpensive cookie cutters can bake you through a year of happy occasions—hearts for Valentine's or any day, shamrocks for St. Patrick's Day, bunnies for Easter, leaves for autumn, stars for Christmas or any festivity, gingerbread people for Christmas, and a round cutter to make circles and half-moons. Cut out half-moons by using only half of a round cookie cutter. Even if all you have is a round cutter, cookie rounds can be decorated with colored sugars, sprinkles, or any of the decorations that appear seasonally in the baking section of supermarkets. Use metal or plastic cookie cutters to cut out nice, precise shapes. Press colored sugar gently onto the cookies before baking them, but add sprinkles or crushed peppermint candy to frosted cookies after baking. If baked, sprinkles and candy melt slightly and tend to lose their shine and shape. Dragees (those little gold or silver balls) can go on before or after baking.

Bottles labeled pure almond extract are made with oil of bitter almond and are preferable to bottles labeled almond extract. The pure version is now available in supermarkets.

Although the cookies can be left plain, I usually brush them with egg white before baking, which adds some shine and helps any decorations adhere to them. Or, I decorate or spread the baked cookies with a simple powdered sugar frosting. The easiest and neatest way to decorate with this frosting is to pipe the frosting from a pastry bag fitted with a small writing tip (page 45, "Measure, Mix and Bake!"). It's fun to try several of the many options for decorating the basic cookie.

A Step Ahead ⌁ Make the dough a day ahead and refrigerate it overnight, but allow time for it to soften before rolling it out.

Baked cooled cookies can be frozen. Wrap the cookies in plastic wrap and put them in a rigid plastic container or metal tin. Separate the layers of cookies with pieces of wax paper. Let any topping firm before wrapping and freezing the cookies. Label them with the date and contents and freeze up to 3 months. Defrost the wrapped cookies at room temperature.

MAKES ABOUT SEVENTY-TWO 1½-INCH COOKIES

Necessities ⌁ *2 heavyweight baking sheets, a rolling pin, appropriate cookie cutters, 2 wire racks for cooling the cookies, and a pastry brush*

COOKIE DOUGH	½ teaspoon pure almond extract
1¼ cups unbleached all-purpose flour	1 large egg white, optional
½ cup cornstarch	
½ teaspoon baking powder	Granulated sugar, colored granulated
½ teaspoon salt	sugar, sprinkles, silver or gold
½ pound (2 sticks) soft unsalted butter	dragees, crushed peppermint-striped
⅔ cup powdered sugar	candy, or edible glitter for decorating,
1½ teaspoons vanilla extract	optional
FROSTING (OPTIONAL)	2 tablespoons water, plus 1 additional
1 cup powdered sugar, sifted	teaspoon if needed
½ teaspoon vanilla extract	

Mix the Dough

⌁ Position 2 oven racks in the middle and upper third of the oven. Preheat the oven to 325°F. Line 2 baking sheets with parchment paper.

Sift the flour, cornstarch, baking powder, and salt together onto a piece of wax paper or into a medium bowl and set aside.

Put the butter and powdered sugar into a large bowl and beat with an electric mixer on medium speed until the mixture looks smooth and creamy and the color lightens, about 1 minute.

Move the beaters around in the bowl if using a handheld electric mixer. Stop the mixer and scrape the mixture from the sides of the bowl and any dough that becomes caught in the beaters as needed. Mix in the vanilla and almond extract until they are blended into the mixture. Decrease the speed to low and add the flour mixture, mixing just until it is incorporated and a smooth dough forms. Divide the dough in 2 portions and pat each into a 5-inch disk. Wrap each disk in plastic wrap and chill in the refrigerator for about 30 minutes or until the dough is firm. Or, refrigerate the dough overnight and let it soften at room temperature just until it is soft enough to roll easily.

Remove the dough from the refrigerator. Lightly brush flour on the rolling surface and rolling pin. Roll 1 piece of dough to a scant ¼-inch thickness. Slide a thin metal spatula under the dough to loosen it from the rolling surface. Use a cookie cutter that is about 1½ to 2 inches in diameter or across the middle to cut out hearts, stars, half-moons, or any desired shape. Place half of a round cookie cutter on the dough to cut half-moons. Using more than half of the cutter makes larger curved half-moons, while using less than half of the cutter makes smaller crescent moons. Use the spatula to lift the cookies and place them ¾ inch apart on a prepared baking sheet. Wrap the scraps in plastic wrap and set aside. Repeat the rolling and cutting with the second piece of dough. Transfer the cookies to a prepared baking sheet. Press all of the dough scraps together to form a smooth dough and repeat the rolling and cutting process, rolling the dough to a scant ¼-inch thickness. Transfer the cookies to the baking sheet. If you still have a lot of scraps of dough, press them together and repeat the rolling and cutting once more. If using the egg white to glaze the cookies, put it in a small bowl and whisk it until foamy. Brush the top of each cookie lightly with some of the egg white, if desired. Sprinkle granulated sugar, or colored sugar, dragees, candy, or glitter lightly over the egg white, if desired. Or, omit the egg white and leave the top of the cookies plain, then glaze the warm baked cookies or decorate the cooled cookies with powdered sugar frosting as directed below.

Bake the Cookies

↝ Bake the cookies about 18 minutes, reversing the sheets top to bottom and back to front after 10 minutes of baking. The edges of the cookies will be light brown but the centers pale. Cool the cookies 5 minutes on the baking sheet. Use a thin metal spatula to transfer them to a wire rack to cool thoroughly.

Make the Optional Frosting

↝ In a small bowl, stir the powdered sugar, vanilla, and enough water together to form a stiff frosting. Use the frosting immediately while it is soft.

Decorate the Cookies

↝ If using the frosting, there are 2 choices. Using a thin spatula to spread the frosting thinly on the warm cookies melts the frosting slightly, so it forms a thin layer of firm glaze on the cookies. Or, if the frosting is spread over or piped on cooled cookies, it keeps its white color and holds its shape. Spoon the frosting into a pastry bag fitted with a small writing tip and pipe dots or stripes of frosting on cooled cookies, then dip the cookies in the decorations and gently shake off any excess. The decorations will adhere to the frosting. Hold the pastry tip about 1 inch above the cookies and press gently on the pastry bag so frosting comes out slowly and evenly. The tips of star-shaped cookies look nice decorated like this. If you have used a gingerbread person cutter, use the pastry bag and writing tip to draw frosting shoes, clothes, and faces on the baked gingerbread people. Play around and have a good time with the frosting and decorating; it will all look good. After decorating a batch, you can step back and choose your favorites for repeating.

Serve the Cookies

↝ Store the cookies in a metal tin for up to 1 week. Let any frosting dry firm before storing the cookies, then layer them carefully between sheets of wax paper so as not to disturb any decorations. Or, freeze as directed above in "A Step Ahead."

Mixing
a Smooth Batter

THESE ARE ALL-IN-ONE CAKES THAT COME OUT OF THE OVEN READY TO EAT. OF COURSE, THEY MUST COOL, BUT WITH THE EXCEPTION OF THE SAUCE FOR THE GINGERBREAD CAKE, IF THESE CAKES HAVE A TOPPING, IT BAKES RIGHT ON THE CAKE. I hope you'll notice how short the directions are for actually mixing these cake batters—they are really easy.

Cake batters are thinner mixtures than the dough mixtures in the previous chapter. However, cake batters vary in thickness, and this influences the finished cake. Sticky-Top Gingerbread with Brown Sugar Toffee Sauce (page 155) is made from a thin batter that produces a fine-grained cake, while the thick batter of a pound cake produces a firm cake with a dense texture. Somewhere in the middle are the batters for the upside-down cakes and Blueberry Crumb Cake (page 153) that result in a soft-textured butter cake. These butter-cake batters have a lower proportion of butter and eggs and more leavening than a batter for a pound cake does. All of these results are desirable for different types of cakes.

Not all cake batters are mixed the same way. Some, such as the Fifty-Fifty Crumb Buns, (page 148) are mixed in a food processor, while the gingerbread cake needs only a thorough stirring to blend its ingredients together. The Blueberry Crumb Cake, pound cake, and upside-down cakes are butter cakes that are mixed by a traditional cake-mixing method. The structure of these cakes develops during the thorough beating of first the butter and sugar, then during the beating when the eggs are added. Careful beating at these stages is important. If a recipe directs beating butter and sugar for 3 minutes, I time it. It is an easy way to ensure that cakes come out just right. The final step of adding the flour alternately with some liquid is only a process of incorporating ingredients.

I find that creaming butter and sugar with a handheld mixer forms large fluffy clumps but not the creamy smooth mass that beating with the flat beater of a standing mixer does. Cakes are equally good when beaten with either type of mixer as long as you don't skimp on the beating time.

Baking powder and baking soda are leavenings that help cakes rise. Baking soda is added when the batter includes such acid ingredients as buttermilk, molasses, or sour cream.

When cold eggs or cold liquids are added to a butter batter, the batter may look curdled since the cold ingredients firm up bits of the butter. When the flour is added, the batter loses the curdled look and becomes smooth. Adding the flour alternately (and in smaller portions) with the liquid reduces the tendency to curdle. This curdling from cold liquids does not harm the finished cake as long as the finished batter has become smooth. If eggs or liquids are at room temperature when they are added, the batter curdles less or not at all.

Sturdy, heavyweight pans bake cakes evenly. Square, round, and tube pans are the shapes most commonly used for cakes. I prefer shiny pans that reflect heat rather than dark ones. The outside of a cake can turn darker than desired in a dark pan. If all you have is a dark pan, try reducing the oven temperature 25°F. and watch the cake carefully as the end of the baking time nears. Take a look at the recipe beforehand and check to see that you have the right-size pan or pans. It's risky to bake cakes in a pan size different from what the recipe calls for, since this affects baking times and how cakes develop during baking. For example, if a batter is meant to bake in a 9-inch square pan but is baked in an 8-inch square pan, it could burn on the edges before the center is done. It could also develop a heavy texture from the weight of so much batter in the pan, or even overflow out of the smaller pan.

I line cake-pan bottoms with parchment or wax paper so cakes never stick to the bottom of the pan. Since the bottoms of cake pans are filled with batter, wax paper will not burn and can substitute for parchment paper. To cut a paper liner that fits into the cake pan use the cake pan bottom rather than the top as a guide. The bottom of the pan is where the liner must fit, and some pans, such as tube pans, are smaller at the bottom than at the top. Also, the top of a cake pan often has a rolled edge, so using this as a pattern would not give a liner that fits exactly. Turn the pan upside down and place the paper on the bottom of the cake pan to use as a guide and cut the paper liner. Then, if the pan has a center tube, use the tip of the scissors to mark the center of the paper liner with the outline of the hole in the bottom of the pan. Set the pan aside. Fold the marked paper circle in half and cut along the outline of the hole. Open the paper circle and fit it inside the bottom of the pan. The bottoms of springform pans do not need to be lined, as the cakes are easy to remove once you release and open the sides of these pans.

To check to see if a cake is done, first gently touch the top to see if it feels firm. When the top feels firm, insert a toothpick into the center of the cake. If the toothpick comes out clean, the cake is done. Check often as the end of the baking time nears, because an overbaked cake also yields a dry toothpick. After testing cakes several times, you'll even be able to judge the doneness by how the toothpick feels as it goes into the cake. Crumb toppings feel firm whether or not a cake is done, so test crumb-topped cakes with a toothpick and skip the step of touching the top. If a cake contains fruit or chocolate pieces, insert the toothpick in the cake rather than the fruit or chocolate. Soft fruit and melted chocolate always give a wet toothpick, so if you hit either with the toothpick, test another spot.

Cakes firm as they cool. Recipes advise letting them sit in their pans for a specified time so they can cool to the point that they are fairly sturdy when turned out of the pan. Cakes cool evenly on a wire rack that allows air to circulate around them. Once they are cool, slide cakes onto a serving plate, if appropriate. The removable bottom of a tart pan works well for supporting a cake while moving it around.

Fifty-Fifty Crumb Buns

A s an avid lover of crumb toppings, I need a lot of crumbs to satisfy me. These cupcake-size buns are half yellow butter cake and half crumb topping and have earned my highest "crumb seal of approval."

Baking Answers ❧ Both the crumbs and the cake batter are made in a food processor. Prepare the crumbs first, then you won't have to wash the work bowl before using it to mix the cake batter.

Bottles labeled pure almond extract are made with oil of bitter almond and are preferable to bottles labeled almond extract. The pure version is now available in most supermarkets.

MAKES 12 BUNS

Necessities ❧ *Muffin tin or tins to hold 12 buns*

CRUMB TOPPING	
1 cup plus 2 tablespoons unbleached all-purpose flour	¼ teaspoon salt
¾ cup packed light brown sugar	3 ounces (¾ stick) cold unsalted butter, cut into 6 pieces
1 teaspoon ground cinnamon	2 tablespoons water

CAKE BATTER	
¾ cup plus 2 tablespoons unbleached all-purpose flour	2 large eggs
¾ teaspoon baking powder	2 tablespoons milk
¼ teaspoon salt	1 teaspoon vanilla extract
3 ounces (¾ stick) soft unsalted butter	½ teaspoon pure almond extract
¾ cup powdered sugar	Powdered sugar for dusting the buns

Make the Topping

❧ Position a rack in the middle of the oven. Preheat the oven to 325°F. Line 12 muffin tin openings with paper muffin liners.

Put the flour, brown sugar, cinnamon, and salt in the work bowl of a food processor and process about 10 seconds to blend them. Add the butter pieces and process with about 25 on/off bursts until the largest pieces of butter are ¼ inch in size. With the machine running, add the water and process for about 15 seconds until it is incorporated and the mixture forms large clumps of crumbs and holds together. Transfer the crumbs to a medium bowl and set aside while you mix the cake batter. It is not necessary to wash the work bowl of the food processor before mixing the cake batter.

Mix the Batter

↦ Sift the flour, baking powder, and salt into a small bowl or onto a piece of wax paper. Set aside.

Put the butter and powdered sugar in the work bowl of the food processor and process for about 10 seconds until smooth. Add the eggs, milk, vanilla, and almond extract and process for about 20 seconds until smoothly blended, stopping the food processor once to scrape down the sides with a rubber spatula. Add the flour mixture, processing just until the flour is incorporated. The batter will be thick. Divide the batter evenly among the 12 muffin liners, spooning about 2 rounded tablespoons of batter into each muffin liner and filling the liners slightly less than half full. Distribute a thick layer of the crumbs evenly over each portion of batter, pressing the crumbs gently onto the batter. Brush off any crumbs that spill onto the top of the muffin tin.

Bake and Serve the Buns

↦ Bake until a toothpick inserted into the center of the buns comes out clean, about 30 minutes. Cool the buns for 10 minutes in their pans. Use a small sharp knife to loosen any of the buns that have risen above the paper liner from the muffin tin. Carefully lift and transfer the buns to a wire rack to cool. Dust with powdered sugar. Serve within 3 days.

Peanut Butter Crumb Cake

When my friend Dianne Hannan told me about her Peanut Butter Crumb Cake, the name alone made me eager to try it. The cake did not disappoint. It has a solid peanut butter taste and a lighter texture than is typical for recipes made with peanut butter. Since part of the cake mixture is used for the crumb topping, it can be mixed in 1 bowl. The cake bakes in a large 13 x 9-inch pan and serves a crowd of peanut butter lovers.

Baking Answers

Smooth peanut butter can be substituted for the chunky variety if you prefer less crunch. Soft peanut butter blends easily into the batter. If the peanut butter has been refrigerated, soften it to room temperature. I use the low-sodium but not the low-fat peanut butter. Use a rubber spatula to scrape the peanut butter out of a jar or measuring cup easily.

Mix the baking soda and water together when you are ready to add it to the batter. If soda sits in the water ahead of time, it reacts with the water and loses its power.

This cake is beaten on low speed and does not require long beating.

Kitchen Experiments

I tried adding 1 cup of milk chocolate chips to the cake batter. It worked fine, but the peanut butter flavor was overpowered by the chocolate chips—not a bad thing, but different.

SERVES 16 TO 20

Necessities ❧ *A 13 x 9-inch baking pan with 2-inch-high sides*

2 large eggs	½ cup chunky peanut butter, room
2½ cups unbleached all-purpose flour	temperature
2 cups packed light brown sugar	1 cup buttermilk (nonfat is fine)
½ teaspoon salt	1 teaspoon vanilla extract
5 tablespoons soft unsalted butter, cut	1 teaspoon baking soda
into 10 pieces	1 teaspoon water

Mix the Cake and Crumbs

❧ Position an oven rack in the middle of the oven. Preheat the oven to 350°F. Butter a 13 x 9 x 2-inch baking pan.

Put the eggs in a small bowl and stir them vigorously with a fork to blend the yolks and whites. Set aside.

Put the flour, brown sugar, and salt in a large bowl and beat with an electric mixer on low speed to blend them together. Add the butter and peanut butter and continue beating until a mealy mixture with some large crumbs forms, about 1 minute. Remove ⅔ cup of the mixture to a small bowl and set aside for the crumb topping. Add the buttermilk, reserved eggs, and vanilla to the mixture in the large bowl and beat until they are blended into the mixture and a thick batter forms. The batter has a few lumps. Stir the baking soda and water together gently in a small bowl, just to dissolve the baking soda. Add the baking soda mixture to the batter, mixing just until it is blended completely into the mixture. Use a rubber spatula to scrape all of the batter into the prepared pan. Sprinkle the reserved crumb mixture evenly over the top.

Bake and Serve the Cake

✷ Bake for about 30 minutes, just until a toothpick inserted into the center of the cake comes out clean. Cool the cake in the pan and cut into squares to serve. The cake can be covered with plastic wrap and stored at room temperature for 2 days. This cake makes a great choice to take along on a picnic or pack in a lunch box.

Cranberry-Walnut Butterscotch Bars

This is the story of the Little Butterscotch Bar That Could. First, it saved itself from the scrap heap of baking history, and then it opened my eyes to a whole new realm of fun with baking.

It began when I was away on a trip. On the phone my husband Jeff told me he was eating a great cranberry bar that he had found in the freezer. I wasn't sure which bar he meant because I had just finished a marathon testing of brown sugar bars and brownies and thrown all the versions in the freezer and forgotten about them. But his description of them sounded so good—very moist, tasting of butter and brown sugar, loaded with cranberries and nuts—that I retrieved my notes, tracked them down, and made them again.

This time, I shared a batch with my editor, Janice. She liked them so much that she demanded a copy of the recipe at once. It happened to be February, time for Valentine's Day. Janice decided to make a batch to send to her grandmother—after all, cranberries are red, and bar cookies travel well. In keeping with the holiday, she used a heart cookie cutter to cut her bars from the pan. Elegant bar cookies for Grandma, divine scraps and crumbs for Janice.

I encourage you to take this spirit of invention to your baking as well. Lemon Chess Bars (page 88) cut into chess pieces? Apple Crumble Bars (page 68) in the shape of apples? The possibilities are endless!

Baking Answers ❧ Bake these bars only to the point that a toothpick comes out with a few moist crumbs clinging to it. The tops of the bars will be golden brown and the edges will be crisp and taste of butter.

Mix the ingredients together just until they are blended smoothly rather than trying to beat a lot of air into them.

Grate only the orange part of the citrus rind for the zest. The white pith is bitter.

A Step Ahead ❧ The bars can be wrapped in plastic wrap, then heavy aluminum foil, and stored in the freezer for up to 3 months. Label them with the date and contents. Defrost the wrapped bars at room temperature.

MAKES 12 TO 16 BARS

Necessities ❧ *One 9-inch square baking pan or an 11 x 7-inch baking pan, both with 2-inch-high sides, a grater for the orange zest, and a wire rack*

1⅓ cups unbleached all-purpose flour
1 teaspoon baking powder
½ teaspoon salt
6 ounces (1½ sticks) soft unsalted
   butter
¾ cup packed light brown sugar
½ cup granulated sugar
1 teaspoon grated orange zest

2 large eggs
2 teaspoons vanilla extract
1⅓ cups (about 6 ounces) dried cranberries
1 cup walnuts, coarsely chopped
Powdered sugar for dusting the top of
   the bars

Mix the Dough

❧ Position a rack in the middle of the oven. Preheat the oven to 325°F. Butter a 9 x 9 x 2-inch or 11 x 7 x 2-inch pan.

Stir the flour, baking powder, and salt together into a small bowl or onto a piece of wax paper and set aside.

Put the butter, brown sugar, granulated sugar, and orange zest in a large bowl and beat with an electric mixer on medium speed until the mixture looks smooth, about 1 minute. Move the beaters around in the bowl if using a handheld electric mixer. Stop the mixer and scrape the mixture from the sides of the bowl and any that becomes caught in the beaters as needed throughout the mixing process. Mix in the eggs and vanilla until they are blended in thoroughly. The batter will look curdled if the eggs are cold. Decrease the speed to low and add the flour mixture, mixing just until it is incorporated. The batter will look smooth again. Add the cranberries and walnuts, stirring just to distribute them evenly in the mixture. Use a rubber spatula to scrape the batter from the bowl and spread it evenly in the prepared pan.

Bake and Serve the Bars

⤙ Bake for about 40 minutes, just until a toothpick inserted in the center comes out with a few moist crumbs clinging to it. The toothpick should not have liquid clinging to it. The top will be golden brown and firm. Cool the bars thoroughly in the pan on a wire rack, about 1 hour. Dust powdered sugar over the top of the bars. Cut the bars into 12 to 16 pieces and use a thin metal spatula to remove them from the pan. Wrap individual bars in plastic wrap and store at room temperature up to 3 days, or freeze the bars as directed above in "A Step Ahead."

Blueberry Crumb Cake

Right after my daughter's wedding we wisely took a relaxing trip to Nantucket with several friends. We stayed at the Pineapple Inn, where we spent a good part of each morning enjoying this warm blueberry cake during our lazy breakfasts on their sunny patio. This especially light cake is brimming with blueberries under a crunchy cinnamon topping. Our stay was made perfect when the owners of the inn offered to share their recipe with us.

Baking Answers

⤙ Use fresh or frozen, but not defrosted, blueberries for the cake. If defrosted frozen blueberries are used, they add moisture to the batter and the cake loses its light texture. I often use small, wild Maine summer blueberries for this cake. If using small blueberries, you will need 2½ cups.

The cake bakes in a springform pan, so it does not have to be inverted to remove it from the pan. This keeps the topping in perfect condition so none of it falls off the cake.

A Step Ahead

⤙ The cake can be baked a day ahead, left in its pan at room temperature, and covered with aluminum foil, ready to be warmed for serving.

Necessities ✍ *One 9-inch springform pan with sides at least 2¾ inches high*

CRUMB TOPPING	1 teaspoon ground cinnamon
⅓ cup unbleached all-purpose flour	3 tablespoons cold unsalted butter, cut
½ cup sugar	into ½-inch pieces

BLUEBERRY CAKE	1 large egg
2 cups unbleached all-purpose flour	1 teaspoon vanilla extract
1½ teaspoons baking powder	½ cup milk (any fat content)
½ teaspoon salt	2 cups fresh or frozen blueberries (2½
5 tablespoons soft unsalted butter	cups if using small wild blueberries)
¾ cup sugar	

Mix the Topping

✍ Put the flour, sugar, and cinnamon in a large bowl and use a large spoon to stir them together. Add the butter pieces, stirring to coat them with flour. Rub the butter pieces and flour mixture between your thumb and fingertips, or cut them together with a pastry blender until coarse crumbs form that are about ½ to ¾ inch in size. Set the topping aside while you mix the cake.

Mix the Cake

✍ Position an oven rack in the middle of the oven. Preheat the oven to 350°F. Butter a 9-inch springform pan with sides at least 2¾ inches high.

Put the flour, baking powder, and salt in a medium bowl and stir them together. Set aside.

Put the butter and sugar in a large bowl and beat with an electric mixer on medium speed until lightened in color and fluffy, about 2 minutes. The mixture will come away from the sides of the bowl. Move the beaters around in the bowl if using a handheld electric mixer. Stop the mixer and scrape the mixture from the sides of the bowl and any that becomes caught in the beaters as needed throughout the mixing process. Add the egg and vanilla and beat for 1 minute. Decrease the speed to low and in 5 additions (3 flour, 2 milk) add the flour mixture and the milk alternately, beginning and ending with the flour mixture. Let each addition of milk or flour incorporate before adding another. The batter may look curdled after the milk additions. Scrape the sides of the bowl again after the last addition of flour. The batter will look smooth. Using a large spoon, gently stir in the blueberries just to distribute them evenly. The batter becomes cold and quite thick if frozen blueberries are used. This is okay. Use a rubber spatula to scrape all of the batter into the prepared pan. Sprinkle the reserved crumb topping evenly over the cake.

Bake and Serve the Cake

❧ Bake for about 55 minutes if using frozen blueberries and about 50 minutes if using fresh blue-berries, until a toothpick inserted in the center of the cake comes out clean. If the toothpick pen-etrates the blueberries, test another spot.

Cool the cake in the pan for 5 minutes. Use a small sharp knife to loosen the sides of the cake from the pan. Remove the sides of the springform pan. Either cut wedges of cake on the pan bottom or slip a thin metal spatula under the cake and carefully slide the cake onto a serving plate. Serve the cake warm or at room temperature. The cake can be baked a day ahead, left in its pan at room temperature and covered with aluminum foil, then heated in a 275°F. oven for about 15 minutes until it is warm.

Sticky-Top Gingerbread with Brown Sugar Toffee Sauce

This dark, spicy cake is great for warming up cold winter evenings. First, the cinnamon, cloves, and ginger create a festive mood as their spicy aroma wafts through the oven door. Then the sticky-top sauce appeals to the child within, who enjoys every gooey lick.

The brown sugar and cream topping of this gingerbread actually does double duty. It bakes into the top of the gingerbread as a toffeelike glaze, while the finished cake is blanketed with additional warm, sticky toffee sauce.

Baking Answers ❧ The toffee sauce cooks at a gentle simmer and there will be tiny bubbles at the surface. The simmering evaporates some of the moisture and the sauce thickens slightly. Some of the toffee sauce bakes on top of the cake and makes the cake especially moist, while at the same time forming an instant glaze for the cake.

Mixing this cake is just a matter of stirring wet ingredients with dry ones. No electric mixer or long beating is needed.

A Step Ahead ❧ The gingerbread can be prepared 3 days ahead and the sauce 5 days ahead. Store the covered gingerbread at room temperature and the covered sauce in the refrigerator.

Necessities ⌁ *One 2-quart saucepan and one 9-inch square baking pan or one 11 x 7-inch baking pan, both with 2-inch-high sides*

**BROWN SUGAR TOFFEE SAUCE—
MAKES ABOUT 1⅓ CUPS**

1 cup whipping cream

2 tablespoons molasses

1 ounce (¼ stick) unsalted butter

1 cup packed light brown sugar

GINGERBREAD

6 ounces (1½ sticks) unsalted butter

½ cup molasses

1 cup packed light brown sugar

2 large eggs

2 cups unbleached all-purpose flour

⅛ teaspoon salt

1 tablespoon ground ginger

1 tablespoon ground cinnamon

¼ teaspoon ground cloves

1¼ cups warm milk

½ teaspoon instant coffee granules

2 teaspoons baking soda

Cook the Sauce

⌁ Put the cream, molasses, butter, and brown sugar in a medium saucepan and cook over medium heat until the butter and brown sugar melt, stirring constantly. Increase the heat to medium-high and bring just to a simmer. You will see tiny bubbles. Continue cooking at a gentle simmer for 5 minutes, stirring often and adjusting the heat if necessary. The sauce will reduce and thicken slightly. Remove it from the heat and set aside.

Mix the Gingerbread

⌁ Position a rack in the middle of the oven. Preheat the oven to 350°F. Butter a 9 x 9 x 2-inch or an 11 x 7 x 2-inch pan.

Put the butter, molasses, and brown sugar in a medium saucepan and cook over low heat just until the butter and brown sugar melt and the mixture is smooth, stirring often. The mixture should be warm but not hot. Remove from the heat and add the eggs, stirring to incorporate them smoothly into the mixture.

Sift the flour, salt, ginger, cinnamon, and cloves into a large bowl. Pour the molasses mixture over the flour mixture and use a large spoon to stir them until they are blended together. Put the warm milk in a small bowl and add the instant coffee, stirring to dissolve the coffee. Gently stir the baking soda into the milk mixture. Add the milk mixture to the flour mixture, stirring it gently into the batter just until it is incorporated. The batter will be thin. Pour it into the prepared pan.

Bake the Gingerbread

↵ Bake 25 minutes. Remove the cake from the oven. Reduce the oven temperature to 250°F. and spoon ½ cup of the reserved warm toffee sauce gently and evenly over the top of the cake. Bake for about another 20 minutes until a toothpick inserted in the center of the gingerbread comes out dry.

Serve the Gingerbread

↵ The gingerbread can be cooled for 20 minutes and served warm, or cooled thoroughly in its pan and served at room temperature. Cut the gingerbread into squares and put them in shallow bowls or dishes. Warm the remaining toffee sauce over low heat and then put it into a small pitcher to pour over the gingerbread squares. The gingerbread can be prepared 3 days ahead and the sauce 5 days ahead. Store the covered gingerbread at room temperature and the covered sauce in the refrigerator. Put the sauce in a small saucepan and warm it on low heat when ready to serve the gingerbread.

Deep South Pound Cake

My daughter's friend John Quattlebaum presented this large butter pound cake to her several years ago as a Christmas gift. It was one of John's first baking attempts and was a huge success. John's mother, Mary Jane, had sent him their family pound cake recipe along with her advice to use real butter and to buy baking powder, which is in the red can, not baking soda, in the yellow box. The real gift that year was the sharing of a family tradition with his friends and the passing of a treasured recipe from one generation to another.

A pound of butter and a generous measure of vanilla work together to make this pound cake special. From the first whiff of vanilla when mixing the batter to a house filled with the scent of butter as the cake bakes, you will relish the combination in every slice of this extremely moist and fine-textured cake.

Baking Answers ↵ The batter mixes especially smooth if the butter is soft and the eggs and milk are at room temperature. Mary Jane Quattlebaum suggests leaving the eggs and milk at room temperature for 1 hour. When butter is soft, you should be able to easily press your finger into a stick of the unwrapped butter.

This is a large amount of batter and should be beaten in a large bowl that has at least a 3½-quart capacity.

For directions for lining a tube pan with parchment or wax paper see page 147.

The cake is mixed by creaming the butter and sugar then beating in the eggs. The flour is added alternately with the milk at the end of the mixing. Thorough beating is important to develop the cake's structure when creaming the butter and sugar and when adding the eggs to the cake batter. Adding dry ingredients and milk to the batter is only a process of blending them into the batter and does not require long beating.

This recipe makes either 1 large tube cake or 2 loaf-size pound cakes. The Zuccotto—Italian Chocolate and Vanilla Cream Cake (page 341) and the Deep-Dish Strawberry Whipped Cream Cake (page 312) each use 1 loaf of pound cake. The batter can also bake in 6 small loaf pans that make nice holiday gifts. Cakes in small loaf pans take about 1 hour and 10 minutes to bake.

A Step Ahead ⭗ This cake keeps well and actually develops more flavor the second day. It also freezes well. Wrap the cooled cake in plastic wrap, then heavy aluminum foil, and label it with the date and contents. Store it in the freezer for up to 3 months. Defrost the wrapped cake at room temperature.

Kitchen Experiments ⭗ Some cooking shops sell attractive heavy brown cardboard disposable loaf pans suitable for baking. The pound cake can bake in these pans and remain in them for gift giving. I tried baking this pound cake in the full-size and small-size cardboard loaf pans and found the only difference was that the cakes did not brown quite as much on top and needed to bake slightly longer in the cardboard pans than in a metal pan. I imagine metal pans hold heat better than the cardboard ones do.

SERVES ABOUT 20

Necessities ⭗ *A 9½- or 10-inch-diameter fixed-bottom tube pan with at least 3¾-inch-high sides or 2 loaf pans with a 6- to 8-cup capacity, and 2 wire racks for cooling and inverting the cake or loaves*

4 cups unbleached all-purpose flour	1 pound (4 sticks) soft unsalted butter
1 teaspoon baking powder	3 cups sugar
⅛ teaspoon salt	2 teaspoons vanilla extract
6 large eggs, at room temperature for 1 hour	½ cup whole milk, at room temperature for 1 hour

Mix the Cake

✎ Position a rack in the middle of the oven. Preheat the oven to 300°F. Butter the bottom, sides, and center tube of a 9½- or 10-inch fixed-bottom tube pan with at least 3¾-inch-high sides or 2 loaf pans, with a 6- to 8-cup capacity. A 9 x 5 x 3-inch loaf pan is a common size. Butter the bottoms of the tube pan or loaf pans, line them with parchment or wax paper, and butter the paper.

Sift the flour, baking powder, and salt together onto a piece of wax paper or into a medium bowl and set aside.

Put the eggs in a medium bowl and beat with an electric mixer on medium speed for 1 minute to combine the yolks and whites thoroughly. Set aside. It is not necessary to clean the beaters before using them to beat the butter and sugar together.

Put the butter and sugar in a large bowl and beat the mixture with an electric mixer on medium speed until it looks creamy and smooth, about 3 minutes. Move the beaters around in the bowl if using a handheld electric mixer. Stop the mixer and scrape the mixture from the sides of the bowl and any that becomes caught in the beaters as needed throughout the mixing process. Add the eggs in 3 additions, beating for 1 minute after each addition and adding the vanilla with the last egg addition. Decrease the speed to low, and in 5 additions (3 flour, 2 milk) add the flour mixture and the milk alternately, beginning and ending with the flour mixture. Let each addition of milk or flour incorporate before adding another. The batter will be smooth and thick. Use a rubber spatula to scrape all of the batter into the prepared pan or pans. Smooth the top.

Bake and Serve the Cake

✎ Bake for about 2 hours if the cake is in a tube pan, just until a toothpick inserted in the center comes out dry but with a crumb or two clinging to it. If baked in loaf pans, the loaves take about 1 hour and 25 minutes. The top of the cake will be firm and golden brown. Cool the cake in the pan for 30 minutes. The cake makes soft sizzling sounds as it begins to cool. Use a small sharp knife to loosen the cake from the sides and the center tube of the pan. Invert the cake onto a wire rack or serving plate. Carefully remove and discard the paper lining the cake bottom. Place another wire rack on the bottom of the cake and invert the cake onto it. The cake is now right side up. Cool the cake thoroughly, about 3 hours. Slide the cooled cake onto a serving platter or cardboard cake circle.

Cut the cake into slices and serve. Fresh berries, sliced peaches, or vanilla ice cream make good accompaniments. Wrap the cake tightly in plastic wrap and store at room temperature up to 5 days.

French Pear and Almond Cake

Recently when I was teaching in San Francisco, I had a free day that I spent with Emily Luchetti and her pastry team at Farallon restaurant. They generously let me help bake the day's desserts with them, including tastes of everything. One of their many impressive dessert ideas was this butter-almond macaroon cake baked with poached pears, which they also made with toasted hazelnuts instead of the almonds.

The cake is a version of a French cake called financier. Financiers are normally baked in small molds and have a unique dense, moist interior and a firm, chewy surface. The soft, dense batter is mixed by stirring the ingredients together and adding melted, browned butter and almonds for a rich nut flavor. This cake has the same desirable texture but is baked as a thin full-size cake. Emily's novel idea was to bake the financier batter with fruit—in this case pears. The cake batter rises up and surrounds the fruit during baking so the round tops of pears nestle into the cake. Although the cake looks complicated you'll be pleased to find that the preparation, including poaching the pears and browning the butter, is not.

Baking Answers ◦ The relatively short baking time of this cake is not long enough to cook the fruit properly, so some precooking in the form of poaching assures tender fruit. Poaching fruit is the process of cooking fruit in a simmering mixture of water and sugar. The fruit softens and the syrup sweetens it slightly. I add strips of lemon and orange peel to enhance the flavor, but wine, cloves, cinnamon sticks, or vanilla beans are other options for enhancing the flavor of poached fruit. Scrape any of the bitter white pith from the lemon and orange peel before using them in the poaching liquid. If the pears are not quite ripe, poaching softens them.

Cooking butter until light brown flecks appear in the bottom of the pan adds a nutty flavor to melted butter. You'll notice a nutty aroma as the butter cooks. When butter is browned, there are tiny brown bits on the bottom of the pan, but the butter itself remains yellow.

To brown butter, melt it over medium heat. At first, the butter will form tiny bubbles that make a low popping noise during about 5 minutes of gentle cooking. Just before the butter browns, the bubbling and popping noise stops. A light brown foam forms around the edge of the pan and brown flecks quickly appear on the bottom of the pan. The butter is now browned. Watch the butter carefully and remove it from the heat as soon as the brown flecks appear.

The whites from 3 large eggs will usually produce ½ cup of egg whites; since this cake is best prepared with ½ cup whites, I've given the cup measurement rather than number of whites.

I prefer to use almonds that have their skins on for the flavor that they add to this cake.

ANY-SEASON FRUIT CRUMBLE (PAGE 63)

Front Plate: Lemon Chess Bars (page 88)
Rear Plate: Cranberry-Walnut Butterscotch Bars (page 151)

PECAN MERINGUES STACKED WITH
WHIPPED CREAM AND STRAWBERRY SAUCE (PAGE 338)

TOP, LEFT TO RIGHT: EBINGER'S ORANGE-GLAZED LAYER CAKE WITH ORANGE BUTTER FILLING (PAGE 193), DARK CHOCOLATE CUPCAKES WITH FUDGE FROSTING (PAGE 296)

BOTTOM, LEFT TO RIGHT: CHOCOLATE COOKIE SANDWICHES (PAGE 287), MOM'S LEMON MERINGUE PIE (PAGE 270)

A PAIR OF APPLE DUMPLINGS BAKED
IN CINNAMON SAUCE (PAGE 218)

ORANGE SPICE SCONES (PAGE 139)

DOUBLE-DECKER RASPBERRY AND
ALMOND PRALINE CHEESECAKE (PAGE 366)

The fluted side of the tart pan adds a nice decorative edge on the cake. The shallow depth of a tart pan allows the cake to brown nicely.

Stainless-steel, ceramic, and nonstick interior saucepans are nonreactive; aluminum is not. If nonstick, the interior of the saucepan should be in good condition and free of scratches.

A Step Ahead ◦ The almonds and powdered sugar can be processed up to 3 days ahead, sealed in a plastic bag, and stored at room temperature.

The pears can be poached and refrigerated with their syrup up to 3 days ahead. Drain the pears and bring them to room temperature before using them.

SERVES 8

Necessities ◦ *One 3-quart nonreactive saucepan, one 9-inch round tart pan with a removable bottom, and a baking sheet to hold the tart pan*

PEAR TOPPING	One 2-inch strip orange peel
4 cups water	*3 medium or 4 small firm but ripe*
1 cup granulated sugar	*pears, peeled, halved, and cored*
One 2-inch strip lemon peel	

ALMOND CAKE	⅔ cup unblanched almonds
1 tablespoon unsalted butter, melted	*⅔ cup powdered sugar*
½ cup cake flour	*¼ pound (1 stick) unsalted butter*
½ cup granulated sugar	*½ cup egg whites (3 large)*

Powdered sugar for dusting the top of the cake

Poach the Pears

◦ Put the water, granulated sugar, lemon peel, and orange peel in a large nonreactive saucepan. Cook over medium heat until the sugar dissolves and the mixture simmers, stirring often. When simmering, the mixture forms tiny bubbles. Add the pear halves. They will float. Cook, uncovered, for 10 minutes in the gently bubbling liquid. Use a large spoon to turn the pear halves over in the syrup. Cook another 5 minutes or just until the pears feel tender when pierced with a 2-pronged fork or the tip of a small knife. Try not to make a lot of large holes in the pears. Drain the pears and set aside. If the pears are going to be refrigerated for later use, put the pears in their syrup in a bowl, cover them, and refrigerate up to 3 days. Drain the pears and bring them to room temperature before using them in the cake.

Mix the Cake

☙ Position a rack in the middle of the oven. Preheat the oven to 350°F. Brush the bottom and sides of a 9-inch round metal tart pan that has a removable bottom with the melted butter.

Sift the cake flour into a large bowl. Stir in the granulated sugar.

Put the almonds and powdered sugar in the work bowl of a food processor fitted with the steel knife and process with a few short bursts to combine the ingredients. Process the mixture about 1 minute until the almonds are finely ground. Add the nut mixture to the flour mixture and stir them together. Set aside.

Put the ¼ pound of butter in a small frying pan and cook it over medium heat for about 6 minutes, just until the butter forms tiny brown flecks on the bottom. The butter will bubble and pop for about 5 minutes, then quiet down and stop bubbling. Light brown foam forms on the sides, then brown flecks on the bottom. Remove the pan from the heat as soon as you see the brown bits on the bottom. Pour the warm butter over the flour mixture and stir the mixture to moisten the flour. There will still be some loose flour. Pour in about half of the egg whites and stir them into the mixture to incorporate them. Add the remaining egg whites, stirring until the egg whites are incorporated and the mixture is smooth. The batter will be thin. Cover and refrigerate the almond batter for 30 minutes. The batter will thicken.

Bake and Serve the Cake

☙ Place the prepared tart pan on a baking sheet for easier handling. Use a rubber spatula to spread the chilled almond batter in the prepared pan. Arrange the pear halves, rounded side up, evenly around the top of the batter, placing the wide end of the pear closest to the edge of the pan. Bake about 35 minutes, just until a toothpick inserted into the center comes out dry, the edges are brown, and the center looks golden.

Cool the cake in the pan for 10 minutes. Use a small sharp knife to loosen the sides of the cake from the pan. It should already be mostly pulled away from the sides of the pan. Remove the tart pan from the baking sheet. If a bit of cake batter has leaked onto the baking sheet, loosen the tart pan from the baking sheet with a metal spatula. Set the tart pan on a shallow bowl, such as a soup bowl, and let the rim slide down, using the knife to loosen any cake that sticks, if necessary. Use a thin metal spatula to loosen the cake from the bottom of the tart pan, but leave the cake on the pan bottom to cool and become firm. When the cake is cool, slide a thin metal spatula under it and slide the cake onto a serving plate. Dust with powdered sugar and serve. The cake can be covered and refrigerated up to 2 days. Serve the cake cold or at room temperature.

Crushed Pineapple Upside-Down Cake

Whing making pineapple upside-down cake, I always feel like a dessert magician. I look in the oven and see a plain golden yellow cake baking. Then, as I unmold the cake to an imaginary drum roll, the cake is magically transformed by its shiny coating of brown sugar–glazed pineapple. Using crushed pineapple in this cake means that every bite of tender yellow cake is covered with the sticky pineapple.

Baking Answers ❧ Dark brown sugar rather than light brown sugar produces the appealing dark, sweet coating on the pineapple. It is easy to mix the butter and brown sugar for the glaze together if the butter is very soft.

The cake is mixed by creaming the butter and sugar and then beating in the eggs. The flour is added alternately with the milk at the end of the mixing. Thorough beating is important to develop the cake's structure when creaming the butter and sugar and when adding the eggs to the cake batter. Adding dry ingredients and milk to the batter is only a process of blending them into the batter and does not require long beating.

Bottles labeled pure almond extract are made with oil of bitter almond and are preferable to bottles labeled almond extract. The pure version is now available in most supermarkets.

Remember to remove the cake from its pan when the glaze and pineapple are warm so it releases easily and doesn't stick to the pan. If any pineapple should stick, replace it on the cake.

SERVES 8

Necessities ❧ *One 9-inch-diameter cake pan with 2-inch-high sides and 2 wire racks for cooling and inverting the cake*

GLAZE AND PINEAPPLE	
3 tablespoons very soft unsalted butter	One 14-ounce can crushed pineapple in its own juice, drained
¾ cup packed dark brown sugar	

CAKE	
1¼ cups cake flour	1 cup granulated sugar
1 teaspoon baking powder	2 large eggs
¼ teaspoon salt	1 teaspoon vanilla extract
¼ pound (1 stick) soft unsalted butter	¼ teaspoon pure almond extract
	½ cup whole milk

Mixing a Smooth Batter

Mix the Glaze

◈ Position a rack in the middle of the oven. Preheat the oven to 350°F. Butter the inside of a 9-inch-diameter cake pan with 2-inch-high sides.

Put the butter and brown sugar in a small bowl and stir them together until the butter is incorporated. Sprinkle the brown sugar mixture over the prepared pan, then pat it in an even layer over the bottom. Spread the crushed pineapple evenly over the brown sugar. Set aside.

Mix the Cake

◈ Sift the flour, baking powder, and salt together onto a piece of wax paper or into a medium bowl and set aside.

Put the butter and granulated sugar in a large bowl and beat with an electric mixer on medium speed until lightened in color and fluffy, about 3 minutes. Move the beaters around in the bowl if using a handheld electric mixer. Stop the mixer and scrape the mixture from the sides of the bowl and any that becomes caught in the beaters as needed throughout the mixing process. Add the eggs one at a time, beating for 1 minute after each addition. Stir in the vanilla and almond extract, mixing just to incorporate them. Decrease the speed to low and in 5 additions (3 flour, 2 milk) add the flour mixture and the milk alternately, beginning and ending with the flour mixture. Let each addition of milk or flour incorporate before adding another. The batter may look curdled after the milk additions. Scrape the sides of the bowl again after the last addition of flour. The batter is ready when the final addition of flour is mixed completely into the batter and the batter is smooth. If any flour is clinging to the sides of the bowl, stir it into the batter. Use a rubber spatula to scrape the batter from the bowl and spread it evenly over the pineapple in the prepared pan.

Bake and Serve the Cake

◈ Bake for about 55 minutes, until the top feels firm when touched lightly, and a toothpick inserted into the center of the cake comes out clean. Be sure to insert the toothpick into the cake, not into the pineapple.

Cool the cake in the pan for 5 minutes. Use a small sharp knife to loosen the sides of the cake from the pan. Place a wire rack against the top of the cake and invert the cake onto the rack to cool. The cake can be cooled for 20 minutes and served warm, or it can be cooled thoroughly and served at room temperature. Vanilla ice cream or whipped cream (page 320) makes a good accompaniment. Store the covered cake at room temperature up to 2 days and serve at room temperature.

Variation ◈ *Two cups of fresh or frozen and defrosted cranberries can be substituted for the pineapple.*

Pear and Gingerbread Upside-Down Cake

Pears and spice cake make a comforting fall idea for an upside-down cake. The sliced pears become coated with butter, honey, and brown sugar as they bake under the ginger-scented cake. When the cake is inverted, the honey-lacquered pear slices form a beautiful pattern over the top. Apple slices can be substituted for the pears.

Baking Answers ❧ Remember to remove the cake from its pan when the glaze and pears are warm, so they release easily and do not stick to the pan. If any pear slices do stick, replace them on the cake.

Cold honey sometimes becomes opaque and hard after long refrigeration. Warming the honey returns it to a clear liquid. Either spoon out some of the honey and warm it in a pan over low heat or let the open jar sit in hot water until the honey softens.

SERVES 8

Necessities ❧ *One 9-inch-diameter cake pan with 2-inch-high sides and 2 wire racks for inverting and cooling the cake*

GLAZE AND PEARS	¼ cup packed light brown sugar
3 tablespoons soft unsalted butter	2 pears, peeled, halved, cored, and cut
2 tablespoons honey	into ¼-inch slices

CAKE	6 ounces (1½ sticks) soft unsalted
2 cups unbleached all-purpose flour	butter
1½ teaspoons baking powder	¾ cup granulated sugar
½ teaspoon baking soda	3 large eggs
1½ teaspoons ground ginger	2 tablespoons unsulphured molasses
1 teaspoon ground cinnamon	1 teaspoon vanilla extract
¼ teaspoon ground cloves	

Mix the Glaze and Arrange the Pears

❧ Position a rack in the middle of the oven. Preheat the oven to 325°F. Have ready one 9-inch-diameter cake pan that is 2 inches deep.

Mixing a Smooth Batter

Heat the butter, honey, and brown sugar in a small saucepan over low heat until the butter and brown sugar melt and the mixture is smooth, stirring constantly. Pour the honey mixture into the cake pan and spread it evenly. Beginning at the edge of the pan, arrange the pear slices over the honey mixture in overlapping concentric circles to cover the bottom of the pan. You will have 2 rows of pear circles. Arrange the pears neatly, as this will become the top of the cake.

Mix the Cake

✑ Sift the flour, baking powder, baking soda, ginger, cinnamon, and cloves together onto a piece of wax paper or into a medium bowl and set aside.

Put the butter and granulated sugar in a large bowl and beat with an electric mixer on medium speed until lightened in color and fluffy, about 2 minutes. Move the beaters around in the bowl if using a handheld electric mixer. Stop the mixer and scrape the mixture from the sides of the bowl and any that becomes caught in the beaters as needed throughout the mixing process. Add the eggs one at a time, beating for 1 minute after each addition. Stir in the molasses and vanilla, mixing just to incorporate them. The batter may look curdled. Decrease the speed to low and add the flour mixture, mixing just until it is incorporated and the batter looks smooth. Spread the batter evenly over the pear slices, spreading it carefully so as not to disturb the pears.

Bake and Serve the Cake

✑ Bake for about 45 minutes until the top feels firm when touched lightly and a toothpick inserted into the center of the cake comes out clean. Be sure to insert the toothpick into the cake, not into the pears.

Cool the cake in the pan for 5 minutes. Use a small sharp knife to loosen the sides of the cake from the pan. Place a wire rack against the top of the cake and invert the cake onto the rack to cool. The cake can be cooled for 20 minutes and served warm, or it can be cooled thoroughly and served at room temperature. Vanilla toffee, caramel, or caramel swirl ice cream makes a good accompaniment. Store the covered cake at room temperature up to 2 days and serve at room temperature.

Variation ✑ *Three apples peeled, halved, cored, and cut in ¼-inch slices can be substituted for the pears.*

Black-and-White Cheesecake Cake

Not one but two well-liked desserts come together in this cake. Vanilla cheesecake bakes on top of chocolate cake, and just for good measure a layer of chocolate chips separates the two. It's a match made in dessert heaven.

Baking Answers ❧ The ingredient list looks a bit long, but sugar, flour, eggs, and vanilla extract all repeat for each layer.

When the vanilla cheesecake bakes on top of the chocolate cake, some of the cheesecake batter sinks into the chocolate cake batter to create an attractive swirled cake.

The large quantity of cream produces a thin cheesecake batter. After baking, the cheesecake layer firms up.

This cheesecake and cake combination does not need to be baked in a water bath.

A Step Ahead ❧ The cooled cake can be stored covered in the refrigerator for up to 5 days.

SERVES 16

Necessities ❧ One 9-inch springform pan with sides at least 2¾ inches high

CHOCOLATE CAKE
1 cup unbleached all-purpose flour
3 tablespoons unsweetened Dutch
   process cocoa powder
¾ teaspoon baking powder
¼ teaspoon salt
3 ounces (¾ stick) soft unsalted butter
½ cup sugar
2 large eggs
⅓ cup milk
1 teaspoon vanilla extract
1 cup (6 ounces) semisweet chocolate
   chips

CHEESECAKE TOPPING
12 ounces cream cheese, softened 3 to
   4 hours at room temperature
⅔ cup sugar
2 tablespoons unbleached all-purpose flour
3 large eggs, room temperature
¾ cup whipping cream
2 teaspoons vanilla extract

Mix the Cake

↪ Position an oven rack in the middle of the oven. Preheat the oven to 325°F. Butter a 9-inch springform pan with sides at least 2¾ inches high.

Sift the flour, cocoa powder, baking powder, and salt into a small bowl. Set aside.

Put the butter and sugar in a large bowl and beat with an electric mixer on medium speed for about 1 minute until the mixture is lightened in color and smooth. Move the beaters around in the bowl if using a handheld electric mixer. Stop the mixer and scrape the mixture from the sides of the bowl and any that becomes caught in the beaters as needed throughout the mixing process. Add the eggs and beat for 2 minutes. The mixture will look slightly curdled. On low speed, add half of the flour mixture, mixing just to incorporate it. Add the milk and vanilla extract, stirring just to blend them into the mixture. Add the remaining flour mixture, stirring just to incorporate it. Spread the batter in the prepared pan. Sprinkle the chocolate chips evenly over the batter. Set the pan aside while you mix the cheesecake batter.

Mix the Topping

↪ Put the cream cheese and sugar in a large bowl and beat with an electric mixer on low speed until the mixture looks smooth. If using a handheld electric mixer, move the beaters around in the bowl. Stop the mixer and scrape the mixture from the sides of the bowl as needed throughout the mixing process. Mix in the flour until it is incorporated. Put the eggs in a small bowl and stir them vigorously with a fork to blend the yolks and whites. Add the eggs in 2 additions. Mix in the cream and vanilla, just to incorporate them. Carefully pour the batter over the chocolate chips in the pan.

Bake and Serve the Cake

↪ Bake for about 55 minutes, until you can give the cake a gentle shake and the cheesecake topping looks firm but is not browned. The center of the cheesecake will be soft. Cover the cake loosely with a paper towel and cool it thoroughly, about 2 hours. Cover with plastic wrap and chill it thoroughly in the refrigerator, at least 6 hours or overnight. For the best flavor, let the cake sit at room temperature about 1 hour before serving. The cake can be covered and stored in the refrigerator for up to 5 days.

Putting
the Frosting
with the Cake

❦

THESE ARE THE PROUD CAKES OF A SOUTHERN GRANDMOTHER, THE COZY CAKES FOR A FALL AFTERNOON, THE FESTIVE CAKES FOR A CHRISTMAS DINNER, AND THE CAKES THAT FORM CHILD-HOOD MEMORIES. THEY COME IN ALL SIZES, FROM A BIG LEMON-Glazed Lemon Pound Cake (page 180), to an orange layer cake, to squares of Pumpkin Cake with Brown Sugar Icing (page 183), to small carrot cake snowballs.

Traditionally frosting covers and sometimes fills a cake, but it can also sandwich individual Whoopie Pies (page 173) together or be served as a dish of frosting that is a do-it-yourself spread to accompany a Cranberry Eggnog Cake (page 177). Adding different flavorings to a frosting turns one recipe into many. A cream cheese frosting can be flavored with lemon, cinnamon, ginger, or orange, while the flavor of a powdered-sugar glaze becomes completely different when the liquid changes from lemon juice to milk or to coffee.

From butter cream and cream cheese frostings to shiny icings and glazes, all kinds of frost-ings cover these cakes. The proportion of butter and powdered sugar used in a frosting determines its consistency. Butter cream and cream cheese frostings have a larger proportion of butter to pow-dered sugar and a somewhat creamier texture than mixtures used as an icing or a glaze. The finish on an icing is slightly shinier than that of a butter cream frosting. Glazes are usually liquid enough to be poured over the top of a cake. Glazes should be allowed to cool if cooked, or made with enough powdered sugar that they are thick enough to cling to the sides of a cake. But remember, a layer of glaze is meant to be a thinner coating than a layer of frosting or icing.

Let butter or cream cheese soften thoroughly before beating them with powdered sugar. This ensures that the frosting becomes silky smooth.

A thin metal spatula is the best tool for spreading frosting smoothly over a cake. On some soft cakes, crumbs fall off the cake when frosting is spread on them. Some cakes benefit from hav-ing a "crumb coat" of frosting that prevents cake crumbs from becoming mixed in with the outer layer of frosting. The crumb coat is a thin layer of frosting that is spread over the outside of the cake before the final thick layer of frosting is added. Since the cakes in this chapter are either quite moist and dense or have firm exteriors, they do not need this crumb coat of frosting. But the light cake of The Groom's Lemon Cake (page 244) and Aunt Elaine's Mocha Whipped Cream Shadow Cake (page 332) benefits from an initial crumb coat of frosting or whipped cream. It is also a good idea to wipe the spatula clean on the sides of the frosting bowl after each spreading before using it to take a new dollop of frosting.

Carrot Cake Coconut Snowballs

By popular request, my lifelong friend Sue Chase used to make this carrot cake with cream cheese frosting for every dinner party. Carrot cakes were just gaining popularity then and there were not all of the pineapple-walnut-raisin variations that have evolved. Recently I dug her recipe out of my files to use for these upside-down cupcakes slathered with cream cheese frosting and covered in coconut. As soon as I tasted the cake again, I remembered why we had relished Sue's pure carrot cake.

Baking Answers ❧ Since these cupcakes are turned bottom side up to frost the bottom and the sides, I want the cupcakes to be small without big flat tops. I leave a ½-inch space at the top of the paper liners and use only about ¼ cup of batter for each cupcake. When turned upside down and frosted, these cupcakes really do look like fluffy snowballs.

Using oil for the shortening in this cake creates a moist, dense cake. The aim of the mixing process is just to blend the ingredients together, so no long beating is required.

A food processor makes quick work of chopping the carrots.

Lining the muffin tin with paper liners makes the cupcakes easy to remove from the pan and the pans easy to clean.

MAKES 12 CUPCAKES

Necessities ❧ *2 muffin tins with 6 openings or 1 muffin tin with 12 openings, paper cupcake liners, and a wire rack for cooling the cupcakes*

CARROT CUPCAKES	
1 cup unbleached all-purpose flour	½ cup canola or corn oil
1 cup granulated sugar	2 large eggs
1 teaspoon baking soda	1 teaspoon vanilla extract
½ teaspoon salt	1½ cups peeled and finely chopped
1 teaspoon ground cinnamon	carrots (about 4 medium carrots)

CREAM CHEESE FROSTING	
¼ pound (1 stick) soft unsalted butter	3¼ cups powdered sugar
6 ounces cream cheese, softened	
2 teaspoons vanilla extract	2⅔ cups (one 7-ounce package)
	shredded sweetened coconut

Mix the Cupcakes

◦ Position a rack in the middle of the oven. Preheat the oven to 350°F. Line 12 muffin tin openings with paper cupcake liners.

Sift the flour, granulated sugar, baking soda, salt, and cinnamon into a large bowl. Add the oil and mix with an electric mixer on low speed just until the oil is incorporated and the mixture forms large crumbs. Move the beaters around in the bowl if using a handheld electric mixer. Add the eggs one at a time, mixing to incorporate them. Stir in the vanilla. The batter will be thick. Stir in the carrots, mixing just to distribute them evenly. The batter becomes thinner after the carrots are added. Fill the paper liners with batter, leaving ½ inch of paper liner unfilled and using about ¼ cup of batter for each.

Bake the Cupcakes

◦ Bake just until a toothpick inserted in the center of a cupcake comes out clean, about 25 minutes. Cool the cupcakes for 5 minutes in the pan, then transfer them in their paper liners to a wire rack to cool thoroughly.

Make the Frosting

◦ Put the butter, cream cheese, and vanilla in a large bowl and beat with an electric mixer on medium speed for about 1 minute until the mixture is smooth and the butter and cream cheese are combined thoroughly. Move the beaters around in the bowl if using a handheld electric mixer. Decrease the speed to low and add the powdered sugar in 2 additions. Continue beating until the powdered sugar is incorporated and the frosting is smooth.

Frost and Serve the Cupcakes

◦ Spread the coconut on a flat plate and set aside.

Remove the paper liners from the cupcakes and turn them upside down. Use a small metal spatula to spread about ¼ cup of frosting over the top and sides of each cupcake. Hold the bottom (which baked as the top) of the cupcake in your hand, turning it to frost it evenly. Gently roll the frosted part of the cupcake in the coconut to cover the frosting with coconut. Place the cupcakes unfrosted side down on a plate and serve at room temperature. These generously frosted cupcakes are best eaten with a fork. The cupcakes can be wrapped carefully in plastic wrap and refrigerated for up to 3 days. Let them sit at room temperature for about 1 hour before serving.

Whoopie Pies

Take a look at any general store checkout counter in Maine and you'll almost always see a basket of Whoopie Pies for sale. Whoopie Pies are cake sandwiches that look as if the tops of two chocolate cupcakes have been sandwiched together with white frosting. Their history is sketchy at best, but the funny name is just right for something that's so much fun to eat.

Wrapped in plastic wrap, Whoopie Pies travel well and make a good dessert for picnics or lunch boxes.

Baking Answers ❧ These little cakes bake on a baking sheet. The batter is thick and the cakes hold their shape and bake into small rounded cakes with flat bottoms. When the cakes are done, they have some small cracks on the top. When cool, the cakes are slightly crisp on the outside and soft in the middle. The outsides soften after being wrapped in plastic wrap.

Bottles labeled pure almond extract are made with oil of bitter almond and are preferable to bottles labeled almond extract. The pure version is now available in most supermarkets.

MAKES NINE 3-INCH-ROUND FILLED WHOOPIE PIES

Necessities ❧ *2 heavyweight baking sheets and 2 wire racks for cooling the cakes*

CHOCOLATE CAKE ROUNDS

1¼ cups unbleached all-purpose flour
¼ cup unsweetened Dutch process cocoa powder, such as Droste or Hershey's European
½ teaspoon baking powder
¾ teaspoon baking soda
¼ teaspoon salt

6 tablespoons (¾ stick) unsalted butter, softened
¾ cup plus 1 tablespoon granulated sugar
1 large egg
1 teaspoon vanilla extract
¾ cup sour cream

FROSTING

¼ pound (1 stick) soft unsalted butter

1½ cups powdered sugar
1 teaspoon vanilla extract
¾ teaspoon pure almond extract

Mix the Cake Rounds

✎ Position 2 oven racks in the middle and upper third of the oven. Preheat the oven to 350°F. Line 2 baking sheets with parchment paper.

Sift the flour, cocoa powder, baking powder, baking soda, and salt together onto a piece of wax paper or into a medium bowl and set aside.

Put the butter and granulated sugar in a large bowl and beat with an electric mixer on medium speed until the mixture looks smooth, about 1 minute. Move the beaters around in the bowl if using a handheld electric mixer. Stop the mixer and scrape dough from the sides of the bowl and any dough that becomes caught in the beaters as needed. Mix in the egg and vanilla until they are blended into the mixture. Decrease the speed to low and mix in the sour cream, just until no white streaks remain. Mix in the flour mixture just until the flour is incorporated. Use a tablespoon to drop 18 rounded tablespoons of batter 3 inches apart on the prepared baking sheets. The batter is thick enough to hold its mound shape on the baking sheet.

Bake the Cake Rounds

✎ Bake the 2 sheets of cake rounds for about 12 minutes, until the tops are firm to the touch and a toothpick inserted into the center of a cake comes out clean. Reverse the baking sheets after 7 minutes, front to back and top to bottom, to ensure the cakes bake evenly. Cool the cakes for 5 minutes on the baking sheet. Use a wide metal spatula to loosen the cakes from the paper and transfer them to wire racks to cool thoroughly.

Mix the Frosting and Serve the Pies

✎ Put the butter, powdered sugar, vanilla, and almond extract in a large bowl and beat with an electric mixer on medium speed until the mixture looks smooth, about 1 minute. Move the beaters around in the bowl if using a handheld electric mixer. Use a thin metal spatula to spread a well-rounded tablespoon of filling over the flat bottom of half of the cooled cake rounds spreading the filling to the edge of the cake. Press the flat bottom of the remaining cake rounds gently onto the filling. Serve at room temperature. Whoopie Pies can be wrapped in plastic wrap and stored at room temperature for up to 2 days.

Texas Chocolate Sheet Cake

This cake has stood the test of baking in the tiniest of kitchens—the galley on a sailboat. Dee Dee Conover and her husband are avid sailors who have sailed their boat across the ocean. Her notes for this recipe said that they enjoyed this cake while sailing the Norwegian fjords.

When Dee Dee gave me this recipe, she told me it was the easiest of cakes and was a good choice when you were expecting a crowd. Both cake and frosting are mixed quickly without an electric mixer. The thin cake batter bakes into a smooth-textured cake, while the frosting is a shiny light chocolate icing that spreads easily over the warm cake. Since the chocolate flavor comes from cocoa powder, there's not even any chocolate to melt.

Baking Answers ❧ This cake is baked in a rectangular jelly roll pan that measures 15½ x 10½ x 1 inches. The thin cake is cut into squares or rectangles for serving. The iced cake will just come to the top edge of the 1-inch pan. You can also use a half-sheet pan that measures about 17 x 12 x 1 inches, but the cake will be thinner and bake for about 3 to 5 minutes less than if baked in the jelly roll pan.

When baking soda is added to a liquid mixture, stir the mixture gently. If stirred vigorously, soda may bubble up and react with the mixture and its leavening power will be lost.

This thin cake cooks quickly, so watch it carefully as the end of the baking time nears. Make the icing while the cake bakes. The icing spreads easily over the warm cake.

MAKES 35 TWO-INCH CAKE SQUARES

Necessities ❧ *One 15½ x 10½ x 1-inch baking pan and a 3-quart saucepan*

FOR THE CAKE
2 large eggs
½ pound (2 sticks) unsalted butter
1 cup water
2 tablespoons unsweetened Dutch process cocoa powder, such as Droste or Hershey's European

2 cups unbleached all-purpose flour
2 cups granulated sugar
½ teaspoon salt
½ cup buttermilk (nonfat is fine)
1 teaspoon baking soda

FOR THE ICING

¼ pound (1 stick) unsalted butter

4 tablespoons unsweetened Dutch process cocoa powder

3½ cups powdered sugar

6 tablespoons milk

1 tablespoon vanilla extract

Mix the Cake

Position a rack in the middle of the oven. Preheat the oven to 375°F. Butter a 15½ x 10½ x 1-inch pan. Dust the bottom of the pan lightly with flour.

Put the eggs in a small bowl and stir about 20 vigorous strokes with a fork to blend the whites and the yolks. Set aside.

Put the butter, water, and cocoa powder in a 3-quart saucepan. Cook the mixture over medium heat until the butter melts and the cocoa powder dissolves, stirring constantly with a whisk to produce a smooth mixture. Remove from the heat and set aside in a medium bowl. Wash and dry the saucepan to use for the icing.

Put the flour, granulated sugar, and salt in a large bowl and stir them together just to blend them. Add the reserved warm butter mixture, stirring to blend the ingredients to a fairly smooth mixture that has a few small lumps. Stir in the reserved eggs until they are incorporated. Add the buttermilk and baking soda, stirring gently but thoroughly to incorporate them. The batter will be thin.

Bake the Cake

Pour the batter into the prepared pan. Bake about 22 minutes until a toothpick inserted in the center comes out clean and the edges are firm. Cool the cake slightly for about 30 minutes while you prepare the icing.

Make the Icing

Put the butter and cocoa powder in a 3-quart saucepan. Cook the mixture over medium heat until the butter melts and the cocoa powder dissolves, stirring constantly with a whisk to produce a smooth mixture. Remove the pan from the heat. Using a large spoon, stir in the powdered sugar. The mixture will be thick and not all of the powdered sugar will be incorporated. Add the milk and vanilla and use a whisk to beat the mixture smooth.

Ice and Serve the Cake

Spoon the icing over the slightly cooled but still warm cake. Use a thin metal spatula to spread the icing evenly. The icing slides easily over the cake. Cool the iced cake thoroughly at room temperature. Cut the cake into squares to serve. I often cut the cake into about 70 small squares and serve it with other small cakes or cookies. To store leftover cake, refrigerate it to firm the frosting, then cover with plastic wrap and refrigerate up to 3 days. For longer storage, wrap pieces of cold cake in plastic wrap, put them in a rigid freezer container, and freeze up to 1 month.

Cranberry Eggnog Cake with Bourbon Butter Frosting

Several years ago we spent Christmas in London with our English cousins, Gillian and Illtyd Lewis. Christmas dinner was a true feast that was crowned with a flaming Christmas pudding cake accompanied by a bowl of brandy butter. As we helped ourselves to big spoonfuls of brandy butter to spread over our cake, I realized that spread your own frosting and take as much as you want is a great idea. The following Christmas, I adapted the idea for our own holiday cake. The cake is a large yellow cake that bakes in a tube pan. It is laced with the familiar nutmeg and bourbon flavorings of a holiday eggnog, studded with colorful cranberries, and dusted with a light snowfall of powdered sugar and nutmeg after it bakes. I bring out a bowl of frosting that is heavy on the bourbon and butter, and we indulge in a cake and frosting feast.

Baking Answers ⋅⋄ Tube pans have a center tube that holds the heat during baking and helps this big cake cook evenly. For directions on lining a tube pan with parchment or wax paper see page 147.

Even with the amount of baking that I do, it is hard for me to finish a can of ground nutmeg before it loses its flavor, so I buy whole nutmeg and use a small nutmeg grater to grate fresh nutmeg whenever I need it.

The easiest way to chop the cranberries is in a food processor fitted with the steel knife and using few quick on/off pulses.

A Step Ahead ⋅⋄ The frosting improves in flavor if made a day ahead. It can be prepared up to a week ahead, put in its serving bowl, covered, and stored in the refrigerator. Bring the frosting to room temperature for serving.

SERVES 12 TO 16

Necessities ⋅⋄ *A 9½- or 10-inch-diameter tube pan with a fixed bottom, with at least 3¾-inch-high sides, and 1 wire rack for cooling the cake*

CAKE

2¾ cups cake flour

1½ teaspoons baking powder

¼ teaspoon salt

1¼ teaspoons ground nutmeg

1 cup fresh or previously frozen and defrosted unsweetened cranberries, coarsely chopped

2 cups plus 2 tablespoons granulated sugar

6 ounces (1½ sticks) soft unsalted butter

4 large eggs

2 teaspoons vanilla extract

¼ cup bourbon

1 cup whipping cream

1 tablespoon powdered sugar mixed with ¼ teaspoon ground nutmeg for dusting the top of the cake

FROSTING

6 ounces (1½ sticks) soft unsalted butter

1½ cups powdered sugar, sifted

2 tablespoons bourbon

1 teaspoon vanilla extract

Mix the Cake

❧ Position an oven rack in the middle of the oven. Preheat the oven to 325°F. Butter the bottom, sides, and center tube of a 9½- or 10-inch fixed-bottom tube pan with at least 3¾-inch-high sides. Line the bottom with parchment or wax paper and butter the paper.

Sift the flour, baking powder, salt, and nutmeg together onto a piece of wax paper or into a medium bowl and set aside.

Put the cranberries and 2 tablespoons of the granulated sugar in a medium bowl and stir them together to coat the cranberries with sugar. Set aside.

Put the butter and remaining 2 cups of granulated sugar in a large bowl and beat with an electric mixer on medium speed until fluffy, for 2 minutes. The mixture looks crumbly, not smooth. Move the beaters around in the bowl if using a handheld electric mixer. Stop the mixer and scrape the mixture from the sides of the bowl and any that becomes caught in the beaters as needed throughout the mixing process. Put the eggs in a small bowl and stir them vigorously with a fork to blend the yolks and whites. Add the eggs in 3 additions to the butter mixture, beating for 1 minute after each addition. Add the vanilla and bourbon to the cup of whipping cream. Decrease the speed to low, and in 5 additions (3 flour, 2 cream) add the flour mixture and the cream alternately, beginning and ending with the flour mixture. Let each addition of cream or flour mixture incorporate before adding another. The batter may look curdled after the cream additions. Scrape the sides of the bowl again after the last addition of flour. The batter should be smooth and all of the flour mixed completely into the batter. If any flour is clinging to the sides of the bowl, stir it into the batter. Use a rubber spatula to stir the cranberries gently into the batter. The batter will be thick. Use a rubber spatula to scrape all of the batter into the prepared pan. Smooth the top.

Bake the Cake

⤙ Bake for about 1 hour and 25 minutes, just until a toothpick inserted in the center comes out dry. If the toothpick penetrates a cranberry, test another spot. The top of the cake will be firm and golden brown. Cool the cake in the pan for 20 minutes. Use a small sharp knife to loosen the cake from the sides and the center tube of the pan. Invert the cake onto a flat serving plate. Carefully remove and discard the paper lining the cake bottom. Place a wire rack on the bottom of the cake and invert the cake onto it. The cake is now right side up. Cool the cake thoroughly, about 3 hours. Slide the cooled cake onto a serving platter or cardboard cake circle. Strain the powdered sugar and nutmeg mixture lightly over the top. The cake can be wrapped tightly in plastic wrap and stored at room temperature for up to 3 days.

Make the Frosting

⤙ Put the butter in a large bowl and beat with an electric mixer on medium speed for about 2 minutes until the butter is smooth. Add the powdered sugar, bourbon, and vanilla and beat until the powdered sugar is incorporated and the frosting is smooth. Put the frosting in a medium serving bowl. Serve the frosting with the cake, or press plastic wrap onto the surface of the frosting and refrigerate it for up to 1 week. Let the frosting soften for 1 hour at room temperature before serving it.

Serve the Cake

⤙ Cut the cake into slices and pass the bowl of frosting to spread on the slices of cake.

Lemon-Glazed Lemon Pound Cake

Not surprisingly, this recipe comes from the Southern family known for its Deep South Pound Cake (page 157). Mary Jane Quattlebaum's mother, Marian Reames, was always a great pie baker, but never made cakes. At an age when many people think about retiring from baking, she learned to make this outstanding lemon pound cake. The cake is extremely fine-textured and is covered with a lemon glaze that is almost as thick as a frosting. Big, proud, and dripping with golden glaze, this cake looks like the epitome of a Southern cake and is a legacy from a superb baker.

Baking Answers ⟡ This cake includes both butter and vegetable shortening for the shortening. Butter adds to the good taste, while vegetable shortening combines smoothly with the other ingredients to produce a cake with an exceptionally smooth, fine texture. Crisco vegetable shortening comes in convenient sticks that are marked in tablespoons and partial cups.

Remember to grate the lemon zest from the lemon before squeezing the juice. Be sure to grate only the yellow skin of the lemon. The white pith is bitter and has no lemon flavor.

This is a large amount of batter, which is best beaten in a large bowl that has at least a 3½-quart capacity.

The cake is mixed by creaming the butter and sugar then beating in the eggs. The flour is added alternately with the milk at the end of the mixing. Thorough beating is important to develop the cake's structure when creaming the butter and sugar and when adding the eggs to the cake batter. Adding dry ingredients and milk to the batter is only a process of blending them into the batter and does not require long beating.

For directions for lining a tube pan with parchment or wax paper see page 147.

The glaze should be poured over the cake while it is warm so some of it soaks into the cake. Since the warm glaze drips down the sides, just keep spreading any drips onto the sides of the cake.

SERVES ABOUT 20

Necessities ⟡ *A 9½- or 10-inch-diameter tube pan with a fixed bottom, with at least 3¾-inch-high sides, a 3½-quart-capacity or larger bowl, and 1 wire rack for cooling the cake*

LEMON POUND CAKE

3½ cups unbleached all-purpose
   flour
1 teaspoon baking powder
½ teaspoon salt
½ pound (2 sticks) soft unsalted
   butter
8 tablespoons (½ cup) room
   temperature vegetable shortening,
   such as Crisco

3 cups granulated sugar
6 large eggs
1 tablespoon lemon juice
2 teaspoons grated lemon zest
1 cup whole milk

THICK LEMON GLAZE

6 tablespoons (¾ stick) unsalted
   butter, melted

2 tablespoons fresh lemon juice
⅛ teaspoon salt
2 cups powdered sugar

Mix the Cake

↬ Position a rack in the middle of the oven. Preheat the oven to 300°F. Butter the bottom, sides, and center tube of a 9½- or 10-inch fixed-bottom tube pan with at least 3¾-inch-high sides. Line the bottom of the pan with parchment or wax paper and butter the paper.

Sift the flour, baking powder, and salt together onto a piece of wax paper or into a medium bowl and set aside.

Put the butter, vegetable shortening, and granulated sugar in a large bowl and beat with an electric mixer on medium speed until it looks creamy and forms fluffy large clumps, about 3 minutes. Move the beaters around in the bowl if using a handheld electric mixer. Stop the mixer and scrape the mixture from the sides of the bowl and any that becomes caught in the beaters as needed throughout the mixing process. Add the eggs one at a time, beating for ½ minute after adding each egg. Add the lemon juice and lemon zest, mixing just to incorporate them. Decrease the speed to low, and in 5 additions (3 flour, 2 milk) add the flour mixture and the milk alternately, beginning and ending with the flour mixture. Let each addition of milk or flour incorporate before adding another. The batter will be smooth and thick and there should be no loose flour. If any lemon zest clings to the beaters, scrape it off and stir it into the batter. Use a rubber spatula to scrape all of the batter into the prepared pan and smooth the top. Wipe any drips off the edges or center tube of the pan.

Bake the Cake

↬ Bake for about 1 hour and 50 minutes, but begin checking the cake after 1 hour and 35 minutes. The cake is done as soon as a toothpick inserted in the center comes out free of batter but with a crumb or two of cake clinging to it. The top of the cake will be firm and golden brown. Cool the cake in the pan for 15 minutes. Use a small sharp knife to loosen the cake from the sides and the center tube of the pan. Invert the cake onto a wire rack or serving plate. Carefully remove and discard the paper lining the cake bottom. Place a wire rack on the bottom of the cake and invert the cake onto it. The cake is now right side up on the wire rack. Place a piece of wax paper under the wire rack to catch the drips when you glaze the warm cake.

Make the Glaze and Glaze the Cake

↪ Put the melted butter, lemon juice, salt, and powdered sugar in a medium bowl and stir them together until the glaze looks smooth and the ingredients are blended. Spoon about two thirds of the glaze over the top of the warm cake, using a small metal spatula to spread it evenly over the top. Some of the glaze drips onto the sides and should be spread also. Spread the remaining glaze over the sides and in the center hole of the cake. Spread any glaze that drips off back onto the cake. The glaze may not look completely smooth. Cool the cake thoroughly. The glaze will firm as the cake cools. Slide the cooled cake onto a serving platter or a cardboard cake circle.

Serve the Cake

↪ Cut the cake into slices and serve. Fresh berries or strawberry or black raspberry ice cream make good accompaniments. The cake can be covered and stored at room temperature up to 5 days.

Pumpkin Cake with Brown Sugar Icing

These big squares of golden pumpkin cake that are dripping with smooth butterscotch-flavored icing will add a warm glow to any chilly day. The cake has a layer of crisp pecan halves that toast as they bake on top of the ginger- and cinnamon-spiced cake while the pourable butter and brown sugar icing almost spreads itself over the top of the cake.

Baking Answers ◆ This pumpkin cake uses oil for the shortening. The liquid oil makes the batter especially easy to mix and gives the cake a moist but light texture. This batter does not require long beating.

Check to see that the label on the can of pumpkin says pumpkin rather than pumpkin pie filling, which would have spices added.

MAKES NINE 3-INCH FROSTED CAKE SQUARES

Necessities ◆ *One 9-inch square baking pan or one 11 x 7-inch baking pan,*
both with 2-inch-high sides

PUMPKIN CAKE
1½ cups unbleached all-purpose
   flour
¾ teaspoon baking powder
¾ teaspoon baking soda
½ teaspoon salt
1¼ teaspoons ground cinnamon
¾ teaspoon ground ginger
1 cup canned pumpkin
1 cup granulated sugar
½ cup canola or corn oil
2 large eggs
¾ cup pecan halves

BROWN SUGAR ICING
5 tablespoons unsalted butter
⅔ cup whipping cream
1 cup packed dark brown sugar
1 teaspoon vanilla extract
1 cup powdered sugar

Mix the Cake

◆ Position a rack in the middle of the oven. Preheat the oven to 325°F. Butter or rub with oil the bottom and sides of a 9 x 9 x 2-inch or 11 x 7 x 2-inch pan.

Sift the flour, baking powder, baking soda, salt, cinnamon, and ginger onto a piece of wax paper or into a medium bowl and set aside.

Put the pumpkin, granulated sugar, and oil in a large bowl and beat with an electric mixer on medium speed until smooth, about 1 minute. Move the beaters around in the bowl if using a handheld electric mixer. Add the eggs one at a time, beating to blend each thoroughly into the mixture. The mixture looks smooth and shiny. Decrease the speed to low and add the flour mixture. The batter is ready when the flour is mixed completely into the batter. If any flour is clinging to the sides of the bowl, stir it into the batter. Use a rubber spatula to scrape the batter from the bowl and spread it evenly in the prepared pan. Scatter the pecans evenly over the top.

Bake the Cake

↝ Bake just until a toothpick inserted into the center of the cake comes out clean, about 30 minutes. The cake can be iced when it is warm or has cooled, but let the cake cool in the pan for at least 10 minutes before adding the icing. Use a small knife to loosen the cake from the sides of the pan before adding the icing.

Make the Icing

↝ Put the butter, cream, and brown sugar in a medium saucepan and cook over medium heat until the butter melts and the sugar dissolves, stirring often. Increase the heat to medium-high and bring the mixture to a boil. Boil for 3 minutes, stirring occasionally. Remove from the heat and stir in the vanilla just to blend it into the mixture. Set aside to cool slightly for about 30 minutes. Sift the powdered sugar into a medium bowl. Pour the slightly cooled sauce over it and use a whisk or electric mixer to beat the icing smooth, about 1 minute or less. It will change from a brown to a light brown color. Immediately pour the icing over the cake in the pan. Use a metal spatula to spread it evenly, if necessary. If the cake is warm, the icing spreads by itself. Icing will drip down around the edges of the pan and thinly coat the sides of the cake. This is good. Cool the cake and icing thoroughly, about 3 hours, but mark the portions in the top of the icing as soon as it is firm enough to hold the mark. Cut the cake into 9 squares. A thin metal spatula and a pancake turner work well together to help lift the cake squares from the pan. Serve the cake cold or at room temperature. Butter pecan ice cream makes a good accompaniment.

Rolling Pin Glazed Almond Cake

For years, my friend Mary Pennell sent me this cake from the Rolling Pin Bakery in Asheville, North Carolina, as a present. But, as generous as she was, it never seemed often enough. Then she outdid herself by talking the bakery into sharing the recipe. No matter that their recipe made a dozen cakes, I quickly adapted the ingredients and pared it down, so I can now mix up this cake whenever I want.

This cake is only about 1¼ inches high and bakes in a pie pan. The extremely moist texture comes from using almond paste and oil in the cake batter, and from the almond-flavored glaze that saturates the warm cake. It's a perfect partner to a cup of tea, or, if left in its pan, this cake travels well and is a good choice to take on a picnic.

Baking Answers ❧ Almond paste is a finely ground mixture of almonds and some sugar. When fresh, it is soft, malleable, and easy to mix into the cake batter. Check to see that you are buying almond paste rather than marzipan, which contains more sugar than almond paste does. Any leftover almond paste can be wrapped tightly in plastic wrap and refrigerated for up to 1 month. Almond paste in cans or sealed tubes of plastic is available in the baking section of most supermarkets. King Arthur Flour, listed in Mail-Order Sources on page 384, ships good-quality canned almond paste. Bottles labeled pure almond extract are made with oil of bitter almond and are preferable to bottles labeled almond extract. The pure version is now available in most supermarkets.

This cake is mixed by an interesting method that produces its unique crumbly texture. The dry ingredients and almond paste are mixed to a crumbly mixture, then when the oil is added, it coats the crumbs. Finally, the addition of the wet ingredients forms the smooth batter.

Poke holes in the warm baked cake with a fork and immediately spread the glaze over the top. The glaze soaks into the warm cake, melts easily over the top, and remains shiny even when it cools.

A Step Ahead ❧ The cooled cake can be wrapped in plastic wrap and aluminum foil and frozen for up to 1 month. Defrost the wrapped cake at room temperature.

SERVES 8

Necessities ❧ *One 9-inch shiny metal or glass pie pan*

ALMOND CAKE	½ teaspoon baking powder
⅓ cup (about 2¾ ounces) firmly packed almond paste, room temperature	¼ teaspoon baking soda
	¼ teaspoon salt
	⅓ cup canola or corn oil
¾ cup cake flour	1 large egg
⅓ cup unbleached all-purpose flour	½ cup sour cream
½ cup packed light brown sugar	1 teaspoon vanilla extract
2 tablespoons granulated sugar	¼ teaspoon pure almond extract

BUTTER ALMOND GLAZE	1 cup powdered sugar, sifted
2 tablespoons (¼ stick) soft unsalted butter	2 tablespoons milk
	⅛ teaspoon pure almond extract

Mix the Cake

↬ Position a rack in the middle of the oven. Preheat the oven to 350°F. Lightly oil a 9-inch pie pan or spray the pie pan with a vegetable oil spray.

Put the almond paste, both flours, brown sugar, granulated sugar, baking powder, baking soda, and salt in a large bowl. Break the almond paste into pieces then beat the mixture with an electric mixer on medium speed until crumbs form, about 1 minute. Move the beaters around if using a handheld mixer. Stop the mixer and scrape the mixture from the sides of the bowl and any that becomes caught in the beaters throughout the mixing process. Add the oil and mix until large, oil-coated crumbs form, about 1 minute. Add the egg, beating just to incorporate it. Add the sour cream, vanilla, and almond extract, mixing until the batter is smooth and the sour cream is incorporated. You may see a few specks of almond paste. Use a rubber spatula to scrape the batter into the prepared pan, spreading it evenly.

Bake the Cake

↬ Bake just until a toothpick inserted into the center of the cake comes out clean, about 20 minutes. Prepare the glaze while the cake bakes.

Mix the Glaze and Glaze the Cake

↬ Stir the butter and powdered sugar together in a small bowl to blend them into a crumbly mixture. Stir in the milk and almond extract until a smooth glaze forms.

Remove the cake from the oven and immediately use a fork to poke rows of holes over the top of the cake. Poke the cake about 25 times. Pour the glaze over the top of the cake and use a knife or small spatula to spread it evenly. Some of the glaze will collect at the edge of the pan. Cool the cake thoroughly. The glaze firms as the cake cools.

Serve the Cake

❧ Cut the cake into wedges and serve at room temperature. Leftover cake can be covered with plastic wrap and stored at room temperature for 3 days.

Hummingbird Cake

My husband Jeff thinks that the purpose of cake is to hold cream cheese frosting, but even he admits that this moist banana, pineapple, and toasted pecan cake is good enough to serve without any frosting at all. The cake is a Southern specialty with a name that may suggest the sweet nectar that hummingbirds gather.

Baking Answers ❧ The cake is mixed by creaming the butter and sugar, then beating in the eggs. The flour is added alternately with the buttermilk at the end of the mixing. Thorough beating is important to develop the cake's structure when creaming the butter and sugar and when adding the eggs to the cake batter. Once the eggs are beaten in, adding the remaining ingredients to the batter is only a process of blending them into the batter and does not require long beating.

Toasting the pecans (page 40) enhances their flavor. Toast the pecans both for the cake layers and for topping the frosting together, then measure out what you need for each.

You can mash the bananas with a fork or with a handheld electric mixer. The mashed bananas are not smooth but have some lumpy pieces.

A Step Ahead ❧ The pecans can be toasted, cooled, tightly covered, and stored at room temperature up to 5 days ahead.

SERVES 12 TO 16

Necessities ❧ *Two 9-inch-diameter cake pans with 2-inch-high sides and 2 wire racks for cooling the cake layers*

CAKE LAYERS

2 cups unbleached all-purpose flour

1 teaspoon baking powder

¾ teaspoon baking soda

½ teaspoon salt

1 teaspoon ground cinnamon

5 ounces (1¼ sticks) soft unsalted butter

1½ cups granulated sugar

3 large eggs

2 teaspoons vanilla extract

1½ cups (about 3 medium) ripe mashed bananas

½ cup buttermilk (nonfat is fine)

One 8-ounce can (1 scant cup) crushed pineapple in its own juice, drained

1 cup coarsely chopped toasted pecans (page 40)

CREAM CHEESE FROSTING

6 ounces (1½ sticks) soft unsalted butter

8 ounces cream cheese, softened

2 teaspoons vanilla extract

4 cups powdered sugar

1 cup coarsely chopped toasted pecans (page 40), for sprinkling over the cake

Mix the Cake

↝ Position a rack in the middle of the oven. Preheat the oven to 350°F. Butter the bottom and sides of two 9-inch-diameter cake pans with 2-inch-high sides. Line the bottom of each pan with parchment or wax paper and butter the paper.

Sift the flour, baking powder, baking soda, salt, and cinnamon together onto a piece of wax paper or into a medium bowl and set aside.

Put the butter and granulated sugar in a large bowl and beat with an electric mixer on medium speed until lightened in color and fluffy, about 3 minutes. You will have small crumbs of butter and sugar rather than a smooth mixture. Move the beaters around in the bowl if using a handheld electric mixer. Stop the mixer and scrape the mixture from the sides of the bowl and any that becomes caught in the beaters as needed throughout the mixing process. Add the eggs one at a time, beating well after each addition, then beat for 1 minute. Add the vanilla and mashed bananas, mixing just until no large pieces of banana remain. On low speed add half the flour mixture just until it is incorporated. Mix in the buttermilk to incorporate it. Add the remaining flour, stopping the mixing as soon as the flour is incorporated. Use a large spoon to stir in the pineapple and pecans. Divide the batter equally between the prepared pans.

Bake the Cake

✧ Bake about 35 minutes, until the top feels firm when touched lightly, and a toothpick inserted in the center of the cake comes out clean. Cool the layers for 10 minutes in the pans. Use a small sharp knife to loosen the sides of the cake from the pans. Place a wire rack on the top of each cake and invert the cakes onto each rack. Carefully remove the paper lining the cake bottoms and replace them loosely on each cake. Let the cake layers cool thoroughly with the top side down. Discard the paper liners.

Make the Frosting

✧ Put the butter, cream cheese, and vanilla in a large bowl and beat with an electric mixer on medium speed for about 1 minute until the mixture is smooth and the butter and cream cheese are combined thoroughly. Move the beaters around in the bowl if using a handheld electric mixer. Decrease the speed to low and add the powdered sugar in 2 additions. Continue beating until the powdered sugar is incorporated and the frosting is smooth.

Frost the Cake

✧ Place a serving plate over the bottom of 1 cake layer and invert the cake onto it. The top side will be up. Tuck wax paper strips just an inch or so under the bottom of the cake all the way around to keep the plate clean. Use a thin metal spatula to spread about 1 cup of frosting over the top of the cake layer, spreading it to the edges. Invert the second layer onto a plate and slide it onto the frosted layer. The sides of the 2 layers should line up evenly. Spread a thick layer of frosting over the top of the cake, then spread the remaining frosting over the sides of the cake. Scrape the spatula clean on the edge of the bowl as you frost the cake to prevent cake crumbs from sticking to the frosting. Sprinkle the pecans over the top. Gently pull out the wax paper strips, while sliding a knife under the cake to avoid pulling out smears of frosting, and discard them.

Serve the Cake

✧ Cut the cake into slices and serve at room temperature. Cover leftover cake with plastic wrap and store it in the refrigerator for up to 3 days, but let it sit at room temperature for about 1 hour before serving.

Chocolate-Covered Banana–Chocolate Chip Cake

With their mild flavor, bananas have a natural affinity for pairing with such flavors as butterscotch, caramel, or chocolate. The banana–chocolate combination rises to new heights with this chocolate chip–studded banana cake that is coated with a dark chocolate glaze.

The very easy dark chocolate glaze takes only about 5 minutes to prepare. It's made by combining warm cream with chocolate chips. Since the warm cream melts the chocolate chips, it eliminates melting the chocolate beforehand.

Baking Answers ⊸ The good structure of this cake develops from beating the butter and sugar and then the eggs thoroughly. Adding dry ingredients and the sour cream mixture to the batter is only a process of blending them into the batter and does not require long beating. After the bananas are mashed they will still have some lumps. These dissolve as the cake is mixed.

For directions on lining a tube pan with parchment or wax paper see page 147.

The chocolate chips sink about halfway down into the cake. If you want them more evenly distributed, use miniature chocolate chips.

This cake is turned bottom side up for glazing and serving. This gives a smooth top and sharp edge to the finished cake.

SERVES 12 TO 16

Necessities ⊸ *A 9½- or 10-inch-diameter tube pan with a fixed bottom with at least 3¾-inch-high sides, and 1 wire rack for cooling the cake*

BANANA CAKE
2½ cups cake flour
1 teaspoon baking powder
¾ teaspoon baking soda
½ teaspoon salt
2 teaspoons ground cinnamon
4 medium bananas
1 cup sour cream

1 teaspoon vanilla extract
6 ounces (1½ sticks) soft unsalted butter
2 cups sugar
4 large eggs
2 cups (12 ounces) semisweet chocolate chips

VERY EASY CHOCOLATE GLAZE—
MAKES ABOUT 1⅓ CUPS

½ cup whipping cream
2 ounces (½ stick) unsalted butter,
  cut into 4 pieces

2 tablespoons light corn syrup
1⅓ cups (8 ounces) semisweet
  chocolate chips

Mix the Cake

↝ Position an oven rack in the middle of the oven. Preheat the oven to 325°F. Butter the bottom, sides, and center tube of a 9½- or 10-inch fixed-bottom tube pan with at least 3¾-inch-high sides. Line the bottom with parchment or wax paper and butter the paper.

Sift the flour, baking powder, baking soda, salt, and cinnamon together onto a piece of wax paper or into a medium bowl and set aside.

Put the bananas in a medium bowl, breaking them into quarters as you put them in the bowl. Use a handheld electric mixer on low speed or a fork to mash the bananas. There will be pieces of banana. This is fine. Stir the sour cream and vanilla into the bananas, just to blend them together. Set aside. It is not necessary to wash the beaters before beating the butter and sugar together.

Put the butter and sugar in a large bowl and beat with an electric mixer on medium speed until lightened in color and fluffy, about 2 minutes. Move the beaters around in the bowl if using a handheld electric mixer. Stop the mixer and scrape the mixture from the sides of the bowl and any that becomes caught in the beaters as needed throughout the mixing process. Add the eggs one at a time, beating for 1 minute after each addition. Decrease the speed to low, and in 5 additions (3 flour, 2 banana) add the flour mixture and the banana mixture alternately, beginning and ending with the flour mixture. Stop mixing as soon as the last addition of flour is incorporated. The batter will be smooth and thick. Stir in the chocolate chips to distribute them evenly. Use a rubber spatula to scrape all of the batter into the prepared pan and smooth the top.

Bake the Cake

↝ Bake until the top feels firm when touched lightly and a toothpick inserted in the center of the cake comes out clean, about 1 hour and 10 minutes. If the toothpick penetrates a chocolate chip, test another spot.

Cool the cake in the pan for 15 minutes. Use a small sharp knife to loosen the cake from the sides and the center tube of the pan. Invert the cake onto a wire rack. Carefully remove and discard the paper lining the cake bottom. Leave the cake bottom side up. Cool the cake thoroughly, about 1½ hours, before applying the chocolate glaze. Make the glaze while the cake cools.

Make the Glaze

~ Heat the cream, butter, and corn syrup in a medium saucepan over medium heat until the mixture is hot and the butter melts. Do not let the mixture boil. Remove the pan from the heat and add the chocolate chips. Let the chocolate chips melt in the warm mixture for about 30 seconds. Gently stir the mixture until all of the chocolate is melted and the glaze is smooth. Let the glaze cool at room temperature for about 30 minutes to thicken slightly. The glaze should be pourable but thick enough to cling to the cake when it is spread. If the glaze becomes too thick to spread, warm it briefly over low heat, just until it is spreadable but remains thick enough to cling to the cake.

Glaze the Cake

~ Spread a piece of wax paper under the wire rack to catch any drips. Gently pour about half of the chocolate glaze over the top of the cooled cake. Use a thin metal spatula to spread the glaze inside the hole in the center and over the top of the cake. Spread a layer of glaze over the sides of the cake. Spread any remaining glaze on the top of the cake. Use a large spatula to slide the cake onto a cardboard cake circle or serving plate. Let the glaze firm for about 1 hour before serving the cake.

Serve the Cake

~ Cut the cake into slices and serve at room temperature. Cover leftover cake with plastic wrap and store it in the refrigerator for up to 3 days, but let it sit at room temperature for about 1 hour before serving. The cake can be served with banana ice cream or Ben and Jerry's Chunky Monkey ice cream.

Ebinger's Orange-Glazed Layer Cake
with Orange Butter Filling

Some people have fond childhood memories of their first kiss, some of their first day at school, but mine are of cakes, cookies, and pies; especially those from Ebinger's, the long gone, but not forgotten, Brooklyn bakery. I have remembered this cake from my summer visits to Ebinger's over forty years ago. It is a 2-layer yellow cake filled with a creamy orange butter cream and covered with a thick shiny glaze full of tiny bits of orange peel. It's one of my sweetest memories.

With its pastel golden yellow color, this cake has a springlike look that makes a nice choice for Easter, Mother's Day, or a wedding shower.

Baking Answers ❧ The orange flavor of this cake comes from freshly grated orange zest. Remember to grate the orange zest from the oranges before squeezing the juice that you will need for the filling. Be sure to grate only the orange skin of the orange. The white pith is bitter and has no orange flavor.

The cake is mixed by creaming the butter and sugar, then beating in the eggs. The flour and milk are added at the end in alternate portions. Thorough beating is important to develop the cake's structure when creaming the butter and sugar and when adding the eggs to the cake batter. Adding dry ingredients and milk to the batter is only a process of blending them into the batter and does not require long beating.

Let the glaze chill in the refrigerator until it cools and thickens enough to stay on the sides of the cake when it is spread.

A Step Ahead ❧ The cake layers can be baked, cooled, wrapped in plastic wrap and heavy aluminum foil, and frozen for up to 1 month. Defrost the cake layers, with the wrapping on, at room temperature. Or, they can be baked a day ahead, wrapped with plastic wrap, and stored at room temperature.

SERVES 12

Necessities ❧ *Two 9-inch-diameter cake pans with 2-inch-high sides and 2 wire racks for cooling the cake layers*

ORANGE BUTTER CAKE LAYERS	2 cups granulated sugar
2½ cups cake flour	4 large eggs
1½ teaspoons baking powder	2 teaspoons vanilla extract
½ teaspoon salt	1 teaspoon grated orange zest
½ pound (2 sticks) soft unsalted butter	1 cup whole milk

ORANGE ICING	2 tablespoons granulated sugar
2 cups powdered sugar	3 ounces (¾ stick) unsalted butter
½ cup water	4 teaspoons grated orange zest

ORANGE BUTTER CREAM FILLING	1¼ cups powdered sugar
¼ pound (1 stick) soft unsalted butter	3 tablespoons fresh orange juice
	½ teaspoon grated orange zest
	½ teaspoon vanilla extract

Mix the Cake

❧ Position a rack in the middle of the oven. Preheat the oven to 350°F. Butter the bottoms and sides of two 9-inch-diameter cake pans with 2-inch-high sides. Line the bottom of each pan with parchment or wax paper and butter the paper.

Sift the flour, baking powder, and salt together onto a piece of wax paper or into a medium bowl and set aside.

Put the butter and granulated sugar in a large bowl and beat with an electric mixer on medium speed until lightened in color and fluffy, about 3 minutes. Move the beaters around in the bowl if using a handheld electric mixer. Stop the mixer and scrape the mixture from the sides of the bowl and any that becomes caught in the beaters as needed throughout the mixing process. Put the eggs in a small bowl and stir them vigorously with a fork to blend the yolks and whites. Add the eggs in 3 additions, beating for 1 minute after each addition, stirring the vanilla and orange zest in with the last addition of eggs. Decrease the speed to low, and in 5 additions (3 flour, 2 milk) add the flour mixture and the milk alternately, beginning and ending with the flour mixture. Let each addition of milk or flour incorporate before adding another. The batter may look curdled after the milk additions. Scrape the sides of the bowl again after the last addition of flour. The batter is ready when the final addition of flour is mixed completely into the batter and the batter is smooth. If any flour clings to the sides of the bowl, stir it into the batter. If any orange zest clings to the beaters, scrape it off and stir it into the batter. Pour the batter into the prepared pans, dividing it evenly between the 2 pans. Use a rubber spatula to scrape all of the batter from the bowl. Smooth the top.

Bake the Cake

⤙ Bake for about 37 minutes, until the top feels firm when touched lightly and a toothpick inserted in the center of the cake comes out clean.

Cool the cakes in their pans for 10 minutes. Use a small sharp knife to loosen the cakes from the sides of each pan. Place a wire rack on the top of each cake and invert the cakes onto it. Carefully remove the papers lining the cake bottoms and replace them loosely on each cake. Let the cake layers cool thoroughly with the top side down. Discard the paper liners.

Mix the Icing

⤙ Sift the powdered sugar into a large bowl. Set aside.

Heat the water, granulated sugar, and butter in a small saucepan over low heat until the sugar dissolves and the butter melts, stirring often. Increase the heat to medium-high and boil the mixture for 3 minutes, stirring occasionally. Pour the hot mixture over the powdered sugar and add the orange zest. Use a whisk to mix the glaze smooth. Refrigerate the icing until it is cool to the touch and firm enough to spread, about 1 hour. Make the filling while the icing cools.

Mix the Filling

⤙ Put the butter and powdered sugar in a medium bowl and beat with an electric mixer on medium speed until smooth, about 1 minute. Add the orange juice, orange zest, and vanilla, mixing just to blend them smoothly into the mixture. Place a serving plate over the bottom of 1 cake layer, and using the wire rack to hold the cake in place, invert the cake onto the serving plate. The top side of the cake layer will be up. Tuck waxed paper strips just an inch or so under the bottom of the cake all the way around to keep the plate clean. Spread the filling over the top of the cake layer, spreading it to the edges. Invert the second layer onto a plate and slide it onto the filled layer.

Glaze the Cake

⤙ When the icing is firm enough to spread and adhere to the cake, use a thin metal spatula to spread it over the top and sides of the cake. The icing will still be pourable, and you should begin by pouring about two thirds of the icing over the top and spreading it evenly. Then spread the remaining icing and any drips onto the sides of the cake. Gently pull out the wax paper strips while sliding a knife under the cake to avoid pulling out smears of frosting, and discard them. Refrigerate the cake, uncovered, to firm the icing, then cover the cake with plastic wrap.

Serve the Cake

⤙ Serve the cake cold or let it sit at room temperature for 1 hour before serving. The covered cake can be refrigerated up to 3 days.

Rolled Crusts
for Pies
and Tarts

LIKE MANY OF YOU, I WAS NOT A BORN PIECRUST MAKER. MY MOM LOVED TO BAKE COOKIES AND CAKES BUT AVOIDED MAKING ANY ROLLED PIECRUST, SO IT WAS NOT UNTIL I PRACTICED WITH MANY DETAILED RECIPES THAT I GAINED COMFORT IN THIS AREA. A good friend, Rosie Levitan, had also shied away from recipes calling for a rolled dough, so I asked her to try out my piecrust recipe. Inherently nervous, she studied my directions for several days before she was ready to take the piecrust plunge. Her crust was a success on the very first try, and we both felt that my recipe was a nice, easy method. Rosie also confirmed my belief that after making a recipe several times, you become familiar and relaxed with it and the process proceeds more quickly.

My Fearless Piecrust (page 199) mixes grated frozen shortening with the flour mixture. These tiny pieces of shortening combine almost instantly with the flour. After stirring cold water into the mixture to make the dough and letting the dough rest in the refrigerator, you are ready to roll it. Once you try it and succeed, the whole pie world awaits you.

Tarts bake in pans with ridged, straight sides rather than the slanted sides of pie pans. Most of the pan bottoms are removable. Since the pan sides are removed once tarts cool, their crusts must be strong enough to stand alone. My tart crust is a lightly sweetened butter cookie dough that mixes as easily as cookie dough and holds its shape while baking and after the pan is removed. It is soft and tender rather than flaky like a piecrust. I've put the piecrust and tart crust at the beginning of this chapter for easy reference.

As long as dough is cold, it does not have a tendency to stick to the rolling surface. A light dusting of flour on the rolling surface and the rolling pin also helps to prevent sticking. In a warm summer kitchen, dough might have more of a tendency to stick. If your rolling surface is movable, chilling it in the refrigerator before rolling out the dough is a great idea. Otherwise, use well-chilled dough and work as quickly as you are comfortable doing—no phone calls in the middle of rolling out the dough. Chilling the rolling pin on a hot day also works well. I roll dough on a ceramic cutting board, which has a rather cool surface. Marble boards are nice but heavy and expensive. Clean plastic cutting boards that are free of odors work fine. I do not recommend wooden cutting boards for rolling dough, unless you have one used specifically for rolling dough that is smooth, odor-free, and has no cuts or gashes from knives. A clean kitchen counter makes a fine rolling surface.

Roll out dough with a light but firm pressure. Roll the dough around the sections of its circle, rolling from the center to the edge. If the dough edges crack, press scraps of dough onto them to repair them as you roll. Before lifting the dough from the board, loosen the dough from the rolling surface with a thin metal spatula. Then you can roll the dough loosely around the rolling pin and unroll it carefully into its pan. If the dough is especially sticky, it can be rolled between 2 pieces of wax paper or a pastry cloth to prevent tears. After the dough is rolled out to the desired size, lift the top piece of wax paper off, put the dough, exposed side down, into the pan, and remove the remaining piece of wax paper. A pastry cloth is a large, smooth heavy piece of cloth that is especially used for rolling pastry. It is sold in kitchen shops and hardware stores and is a heavier version of the wax paper method.

If a pie or tart filling cooks separately from or not at all with the crust, the crust must bake unfilled. This baking of an empty crust is called baking it "blind." Piecrust dough has a tendency to shrink if baked empty, so it must be lined with aluminum foil or parchment paper and weighted with pie weights, dried beans, or uncooked rice for about the first 10 minutes. Heavy aluminum foil liners are less likely to tear than regular weight aluminum foil. For Mom's Lemon Meringue Pie (page 270) the crust is baked without its filling because the lemon filling cooks separately, while the Bountiful Apricot, Cranberry, and Walnut Pie (page 210), Pear and Cranberry Cream Crunch-Top Pie (page 208), and New England Maple Pumpkin Pie (page 316) are examples of partially baking crusts so that they remain firm beneath their moist filling. Once the crust bakes enough to be set, the foil and weights are removed to allow the crust to brown. The Butter Cookie Tart Crust (page 203) does not need to be weighted when baked blind. It holds its shape beautifully.

After testing many methods for trying to keep a bottom crust crisp, I've come to the realization that it is the top crust and the browned edges of a crust that should play the crisp role. The bottom crust should be firm enough to hold together and retain its own texture, but it is perfectly natural that it will inevitably soften from its filling. Pies should bake until the top crusts are browned lightly. A golden crust has the rich taste of browned butter and flour.

I prefer shiny metal or ovenproof glass pans for baking pies. Ceramic or ovenproof stoneware pie pans work fine also. If your pie pan does have a dark finish, reduce the baking temperature 25°F. and watch the pies carefully at the end of their baking time. Dark metal pans do not reflect the heat as shiny metal pans do, so crusts can darken or burn quickly. My tart pan has a dark finish, and the oven temperatures and baking times in these recipes are adjusted to that. Shiny metal tart pans work fine also, but if baked in them, crusts may require a few minutes longer of baking time.

As intimidating as piecrusts are to bakers, the opposite is true of pie fillings. Nutty-type fillings need only to be stirred together, while most fruit pies need only to be filled with fruit that has been peeled, cut, and mixed with any flavorings. The actual preparation time for such other additions as the hazelnut filling for the Apple and Hazelnut Macaroon Tart (page 222) or the roasted tomato mixture for the Roasted Tomato, Basil, and Parmesan Pie (page 228) is short. It is only the baking itself that takes time, but you can be doing other things.

In this chapter alone, there are 4 different versions of apple pie for the apple-pie-lover crowd. The varied assortment includes a classic 2-crust apple pie, a free-form double-crust apple pie with a powdered sugar glaze, individual apples wrapped in crust and baked with a cinnamon sauce, and a fancy tart with apples baked on top of a hazelnut filling.

Fearless Piecrust

Since my mother was not comfortable making piecrusts, it followed in my mind that if my great-baker mom couldn't make piecrust, it must be hard. I was over thirty when I attempted my first crust. It was too bad that I waited so long, because a flaky, buttery, homemade piecrust has no equal, and it isn't hard after all, but rather a matter of paying attention to a few guidelines. As long as I kept the shortening cold, mixed the shortening into the flour quickly to produce a flour-coated crumbly mixture, and added as little cold water as possible to form the soft dough, I was rolling out pie dough with ease. Even my mom was impressed.

When I set out to develop this piecrust recipe, I wanted anyone to feel comfortable making it. At the same time I was asked to edit some recipes for the Culinary Institute of America in Hyde Park, New York. Their piecrust recipe had a clever technique that worked so well I adapted it from then on for all of my piecrusts. The butter and vegetable shortening are softened and blended to a smooth mass, then frozen for at least 5 hours. The frozen shortening is coarsely grated and then immediately stirred into the flour. The frozen shortening can even be grated in a food processor. The small grated pieces produce the desired crumbly shortening-and-flour mixture effortlessly. The final step is to stir in enough cold water to form a dough. This is a yes-you-can piecrust that I hope you'll try.

Please don't be put off by the length of these directions. The pie dough actually takes minutes to prepare and roll, but I wanted to pass on what I've learned so you would feel confident making piecrust.

Baking Answers ⋄ This piecrust includes butter for flavor and vegetable shortening for flakiness. A combination of all-purpose and cake flour for the flour lowers the gluten content of the total flour and ensures a more tender crust. It's like a little safety net to make the crust tender. The butter and shortening mixture must be frozen and should be added to the flour as soon as it's grated. Grate the shortening on the large holes of a grater, holding the frozen piece of shortening with a clean dish towel or several layers of aluminum foil so the warmth of your hand doesn't warm it. Even better, grate the shortening in a food processor fitted with the grating blade.

Pie dough often requires slightly less liquid on a warm, humid day and slightly more liquid on a cold, dry day. The same brand of flour may use more liquid at different times of the year. This is why recipes for piecrust often give a flexible measurement that usually varies by 1 to 2 teaspoons for the amount of liquid that is used.

Cold tiny pieces of shortening form little fat pockets in the crust that make a crust with flaky layers. You'll actually be able to see the layers in a piece of baked crust. Use ice water for the liquid to avoid warming the shortening. Once the dough is mixed you can gather it into a ball without worrying. It would take a lot of handling with warm hands to toughen the dough. The dough rests in the refrigerator to relax the gluten in the flour that has become stretched by the mixing process. Once chilled, the cold dough rolls out easily and doesn't stick to the rolling surface. A clean kitchen counter works well for rolling dough.

One of the problems people have mentioned that they have with piecrust is that it becomes hard after it bakes. This happens when the fat is not mixed enough with the flour to form small crumbs, which requires additional liquid to be added to form a dough. As you know from playing with it as a child, flour and water make paste, so a dough that has too much water bakes into a firm pastelike crust. My method of grating the frozen shortening makes it so easy to blend the fat and flour that it virtually eliminates this possible problem.

I use Crisco for the vegetable shortening. Try to buy the easy-to-measure sticks of vegetable shortening rather than the cans of shortening. Do not use butter-flavor Crisco.

In the unlikely event that the piecrust tears or cracks when you transfer it to the pie pan, press scraps of dough onto any holes to seal them.

A Step Ahead ❧ Disks of piecrust dough can be covered and refrigerated overnight and rolled out the next day. The dough will need to soften until it rolls out easily. Or pie pans can be lined with the rolled piecrust, covered, and refrigerated overnight.

Unbaked piecrust can be rolled, pressed into its pan, wrapped tightly, and frozen for up to 1 month. Frozen piecrust in a metal pan does not need to defrost before baking but will take about 5 minutes longer to bake than cold, defrosted piecrust. The unrolled disks of dough can also be wrapped with plastic wrap and foil and frozen for up to 1 month. Defrost the wrapped frozen dough overnight in the refrigerator and let it soften at room temperature just until it is soft enough to roll out easily. I defrost piecrusts that are frozen in ovenproof glass pans in the refrigerator to avoid the possibility of the frozen pie dish breaking when it is put in a hot oven. With a piecrust ready to go in the freezer, many pie fillings such as the Sticky Walnut Pie (page 205) or the Pecan–Chocolate Chip Pie (page 207) can be mixed so quickly that the pies can be ready to bake in about 10 minutes.

MAKES 1 OR 2 PIECRUSTS FOR A 9-INCH PIE PAN

Necessities ❧ *One 9-inch pie pan, a grater for the frozen shortening mixture (which freezes for at least 5 hours), and a rolling pin*

<table>
<tr><td>

For 1 piecrust

</td><td>

For 2 piecrusts or a 2-crusted pie

</td></tr>
<tr><td>

5 tablespoons soft unsalted butter

4 tablespoons (¼ cup) soft vegetable shortening

1 cup unbleached all-purpose flour

⅓ cup cake flour

1 tablespoon sugar

¼ teaspoon salt

3 tablespoons plus 2 to 3 teaspoons ice water

</td><td>

10 tablespoons (1¼ sticks) soft unsalted butter

8 tablespoons (½ cup) soft vegetable shortening

2 cups unbleached all-purpose flour

⅔ cup cake flour

2 tablespoons sugar

½ teaspoon salt

7 to 8 tablespoons ice water

</td></tr>
</table>

Mix the Dough

~ Butter a 9-inch-diameter metal or glass pie pan.

Put the butter and vegetable shortening in a medium bowl and beat with an electric mixer on medium speed until they are blended smoothly together, about 1 minute. Scrape the mixture onto a piece of plastic wrap and form it into a rectangle about 4 x 2½ inches and about 1 inch thick. This shape is easy to hold for grating and can fit or be cut to fit in the feed tube of a food processor. Wrap in the plastic wrap and freeze firm, at least 5 hours or overnight. If making 2 piecrusts, form the shortening into 2 rectangles for easier grating.

Put both flours, sugar, and salt in a large bowl and stir to combine the ingredients. Set aside.

Remove 1 piece of frozen shortening (if there are 2 pieces) from the freezer and unwrap it. Holding the shortening with a clean dish towel to prevent warm hands from melting it and using the large holes of a grater, grate the shortening onto a piece of wax paper. If there is a little piece left at the end, cut it into tiny pieces to add to the flour. Grate the second frozen piece, if making 2 crusts. Or, grate the frozen shortening in a food processor fitted with the grating blade. Immediately add the grated shortening to the flour mixture. Use a fork to stir the shortening into the flour until it is completely blended and looks crumbly, about 40 strokes. Or, use an electric mixer to mix the shortening and flour for about 15 seconds until it forms crumbs. The largest crumbs will be about ¼ inch in size. Sprinkle 3 tablespoons of ice water (or 7 tablespoons of ice water for 2 piecrusts) over the mixture, stirring it with the fork or electric mixer. Add additional water by teaspoonfuls, stirring it in just until there is no loose flour and a dough forms that holds together in clumps. The dough should feel cold.

Gather the dough together and turn it out onto a lightly floured rolling surface. With the heel of your hand push the dough down and forward against the rolling surface 3 or 4 times to form a smooth dough (6 or 7 times for 2 piecrusts). A couple of additional strokes with the heel of your hand in order to form a smooth dough is fine. Gather the dough into a ball, then press it into a disk about 5 inches in diameter (2 disks if making 2 piecrusts). The dough feels soft and malleable, but not sticky. The dough is easier to roll into a circle if it is round and the edges are smooth, but don't handle it a lot just to get smooth edges or a perfect circle. Wrap the dough in plastic wrap and chill it in the refrigerator for at least 30 minutes or as long as overnight.

At this point the dough can be wrapped in plastic wrap and heavy aluminum foil, labeled with the date and contents, and frozen for up to 1 month.

Roll the Dough

↶ Remove the dough from the refrigerator and unwrap it. If the dough has become cold and hard, let it sit at room temperature until it is easy to roll. The time it takes to soften depends on the temperature in your kitchen and how long it has been in the refrigerator. After a 30-minute rest in the refrigerator the dough is usually just right for rolling. Lightly flour the rolling surface and rolling pin. Roll the dough from the center out into a circle about 4 inches wider than the bottom of the pie pan. Move the rolling pin around the circle to roll the dough evenly. Don't flip the dough over while rolling, but gently lift and turn the dough several times as you roll it to prevent it from sticking to the rolling surface. The rolled dough should be about ⅛ inch thick. Unless the day is quite warm, this dough does not have a tendency to stick.

Transfer the Dough to the Pie Pan

↶ Roll up the dough circle loosely over the rolling pin and unroll it carefully into the pie pan. Press the dough into the pie pan to fit the pan, but don't pull or stretch it. Trim the dough edges evenly to overhang ¾ inch over the edge of the pie pan. To form a smooth edge all around, press about ½ inch of the edge of dough under itself. Then, form a crimped edge around the top of the pie pan by pressing the edge of the dough between your thumb and forefinger. Crimp about ⅝ inch of dough at a time and move your fingers around the rim of the pan to crimp dough all the way around. Or, use a fork to press the edge of the crust onto the rim of the pan. The crust is ready to be filled. There may be some scraps that can be sprinkled with sugar, baked in a separate pan, and used for snacks.

See the Well-Filled Two-Crust Apple Pie recipe (page 214) for crust directions for making a 2-crust pie, but leave the bottom crust edges flat and not crimped. A 2-crust pie is filled before the top crust is added, and then the top and bottom crust are crimped together.

Variation Using Milk ↶ *Prepare the piecrust substituting cold whole-fat milk for the water. This is used in the Farmhouse Apple Pie (page 212).*

Butter Cookie Tart Crust

I f you can mix a cookie dough together, you can make this crust for sophisticated-looking tarts. The baked crust is exceedingly tender and is good enough to eat as a vanilla butter cookie, which is a good reason to bake any scraps. Tart crusts are often baked "blind," without any filling, then filled with fresh fruit or custard; they usually need to be pricked and then weighted with pie weights or beans to keep them in place during baking. But not this friendly crust, which has the nice cookie-like quality of keeping its shape during baking. It can be pressed into its pan and baked with confidence without further ado.

Baking Answers ⭗ Tarts bake in a special tart pan with a removable bottom. The sides of the pan are usually 1 inch high and are fluted. The edge of the pan produces perfectly ridged sides on the baked crust. Spraying the inside of the pan with unflavored cooking spray is a good way to grease the ridged sides evenly.

I used a 9-inch-diameter black steel tart pan with a removable bottom for these tarts. Since tarts usually have a thinner layer of filling and bake for a shorter time than pies, black steel pans retain the heat efficiently and help the crust brown even more quickly than aluminum. Dry these pans thoroughly after washing to prevent rust from forming.

Since the sides of a tart pan are removed after baking, the sides of the baked crust should be strong enough to carry the weight of the filling. Folding the overhanging edges of dough into the pan and pressing them into the sides of the tart pan produces thickened pastry sides that are strong enough to hold the filling once the support of the pan is removed. After tarts bake and cool, the crust becomes firm and crisp.

The soft dough for this crust is easy to move around if rolled between 2 pieces of wax paper. If the crust should break when moving it to the tart pan, just press any breaks together once the dough is in the pan. The soft dough repairs easily.

If the dough is refrigerated for 30 minutes, it should be just right for rolling.

The tart pan is easy to move in and out of the oven if it is placed on a baking sheet.

A Step Ahead ⭗ Disks of tart crust dough can be refrigerated overnight and rolled out the next day. The dough will need to soften until it rolls out easily. The temperature of the kitchen determines how long this takes. On a cold day, it could take up to 1 hour.

Unbaked tart crust dough can be rolled, pressed into its pan, wrapped tightly, and frozen for up to 2 weeks. It does not need to defrost before baking, but it will take about 5 minutes longer to bake than a cold, defrosted tart crust.

Necessities ⤙ *One 9-inch metal tart pan with a removable bottom, a rolling pin, and a baking sheet for holding the pan during baking*

1 cup unbleached all-purpose flour
½ cup cake flour
¼ teaspoon salt
5 ounces (1¼ sticks) soft unsalted
   butter

¼ cup sugar
1 large egg yolk
½ teaspoon vanilla extract

Mix the Dough

⤙ Butter or spray with unflavored cooking spray the bottom and sides of a 9-inch metal tart pan with a removable bottom. Butter or spray the ridged sides of the pan carefully. The cooking spray is a good way to coat the ridged sides completely.

Sift both the flours and the salt onto a piece of wax paper or into a medium bowl and set aside.

Put the butter and sugar in a large bowl and beat with an electric mixer on medium speed until the mixture looks smooth and creamy, and the color lightens, about 1 minute. Move the beaters around in the bowl if using a handheld electric mixer. Stop the mixer and scrape dough from the sides of the bowl and any dough that becomes caught in the beaters as needed. Mix in the egg yolk and vanilla until they are blended into the mixture. Decrease the speed to low and add the flour mixture, mixing just until it is incorporated and a smooth mixture forms. At first the dough forms small crumbs, then it forms large clumps that hold together and pull away from the side of the bowl. Gather the dough into a ball, then press it into a disk about 6 inches in diameter. Wrap the dough in plastic wrap and chill it in the refrigerator for at least 30 minutes or as long as overnight.

Roll the Dough

⤙ Remove the dough from the refrigerator and unwrap it. If the dough has become cold and hard, let it sit at room temperature until it is easy to roll. After a 30-minute rest in the refrigerator the dough is usually just right for rolling, but if left in the refrigerator for a longer time, the dough will need time to soften at room temperature. Put the dough between 2 large pieces of wax paper. Roll the dough from the center out into a circle 3 inches wider than the bottom of the tart pan; for a 9-inch tart pan you should have a 12-inch circle. The rolled dough should be about a scant ¼ inch thick. Carefully peel off the top piece of wax paper and discard. Turn dough with the wax paper side up and center the crust over the prepared pan. Peel off the remaining piece of wax paper and discard. Gently press the dough into the pan, trimming the edges to leave a ½-inch overhang. Fold the overhang into the pan and press it against the edge of the pan to form slightly thickened sides. The edge of the tart pan may cut off the overhang. If this happens, press the strip of dough onto the inside of the sides of the crust to form the slightly thickened sides. Repair any cracks or tears by pressing a small scrap of the dough onto the crack. Whether or not the recipe you're following calls for filling a baked or unbaked crust, the dough should be covered and refrigerated for 30 minutes before proceeding.

Bake the Crust

↶ If the crust is going to be baked before filling it as in the Shimmering Fresh Berry Tart (page 224), position an oven rack in the middle of the oven and preheat the oven to 375°F. Place the tart pan on a baking sheet. Use a fork to prick the bottom of the crust gently in about 8 places. Bake the crust until the edges brown and the center is firm and lightly colored, about 17 minutes. Fill the baked crust as recipes direct.

Sticky Walnut Pie

This pie from my friend Rosalee Glass stands out far and wide as a great walnut pie. The top of the pie is completely coated with crisp walnuts that have become sugar-glazed from the sticky, golden filling underneath. But best of all, the filling can be mixed in less than 5 minutes, and the walnut topping forms all by itself when the nuts float to the top as the pie bakes.

Baking Answers ↶ To prevent any filling from seeping under the crust while the pie bakes, check to see that there are no holes in the piecrust. Patch any holes by pressing a scrap of pie dough firmly onto the hole to cover it. If filling seeps under a hole in the crust, it pushes the crust up into the middle of the pie. It makes a strange-looking pie, but still tastes fine.

Sweetening this pie filling with light corn syrup and granulated sugar makes a filling that is not overly sweet and has a firm but light, syrupy texture.

Baking the pie for the first 10 minutes at a higher temperature gives the crust a good start for baking to a golden brown.

A Step Ahead ⤶ Roll the piecrust, put it in its pan, cover, and refrigerate overnight.

Necessities ⤶ *1 unbaked cold Fearless Piecrust (page 199) in a 9-inch shiny metal or glass pie pan*

3 large eggs	1½ cups coarsely chopped walnuts
½ cup sugar	One 1-crust recipe unbaked cold
1 cup light corn syrup, such as Karo	Fearless Piecrust (page 199), in a
syrup	9-inch pie pan
1 teaspoon vanilla extract	
¼ pound (1 stick) unsalted butter,	
melted	

Mix the Filling

⤶ Position a rack in the bottom third of the oven. Preheat the oven to 400°F.

Put the eggs in a large bowl and use a whisk to beat them until foamy, 30 seconds. Add the sugar, corn syrup, and vanilla and whisk until blended to a smooth mixture, 30 seconds. Add the melted butter, whisking to incorporate it. Use a large spoon to stir in the walnuts. Pour the mixture into the cold, unbaked piecrust.

Bake and Serve the Pie

⤶ Bake 10 minutes. Reduce the oven temperature to 350°F. and continue baking until the filling is set, about 40 more minutes. The walnuts will have risen to the top and the top will look golden. Check to see that the pie is set by giving it a gentle shake; the center should remain firm. The pie puffs during baking, then deflates slightly, but does not sink, as it cools. Cool thoroughly at room temperature.

Serve at room temperature. The covered pie can be stored refrigerated up to 3 days.

Pecan–Chocolate Chip Pie

I don't know where the idea first came from for adding chocolate to a pecan pie. It might have been the Tar Heel pie from North Carolina or maybe the Derby pie from Kentucky. Wherever it came from, the idea inspired me to create this chewy pecan and chocolate chip pie that any state would be glad to claim.

Baking Answers

To prevent any filling from seeping under the crust while the pie bakes, check to see that there are no holes in the piecrust. Patch any holes by pressing a scrap of pie dough firmly onto the hole to cover it.

Baking the pie for the first 10 minutes at a higher temperature gives the crust a good start for baking to a golden brown.

A Step Ahead

Roll the piecrust, put it in its pan, cover, and refrigerate overnight.

SERVES 8

Necessities

1 unbaked cold Fearless Piecrust (page 199) in a 9-inch shiny metal or glass pie pan

2 large eggs
½ cup granulated sugar
½ cup packed light brown sugar
1 teaspoon vanilla extract
¼ cup unbleached all-purpose flour
1¼ cups coarsely chopped pecans
1 cup (6 ounces) semisweet chocolate chips

One 1-crust recipe unbaked cold Fearless Piecrust (page 199), in a 9-inch shiny metal or glass pie pan
Vanilla ice cream for serving with the pie, optional

Mix the Filling

Position a rack in the bottom third of the oven. Preheat the oven to 400°F.

Put the eggs in a large bowl and use a whisk to beat the eggs until foamy, 30 seconds. Add the granulated sugar, brown sugar, and vanilla and whisk until blended to a smooth mixture, 30 seconds. Add the flour, whisking to incorporate it. Use a large spoon to stir in the pecans and chocolate chips. Pour the mixture into the cold, unbaked piecrust.

↝ Bake 10 minutes. Reduce the oven temperature to 350°F. and continue baking until the top is firm and the filling is set, about 25 more minutes. The top will be smooth and crisp. The pie can be served warm or at room temperature. Warm pie has soft chocolate chips, but crunchy pecans. Once the pie cools, the pecans and chocolate chips form a firm, chewy filling. Serve with vanilla ice cream, if desired. The covered pie can be stored refrigerated up to 3 days.

Pear and Cranberry Cream Crunch-Top Pie

This pie is a study in contrasts. Tart cranberries make a perfect foil for ripe, sweet pears, while the sweetened sour cream filling is a creamy complement to the soft fruit. Then it is all topped off with an especially crisp pecan crumb topping.

Baking Answers ↝ Use pears that are ripe but still firm so they hold their shape when baked. To check to see if a pear is ripe, press the narrow top of the pear at the stem end. If the pear gives slightly at this point, it is ripe. Cut the pears into small uniform pieces, so they become soft in the time that it takes the crumb topping to bake.

The crust for this pie is partially baked without the filling to help firm the crust before baking it with the moist filling. Line the unbaked crust with aluminum foil and weight it with metal pie weights or dried beans to keep it from shrinking. Once the crust bakes for about 10 minutes, it is set enough so that the foil and weights can be removed. Cool the pie weights or beans before storing them for another use.

Using melted butter for the crumb mixture produces an especially crisp topping, which is made even crunchier by adding pecans to it.

A Step Ahead ↝ Roll the piecrust, put it in its pan, cover, and refrigerate overnight.

SERVES 8

Necessities ↝ *1 unbaked cold Fearless Piecrust (page 199) in a 9-inch shiny metal or glass pie pan, metal pie weights or 2½ cups dried beans, and a rolling pin*

One 1-crust recipe unbaked cold
Fearless Piecrust (page 199), in a
9-inch shiny metal or glass pie pan

PECAN CRUMB TOPPING	1 teaspoon ground cinnamon
⅓ cup granulated sugar	5 tablespoons unsalted butter,
⅓ cup packed light brown sugar	melted
1¼ cups unbleached all-purpose	¾ cup coarsely chopped pecans
flour	

PEAR, CRANBERRY, AND SOUR	2 teaspoons vanilla extract
CREAM FILLING	½ teaspoon salt
1½ cups sour cream	5 ripe pears, peeled, cored, and cut
1 cup granulated sugar	into ½- to ¾-inch pieces
⅓ cup unbleached all-purpose flour	1 cup unsweetened cranberries, fresh or
1 large egg	frozen and defrosted

Partially Bake the Crust

↪ Position a rack in the bottom third of the oven. Preheat the oven to 375°F. Line the prepared crust with heavy aluminum foil or a double layer of standard foil, pressing the aluminum foil gently over the edges of the pie pan. Fill the aluminum foil with metal pie weights or dried beans, about 2½ cups of beans. Check to see that the weights evenly cover the entire bottom of the crust. The weights should make a thick layer over the bottom, but they do not have to come to the top of the pan. Bake the crust for 10 minutes. Protect your hands with potholders and carefully remove the aluminum foil by lifting it and the pie weights from the crust. Set the weights aside to cool and store for another use. Bake the uncovered crust for 5 more minutes to firm it slightly. Remove the crust from the oven and set aside. Leave the oven on for baking the filled pie.

Mix the Topping

↪ Stir the granulated sugar, brown sugar, flour, and cinnamon together in a medium bowl. Pour the melted butter over the mixture, stirring until the mixture is evenly moistened and fine crumbs form. Stir in the pecans to distribute them. Set aside.

continued

Mix the Filling

~ Put the sour cream, granulated sugar, flour, egg, vanilla, and salt in a large bowl and use a whisk to mix them smooth. Stir in the pears and cranberries. Pour the filling into the partially baked piecrust. Sprinkle the reserved crumb mixture evenly over the filling.

Bake and Serve the Pie

~ Bake for 10 minutes, then reduce the oven temperature to 350°F. Continue to bake until the crumb topping is golden brown and the pears and cranberries are soft when tested with a toothpick, about 35 minutes. Let the pie cool and firm for at least 1 hour before serving. Cut the pie into slices and serve. I prefer to serve this pie the same day it is baked. If it is kept overnight, cover and refrigerate it.

Variations ~ *Peeled and cored apples that are sliced ¼ inch thick can be substituted for the pears. The cranberries can be omitted. The crumb topping can be made with walnuts or the nuts can be omitted.*

Bountiful Apricot, Cranberry, and Walnut Pie

After spending much of my life in Florida with the air conditioning usually going full blast on Thanksgiving Day, I really appreciate the brisk fall temperatures and autumn leaves that have been a reliable part of our Maine Thanksgivings for the past twenty years. November may not be a month known for its abundance of fruit, but this pie is a Thanksgiving dessert that takes advantage of always-in-season dried cranberries and apricots and the fall crop of new walnuts. The pie is filled to the brim with this colorful mixture, which imitates the final blaze of color from those fallen leaves.

Baking Answers ~ Look for the new crop of walnuts that usually appears in supermarkets sometime in October. You'll begin to see well-stocked shelves and displays of nuts when the fresh crop arrives.

The crust for this pie is partially baked without the filling to help firm the crust before baking it with the moist filling. Line the unbaked crust with aluminum foil and weight it with metal pie weights or dried beans to keep it from shrinking. Once the crust bakes for about 10 minutes, it is set enough so that the foil and weights can be removed. Cool the pie weights or beans before storing them for another use.

A Step Ahead ❧ Roll the piecrust, put it in its pan, cover, and refrigerate overnight.

Necessities ❧ *1 unbaked cold Fearless Piecrust (page 199) in a 9-inch shiny metal or glass pie pan, metal pie weights or 2½ cups dried beans, and a rolling pin*

1 unbaked cold recipe Fearless
  Piecrust (page 199), and in a 9-
  inch shiny metal or glass pie pan
2 large eggs
1 cup packed light brown sugar
1 teaspoon vanilla extract
¼ teaspoon salt
¾ teaspoon ground cinnamon

¼ cup whipping cream
3 tablespoons unsalted butter, melted
1½ cups coarsely chopped walnuts
1½ cups dried apricots (about 7
  ounces), cut into ½-inch pieces
1 cup dried cranberries (about 2½
  ounces)

Partially Bake the Crust

❧ Position a rack in the bottom third of the oven. Preheat the oven to 375°F. Line the prepared crust with heavy aluminum foil or a double layer of standard foil, pressing the aluminum foil gently over the edges of the pie pan. Fill the aluminum foil with metal pie weights or about 2½ cups of dried beans. Check to see that the weights evenly cover the entire bottom of the crust. The weights should make a thick layer over the bottom, but they do not have to come to the top of the pan. Bake the crust for 10 minutes. Protect your hands with potholders and carefully remove the aluminum foil by lifting it and the pie weights from the crust. Set the weights aside to cool and store for another use. Bake the uncovered crust for 5 more minutes to firm it slightly. Remove the crust from the oven and set aside. Reduce the oven temperature to 350° F.

Mix the Filling

❧ Put the eggs, brown sugar, and vanilla in a large bowl and use a whisk to mix them smooth. Add the salt, cinnamon, cream, and melted butter, whisking to incorporate them. Use a large spoon to stir in the walnuts, apricots, and cranberries. Pour the filling into the partially baked crust.

Bake and Serve the Pie

↬ Bake until the pie is set, about 30 minutes. Check to see that the pie is set by giving it a gentle shake; the center should remain firm. The fruit and nuts will have risen to the top of the pie. Cool thoroughly at room temperature.

Serve at room temperature. The covered pie can be stored refrigerated up to 3 days.

Farmhouse Apple Pie

This free-form apple pie bakes on a baking sheet rather than in a pie pan. It's a large round mound of a rustic-looking 2-crust pie with an especially tender and crisp crust. The Fearless Piecrust (page 199) is prepared with milk rather than water, giving the crust a slightly softer quality than a crust made with water.

Baking Answers ↬ Baking apples for a short time before they bake with the crust releases some of their water and gives the apple filling just the right amount of moistness. It also assures that the apples soften by the time the pie bakes. Cool the apples thoroughly before putting the pie together. Warm apples soften the dough and make the pie difficult to assemble.

Use the freshest apples available. Fall brings a succession of recently harvested apple varieties that work well. If an apple is firm and crisp, it is usually a good choice for pies. I find Granny Smith apples to be the most reliable variety on a year-round basis. See the Any-Season Fruit Crumble (page 63) for advice on peeling, coring, and cutting apples.

The crust is glazed twice: first with an egg wash to brown it during baking, then with a powdered-sugar-and-water mixture that forms a shiny, clear finish over the warm crust.

A Step Ahead ↬ Prepare the 2 disks of piecrust dough 1 day ahead, cover with plastic wrap, and refrigerate.

SERVES 8 TO 10

Necessities ↬ *1 baking sheet with 1-inch-high sides for prebaking the apples, 1 heavyweight baking sheet or pizza pan, preferably with flat edges, for baking the pie, 1 wire rack for cooling the pie, a pastry brush, a rolling pin, and one 2-crust recipe of Fearless Piecrust prepared with milk (see variation, page 202)*

APPLE FILLING	3 tablespoons granulated sugar
5 large apples, peeled, cored, sliced ¼ inch thick, and cut into 1-inch pieces	2 tablespoons unsalted butter, melted
	2 teaspoons fresh lemon juice

One 2-crust recipe Fearless Piecrust prepared with milk (see variation, page 202), formed into 2 disks, with 1 disk slightly larger than the other, chilled, and ready to roll	1 egg beaten with a fork with 2 tablespoons whipping cream for the egg wash
	½ cup powdered sugar stirred in a small bowl with 1 tablespoon water to a smooth thin syrup for the sweet glaze

Mix the Filling

ꞏ❧ Position a rack in the bottom third of the oven. Preheat the oven to 350°F. Butter a pizza pan or baking sheet that preferably has flat rather than raised edges. The pie bakes on this pan.

Spread the apple pieces on a baking sheet with 1-inch-high sides. Sprinkle the sugar, melted butter, and lemon juice over the apples, tossing the mixture to coat the apples. Bake, uncovered, for 15 minutes, stirring once. Remove the apple mixture from the oven. Drain off any liquid, and set the apples aside until they are cool to the touch.

Raise the oven temperature to 375°F.

Roll the Crust and Fill the Pie

ꞏ❧ On a lightly floured surface, roll the smaller disk of dough into an 11-inch circle. Slide a thin metal spatula under the dough to loosen it from the rolling surface. Roll up the dough circle loosely over the rolling pin and unroll it onto the pizza pan or baking sheet. Trim the dough to an even circle, about 10 inches. Leaving a 1-inch edge bare, spoon the cooled apple mixture over the crust, mounding it slightly toward the center. Roll the remaining piece of dough into a 12-inch circle. Trim it to even it up into an 11-inch circle. Slide a thin metal spatula under the dough to loosen it from the rolling surface. Roll up the dough circle loosely over the rolling pin and unroll it onto the apple filling. Use a fork to press the edges of the dough together to seal them tightly. Avoiding the edges that were pressed with the fork, use a pastry brush to brush the top of the pie with the egg mixture. You will not use all of the egg wash. Cut four 2-inch slits in the top crust to release the steam. If desired, for decoration you can cut 4 to 6 small leaf shapes from the dough scraps and press them gently onto the top center of the pie. Brush the leaves with the egg wash.

continued

↶ Bake about 40 minutes until the crust is golden brown. The top may look bumpy as the crust settles in around the apples. This is fine. Wash the pastry brush thoroughly before using it to brush the powdered sugar glaze over the baked pie. Remove the pie from the oven and immediately use the clean pastry brush to brush the top with the powdered-sugar syrup mixture. Cool about 20 minutes to firm the pie. Slide the pie onto a wire rack to cool for at least 30 minutes before serving. The pie can be covered and stored at room temperature up to 2 days.

A Well-Filled Two-Crust Apple Pie

If "A" is for apple and "A" is for American, then it must certainly follow that our all-American apple pie has an A+ rating. And well it should. After all, what would family reunions, county fair contests, and Thanksgiving dessert be without a double-crusted apple pie with its top crust forming crisp, browned waves over the thick layer of sweet sliced apples nestling in the soft bottom crust? No pie in the sky is our beloved American dessert.

Prebaking the apples is the secret to the exceptional amount of apples that this apple pie can hold. When apple slices bake for a short time before they are put in their crust, they give off moisture and shrink ahead of time. The softened apple slices also allow you to put more apples in the pie, since they can be layered more closely together than raw apples can. The result is one of the most intensely flavored apple pies that you'll ever savor.

Two-crust pies can be filled with almost any fruit. The method of putting the pie together remains the same, but the filling requirements and baking times change. I have given some suggestions for a year of pies in the chart on the opposite page.

Baking Answers ↶ Use the freshest apples available. If an apple is firm and crisp, it is usually a good choice for pies. I find Granny Smith apples to be the most reliable variety on a year-round basis. See the Any-Season Fruit Crumble (page 63) for advice on peeling, coring, and slicing apples.

After baking the apple slices by themselves, cool them thoroughly before assembling the pie. Hot apple slices soften the crust. Baking the apple slices for 15 minutes produces a pie filling with tender but firm apple slices that hold their shape. If you want a softer result for the apple filling, bake the apple slices for 20 minutes.

Apples vary in their sweetness. Add sugar to the point that it brings out the flavor of the apples without overpowering them with sweetness. Mix some of the brown sugar with the apples, then taste a piece of apple. Add enough sugar so that the apples taste pleasingly sweet to you but strongly of apple rather than sugar.

Flour, cornstarch, and quick-cooking tapioca are starches used to thicken the juices in pie fillings. As a general guideline, I prefer to use flour to thicken the fillings for fruits that produce lesser amounts of liquid during baking and quick-cooking tapioca for fruits (or rhubarb) that produce larger quantities of liquid as they cook. The quick-cooking tapioca gives a lighter, less-thick result than the quantity of flour that would be required to thicken a very moist filling. Fruit pie fillings should be thickened just to the point that slices of pie hold a soft rather than rigid shape. Some fruit spilling slightly from a slice of pie is appealing and natural-looking.

The crust is brushed before baking with an egg-wash mixture of egg and cream, then sprinkled with cinnamon sugar. The egg wash browns the crust while the sugar mixture adds additional crunch to the top of the pie.

AMOUNT OF FRUIT	SUGAR AND FLAVORINGS	BAKING TIME AT 375°F.
9 cups peeled, cored, sliced, and prebaked apples or pears, or 1 cup cranberries with 8 cups cored, sliced, and prebaked apples or pears	3 tablespoons granulated or light brown sugar, 1 tablespoon fresh lemon juice, ½ teaspoon ground cinnamon	about 30 minutes, until the fruit is tender
6 cups fresh blueberries, 7 cups if using small wild blueberries	⅓ cup packed light brown sugar, 1 teaspoon ground cinnamon, ¼ cup flour	about 25 minutes, just until the crust browns
6 cups peeled (see page 38), pitted, and sliced peaches	2 to 3 tablespoons granulated sugar, 1 tablespoon lemon juice, ¼ cup flour	about 25 minutes, just until the crust browns
5 cups peeled (see page 38), pitted, and sliced peaches and 1 cup fresh raspberries	3 to 4 tablespoons granulated sugar, ¼ cup flour	about 25 minutes, just until the crust browns
6 cups rhubarb cut in ½-inch pieces plus 2 cups sliced strawberries, if desired	about ¾ cup granulated sugar, ¼ cup quick-cooking tapioca, 1 teaspoon ground cinnamon	about 30 minutes, until the rhubarb is tender and the crust browns

The chart on page 215 gives guidelines to bake you through a year of 2-crust fruit pies. Begin by baking the pies at 400°F. for 10 minutes to give the crust a good start to its browning. Some moist fruits have unbleached all-purpose flour or quick-cooking tapioca mixed with the fruit to thicken the juices.

A Step Ahead ⤳ Prepare the 2 disks of piecrust dough 1 day ahead, cover with plastic wrap, and refrigerate.

SERVES 8 TO 10

Necessities ⤳ *One 2-crust recipe of Fearless Piecrust (page 199), formed into 2 disks, chilled, and ready to roll, one baking sheet with 1-inch-high sides for prebaking the apples, one 9-inch-diameter shiny metal or glass pie pan, a rolling pin, and a pastry brush*

9 large apples, peeled, cored, halved, and sliced ¼ inch thick

2 teaspoons fresh lemon juice

2 tablespoons granulated sugar

2 tablespoons unsalted butter, melted

One 2-crust recipe Fearless Piecrust (page 199), formed into 2 disks, chilled, and ready to roll

3 to 4 tablespoons (to taste) packed light brown sugar

1½ teaspoons ground cinnamon

⅛ teaspoon fresh ground nutmeg, optional

1 egg beaten with a fork with 2 tablespoons whipping cream for the egg wash

1 tablespoon granulated sugar mixed with ¼ teaspoon ground cinnamon for sprinkling on top of the piecrust

Mix the Filling

⤳ Position a rack in the bottom third of the oven. Preheat the oven to 350°F. Butter the pie pan.

Spread the apple slices on a baking sheet with 1-inch-high sides. Sprinkle the lemon juice, granulated sugar, and melted butter over the apples, stirring the mixture to coat the apples. Bake, uncovered, for 15 minutes, stirring once during the baking. Remove the apple mixture from the oven. Drain off any liquid and set aside until the apples are cool to the touch.

Increase the oven temperature to 400°F.

Roll the Crust and Fill the Pie

⤳ On a lightly floured surface, roll 1 disk of dough into a circle that is 4 inches wider than the bottom of the pie pan. Move the rolling pin around the circle to roll the dough evenly. Don't flip the dough over while rolling, but gently lift and turn the dough several times as you roll it to prevent it from sticking to the rolling surface. The rolled dough should be about ⅛ inch thick. Slide a thin metal spatula under the dough to loosen it from the rolling surface. Roll up the dough circle loosely over the rolling pin and unroll it onto the pie pan. Press the dough into the pie pan, but don't pull or stretch it. Trim the edges evenly to overhang ½ inch over the edge of the pie pan.

Stir 3 tablespoons of the brown sugar, cinnamon, and nutmeg, if desired, into the cooled apples. Taste a piece of apple and add more brown sugar if needed. Spoon the apple mixture into the crust, mounding it slightly higher toward the center. The apples in the center of the pie will be about 1 inch above the rim of the pan. Roll the remaining piece of dough into a 12-inch circle. Slide a thin metal spatula under the dough to loosen it from the rolling surface. Roll up the dough circle loosely over the rolling pin and unroll it onto the apple filling. Trim the edge of the top crust to meet the edge of the bottom crust. Press the edges together to seal them. Form a crimped edge around the top of the pie pan by pressing them between your thumb and forefinger to crimp them. Or, use a fork to press both edges of the trimmed crust onto the rim of the pan. Leaving the crimped edges plain, use a pastry brush to brush the top of the pie with the egg and cream mixture. You will not use all of the egg wash. Sprinkle the cinnamon sugar mixture evenly over the top of the pie. Cut four 2-inch slits in the top crust to release the steam.

Bake and Serve the Pie

↦ Bake 10 minutes. Reduce the oven temperature to 375°F. and continue baking until the top crust is lightly browned, about 30 minutes. Cool about 20 minutes and serve warm, or cool completely and serve at room temperature. The covered pie can be stored at room temperature up to 2 days. The cooled pie can be warmed, uncovered, in a preheated 275°F. oven for about 15 minutes. Scoops of vanilla ice cream make a good accompaniment.

A Pair of Apple Dumplings Baked in Cinnamon Sauce

Need something warm to soothe you on a cold winter evening? Forget the soup. Sit down in front of a crackling fire with one of these warm apple dumplings, and you'll forget all about the cold temperatures outside. Whole peeled apples are wrapped in piecrust and basted during the baking with a cinnamon sauce that forms a brittle, candylike coating wherever it coats the crust. It's the perfect ending to a cozy dinner for two.

Baking Answers ⤏ Apples are peeled and cored but left whole for apple dumplings. An apple corer is the best tool for coring a whole apple, but a small paring knife will do the job. Use the knife to cut a cone out of the center of the apple, cutting out the stem and cutting the cone as deeply as you can. Turn the apple over and cut a cone from the bottom. Stand the apple stem end up and work the knife around the hole in the center to make a hole through the center of the apple that removes the core and any seeds.

    Cool the cinnamon sauce slightly before pouring it over the apples. Hot cinnamon sauce can melt the butter in the dough and soften the dough before it bakes and sets.

A Step Ahead ⤏ Mix the piecrust dough 1 day ahead, cover with plastic wrap, and refrigerate. The dumplings can be assembled and put in their pan, but without the sauce, 4 to 5 hours ahead of time. Cover with plastic wrap and refrigerate until ready to pour over the sauce and bake them.

    You can bake the dumplings a day ahead, then warm them before serving them.

SERVES 2

Necessities ⤏ *One 9-inch-diameter shiny metal or glass pie pan or 2 individual oval or round shallow-sided ovenproof dishes about 6 inches across (such as au gratin dishes), a rolling pin, and one 1-crust recipe cold Fearless Piecrust dough (page 199)*

CINNAMON SAUCE
½ cup water
¼ cup sugar

½ teaspoon ground cinnamon
1 tablespoon unsalted butter

1 recipe cold Fearless Piecrust dough
   (page 199)

APPLE FILLING

2 medium apples, peeled, cored, and
   left whole

2 teaspoons unsalted butter

2 teaspoons sugar

⅛ teaspoon ground cinnamon

Cook the Sauce

↝ Position a rack in the middle of the oven. Preheat the oven to 400°F. Butter a 9-inch pie pan or 2 individual baking dishes with shallow sides about 1 inch high and about 6 inches across at the widest point.

Put the water, sugar, cinnamon, and butter in a small saucepan and cook over medium heat, stirring often, until the sugar dissolves and the butter melts. Set the sauce aside to cool while you prepare the dumplings.

Make the Dumplings

↝ Lightly flour the rolling surface and rolling pin. Roll the piecrust dough into a long rectangle 17 x 8½ inches. Trim the edges and cut two 8-inch squares. Use a thin metal spatula to loosen the dough from the rolling surface and transfer each square to the baking pan. Cut a thin slice off the bottom of each apple so the bottom is flat. Put 1 apple in the center of each square of dough. Then, press 1 teaspoon of butter into the center of one of the apples and sprinkle with half of the sugar and cinnamon. Bring up the corners of the square to the top center of the apple and seal. Pinch the seams to seal them well, but don't press them flat against the apple. Leave them poking out so they look like 4 segments of thin wings coming out from the apple. If thick seams form, trim them slightly with a small knife. Check for any breaks in the dough and press dough scraps onto any breaks to repair them. Repeat with the second piece of dough and apple, placing the dumplings at least 1 inch apart. Use a fork to prick the pastry twice on the top of each dumpling. You can cut out 4 oval leaf shapes from scraps of dough and press 2 each onto the top of each dumpling for decoration. Pour all of the cinnamon sauce over the apples. It will be thin and run off the dumplings.

Bake the Dumplings

↝ Bake 35 minutes, until the crust is light brown. The edges of the seams turn slightly darker. Use a large spoon to baste the dumplings with the sauce after the first 15 minutes of baking and again after an additional 10 minutes of baking. The dumplings will have baked for 25 minutes before the second basting and the sauce will be thick and syrupy and cling to the crust. Spoon as much sauce as possible over the dumplings during this second basting. The baked dumplings are glazed over much of the crust with a crisp, shiny layer of cinnamon sauce.

Serve the Dumplings

❧ If the dumplings are baked in a pie pan, immediately use a wide flat spatula to carefully transfer each dumpling to a shallow bowl or dish. Transfer them before the glaze sets so they don't stick to the pan. If baked in individual dishes, serve the dumplings in their baking dishes. Cool slightly for about 10 minutes. Serve warm with fresh cream to pour over, if desired. If the crust should split slightly while the dumplings bake (which seldom happens), press the crust edges together gently. The sticky glaze holds the crust together. However, a small split in the crust gives the dumpling an appealing, homey look. The dumplings can be baked a day ahead and left in their baking pan to be cooled, covered, and stored at room temperature. Uncover the dumplings and warm them in a preheated 275°F. oven for 20 minutes. Warming the dumplings releases the bottoms from the baking pan again.

Especially Crumbly Rhubarb Tart

Maine is at the end of the line for any signs of spring. Every year as I decide that springtime is some far-fetched fantasy, the first stalks of bright red rhubarb arrive in my market. Then I know the daffodils are just around the corner, and it's my spring wake-up call to make this tart. It has a thin layer of rhubarb filling between a Butter Cookie Tart Crust (page 203) and a thick and generous crumb topping.

Baking Answers ❧ When rhubarb is fresh, it is crisp and bright red or rosy pink. A pink color usually signals that the rhubarb has been grown in a hothouse. I try to pick the darkest red stems to produce the most colorful fillings. When rhubarb is fresh, the stem end is firm, clean, and has no signs of rotting. If you wave a stalk in the air, it won't flop around.

Remember that the leaves are toxic, so remove any that remain on the stem and discard them.

Cook rhubarb in a nonreactive pan that does not react with acid. Stainless steel is nonreactive, aluminum is not.

This cookie crust does not need to be weighted when it is baked without its filling.

A Step Ahead ◦ The crust can be prepared, put in the tart pan, covered, and refrigerated overnight.

Necessities ◦ *1 cold unbaked Butter Cookie Tart Crust (page 203) in a 9-inch metal tart pan with a removable bottom, and a baking sheet for holding the tart pan during baking*

RHUBARB FILLING	3 tablespoons water
2½ cups (about 10 ounces) rhubarb cut into ½-inch pieces	¼ cup granulated sugar

CRUMB TOPPING	¼ teaspoon salt
1¼ cups unbleached all-purpose flour	¾ teaspoon ground cinnamon
1¼ cups packed light brown sugar	7 tablespoons unsalted butter, melted
	1 teaspoon vanilla extract

1 recipe cold unbaked Butter Cookie
Tart Crust (page 203) in a 9-inch
tart pan with a removable bottom

Cook the Filling

◦ Put the rhubarb, water, and granulated sugar in a nonreactive saucepan and stir them together. Cover the pan and cook the mixture over low heat until it comes to a simmer and begins to release liquid, about 5 minutes. Remove the cover and increase the heat just so the mixture boils gently, stirring often. Cook just until the rhubarb softens and most of the water evaporates, about 5 minutes. Set aside to cool.

Mix the Topping

◦ Put the flour, brown sugar, salt, and cinnamon in a large bowl and stir them together. Mix the melted butter and vanilla together in a small bowl. Add the melted butter mixture to the flour mixture, stirring until crumbs form and the mixture looks evenly moist. Set aside.

Partially Bake the Crust

◦ Position an oven rack in the middle of the oven. Preheat the oven to 375°F. Place the crust-lined tart pan on a baking sheet. Bake the crust 10 minutes and remove it from the oven.

Reduce the oven temperature to 350° F.

Assemble and Bake the Tart

✧ Spread the cooled rhubarb mixture evenly over the crust. Sprinkle the reserved crumb topping over the rhubarb filling. Bake about 25 minutes until the crumb topping and the edges of the crust are lightly browned. Cool the tart thoroughly in its pan. Use a small sharp knife to loosen the sides of the crust from the pan. Set the tart pan on a shallow bowl, such as a soup bowl, and let the rim slide down. Loosen the bottom of the tart with a thin spatula and slide the tart onto a serving plate. Use a large, sharp knife to cut the tart into slices and serve at room temperature. The tart can be made up to 3 days ahead, cooled, covered, and stored at room temperature.

Apple and Hazelnut Macaroon Tart

Although this tart looks as if it came from a fancy French bakery, the components are a butter cookie dough crust, a filling that can be made in about 2 minutes in a food processor, and a topping of thinly sliced apples. The hazelnut filling will remind you of a soft and lightly sweetened hazelnut macaroon cookie. Spiral rows of apple slices, brushed to a sheen with apricot jam, crown the top. The tart looks as if it takes hours to prepare, but you can put it together in about 30 minutes or less. But maybe you should keep that to yourself and show off a bit.

Baking Answers ✧ If the apples are thinly sliced, 1 large apple will cover the top of the tart. Overlap the apple slices carefully to form neat rows.

Let the filling chill before adding the apple slices. This firms the filling slightly so that the thin slices don't sink into it.

A pastry brush is a good tool for brushing the apricot glaze over the apples. Buy a good-quality brush that will not drop its bristles on the tart.

SERVES 8

Necessities ✧ *1 cold unbaked Butter Cookie Tart Crust (page 203) in a 9-inch metal tart pan with a removable bottom, a baking sheet for holding the tart pan during baking, and a pastry brush*

1 recipe cold unbaked Butter Cookie
    Tart Crust (page 203) in a
    9-inch tart pan

APPLE HAZELNUT FILLING	1 teaspoon vanilla extract
1 cup toasted peeled hazelnuts	2 large eggs
(page 40)	2 ounces (½ stick) soft unsalted
¾ cup sugar	butter
¼ teaspoon salt	

2 medium apples or 1 large apple,	2 tablespoons sugar
peeled, halved, cored, and sliced	1 tablespoon unsalted butter, melted
⅛ inch thick	¼ cup apricot preserves for glazing the
1 teaspoon fresh lemon juice	baked tart

Mix the Filling

~ Position a rack in the middle of the oven. Preheat the oven to 400°F. Have the cold tart crust ready to fill. Put the hazelnuts, sugar, salt, vanilla, and eggs in the work bowl of a food processor. Process until a thick mixture forms, about 1 minute. Add the soft butter and process until it is incorporated. The mixture lightens in color and you will see some tiny pieces of hazelnuts. Use a rubber spatula to scrape the filling into the chilled crust, spreading it evenly. Place the filled tart pan on a baking sheet, so it is easy to move around. Refrigerate 30 minutes to firm the filling.

Put the apple slices, lemon juice, and 1 tablespoon sugar in a small bowl and stir them gently together. Be careful not to break the apple slices. Let the apple mixture sit while the filling chills. Drain and discard any liquid, and arrange the apples in 2 circular rows of overlapping slices over the cold hazelnut mixture. Drizzle with the melted butter. Sprinkle the remaining tablespoon of sugar evenly over the apples.

Bake and Glaze the Tart

~ Bake 15 minutes. Reduce the oven temperature to 350°F. Continue to bake until the apples are soft and the edges are browned, about 30 minutes. The filling will look puffed and set. Cool the tart in its pan.

Put the apricot preserves in a small frying pan or saucepan. Cook them over medium heat just until the preserves melt, stirring constantly, about 3 minutes. Strain the preserves into a small bowl. Discard any pieces of apricot in the strainer. When the tart has cooled enough so that the filling is firm, use a pastry brush to brush the apples gently and generously with the strained preserves.

Serve the Tart

✦ Cool the tart thoroughly. Use a small sharp knife to loosen the sides of the crust from the pan. Set the tart pan on a shallow bowl, such as a soup bowl, and let the rim slide down. Loosen the bottom of the tart with a thin spatula and slide the tart onto a serving plate. Use a large, sharp knife to cut the tart into slices and serve at room temperature. The tart can be made up to 1 day ahead, cooled, covered, and stored refrigerated.

Shimmering Fresh Berry Tart

Upon entering a French restaurant, you will often see a pastry cart that displays an extravagant choice of glistening berry tarts. Although these tarts look complicated, making one is not. All you will need to do to make this big-night-out dessert is to arrange some ripe strawberries, red raspberries, dark blueberries, plump blackberries, or a combination in a baked Butter Cookie Tart Crust (page 203) and brush them with jam to make the berries shine. A middle layer of pastry cream can be included, but berries alone are fine.

Baking Answers ✦ Look for the prettiest, ripest berries for this tart. If the berries need to be washed, dry them carefully before adding them to the tart. Drain the berries on a paper towel, patting them gently with more paper towels, if necessary.

A Step Ahead ✦ The crust can be baked a day ahead, cooled, covered, and stored at room temperature. Add the filling on the day you serve it.

SERVES 8

Necessities ✦ *1 Butter Cookie Tart Crust (page 203) baked in a 9-inch metal tart pan with a removable bottom, a baking sheet for holding the tart during baking, and a pastry brush*

1 recipe cold pastry cream (page 106, from Cherry Custard Tart with Pouring Crust), optional

1 Butter Cookie Tart Crust, baked, cooled, in a 9-inch tart pan (page 203)

3 cups cleaned berries: stemmed strawberries cut in half lengthwise; about 1½ pints blueberries, raspberries, blackberries; or a combination of these berries

3 tablespoons jelly or seedless jam (use raspberry jam to glaze strawberries or raspberries, and apricot jam to glaze blueberries, blackberries, or a berry combination)

Assemble the Tart

~ Use a thin metal spatula to spread the pastry cream, if you are including it, over the bottom of the baked tart crust.

For strawberries, begin at the rim of the pan and arrange strawberry halves in a circular pattern to cover the pastry cream or crust. Place strawberry halves, cut side down, with the point of each strawberry overlapping the bottom of the strawberry in front of it to make solid rows. For other berries, gently spoon a solid layer of blueberries, raspberries, or blackberries neatly and thickly over the pastry cream or crust. Or, arrange alternating rings of a combination of blueberries, blackberries, or raspberries over the tart. Another choice is to make a border of whole strawberries around the edge of the tart, then add a thick layer of small berries to fill in the center, mounding the berries slightly higher in the center.

Make the Glaze and Serve the Tart

~ Heat the raspberry or apricot jam or jelly in a small saucepan over low heat to melt it. Strain the apricot jam into a small bowl. Jelly and seedless jam can be used without straining. Cool the jam or jelly slightly. Use a pastry brush to brush the berries gently and generously with the melted jam or jelly. Serve or refrigerate and serve the same day.

Chile, Cheese, and Chorizo Quiche

It was probably inevitable that quiches would suffer from overexposure. They are foolproof and easy to put together, use simple ingredients, and are suitable for a fancy lunch or Sunday supper. The fillings have countless variations that can suit your tastes or whatever is handy in the refrigerator. I recommend forgetting any overexposure and trying this spiced-up quiche that has a savory custard filling flavored with green chiles, Jack cheese, cooked onions, and chorizo sausage.

Baking Answers ❧ Liquid fillings can turn even a freshly baked crust quite soggy, so this crust is baked blind and brushed with egg white during its prebaking. The egg white seals the crust so it remains pleasantly firm after baking with the filling.

To roast fresh chiles, cook them under a broiler until their skins blister, turning to cook all sides. Remove them from the oven and cover with wet paper towels. When they are cool, peel off the skin.

A Step Ahead ❧ The crust can be prebaked and the onion and chile mixture can be cooked early in the day. Both of them can be cooled then covered to wait at room temperature until the quiche is ready to be filled and baked.

This quiche is also delicious when baked ahead and served at room temperature. It can be refrigerated overnight then brought to room temperature.

MAKES 8 SLICES

Necessities ❧ *One 1-crust recipe cold unbaked Fearless Piecrust (page 199) in a 9-inch ovenproof glass or ceramic pie pan, metal pie weights or 2½ cups dried beans, and a pastry brush*

One 1-crust recipe cold unbaked
    Fearless Piecrust (page 199) in a
    9-inch pie pan
1 large egg white, lightly beaten with
    a fork
1 tablespoon unsalted butter
1 cup chopped onion (1 medium)
One 4-ounce can whole green chiles,
    drained and cut in ½-inch pieces,
    or 3 fresh mild or hot green
    chiles, roasted (page 226), peeled,
    and chopped

3 large eggs
1 tablespoon unbleached all-purpose
    flour
½ teaspoon chili powder
¼ teaspoon salt
1 tablespoon unsalted butter, melted
1½ cups half-and-half
1 spicy chorizo sausage (about 4
    ounces), cooked and cut into
    ¼-inch slices
4 ounces (about 1 cup) Jack cheese,
    grated

Prebake the Crust

❧ Position a rack in the bottom third of the oven. Preheat the oven to 375°F. Line the prepared crust with aluminum foil. Fill the aluminum foil with metal pie weights or about 2½ cups of dried beans. Check to see that the weights evenly cover the entire bottom of the crust. The weights should make a thick layer over the bottom, but they do not have to come to the top of the pan. Bake the crust for 15 minutes. Protect your hands with potholders and carefully remove the aluminum foil by lifting it and the pie weights from the crust. Set the weights aside to cool and store for another use.

Reduce the oven temperature to 350°F. Prick the piecrust in about 6 places with a fork. Use a pastry brush to brush the egg white over the bottom of the crust. You will not use all of the egg white. Bake the uncovered crust for about 10 more minutes until the crust is beginning to brown lightly. Remove the crust from the oven and set aside while you prepare the filling. Leave the oven temperature at 350°F.

Prepare and Mix the Filling

❧ Heat the butter over medium heat in a medium fry pan to melt it. Add the onion and cook for about 7 minutes until the onion softens, stirring often. Add the chopped chiles and cook about 3 minutes more until the onion just begins to brown at the edges, stirring often. Set aside.

Put the eggs, flour, chili powder, and salt in a medium bowl and stir them with a whisk to break up the egg yolks and blend the ingredients together. Add the melted butter and half-and-half, whisking to blend them into the mixture. Put the reserved onion mixture into the prebaked crust. Place the sausage slices evenly over the onion mixture. Sprinkle the grated cheese over the sausage. Pour the egg mixture through a strainer into the crust.

~ Bake for about 35 minutes, until you can give the quiche a gentle shake and the filling looks set and the top of the filling begins to turn golden. Some of the chili powder, chiles, and onion will float to the top during baking. Cool for at least 15 minutes. Cut into slices and serve warm. Or, cool for about an hour to serve at room temperature. The slightly cooled quiche can be covered and refrigerated overnight then brought to room temperature for serving.

Roasted Tomato, Basil, and Parmesan Pie

Sun-ripened tomatoes are weighing down their vines, bunches of fresh basil are plentiful, and this savory pie is ready to hold the summer bounty. The pie is packed with tomato halves that have been roasted with garlic and basil and covered with a topping of melted Parmesan cheese and additional basil. The long roasting brings out such sweetness in the tomatoes that they almost seem to be candied. Equally good served warm or at room temperature, this pie can be served with a salad and bread for a light summer dinner or it can highlight a summer picnic.

Baking Answers ~ The tomatoes are peeled before they are roasted. This is a process of quick-cooking the tomatoes in boiling water for a minute or less until the skins slip easily off the tomatoes. Detailed directions for peeling tomatoes are on page 38.

The tomatoes shrink significantly as they roast.

Tomatoes have a lot of acid, so I prefer to bake this tomato-filled pie in an ovenproof glass or ceramic pie pan rather than a metal pie pan.

A Step Ahead ~ The tomato mixture can be baked early in the day, up to 8 hours ahead, and added to the piecrust when you are ready to bake it.

Kitchen Experiments ~ When I first began roasting tomatoes for this pie, the juices from the tomatoes formed a baked-on crust on the pan that was difficult to clean. I tried lining the pan with aluminum foil but the tomatoes stuck to the foil, and I lost pieces of tomato when I lifted them off. I tried using a disposable aluminum pan rubbed with olive oil. The tomatoes baked onto this pan also. Finally, I tried lining the baking pan with a double layer of parchment paper. It worked perfectly. The juices don't soak through the 2 layers of paper and the tomatoes don't stick.

Necessities ⤙ *One 1-crust recipe cold unbaked Fearless Piecrust (page 199) in a 9-inch ovenproof glass or ceramic pie pan, 1 baking sheet or roasting pan with low sides (preferably about 1 inch high), and parchment paper*

ROASTED TOMATOES FOR FILLING	¼ teaspoon salt
5 to 7 tomatoes, 5 large (8 ounces or larger) or 7 medium (at least 6 ounces), skins removed (page 38), and halved horizontally	1 teaspoon (about 2 cloves) finely chopped peeled garlic, green center removed if any
	15 whole fresh basil leaves
	2 tablespoons olive oil
One 1-crust recipe unbaked cold Fearless Piecrust (page 199) in a 9-inch ovenproof glass or ceramic pie pan	Freshly ground black pepper
½ cup freshly grated Parmesan cheese, Parmigiano-Reggiano preferred	2 tablespoons tightly packed fresh basil, torn into approximately ½-inch pieces
4 ounces fresh mozzarella, cut into ½-inch pieces	15 black olives, pitted (oil-cured olives preferred)
	1 tablespoon extra-virgin olive oil

Roast the Tomatoes for the Filling

⤙ Position a rack in the middle of the oven. Preheat the oven to 400°F. Line a shallow roasting pan or baking sheet with 1- to 2-inch-high sides with 2 layers of parchment paper. Put the tomato halves cut side up in the pan. Sprinkle the tomatoes with the salt and chopped garlic. Top each tomato with 1 or 2 basil leaves, placing 2 leaves on the largest tomatoes. Drizzle the 2 tablespoons of olive oil over the basil leaves. Bake for 1 hour and 15 minutes for large tomatoes or 1 hour for medium tomatoes. The basil leaves turn dark and crisp, but they are not burned. The edges of the tomatoes may darken. Remove the tomato mixture from the oven and set aside. Decrease the oven temperature to 375°F.

Fill and Bake the Pie

⤙ Remove the crust from the refrigerator and sprinkle ¼ cup of the Parmesan cheese over the bottom of the crust. Use a large spoon to place the reserved tomatoes and their basil topping, cut side up and close together, in an even layer in the crust. Let any watery liquid from the tomatoes drip back into the baking pan, and discard this liquid with the used parchment paper. Press the tomatoes against each other tightly to fill the crust generously. Bake about 40 minutes until the crust edges are lightly browned and the filling begins to bubble. Remove from the oven and use a small spoon to place the mozzarella cheese pieces between the tomatoes, placing them evenly around the pie. Grind fresh pepper lightly over the top of the pie. Put the torn basil and the remaining ¼ cup of Parmesan in a small bowl and stir them together. Sprinkle the basil mixture over the tomatoes. Arrange the olives evenly over the tomatoes. Drizzle with the 1 tablespoon of olive oil. Bake 10 additional minutes until the cheese melts.

Serve the Pie

✒ Let the pie rest for 10 minutes and serve warm. Or, let the pie come to room temperature and serve. Use a large knife to cut the pie into slices. Leftover pie can be refrigerated overnight and brought to room temperature for serving.

Deep-Dish Wild Mushroom Pie

Jeff's Grandma Tillie often served a great mushroom pie from Hough Bakery in Cleveland for a first course at her dinner parties. It had a crisp top crust and a creamy, but not too thick, filling loaded with fresh mushrooms. Hough Bakery is no more, and multicourse dinner parties are rare, but this pie served with a salad has become a regular for our Sunday supper.

Deep-dish pies have some special qualities. Since there is only one crisp top crust, any chance of a soft bottom crust is eliminated, and you only have to prepare a single crust. The deeper-than-a-pie-pan dishes that these pies bake in can hold a generous amount of filling. For serving, digging into the pie to spoon out generous helpings of crust and filling is all there is to do.

Baking Answers
✒ Even the smallest of markets now seems to offer a variety of fresh mushroom choices. A mixture of crimini, shiitake, and white mushrooms makes a good combination for this pie. The mushrooms shrink during cooking, which evaporates much of their moisture.

Let the filling cool before adding the top crust. A steaming filling could soften the dough and make it difficult to put in place.

Clean mushrooms by wiping any dirt off with a damp paper towel, or rinse quickly with cold water. Soaking them in water can make them watery. Discard the stems of the shiitake mushrooms.

The choice of baking container is flexible. A baking dish that is about 2 inches high is best. If the dish is too deep and there is a lot of space between the filling and the top of the dish, press the crust down in the dish and onto the filling. Round or oval baking dishes are fine; just roll and cut the crust to fit the shape of the top of the baking dish.

An egg and water mixture is brushed over the top of the crust to help the crust brown. This mixture is an egg wash and can also be made with egg and cream.

A Step Ahead ◦ Mix the piecrust dough 1 day ahead, cover with plastic wrap, and refrigerate.

SERVES 4 FOR DINNER OR 8 AS SIDE DISH

Necessities ◦ *A 9-inch-diameter layer pan with 2-inch-high sides or a shallow ovenproof baking dish or casserole about 9 inches in diameter that is about 2 inches high, a pastry brush, one 1-crust recipe Fearless Piecrust dough (page 199), and a rolling pin*

2 tablespoons unsalted butter	1 cup chicken broth, low-sodium
½ cup finely chopped onion	preferred if canned
(1 small)	2 tablespoons dry sherry or white
4 cups cleaned and thinly sliced	wine
fresh mushrooms; mixture of	Salt and freshly ground black pepper
crimini, white, and shiitake is	to taste
preferred (discard stems on	One 1-crust recipe cold Fearless
shiitake mushrooms)	Piecrust dough (page 199)
2 tablespoons unbleached all-purpose	1 large egg beaten with a fork with 2
flour	tablespoons water
¾ cup half-and-half	

Make the Filling

◦ Position a rack in the middle of the oven. Preheat the oven to 400°F. Have ready a 9-inch-diameter layer pan with 2-inch-high sides or a shallow ovenproof baking dish at least 2 inches high that is about the same size as the layer pan.

Melt the butter in a large saucepan over medium heat. Add the onion and cook until soft, about 5 minutes, stirring often. Add the mushrooms, cooking until they soften and the moisture from the mushrooms has evaporated, stirring often, about 8 more minutes. Add the flour and cook, stirring constantly, for 1 minute. Remove from the heat and, stirring constantly, add the half-

and–half, chicken broth, and sherry. The liquid in the mixture should be smooth. Return to the heat and cook for about 1 minute, stirring constantly, until the mixture just begins to boil and thickens slightly. Remove from the heat. Add salt and pepper to your taste. Pour the mixture into the baking dish. Set aside to cool slightly while rolling the crust.

Assemble the Pie

✺ Lightly flour the rolling surface and rolling pin. Roll the piecrust dough to a shape that fits the shape of the top of the baking dish but is 1 inch larger than the top of the dish. Roll up the piecrust over the rolling pin and unroll it over the cooled mushroom filling. Fold ½ inch of the edge of the crust under itself to form a smooth edge that rests on the edge of the pan. Use a fork to press the dough firmly onto the rim of the baking dish. Brush the top of the crust evenly with the egg and water mixture. You will not use all of the mixture. Cut four 2-inch-long slits in the top of the crust to release the steam while the pie bakes.

Bake and Serve the Pie

✺ Bake about 25 minutes until the crust is light brown. Let cool for 5 minutes and serve hot.

Whipping Eggs for Cakes and Meringues

WONDROUS THINGS HAPPEN TO EGGS AS YOU WHIP AIR INTO THEM. EGG WHITES ARE TRANSFORMED INTO CRISP MERINGUES, SOFT TOPPINGS FOR PIES, OR EVEN THE BASE FOR A FLUFFY WHITE FROSTING, WHILE WHIPPED WHOLE eggs or yolks become the foundation for light, billowy cakes.

Happily, an electric mixer does all of the work of beating, so all you have to do is hold the mixer, watch the process, and note when the beaten eggs or whites reach the desired stage. Some of the cakes in this chapter depend on whole eggs beaten with sugar to a fluffy, light stage, while other cakes and meringues use only whipped egg whites.

Whipping eggs and sugar is a simple process. The usual mixing procedure is to beat whole eggs and sugar in a large bowl until the color lightens from light yellow to cream, the mixture thickens, and the movement of the beaters forms lines in the mixture. To reach this point usually takes 2 minutes using the medium speed on a handheld mixer, but a large quantity of eggs may take longer to beat. Move handheld mixers around the mixing bowl so the ingredients beat evenly. Beating the whole eggs with sugar is a step that lightens cakes, and an extra minute of beating is fine and does no harm. The usual order for the rest of the mixing process is to add the ingredients in the order given and mix them until they are blended smoothly. Liquid ingredients are usually added to the batter before the dry ingredients.

Some of these cakes, such as the Almond Angel Cake (page 248), have no added leavening but depend on the air beaten into egg whites and the evaporation of steam during baking to lift and lighten them. Chiffon cakes, on the other hand, achieve their high rise from the triple combination of whipped egg whites, whipped egg yolks, and baking powder.

Although beating egg whites to the proper stage is an important step in these cakes, it is as simple as watching the changes that take place as they whip to a firm froth. Egg whites do not whip properly if there is any fat present, so whip them in a clean, grease-free bowl and remove even 1 speck of egg yolk. Using half an eggshell is a good way to scoop out any stray egg yolk.

If you are using a handheld mixer, be sure to move it around the bowl so all of the egg whites receive an even beating. As egg whites whip, they change from a pale yellow color to pure white. Beating egg whites with some cream of tartar helps stabilize this delicate foam. When the egg whites look smooth, moist, and shiny, they are beaten to the correct stage. Another sure sign is that the movement of the beaters forms a pattern of lines in the egg-white mixture. Recipes often say to beat the egg whites to the soft-peak stage. To check egg whites to see if they have reached this stage, stop the mixer for a moment and lift the beaters out of the mixture. If the egg whites are ready, they will cling to the beaters and form a soft point or peak. The larger the quantity of egg whites to be whipped, the longer the process takes. When beaten properly, egg whites combine easily with other mixtures.

Egg whites that have been beaten without sugar should be used immediately, but if sugar is beaten into egg whites, it stabilizes the foam and the mixture can sit for about 30 minutes before it must be used. Begin adding any sugar just as the egg whites reach the soft-peak stage, and add it slowly so the egg whites have time to absorb it. It is better to underbeat egg whites slightly than to overbeat them. Overbeaten egg whites look dry and dull and form big white clumps if you try to fold them into another mixture. If this should happen, it is best to throw out the egg whites and begin again. After seeing the dry look that egg whites have when beaten too long, you'll know exactly what to look for and be able to prevent it from happening again.

When egg whites are beaten to make a crisp meringue, about ¼ cup of sugar per egg white is slowly beaten into the whipped egg whites. Once the sugar is added, meringues can be spread into layers, dropped into cookies, spread onto bars for a crisp topping, or formed into thick meringue shells that can hold fruit or cream fillings.

The baking of a crisp meringue is a drying-out process of baking the meringues slowly at a low temperature, usually at about 225°F. The low baking temperature bakes the moisture out while keeping the meringue lightly colored. Because of this low baking temperature, a few additional minutes of baking make no difference.

Egg whites can be beaten with about 1½ to 2 tablespoons of sugar per egg white to produce a soft meringue. Soft meringues bake quickly at around 375°F. to a golden color and make a soft and melting swirled topping for such pies as Mom's Lemon Meringue Pie (page 270).

Finally, egg whites and sugar can also be beaten into a billowy old-fashioned marshmallow-like frosting. The frosting mixture is beaten in a pot over hot water until it increases in volume and becomes fluffy and firm enough to hold its shape. It's a foolproof preparation that dissolves the sugar during the beating to produce a smooth-as-silk frosting that's a pleasure to spread over any cake.

Pans for chiffon cakes or angel food cakes are not greased. These cakes must climb slowly up the pan as they bake and stay put. Absentmindedly, I once forgot and greased a tube pan for a chiffon cake. It rose quickly and unusually high, formed a big air pocket, then collapsed as soon as it came out of the oven. I normally line the bottoms of cake pans with parchment paper for easy removal, but I do not line the bottom of the tube pan when baking a chiffon cake. When I have tried a paper lining, the cake has often fallen out of its pan during the long, slow cooling process.

The Coffee Lover's Layer Cake (page 256) has a moist sponge cake. Sponge cakes develop their light sponge texture from whipped eggs. Whipping the eggs with sugar stabilizes the batter. This sponge cake includes hot milk. The milk adds additional richness to the sponge cake, and the hot milk cooks the eggs slightly, thereby stabilizing the mixture even further.

Cinnamon Pecan Swirl Coffee Cake

Although I'm partial to coffee cakes with plenty of filling, I discovered that there are limits to how much filling a cake can hold. When I was testing ideas for this cake, I used so much filling in one attempt that the filling sank through the cake batter and made the whole cake collapse and fall apart when it came out of the pan. I backed off a bit so I could end up with this version with just enough sweet cinnamon pecan mixture to be swirled throughout the tender, fine-grained cake. And, because I couldn't resist, the same cinnamon-pecan mixture covers the top of the cake with a crunchy topping.

Baking Answers ∽ The light structure of the cake develops during a thorough beating of the eggs with the sugar. Once this fluffy mixture is achieved, the remainder of the mixing process is just a matter of blending ingredients together to incorporate them into the batter.

For directions on lining a tube pan with parchment or wax paper, see page 147.

Cake flour gives this cake a lighter texture than all-purpose flour would.

A food processor works best for preparing the pecan filling, but if you don't have one you can chop the pecans very finely, then mix them with the sugar and cinnamon.

A Step Ahead ∽ Prepare the cinnamon-pecan mixture up to 3 days ahead. Cover it and store at room temperature until you are ready to add it to the cake.

The cooled cake can be frozen for up to 3 months. Cover it with plastic wrap, then heavy aluminum foil, and label it with the date and contents. Defrost the wrapped cake at room temperature.

SERVES 12 TO 16

Necessities ∽ *A 9½- or 10-inch-diameter tube pan with a fixed bottom with at least 3¾-inch-high sides, and 2 wire racks for inverting and cooling the cake*

FILLING AND TOPPING— MAKES 1½ CUPS	½ cup sugar
1 cup pecans	1 tablespoon ground cinnamon

CAKE	3 large eggs
2¾ cups cake flour	2 cups sugar
1 teaspoon baking powder	1 cup canola or corn oil
½ teaspoon baking soda	2 teaspoons vanilla extract
½ teaspoon salt	1 cup sour cream

Powdered sugar for dusting the top
   of the cake

Prepare the Filling and Topping

↝ Put the pecans, sugar, and cinnamon in the work bowl of a food processor and process them until the nuts are a combination of finely chopped and ground, about 15 seconds.

Mix the Cake

↝ Position an oven rack in the middle of the oven. Preheat the oven to 350°F. Oil or spray with vegetable oil spray the bottom, sides, and center tube of a 9½- or 10-inch fixed-bottom tube pan with at least 3¾-inch-high sides. Line the bottom with parchment or wax paper and oil the paper.

Sift the cake flour, baking powder, baking soda, and salt together onto a piece of wax paper or into a medium bowl. Set aside.

Put the eggs and sugar in a large bowl and beat with an electric mixer on medium speed for about 2 minutes until the mixture looks fluffy, thickens, and lightens to a cream color. This is the stage of the mixing that lightens the cake, so don't skimp on the mixing time. If using a handheld electric mixer, move the beaters around in the bowl. Stop the mixer and scrape the mixture from the sides of the bowl as needed throughout the mixing process. On low speed slowly add the oil and vanilla, mixing just to blend them into the batter. Mix in the flour mixture just until it is incorporated. Add the sour cream, mixing until it is blended and no white streaks remain. Pour about two thirds of the batter evenly into the prepared pan. Set aside ¼ cup of the cinnamon-pecan mixture for the top of the cake. Sprinkle half of the remaining nut mixture over the batter. Dip a knife about halfway into the batter and run the knife once around the nut mixture to swirl it lightly through the batter. Sprinkle the remaining half of the nut mixture over the batter, but do not swirl it. Use a rubber spatula to scrape the remaining batter into the pan, letting the batter fall gently on top of the nut mixture and gently spreading it evenly. The batter will not cover all of the nut mixture. Sprinkle the reserved ¼ cup of nut mixture evenly over the top of the batter.

Bake and Serve the Cake

◦ Bake about 55 minutes until a toothpick inserted in the center of the cake comes out clean. Cool the cake in the pan for about 45 minutes. Run a thin knife around the sides and center tube of the pan to loosen the cake. Turn the cake out onto a plate or a wire rack. Carefully remove and discard the paper lining the bottom. Place a wire rack over the bottom of the cake and invert the cake so it is nut side up. Cool thoroughly. Dust the top with powdered sugar. Use a large spatula to slide the cake onto a serving plate.

Cut the cake into slices and serve at room temperature. Cover leftover cake with plastic wrap and store at room temperature up to 3 days.

Variation ◦ *Bake the cake in two 7½-inch-diameter tube pans that are 2½ inches high rather than one large pan. The cakes will bake in about 40 to 45 minutes. These smaller cakes make nice holiday gifts. Put each cake on a cardboard cake circle, wrap it in cellophane, and tie with a bow.*

Lemon Ripple Crunch Cake

Swirls of a simple lemon filling play 2 roles in this best-of-everything cake. The lemon mixed into the filling produces a cake that is especially moist, and the lemon swirled into the batter adds moist ripples of intense lemon flavor throughout the golden cake. The crumb topping adds an unexpected crunch.

Baking Answers ◦ Beating the eggs and sugar to a fluffy mixture is the step that gives the cake its light texture, and an additional minute or two of beating is okay. Once this fluffy mixture is achieved, the remainder of the mixing process is just a matter of blending ingredients together to incorporate them into the batter.

Bottles labeled pure almond extract are made with oil of bitter almond and are preferable to bottles labeled almond extract. The pure version is now available in most supermarkets.

For directions on lining a tube pan with parchment or wax paper see page 147.

Add the crumb topping after the cake partially bakes so the crumbs remain on top of the cake rather than sinking into the batter. Add them about halfway through the baking time so they adhere to the cake. Since the crumb topping makes this cake feel firm on top during baking, I depend on a toothpick to test it for doneness.

Remember to grate the lemon zest from the lemon before squeezing the juice. For the zest, grate only the yellow skin of the lemon. The white pith is bitter and has no lemon flavor.

A Step Ahead ◦ Mix the crumb topping up to 3 days ahead. Cover and refrigerate it until you are ready to bake it with the cake. The cooled cake can be frozen for up to 3 months. Cover it with plastic wrap, then heavy aluminum foil, and label it with the date and contents. Defrost the wrapped cake at room temperature.

SERVES 12 TO 16

Necessities ◦ *A 9½- or 10-inch-diameter tube pan with a fixed bottom with at least 3¾-inch-high sides, and 2 wire racks for inverting and cooling the cake*

CRUMB TOPPING	2 tablespoons granulated sugar
¼ cup unbleached all-purpose flour	¼ teaspoon ground cinnamon
2 tablespoons packed light brown sugar	3 tablespoons cold unsalted butter, cut into ½-inch pieces

LEMON CAKE AND FILLING	½ teaspoon salt
2 large egg yolks	3 large eggs
One 14-ounce can sweetened condensed milk	2 cups granulated sugar
⅓ cup fresh lemon juice	1 cup canola or corn oil
2 teaspoons grated lemon zest	2 teaspoons vanilla extract
2¾ cups cake flour	½ teaspoon pure almond extract
1 teaspoon baking powder	1 cup sour cream
½ teaspoon baking soda	Powdered sugar for dusting the top of the cake

Mix the Topping

◦ Put the flour, brown sugar, granulated sugar, and cinnamon in a medium bowl. Mix just to blend the ingredients together. Add the butter pieces and use a fork, pastry blender, or your fingertips to break up the butter pieces, then mix them until crumbs form. Set aside.

Mix the Cake

◦ Position an oven rack in the middle of the oven. Preheat the oven to 325°F. Oil the bottom, sides, and center tube of a 9½- or 10-inch-diameter fixed-bottom tube pan with at least 3¾-inch-high sides. Line the bottom with parchment or wax paper and oil the paper.

Put the egg yolks, sweetened condensed milk, lemon juice, and 1 teaspoon of the lemon zest for the lemon filling in a small bowl, stirring them until smoothly blended. Set aside.

Sift the cake flour, baking powder, baking soda, and salt together onto a piece of wax paper or into a medium bowl. Set aside.

Put the eggs and granulated sugar in a large bowl and beat with an electric mixer on medium speed for about 2 minutes until the mixture looks fluffy, thickens, and lightens to a cream color. This is the stage of the mixing that lightens the cake. Move the beaters around in the bowl if using a handheld electric mixer. Reduce the speed to low and slowly add the oil, vanilla, almond extract, and the remaining teaspoon of lemon zest, mixing until blended together. Mix in the flour mixture just until it is incorporated. Add the sour cream, mixing until it is blended and no white streaks remain. Use a rubber spatula to scrape about two-thirds of the batter into the prepared pan. Leaving about a ½-inch plain edge, spoon the reserved sweetened condensed milk and lemon mixture over the batter. Dipping a spoon about 1 inch into the batter, run it once around the lemon mixture in the pan to swirl it lightly through the batter. There should be dark yellow marbleized streaks of lemon. Use a rubber spatula to scrape the remaining batter into the pan, spreading it evenly.

Bake and Serve the Cake

◦ Bake 35 minutes. Gently sprinkle the reserved crumb topping over the top of the cake. Bake about 40 minutes more until a toothpick inserted in the center of the cake comes out clean. If the toothpick penetrates a large area of lemon filling, test another spot. Cool the cake in the pan for 15 minutes. Run a thin knife around the sides and center tube of the pan to loosen the cake. Turn the cake out onto a plate or wire rack. Carefully remove and discard the paper lining the bottom. Place a wire rack over the bottom of the cake and invert the cake onto it so the cake is crumb topping side up. Cool thoroughly. Dust the top with powdered sugar. Use a large spatula to slide the cake onto a serving plate.

Cut the cake into slices and serve at room temperature. Fresh berries can be served with this cake. Cover leftover cake with plastic wrap and store refrigerated up to 3 days.

Variation ◦ *Bake the cake in two 7½-inch-diameter tube pans that are 2½ inches high rather than one large pan. Add the crumbs after 30 minutes and bake about 35 more minutes. These smaller cakes make nice holiday gifts. Put each cooled cake on a cardboard cake circle, wrap in cellophane, and tie with a bow.*

Italian Cream Cake

When my first editor, Janice Easton, mentioned that she was going home for her father's birthday to bake him his favorite Italian Cream Cake, my baking antenna began to quiver. With such an appealing name and if it was good enough to be a birthday choice, I knew this cake must be special. Pecans and shreds of coconut float throughout the yellow cake that bakes in a tube pan and is large enough to serve a crowd. The outside of the cake is thickly covered with cream cheese frosting and sprinkled with a shower of coconut. I don't know whether the cream part of the name originated from the creamy, soft texture of the cake or from the creamy frosting, but it certainly lives up to its promise.

The recipe for this cake originally came from the Eastons' neighbor, Pat Mesnig, but there are many different family versions out there. A cake like this is too good to be kept to yourself!

Baking Answers ✧ The cake is mixed by creaming shortening and sugar, beating in egg yolks, and adding flour alternately with buttermilk. Then, using an old-fashioned method for lightening the cake's texture, the egg whites are beaten to soft peaks and folded into the cake batter at the end of the mixing process. These whipped egg whites incorporate additional air into the cake batter. Thorough beating is important to develop the cake's structure when creaming the shortening and the sugar and when adding the egg yolks to the cake batter. Adding dry ingredients and milk to the batter is only a process of blending them into the batter and does not require long beating. The beaten eggs whites are folded gently into the batter, so as to deflate them as little as possible.

Beat the egg whites until they form a shiny, pure white mass that clings to the beaters if you stop the mixer and lift the beaters. They will also form a soft point or peak if the beaters are lifted out of the egg whites. A further sign is when an indentation remains in the whites in the bowl if you scoop out a spoonful of perfectly beaten egg whites.

Egg whites need to be free of any yolk to whip properly. Be sure to whip them in a clean grease-free bowl. Separate eggs one a time, putting each egg white as you separate it into a small bowl, then transferring it to a larger bowl before adding another egg white to the small bowl. If the egg yolk breaks up and mixes into the egg white to the point that it is difficult to remove from the whites and you cannot use it, only 1 egg white will have been lost rather than several. On the other hand, a little white that mixes into yolks is not a problem.

Begin adding the sugar just as the egg whites reach the soft-peak stage, adding it slowly to give the egg whites time to absorb it.

Necessities ∾ *A 9½- or 10-inch-diameter tube pan with a fixed bottom with at least 3¾-inch-high sides, 2 large mixing bowls, and 1 wire rack for cooling the cake*

CAKE
5 large eggs, separated
2 cups granulated sugar
¼ pound (1 stick) soft margarine
  (not reduced-fat)
8 tablespoons (½ cup) soft vegetable
  shortening, such as Crisco

2 teaspoons vanilla extract
1 cup buttermilk (nonfat is fine)
1 teaspoon baking soda
2 cups unbleached all-purpose flour
1 cup coarsely chopped pecans
2 cups shredded sweetened coconut

CREAM CHEESE FROSTING
6 ounces cream cheese, softened
6 tablespoons (¾ stick) softened
  margarine (not reduced-fat)

1 teaspoon vanilla extract
3 cups powdered sugar

1½ cups shredded sweetened coconut
  for sprinkling over the frosting

Mix the Cake

∾ Position an oven rack in the middle of the oven. Preheat the oven to 350°F. Butter the bottom, sides, and center tube of a 9½- or 10-inch fixed-bottom tube pan with at least 3¾-inch-high sides. Line the bottom with parchment or wax paper (see page 147) and butter the paper.

Have the egg whites ready in a clean, large bowl.

Put the granulated sugar, margarine, and vegetable shortening in a large bowl and beat with an electric mixer on medium speed until lightened in color and fluffy, about 3 minutes. Move the beaters around in the bowl if using a handheld electric mixer. Stop the mixer and scrape the mixture from the sides of the bowl and any that becomes caught in the beaters as needed throughout the mixing process. Add the egg yolks one at a time, beating for 1 minute after each addition. Stir in the vanilla to incorporate it. Put the buttermilk in a small bowl, add the baking soda, and stir them together gently just to dissolve the baking soda. Decrease the speed to low, and in 5 additions (3 flour, 2 buttermilk) add the flour and the buttermilk alternately, beginning and ending with the flour. Let each addition of milk and flour incorporate before adding another. The batter may look curdled after the milk additions. Scrape the sides of the bowl again after the last addition of flour. The batter will look smooth. Use a large spoon to stir in the pecans and coconut. Set the batter aside and immediately whip the egg whites.

Use an electric mixer with clean, dry beaters to beat the egg whites on medium-high speed until they look white, shiny, and smooth. As the egg whites become firm, the movement of the beaters begins to form lines in them. If you stop the mixer and lift up the beaters, the whites should cling to the beaters rather than drip off them. Remember to move the beaters around in the bowl if using a handheld electric mixer so the egg whites beat evenly. Pour about half the whipped egg whites over the reserved batter and use a rubber spatula to fold the egg whites into the batter by digging down to the bottom of the bowl with the rubber spatula and bringing the 2 mixtures up and over each other to combine them. This lightens the batter slightly, but it is not necessary to fold every bit of egg white in at this point. Pour over the remaining egg whites and fold them into the batter until thoroughly incorporated and no white streaks remain. Use the rubber spatula to scrape all of the batter into the prepared pan. Smooth the top.

Bake the Cake

↝ Bake for about 1 hour, just until a toothpick inserted in the center comes out dry or with a few moist crumbs clinging to it. The top of the cake will be firm and golden brown. Cool the cake in the pan for 20 minutes. Use a small sharp knife to loosen the cake from the sides and the center tube of the pan. Hold a serving plate on top of the cake in the pan and invert the cake onto the plate. Carefully remove and discard the paper lining the cake bottom. Place a wire rack on the bottom of the cake and invert the cake onto it. The cake is now right side up. Cool the cake thoroughly on the wire rack before frosting it, about 2 hours.

Make the Frosting

↝ Put the cream cheese, margarine, and vanilla in a large bowl and beat with an electric mixer on medium speed for about 1 minute until the mixture is smooth and the margarine and cream cheese are combined thoroughly. Move the beaters around in the bowl if using a handheld electric mixer. Decrease the speed to low and add the powdered sugar in 2 additions. Continue beating until the powdered sugar is incorporated and the frosting is smooth.

Frost the Cake

↝ Slide the cake onto a serving plate. Tuck waxed paper strips just an inch or so under the bottom of the cake all the way around to keep the plate clean. Use a thin metal spatula to spread the cream cheese frosting over the top and sides of the cake and inside the hole in the center. Sprinkle the shredded coconut thickly over the top. Let some random shreds fall onto the sides of the cake and press them onto the sides. Gently pull out the wax paper strips, while sliding a knife under the cake to avoid pulling out smears of frosting, and discard them.

Serve the Cake

↶ Cut the cake into slices and serve at room temperature. Cover leftover cake with plastic wrap and store it in the refrigerator for up to 3 days, but let it sit at room temperature for about 1 hour before serving.

The Groom's Lemon Cake

When my chocolate-loving daughter married her lemon-loving husband their wedding cake was all chocolate, so this was the cake that Laura's husband, Michael, chose for his groom's cake. In between the light-textured yellow cake layers is a quickly cooked lemon filling, and the outside of the cake is covered with an ivory-colored cream cheese frosting. For the wedding, I decorated the top with edible pastel royal icing flowers that I ordered from the New York Cake and Baking Center listed in Mail-Order Sources (page 384). A border of halved lemon slices arranged with fresh mint leaves or a sprinkling of lemon zest over the top also makes a nice decoration.

This large cake measures a majestic 4 inches high after it is filled and frosted. Although the finished cake has 4 layers, you need only to bake 2 layers and split them to make 4.

Baking Answers ↶ This light-textured butter cake is mixed by beating eggs and sugar to a thick, fluffy mass, then mixing in flour, warm milk, and melted butter. The structure of the cake develops from the thorough beating of eggs and sugar. The warm milk mixture helps to stabilize the beaten eggs. It would be very difficult to overbeat this egg and sugar mixture, so if in doubt as to whether it is sufficiently beaten, it is fine to continue beating for another minute or two. The purpose of the remainder of the mixing process is just to incorporate ingredients smoothly. The batter is thin and bakes into a cake with a fine grain.

Bottles labeled pure almond extract are made with oil of bitter almond and are preferable to bottles labeled almond extract. The pure version is now available in supermarkets.

Remember to grate the lemon zest from the lemon before squeezing the juice. For the zest, grate only the yellow skin of the lemon. The white pith is bitter and has no lemon flavor.

This cake has a tender, soft crumb, and crumbs can cling to the frosting as you spread it on the cake. To keep the frosting free of crumbs, frost the outside of this cake first with a thin crumb coat of frosting. This is a thin layer of frosting that is spread over the cake and prevents cake crumbs from adhering to the frosting. It acts like frosting glue to hold the cake crumbs on the cake. You will be able to see the cake through this thin layer of frosting. After spreading the crumb coat, spread the remaining frosting over the cake.

A Step Ahead ❧ The lemon filling needs to chill in the refrigerator for at least 3 hours, but it could also be prepared a day ahead, covered, and refrigerated overnight.

SERVES 12 TO 16

Necessities ❧ *Two 9-inch-diameter cake pans with 2-inch-high sides and 2 wire racks for cooling the cake layers*

YELLOW CAKE LAYERS	5 ounces (1¼ sticks) unsalted butter,
2½ cups unbleached all-purpose	cut into 10 pieces
flour	5 large eggs
2 teaspoons baking powder	2½ cups sugar
½ teaspoon salt	1 teaspoon vanilla extract
1¼ cups whole milk	¾ teaspoon pure almond extract

LEMON FILLING—	3 large egg yolks
MAKES ABOUT 2 CUPS	1½ cups sugar
¼ cup cornstarch	½ cup fresh lemon juice
1 cup water	1 teaspoon grated lemon zest

1 prepared recipe cream cheese	6 lemon slices, halved, and fresh
frosting for Hummingbird Cake	mint leaves, or 2 teaspoons grated
(pages 188–89)	lemon zest for garnishing the
	cake, optional

Mix the Cake

❧ Position a rack in the middle of the oven. Preheat the oven to 350°F. Butter the bottom and sides of two 9-inch-diameter cake pans with 2-inch-high sides. Line the bottom of each pan with parchment or wax paper and butter the paper.

Sift the flour, baking powder, and salt together onto a piece of wax paper or into a medium bowl and set aside.

Put the milk and butter in a small saucepan and heat over low heat until it is hot, about 150°F. if measured on a food thermometer. Do not let the milk mixture boil, and remove it from the heat if it becomes too hot. While the milk mixture is heating, put the eggs and sugar in a large bowl and beat with an electric mixer on high speed for about 3 minutes until the mixture is fluffy, thick, and lightened in color. Move the beaters around in the bowl if using a handheld electric mixer. Add the vanilla and almond extract, mixing just to blend them into the mixture. Add the flour mixture, mixing just until it is incorporated. Stop the mixer and scrape the batter from the sides of the bowl. Slowly add the hot milk mixture and continue mixing for about 30 seconds, until the mixture is smooth. The batter will be thin. Pour the batter into the prepared pans, dividing it evenly.

Bake the Cake

~ Bake about 40 minutes until the top feels firm when touched lightly and a toothpick inserted into the center of each cake layer comes out clean. Cool the layers for 10 minutes in the pans. Use a small sharp knife to loosen the sides of each cake from the pan. Place a wire rack on the top of each cake and invert the cakes onto each rack. Carefully remove the papers lining the cake bottoms and replace them loosely on each cake. Let the cake layers cool thoroughly with the top side down. Discard the paper liners. When cooled thoroughly, the cake layers are quite sturdy and easy to move around.

Cook the Filling

~ Stir the cornstarch and ½ cup of the water together in a small bowl until the cornstarch dissolves. Set aside.

Put the egg yolks, sugar, lemon juice, and remaining ½ cup water in a heavy 2-quart saucepan and whisk them together to blend them. Add the cornstarch mixture and whisk to blend it into the mixture.

Cook over low-medium heat just until the mixture is hot and the sugar dissolves, whisking slowly but constantly. The mixture will look opaque. Increase the heat to medium-high and bring to a boil, using a large spoon to stir the mixture constantly. Stir the mixture carefully where the bottom and sides of the pan meet to prevent burning. It will take about 6 minutes to come to the boil. Cook just until the mixture thickens and becomes clear. This is soon after the boil is reached. Remove from the heat. Pour the lemon filling through a strainer into a medium bowl. Discard any bits in the strainer. Stir in the lemon zest. Press a piece of plastic wrap onto the filling and poke a few holes in the plastic wrap with the tip of a knife or toothpick to let the steam escape. Refrigerate the filling for a least 3 hours or overnight until it is cold. The filling thickens further as it cools.

Fill and Frost the Cake

~ Place a serving plate over the bottom of 1 cake layer, and using the wire rack to hold the cake in place, invert the cake onto the serving plate. The top side of the cake layer will be up. Tuck waxed paper strips just an inch or so under the bottom of the cake all the way around to keep the plate clean. Use a long serrated knife to cut the cake layer horizontally into 2 even layers. Cut into the cake layer with the serrated knife, turning the cake as you cut through to the middle until you have cut through the cake layer. Use the removable bottom of a tart pan to lift up the top half of the cake layer and set it aside. Leaving a ½-inch plain edge, spread a scant ¾ cup of lemon filling over the cake. Slide the top half of the cake layer carefully over the lemon filling, centering it over the bottom layer, and spread it with another scant ¾ cup of lemon filling. Invert the second layer onto another plate or wire rack so it is top side up and cut it horizontally into 2 even layers. Use the tart pan bottom to lift up the top half of the cake layer and set it aside. Slide the bottom layer onto the filling and, leaving a ½-inch plain edge, spread the remaining lemon filling over the cake. Slide the remaining top half of the cake layer carefully onto the filling, centering it onto the cake. You will have 4 cake layers with 3 layers of filling.

Use a thin metal spatula to spread a thin layer of frosting over the top and sides of the cake so the cake crumbs adhere to the cake. You will see the cake through this thin layer of frosting. Spread a thick layer of frosting over the top of the cake, then spread the remaining frosting over the sides of the cake. Scrape the spatula clean on the edge of the bowl as you frost the cake to keep the frosting clean of any stray crumbs. Gently pull out the wax paper strips, while sliding a knife under the cake to avoid pulling out smears of frosting, and discard them. Then, arrange a border of halved lemon slices and fresh mint leaves, or sprinkle on grated lemon zest, if desired.

Serve the Cake

↶ Cut the cake into slices and serve at room temperature. Cover leftover cake with plastic wrap and store it in the refrigerator for up to 2 days, but let it sit at room temperature for about 30 minutes before serving.

Almond Angel Cake

The batter for this cake looks like a fluffy white cloud and bakes into a pure white, moist cake that has the unexpected bonus of having no fat. I drizzle the cake with an almond-flavored glaze, but a dusting of confectioners' sugar over the top works as well. Incidentally, it was this cake that convinced my editor to publish *Fearless Baking,* because it came out perfectly the first time she tried it, despite her history of problems with egg whites. Let's hope it makes a believer out of you, too.

Since this impressive cake is easy to transport and keeps well, it makes a good choice to carry to a potluck dinner or to take along on a picnic.

Baking Answers ❧ The lofty rise of this cake depends solely on carefully beaten egg whites. Beat the egg whites until they form a shiny, pure white mass that clings to the beaters if you stop the mixer and lift the beaters. If you scoop out a spoonful of perfectly beaten egg whites, the indentation remains in the whites in the bowl.

Use bottles labeled pure almond extract to give a clear almond flavor to the cake and glaze. There are special angel food cake pans with a center tube and a removable bottom, but a tube pan with a fixed bottom works fine. I line the fixed bottom with wax paper or parchment paper, but a pan with a removable bottom needs no liner. For directions on lining a tube pan with parchment or wax paper, see page 147.

Remember that this cake bakes in an ungreased pan. The cake climbs up the sides as it bakes and the ungreased pan helps the cake to rise slowly and hug the sides firmly. Nonstick pans should not be used.

Although delicate when warm, this large, light-textured cake is quite sturdy when cool. It must be inverted and cooled thoroughly before it is removed from the pan. To achieve good air circulation around the cooling cake, place the open tube of the cake pan over the narrow neck of a bottle. A wine bottle works well. Put the pan over the bottle before filling the pan to check to see that the pan fits easily over it. I use a filled bottle, which is less likely to tip over. The cake should remain snugly in the pan until it is loosened from the pan sides. If cooled on a wire rack, this cake could become soggy from the steam produced by being so close to the counter.

SERVES 12

Necessities ❧ *A 9½- or 10-inch-diameter tube pan with a fixed bottom or a removable bottom, not nonstick, with at least 3¾-inch-high sides, and a filled narrow-necked bottle for cooling the cake—the hole in the tube of the pan should fit over the neck of the bottle*

CAKE	1 teaspoon cream of tartar
1 cup cake flour	¼ teaspoon salt
1¾ cups granulated sugar	1 teaspoon vanilla extract
1¾ cups egg whites (about 11 large)	1 teaspoon pure almond extract

GLAZE	¼ cup whipping cream
1 cup powdered sugar	¾ teaspoon pure almond extract

Mix the Cake

☙ Position an oven rack in the middle of the oven. Preheat the oven to 325°F. Have ready a 9½- or 10-inch-diameter tube pan with at least 3¾-inch-high sides. If the pan does not have a removable bottom, line the bottom with parchment or wax paper. Have ready a narrow-necked bottle for cooling the baked cake.

Sift the cake flour and ¾ cup of the granulated sugar together. Set aside. Use an electric mixer on medium speed to beat the egg whites, cream of tartar, and salt in a large bowl on medium speed until they look foamy and the cream of tartar is dissolved, about 1 minute. Move the beaters around in the bowl if using a handheld electric mixer. Increase the speed to high and beat the egg whites until they look shiny and smooth and the movement of the beaters forms lines in the mixture, about 4 minutes. Move the beaters around in the bowl if using a handheld electric mixer. If you stop the mixer and lift up the beaters, the whites should cling to the beaters rather than drip off them. Slowly beat in the remaining 1 cup of granulated sugar, 2 tablespoons at a time about every 15 seconds, then beat the mixture for 1 minute. Add the vanilla and almond extract, mixing just to incorporate them. Reduce the speed to low and mix in the flour mixture by sprinkling ½-cup additions gently over the egg whites. Incorporate each addition of flour before adding more. Move the mixer around the bowl, giving it a few up-and-down movements, if using a handheld mixer, to incorporate all of the flour mixture. Pour the batter into the tube pan, using a rubber spatula to scrape out any batter that clings. Smooth the batter evenly in the pan.

Bake the Cake

☙ Bake about 50 minutes, until the top is golden and feels firm when gently pressed. Invert the pan onto a narrow-necked bottle to cool thoroughly, about 90 minutes. Remove the pan from the bottle, and run a thin knife around the sides and center tube of the pan to loosen the cake. Remove the cake from the pan by inverting it onto a flat serving plate. Discard any paper lining on the cake bottom. Turn the cake top side up on the serving plate. This now sturdy cake is easy to turn over on the plate.

Mix the Glaze

↬ Put the powdered sugar, cream, and almond extract in a small bowl and stir them together until smooth. Use a small spoon to drizzle the glaze over the top of the cake, letting some of the glaze drip down onto the cake sides.

Serve the Cake

↬ Use a serrated knife and a sawing motion to cut the cake into slices. Serve at room temperature. Cover the cake with plastic wrap and store at room temperature up to 3 days. Fresh strawberries, raspberries, or a mixture of berries, sweetened with sugar if desired, make a good accompaniment.

Chocolate Chiffon Cake

It has been more than 50 years since Harry Baker's "secret recipe" for orange chiffon cake starred at Hollywood parties. When he finally sold the recipe to the General Mills company, the cake turned out to be a combination of a light angel food cake batter and a moist sponge cake batter enriched with oil. Today, there is no secret to making a chiffon cake. It is as easy as combining a whipped egg-white mixture with a whipped egg-yolk mixture. Folding these two soft mixtures together is so pleasant that it makes me think of what it must be like to fold clouds together.

Chiffon cakes lend themselves to many flavorings, and this chocolate version replaces some of the flour with cocoa powder. The cocoa powder adds a bit more fat and richness to the cake plus a deep dark chocolate color. The top of the cake can be drizzled with swirls of chocolate glaze or simply dusted with a combination of powdered sugar and cocoa powder.

Baking Answers ↬ The process for mixing this cake is to beat the dry ingredients, oil, and egg yolks to a smooth, thick mixture that looks fluffy. You can relax when whipping this fluffy egg-yolk mixture, since a combination of fat and dry ingredients would be difficult to overwhip. If you are uncertain as to whether it has been beaten sufficiently, it is fine to continue beating for another minute or two.

On the other hand, the egg whites should be beaten to a shiny, pure white mass that clings to the beaters if you stop the mixer and lift the beaters. If you scoop out a spoonful of perfectly beaten egg whites, the indentation should remain. Begin adding the sugar just as the egg whites reach the soft-peak stage, adding it slowly to give the egg whites time to absorb it.

To fold these two mixtures together, stir some of the lighter egg-white mixture into the heavier egg-yolk mixture to lighten the heavier mixture. Add the remainder of the egg-white mixture and use a large rubber spatula to dig down to the bottom of the bowl and bring the 2 mixtures up and over each other. Using a large bowl and turning the bowl as you fold blends the mixtures quickly and easily.

Since the oil produces a heavier batter than an angel food cake does, chiffon cakes include baking powder to ensure a light texture and dependable rise.

Chiffon cakes cool upside down in their pans so they don't collapse under their own weight. While cooling, they should be held above the counter in some way to allow good air circulation. One method is to place the open tube of the cake pan over the narrow neck of a bottle. A wine bottle works well. Put the pan over the bottle before filling the pan to check to see that the pan fits easily over it. I use a filled bottle, which is less likely to tip over. Or, if your tube pan has several metal "feet" rising above its edges, this is sufficient to hold the chiffon cake above the counter. Occasionally, I have had a chiffon cake slip out of its ungreased pan while it is cooling. I think it's from the oil that is included in the batter, since this never happens to my angel food cakes. Not lining the bottom of the tube pan with paper deters a chiffon cake from slipping out of its pan. If it should fall out of the pan and onto the neck of the bottle, carefully remove it from the bottle and pan and continue cooling it. Remove the chiffon cake from its pan as soon as it feels cool and firm. It is only the warm cake that is delicate; once it cools, the cake is tender yet stable and fairly indestructible.

SERVES 12 TO 14

Necessities ❧ *A 9½- or 10-inch-diameter tube pan with a fixed bottom (not nonstick) and at least 3¾-inch-high sides, 2 large mixing bowls, a wire rack, and a filled narrow-necked bottle for cooling the cake—the hole in the tube of the pan should fit over the neck of the bottle*

CAKE	
1¾ cups cake flour	½ teaspoon salt
½ cup unsweetened Dutch process cocoa powder	½ cup canola or corn oil
1½ cups granulated sugar	7 large eggs, separated
1 teaspoon ground cinnamon	¾ cup water
2 teaspoons baking powder	2 teaspoons vanilla extract
	1 teaspoon cream of tartar

Mix the Cake

↪ Position an oven rack in the middle of the oven. Preheat the oven to 325°F. Have ready a 9½- or 10-inch fixed-bottom tube pan with at least 3¾-inch-high sides. Do not line the bottom of the pan with paper and do not use a nonstick pan.

Sift the cake flour, cocoa powder, 1 cup of the granulated sugar, cinnamon, baking powder, and salt into a large bowl. Use a large spoon to make an indentation in the center of the flour mixture and put in the oil, egg yolks, water, and vanilla. Beat with an electric mixer on medium speed until the mixture is smooth and thick, about 3 minutes. Move the beaters around in the bowl if using a handheld electric mixer. Stop the mixer and scrape the mixture from the sides of the bowl as needed. Set aside.

Put the egg whites and cream of tartar in a clean, large bowl and use an electric mixer with clean, dry beaters on medium speed to beat the egg whites until they are foamy and the cream of tartar is dissolved. Increase the speed to high and continue beating the egg whites until they look white, shiny, and smooth, and the movement of the beaters forms lines in the mixture. Move the beaters around in the bowl if using a handheld electric mixer. If you stop the mixer and lift up the beaters, the whites should cling to them. Slowly beat in the remaining ½ cup of granulated sugar, 2 tablespoons at a time about every 15 seconds, then beat the mixture for 1 minute. Use a rubber spatula to gently stir about one third of the egg whites into the yolk mixture. This lightens the batter slightly. Use a rubber spatula to fold in the remaining egg whites by digging down to the bottom of the bowl and bringing the 2 mixtures up and over each other until no white streaks of egg whites remain. Pour the batter into the tube pan, using the rubber spatula to scrape out any batter that clings. Smooth the top.

Bake the Cake

↪ Bake about 1 hour, until you can gently press your fingers on the top of the cake and it feels firm and any small cracks on the top look dry. Invert the pan onto a narrow-necked bottle to cool for 1 hour. Remove the pan from the bottle and run a thin knife around the sides and center tube of the pan to loosen the cake. Remove the cake from the pan by inverting it onto a flat serving plate; then place a wire rack on the bottom of the cake and invert the cake onto the rack. The cake is now right side up. Cool the cake thoroughly on the wire rack.

 ⌁ Use a small spoon to drizzle the chocolate glaze in swirling lines over the top of the cake, letting some glaze drip down the sides. Or, put the powdered sugar and cocoa powder mixture in a strainer and dust it evenly over the top of the cake. Slip a metal spatula under the cake and slide it onto a serving plate. The cake is sturdy and easy to move.

Use a serrated knife to cut the cake into slices, and serve at room temperature. The covered cake can be stored at room temperature for up to 3 days.

Almond Crunch and Chocolate Confetti Chiffon Cake

I f ever a cake was a pleasure to make and certain to make a grand impression, it's this towering chiffon cake. The almond-accented cake is flavored with almond liqueur, dripping with an almond glaze, and topped with crunchy sugar-coated almonds. The tiny bits of chocolate dotted throughout the cake make it exceptionally moist.

Baking Answers ⌁ The almonds for the topping bake with a coating of egg white and sugar. These nuts remain crisp for several days.

Bottles labeled pure almond extract are made with oil of bitter almond and are preferable to bottles labeled almond extract. The pure version is now available in most supermarkets.

I process miniature chocolate chips in the food processor to form the bits of finely chopped chocolate. Miniature chocolate chips process most easily into small crumbs of chocolate, but standard-size chocolate chips process almost as well.

Check the Baking Answers on page 250 for the Chocolate Chiffon Cake for information on mixing chiffon cakes.

A Step Ahead ⌁ The nuts can be baked up to 3 days ahead. Store the cooled nuts in a tightly sealed tin lined with wax paper.

SERVES 12 TO 14

Necessities ⌁ *A 9½- or 10-inch-diameter tube pan with a fixed bottom (not nonstick) and at least 3¾-inch-high sides, a nonstick baking sheet, 2 large mixing bowls, a wire rack, and a filled narrow-necked bottle for cooling the cake—the hole in the tube of the pan should fit over the neck of the bottle*

CRISP ALMOND TOPPING— MAKES ABOUT 1¼ CUPS	1¼ cups sliced almonds, blanched (page 40) or unblanched
1 large egg white	2 tablespoons granulated sugar

CAKE	7 large eggs, separated
1½ cups (9 ounces) miniature semisweet chocolate chips	⅔ cup water
2¼ cups cake flour	1 teaspoon vanilla extract
1½ cups granulated sugar	1 teaspoon pure almond extract
1 teaspoon baking powder	2 tablespoons amaretto liqueur (or almond-flavored liqueur)
½ teaspoon salt	½ teaspoon cream of tartar
½ cup canola or corn oil	

ALMOND GLAZE	¾ teaspoon pure almond extract
1½ cups powdered sugar	
3 to 4 tablespoons milk (any fat content)	

Make the Topping

❧ Position an oven rack in the middle of the oven. Preheat the oven to 325°F. Have ready an ungreased nonstick baking sheet.

Put the egg white in a medium bowl and beat it with a fork or whisk until foamy, about 30 seconds. Add the nuts and stir them with a large spoon until they are evenly coated with egg white. Sprinkle the sugar over the nuts and stir the mixture together. Spread the nuts in a single layer on the baking sheet. Bake 8 minutes. Stir the nuts with a wooden spoon to loosen them from the baking sheet. Bake 7 to 10 more minutes until the nuts look golden and dry. Remove the nuts from the oven and immediately stir the warm nuts to loosen them from the baking sheet. Cool the nuts on the baking sheet. The nuts become crisp as they cool. Set aside. Leave the oven on if you are ready to mix the cake batter.

Mix the Cake

❧ Position an oven rack in the middle of the oven and preheat the oven to 325°F., if this is not already done. Have ready a 9½- or 10-inch fixed-bottom tube pan with at least 3¾-inch-high sides. Do not line the bottom of the pan with paper.

Put the chocolate chips in a food processor. Process, beginning with a few on/off bursts, for about 20 seconds. Some of the chocolate chips will be finely grated, and some will form small chocolate crumbs. Set aside.

Sift the cake flour, 1 cup of the granulated sugar, baking powder, and salt into a large bowl. Use a large spoon to make an indentation in the center of the flour mixture and put in the oil, egg yolks, water, vanilla, almond extract, and amaretto. Beat with an electric mixer on medium speed until the mixture is smooth and thick, about 3 minutes. Move the beaters around in the bowl if using a handheld electric mixer. Stop the mixer and scrape the mixture from the sides of the bowl as needed. Use a rubber spatula to fold in the reserved chocolate pieces. Set aside.

Put the egg whites and cream of tartar in a clean, large bowl and use an electric mixer with clean, dry beaters on medium speed to beat the egg whites until they are foamy and the cream of tartar is dissolved. Increase the speed to high and continue beating the egg whites until they look white, shiny, and smooth, and the movement of the beaters forms lines in the mixture. Move the beaters around in the bowl if using a handheld electric mixer. If you stop the mixer and lift up the beaters, the whites should cling to them. Slowly beat in the remaining ½ cup of granulated sugar, 2 tablespoons at a time about every 15 seconds, then beat the mixture for 1 minute. Use a rubber spatula to gently stir about one third of the egg whites into the yolk mixture. This lightens the batter slightly. Use a rubber spatula to fold in the remaining egg whites by digging down to the bottom of the bowl and bringing the 2 mixtures up and over each other until no white streaks of egg whites remain. Pour the batter into the tube pan, using the rubber spatula to scrape out any batter that clings. Smooth the top.

Bake the Cake

❧ Bake about 1 hour, until you can gently press your fingers on the top of the cake and it feels firm and any small cracks on the top look dry. Invert the pan onto a narrow-necked bottle to cool for 1 hour. Remove the pan from the bottle and run a thin knife around the sides and center tube of the pan to loosen the cake. Remove the cake from the pan by turning it out onto a flat serving plate, then place a wire rack on the bottom of the cake and invert the cake onto the rack. The cake is now right side up. Cool the cake thoroughly on the wire rack.

Make the Glaze

❧ Put the powdered sugar in a small bowl. Stir in the milk and almond extract, adding enough milk to make a smooth glaze that has the consistency of a thick syrup. Reserve 2 tablespoons of the glaze. Spread the remaining glaze over the top of the cooled cake, letting it drip down the sides and into the center hole of the cake. Cover the top of the cake with glaze.

Add the Topping and Serve the Cake

❧ Spoon the reserved crisp almonds over the top of the cake, pressing them gently into the soft glaze. Drizzle the reserved 2 tablespoons of glaze over the almonds. This drizzle helps to hold the almonds together so they stay in place on the top of the cake. Slip a metal spatula under the cake and slide it onto a serving plate. The cake is sturdy and easy to move.

Use a serrated knife and a slight sawing motion to slice the cake. Serve at room temperature. The covered cake can be stored at room temperature for up to 3 days.

Coffee Lover's Layer Cake

My mom was famous for her beautiful sponge cakes, but they were quite a production to make. I can still picture her counter filled with bowls of whipped egg yolks, whipped egg whites, and the mound of flour that had to be carefully folded in at the end. Happily, these coffee sponge cake layers use a simpler method of beating whole eggs to produce the same type of light and airy cake that I remember.

The cake layers are filled with a soft coffee butter cream and covered with smooth coffee icing. Both filling and icing need no cooking and mix together quickly.

Baking Answers ❖ This sponge cake achieves its airy texture from the beating of whole eggs with sugar to a thick, fluffy mixture. It would be difficult to overbeat this mixture, and a minute or two of additional beating does no harm. The hot milk cooks the eggs slightly, stabilizes the fluffy batter, and consistently produces a moist yet light cake. This thin batter produces a fine-grained cake.

SERVES 12

Necessities ❖ *Two 9-inch-diameter cake pans with 2-inch-high sides and 2 wire racks for cooling the cake layers*

COFFEE SPONGE CAKE LAYERS
1¾ cups cake flour
1¼ teaspoons baking powder
¼ teaspoon salt
1 cup milk
6 large eggs

2 cups granulated sugar
1 teaspoon vanilla extract
1 tablespoon plus 1 teaspoon instant
   coffee granules dissolved in 1
   tablespoon plus 1 teaspoon water

COFFEE ICING	2 ounces (½ stick) unsalted
2 cups powdered sugar	butter
½ cup water	1 teaspoon instant coffee granules
2 tablespoons granulated sugar	dissolved in 1 teaspoon water

COFFEE FILLING	1 cup powdered sugar
4 ounces (1 stick) soft unsalted	1 teaspoon instant coffee granules
butter	dissolved in 1 teaspoon water

Mix the Cake

↪ Position a rack in the middle of the oven. Preheat the oven to 350°F. Butter the bottom and sides of two 9-inch-diameter cake pans with 2-inch-high sides. Line the bottom of each pan with parchment or wax paper and butter the paper.

Sift the flour, baking powder, and salt together onto a piece of wax paper or into a medium bowl and set aside.

Put the milk in a small saucepan and heat it over low heat until it is hot, about 150°F. if measured on a food thermometer. Do not let the milk boil, and remove it from the heat if it becomes too hot. While the milk is heating, put the eggs in a large bowl and beat them with an electric mixer on medium speed just to combine the yolks and whites. Move the beaters around in the bowl if using a handheld electric mixer.

Add the granulated sugar and beat on high speed for about 4 minutes until the mixture is fluffy, thickened, and lightened in color. Decrease the speed to low and add the vanilla and dissolved coffee, mixing to incorporate it. Add the flour mixture, mixing just until it is incorporated. Slowly add the hot milk and continue mixing for about 30 seconds, until the mixture is smooth. The batter will be thin. Use a rubber spatula to scrape all of the batter into the prepared pans, dividing it evenly. Wash and dry the saucepan so it is ready to cook the icing.

Bake the Cake

↪ Bake about 25 minutes until the top feels firm when touched lightly and a toothpick inserted in the center of each cake layer comes out clean. Cool the layers for 5 minutes in the pans. Use a small sharp knife to loosen the sides of each cake from the pan. Place a wire rack on the top of each cake and invert the cakes onto each rack. Carefully remove the papers lining the cake bottoms and replace them loosely on each cake. Let the cake layers cool thoroughly with the top side down. Discard the paper liners. The cooled cake layers are quite sturdy and easy to move around.

Mix the Icing

↶ Sift the powdered sugar into a large bowl. Set aside.

Put the water, granulated sugar, and butter in a small saucepan and cook over low heat until the sugar dissolves and the butter melts, stirring often. Increase the heat to medium-high, and boil the mixture for 3 minutes, stirring occasionally. Pour the hot mixture over the powdered sugar and add the dissolved coffee. Use a whisk to mix the icing smooth. It will be the color of coffee with milk. Refrigerate the icing until it is cool to the touch and firm enough to spread, about 1 hour. Make the filling while the icing cools.

Mix the Filling and Assemble the Cake

↶ Put the butter, powdered sugar, and dissolved coffee in a medium bowl and beat with an electric mixer on medium speed until smooth. Move the beaters around in the bowl if using a hand-held electric mixer. Place a serving plate on the bottom of 1 cake layer. Using the wire rack to hold the cake in place, invert the cake onto the serving plate. The top side of the cake layer will be up. Tuck waxed paper strips just an inch or so under the bottom of the cake all the way around to keep the plate clean. Use a thin metal spatula to spread the filling over the top of the cake layer. Turn the second cake layer top side up and lift it onto the filled cake layer. The sides of the 2 layers should line up evenly.

Use a clean thin metal spatula to spread the chilled icing smoothly over the top and sides of the cake. Gently pull out and discard the wax paper strips. Refrigerate the cake, uncovered, to firm the glaze, then cover the cake with plastic wrap and store in the refrigerator.

Serve the Cake

↶ Serve the cake cold or let it sit at room temperature for 1 hour before serving. Use a large knife to cut the cake into slices. The covered cake can be stored refrigerated for up to 3 days.

Tiramisù Ice Cream Loaf

Thanks to the popularity of the Italian dessert by the same name, the word "tiramisù" is now universally understood. This ice cream cake is a do-way-ahead take on the tiramisù theme. It has a loaf of coffee-soaked coffee sponge cake that is split horizontally into 4 layers and layered with coffee ice cream and sweetened mascarpone. The mascarpone mixture that is poured into the bottom of the loaf pan mold becomes the top of the ice cream cake when it is unmolded, and makes a smooth white creamy frosting on top of the frozen cake.

Baking Answers ❧ The cake used to make the loaf of cake for this tiramisù is a half recipe of the preceding coffee sponge layer. The full recipe (page 256) can be made into 2 loaves for 2 ice cream cakes or for storing 1 loaf in the freezer to use at a later date.

Loaf pans come in many sizes, but a pan that measures 9 x 5 x 3 inches and has an 8-cup capacity is a good size for this dessert. Bake the cake in the loaf pan, then clean the pan and use it as a mold to hold the ice cream cake. The split cake layers fit perfectly into the same pan where they baked. The assembled ice cream cake comes to just over the top of the pan.

Mascarpone is a rich, sweet Italian cream cheese that is usually sold in 8-ounce (1 cup) containers. It can be found in many supermarkets, Italian groceries, and specialty food shops in the dairy or fancy cheese section. Check the expiration date on the container to ensure that the mascarpone is fresh.

A Step Ahead ❧ One or two coffee sponge loaves can be baked up to 2 months ahead and frozen. Wrap the cooled loaves in plastic wrap then heavy aluminum foil, label with the date and contents, and freeze. Defrost the wrapped loaves at room temperature.

SERVES 10

Necessities ❧ *1 loaf pan with an 8-cup capacity that often measures 9 x 5 x 3 inches, 1 wire rack for cooling the loaf, and a pastry brush*

COFFEE SPONGE LOAF

¾ cup plus 2 tablespoons cake flour

¾ teaspoon baking powder

⅛ teaspoon salt

½ cup milk

3 large eggs

1 cup granulated sugar

½ teaspoon vanilla extract

2 teaspoons instant coffee granules
dissolved in 2 teaspoons water

COFFEE SYRUP

2 teaspoons instant decaffeinated
espresso (or coffee) granules

1 tablespoon granulated sugar

¼ cup warm water

¼ cup Kahlúa or coffee-flavored
liqueur

MASCARPONE CREAM—
MAKES ABOUT 2 CUPS

1 cup cold mascarpone

½ cup cold whipping cream

½ cup powdered sugar

½ teaspoon vanilla extract

1 tablespoon Kahlúa or coffee-
flavored liqueur

2 pints coffee ice cream, softened
until spreadable but not melted

Mix the Cake

❧ Position a rack in the middle of the oven. Preheat the oven to 350°F. Butter the bottom and sides of a loaf pan with an 8-cup capacity. Line the bottom of the pan with parchment or wax paper and butter the paper.

Sift the flour, baking powder, and salt together onto a piece of wax paper or into a medium bowl and set aside.

Put the milk in a small saucepan and heat it over low heat until it is hot, about 150°F. if measured on a food thermometer. Do not let the milk boil, and remove it from the heat if it becomes too hot. While the milk is heating, put the eggs in a large bowl and beat with an electric mixer on medium speed just to combine the yolks and whites. Add the granulated sugar and beat on high speed for about 4 minutes until the mixture is fluffy, thickened, and lightened in color. Move the beaters around in the bowl if using a handheld electric mixer. Decrease the speed to low and add the vanilla and dissolved coffee, mixing to incorporate them. Add the flour mixture, mixing just until it is incorporated. Slowly add the hot milk and continue mixing for about 30 seconds, until the mixture is smooth. The batter will be thin. Use a rubber spatula to scrape all of the batter into the prepared pan.

Bake the Cake

◦ Bake about 35 minutes until the top feels firm when touched lightly and a toothpick inserted in the center of the cake comes out clean or with a few crumbs clinging to it. Cool the loaf for 5 minutes in the pan. Use a small sharp knife to loosen the sides of the cake from the pan. Place a wire rack on the top of the cake and invert it onto the rack. Carefully remove the paper lining the cake bottom and replace it loosely on the cake. Let the loaf cool thoroughly with the top side down. Discard the paper liner. Wash and dry the loaf pan.

Cut a long piece of parchment or wax paper that is long enough to fit the bottom and overlap the ends of the now clean loaf pan that was used to bake the cake. Press the paper strip into the bottom and drape it over the ends of the pan. Set aside.

Mix the Syrup

◦ Stir the instant coffee, granulated sugar, and warm water in a small bowl until the coffee and sugar dissolve. Stir in the Kahlúa. Set aside.

Mix the Cream and Assemble the Loaf

◦ Put the mascarpone, whipping cream, powdered sugar, vanilla, and Kahlúa in a medium bowl, and use a whisk to blend them smoothly together. Pour 1 cup of the mascarpone mixture into the bottom of the paper-lined loaf pan and refrigerate it. Cover and refrigerate the remaining mixture for about 1 hour, until it thickens slightly. Before it is chilled, the mascarpone mixture is quite liquid and pours easily. You will have a scant cup remaining.

Use a large serrated knife to cut the cooled loaf into 4 horizontal layers. The loaf is about 2 inches high, so each layer will be about ½ inch thick. Use the knife to mark the 4 layers, then begin your cuts at each mark. Brush one side of each of the 4 layers generously with the reserved coffee syrup. Remove the prepared loaf pan and remaining mascarpone mixture from the refrigerator. Carefully place 1 layer, syrup side up, on the cold mascarpone layer in the pan. Spread 1 pint of coffee ice cream evenly over the cake, spreading it to the edges. Place a second cake layer, syrup side down, on the ice cream. Pour the remaining cold mascarpone mixture evenly over the cake, spreading it evenly if necessary. Place a third cake layer, syrup side up, on the mascarpone. Spread the remaining 1 pint of ice cream evenly over the cake. Place the fourth cake layer, syrup side down, on the ice cream. The loaf has 2 layers of mascarpone, 2 layers of ice cream, and 4 layers of cake. Cover with plastic wrap and heavy aluminum foil and freeze the loaf firm, at least 5 hours or up to 1 week.

Serve the Loaf

◦ Remove the ice cream loaf in its pan from the freezer and unwrap it. Use a small sharp knife to loosen the cake from the sides of the pan. Place a serving plate on top of the loaf and invert it.

Dip a dish towel in hot water and wring out the water. Hold the hot towel around the sides of the pan for about 20 seconds. Release the ice cream loaf from the pan by pulling on the ends of the paper and removing the pan. Remove the paper and discard it. The top of the ice cream cake has a gorgeous smooth layer of mascarpone cream. Let the ice cream loaf soften at room temperature for about 15 minutes or until it is easy to slice. The softening time depends on how cold your freezer is and how warm the room is. The cake insulates the ice cream and the ice cream keeps the cake cold, so it is important to allow time for the cake and ice cream to soften before serving. Use a large sharp knife to cut the cake into generous ¾-inch slices and serve. Cover tightly and return any leftover ice cream cake to the freezer before melting occurs.

Coconut, Fig, and Pecan Cake with Fluffy White Frosting

Snow-white swirls of billowy, marshmallow-like frosting surround this big festive cake. The 2 white cake layers are split to make 4 layers, so the cake can hold plenty of the sticky fruit and nut filling. Toasted coconut pressed onto the sides of the cake accentuates the pure white frosting.

Baking Answers ❧ Since white cake batters include egg whites but no egg yolks, they have a pure white color and light texture. This white cake uses 6 egg whites and the frosting uses 3 egg whites. The filling calls for only 4 egg yolks, so you will end up with an egg-yolk surplus. Making The Groom's Lemon Cake (page 244) is a good way to use up some of the remaining egg yolks. If you have egg whites in the freezer (page 24), they can be defrosted and used in this cake. The egg whites for the cake are beaten to soft peaks then folded into the cake batter. This adds to the lightness of the cake.

The egg yolks, sugar, butter, and cream for the creamy custard–type filling cook gently in a heatproof container over simmering water until they thicken. The cooking should stop as soon as the custard thickens. The easiest way to know if it is done is to check with a food thermometer. When the thermometer registers 180°F., the mixture will have thickened to a thin puddinglike consistency and will be ready. Another test is to dip a spoon in the hot mixture and run your finger down the back of the spoon; when the sauce is thickened sufficiently, a path remains. Cooking the filling in a pan over hot water is a gentle method of cooking that prevents the egg yolks from overheating and possibly curdling the mixture. This light-textured custard mixture does not contain cornstarch or flour as a thickening agent and should not boil. Boiling would curdle it.

The frosting is an old-fashioned 7-minute frosting that calls for cooking a sugar-and-egg-white mixture while it is being beaten in a heatproof container over hot water. This frosting is done in about 7 minutes after it increases in volume and becomes fluffy and firm enough to hold its shape. The egg whites cook gently as the beaters whip air into them, and the result is soft and stable like meringue. This is a foolproof preparation that dissolves the sugar during the beating to produce a smooth-as-silk frosting that's a pleasure to spread over any cake.

A food thermometer is useful for measuring the temperature of the custard filling during cooking and the temperature of the frosting when it is beaten after it cooks.

Bottles labeled pure almond extract are made with oil of bitter almond and are preferable to bottles labeled almond extract. The pure version is now available in supermarkets.

SERVES 12 TO 14

Necessities ◈ *Two 9-inch-diameter cake pans with 2-inch-high sides, 2 wire racks for cooling the cake layers, a 2-quart capacity double boiler or a 2-quart capacity heatproof container that can sit firmly on top of a pot of simmering water for cooking the filling and later the frosting, a baking sheet, and a handheld electric mixer for beating the frosting while it cooks*

WHITE CAKE LAYERS

2¾ cups cake flour
2 teaspoons baking powder
¼ teaspoon salt
6 ounces (1½ sticks) soft unsalted
    butter
2 cups sugar
¾ cup whole milk
¾ cup water
2 teaspoons vanilla extract
½ teaspoon pure almond extract
6 large egg whites

FRUIT AND NUT FILLING

4 large egg yolks
1 cup sugar
6 tablespoons (¾ stick) unsalted
    butter, room temperature
½ cup whipping cream
2 tablespoons bourbon
1 teaspoon vanilla extract
2⅔ cups (one 7-ounce package)
    sweetened shredded coconut,
    toasted (page 40)
1 cup toasted pecans (page 40),
    coarsely chopped
1¼ cups dried figs (about 6 ounces),
    stemmed and chopped

7-MINUTE FROSTING

1¼ cups sugar
⅓ cup water
3 large egg whites
¼ teaspoon cream of tartar
1 teaspoon vanilla extract
½ teaspoon pure almond extract

Mix the Cake

✏ Position a rack in the middle of the oven. Preheat the oven to 350°F. Butter the bottoms and sides of two 9-inch-diameter cake pans with 2-inch-high sides. Line the bottom of each pan with parchment or wax paper and butter the paper.

Sift the flour, baking powder, and salt together onto a piece of wax paper or into a medium bowl and set aside.

Put the butter and sugar in a large bowl and beat with an electric mixer on medium speed until lightened in color and fluffy, about 3 minutes. Move the beaters around in the bowl if using a handheld electric mixer. Stop the mixer and scrape the mixture from the sides of the bowl and any that becomes caught in the beaters as needed throughout the mixing process. Put the milk, water, vanilla, and almond extract in a small bowl and stir together. Decrease the speed to low, and in 5 additions (3 flour, 2 milk) add the flour mixture and the milk mixture alternately, beginning and ending with the flour mixture. Let each addition of milk or flour incorporate before adding the next. The batter may look curdled after the milk additions. Scrape the sides of the bowl again after the last addition of flour. The batter will look smooth. Set aside while you beat the egg whites.

Put the egg whites in a clean, large bowl and use an electric mixer with clean, dry beaters on high speed to beat the egg whites until they look white, shiny, and smooth, and the movement of the beaters forms lines in the mixture. Move the beaters around in the bowl if using a handheld electric mixer. If you stop the mixer and lift up the beaters, the whites should cling to them. Use a rubber spatula to gently stir about one third of the egg whites into the reserved batter to lighten the batter slightly. Use the rubber spatula to fold in the remaining egg whites by digging down to the bottom of the bowl and bringing the 2 mixtures up and over each other until no white streaks of egg whites remain. Pour the batter into the prepared pans, dividing it evenly. Use the rubber spatula to scrape out any batter that clings to the bowl. Smooth the top.

Bake the Cake

✏ Bake for about 35 minutes, until the top feels firm when touched lightly and a toothpick inserted into the center of the cake comes out clean. Lower the oven temperature to 300°F. for toasting the coconut.

Cool the cakes in their pans for 10 minutes. Use a small sharp knife to loosen the cakes from the sides of each pan. Place a wire rack on the top of each cake and invert the cakes onto it. Carefully remove the papers lining the cake bottoms and replace them loosely on each cake. Let the cake layers cool thoroughly with the top side down. Discard the paper liners.

Cook the Filling

~ Put the egg yolks, sugar, butter, and whipping cream in a heatproof container and place it over barely simmering water. Cook the mixture, stirring constantly, for about 10 minutes, until it thickens and reaches 180°F. if tested with a food thermometer. If a spoon is dipped in the custard, it will coat the spoon and leave a path on the back of the spoon if you run your finger down it. Remove the container from over the water. Strain the custard into a medium bowl. Stir in the bourbon, vanilla, 1 cup of the toasted coconut, toasted pecans, and chopped figs. Cover and refrigerate until it is thick enough to spread on the cake, about 20 minutes.

Fill the Cake

~ Place a serving plate on the bottom of 1 cake layer. Using the wire rack to hold the cake in place, invert the cake onto the serving plate. The top side of the cake layer will be up. Tuck strips of waxed paper just an inch or so under the bottom of the cake all the way around to keep the plate clean. Use a long serrated knife to cut the cake layer horizontally into 2 even layers. Cut into the cake layer with the serrated knife, turning the cake as you cut through to the middle until you have cut through the cake layer. Use the removable bottom of a tart pan to lift the top half of the cake layer and set it aside. Leaving a ½-inch edge bare, spread a third of the filling, a generous ¾ cup, over the cake. Slide the top layer carefully onto the filling and repeat with another third of the filling. Invert the second layer and cut it horizontally into 2 even layers. Use the tart pan bottom to lift up the top of the layer and set it aside. Slide the bottom layer onto the filling and, leaving a ½-inch edge bare, spread the remaining filling over the cake. Slide the remaining top layer carefully onto the filling. Refrigerate the cake while you prepare the frosting.

Cook the Frosting

~ Put the sugar, water, egg whites, and cream of tartar in a heatproof container or the top of a double boiler with at least a 2-quart capacity and beat with a handheld electric mixer on high speed for 1 minute, until it is opaque white and foamy. Put the mixture in the container over, but not touching, a saucepan of barely simmering water and beat on high speed for about 7 minutes. At this time, the motion of the beaters should form lines in the mixture, and a soft point or peak forms if you stop the beaters and lift them out of the mixture. The egg-white container should sit firmly on and should not wobble over the pan of hot water. Be sure to keep the electric mixer cord away from the burner. Move the beaters around in the heatproof container, lowering the heat if the water begins to boil. If you lift up the beaters before the frosting is ready, a point forms and immediately flops over. If you stop mixing and the frosting is ready, the pattern of lines remains in the mixture. The mixture registers about 165°F. if measured with a food thermometer and has increased in volume to about 5½ cups. Remove the container of frosting from over the water. Immediately add the vanilla and almond extract and continue beating for 2 minutes more to slightly cool and thicken the frosting further. The mixture will now register about 120°F. if measured with a food thermometer.

Use a thin metal spatula to spread the frosting generously over the top and sides of the filled cake. Dip a spatula or spoon gently into the frosting and lift it to form swirls. Press the remaining 1⅔ cups of toasted coconut onto the sides of the cake. Gently pull out the wax paper strips from under the cake and discard them.

Serve the Cake

↦ Serve the cake or cover it carefully and refrigerate it up to 2 days. Placing a few toothpicks carefully on top of the cake before covering it with plastic wrap protects the frosting, but a large plastic cake cover is ideal for covering the soft frosting. Once the cake has been refrigerated, serve it cold rather than bringing it to room temperature.

Orange Meringue Ice Cream Cake

Remember those vanilla ice cream pops covered with orange sherbet when you were a kid? This ice cream cake takes the same refreshing combination and turns it into a fancy ice cream dessert. It has a crisp nest-shaped meringue shell that holds the scoops of vanilla ice cream and brightly colored orange sauce. Even when frozen, the orange sauce remains soft and the meringue has a melt-in-your-mouth consistency. The whole cake can be prepared and frozen days ahead of time so it is ready to serve at a moment's notice. Since the ice cream softens while the cake is put together, the cake should be assembled at least 5 hours before it is served to allow time for the ice cream to firm up. This ice cream cake is a cool idea to serve for a spring party or a warm summer evening.

Baking Answers
↦ A basic meringue mixture requires only 2 ingredients—egg whites and sugar. Cream of tartar is usually added to stabilize the egg whites, and such flavorings as vanilla extract, ground nuts, or citrus zest can also be included but are not essential. The mixing process for meringues calls for beating the egg whites to soft peaks, then adding sugar slowly to form the meringue. The egg whites are beaten until they are shiny and form a soft point or peak if you dip a spoon or the beater into the egg whites and lift it out. At this point begin beating in the sugar, but

add it slowly so that the egg whites have time to absorb it. This takes a bit of patience, but it is important to give the sugar time to dissolve. Once the sugar is absorbed, add any flavorings, then spread the meringue mixture on a baking sheet into the desired shape.

Baking a crisp meringue is actually a drying-out process of long, slow baking. As the moisture evaporates during baking, the meringue becomes dry and crisp. Although the baked meringues feel dry on the outside, the interiors become firm only after they cool. Since humidity puts moisture back into crisp meringues and softens them, they should be stored in a dry place. When the weather is humid, I usually wrap the meringues and put them in the freezer until I am ready to use them.

Remember to grate the orange zest from the orange before squeezing the juice. For the zest, grate only the orange skin of the orange. The white pith is bitter and has no orange flavor.

A Step Ahead ❧ In addition to assembling the whole cake ahead of time, the meringue nest can be baked, cooled, and stored in the freezer for up to 1 month. To freeze the meringue, place it on a cardboard cake circle or plate to support it and carefully wrap it with plastic wrap then heavy aluminum foil. Put the meringue in a safe place in the freezer where it will not get moved around or broken. It is not necessary to defrost the meringue before filling it.

The orange sauce can be prepared a day ahead, covered, and refrigerated overnight

It is nice but not essential to have an ice cream scoop or spade. Using a scoop fills the meringue shell with round balls, while a spade makes appealing mounds of ice cream in the shell. A large spoon does the job if that is all that is available.

Kitchen Experiments ❧ I wanted to check to see if there was a notable difference in volume in egg whites if they were at room temperature or were cold when they were beaten. Using the same handheld electric mixer to beat each mixture, I tried making separate meringue mixtures with room-temperature egg whites and with cold ones. After measuring the volume of both mixtures of beaten egg whites before adding the sugar and after adding the sugar, I found no noticeable difference in the volume of the 2 mixtures. Both measured as 4 cups of meringue mixture after the sugar was beaten into them. I used a ceramic mixing bowl to beat the egg whites. A copper bowl might have increased their volume, but I don't own one, and the fluffy mixture that I produced in either mixture was satisfactory to me.

SERVES 10

Necessities ❧ *1 heavyweight baking sheet; an ice cream scoop or spade is useful*

VANILLA MERINGUE	1 cup sugar
3 large egg whites	½ teaspoon vanilla extract
¼ teaspoon cream of tartar	

ORANGE SAUCE— MAKES ABOUT 1¾ CUPS	¾ cup sugar
	¾ cup fresh orange juice
2 tablespoons cornstarch	2 tablespoons fresh lemon juice
¾ cup water	2 teaspoons grated orange zest
3 large egg yolks	

2 pints vanilla ice cream

Mix the Meringue

➤ Position an oven rack in the middle of the oven. Preheat the oven to 250°F. Line a baking sheet with parchment paper. Butter the paper lightly and dust it with powdered sugar. With the tip of a dull knife and pressing lightly, mark one 9-inch circle on the parchment paper. A 9-inch round cake pan makes a good guide to use for marking the circle.

Put the egg whites and cream of tartar in a clean, large bowl and use an electric mixer with clean, dry beaters on medium speed to beat the egg whites until they are foamy and the cream of tartar is dissolved, about 15 seconds. Increase the speed to high and continue beating the egg whites until they look white, shiny, and smooth, and the movement of the beaters forms lines in the mixture, about 30 seconds. Move the beaters around in the bowl if using a handheld electric mixer. If you stop the mixer and lift up the beaters, the whites should cling to them. Slowly beat in the sugar, 1 tablespoon every 15 seconds, beating for another 15 seconds after the last addition of sugar. I time the seconds when adding the sugar, so I don't have a tendency to rush the additions. Stir in the vanilla. The tiny bubbles that were visible before the sugar was added have disappeared and the mixture is silken smooth and soft yet firm in texture. It looks like whipped marshmallow.

Put a dab of meringue on the baking sheet underneath each corner of the parchment paper to hold the paper in place. Drop large spoonfuls of the meringue mixture over the marked circle. Use a thin metal spatula to spread the mixture over the circle. Then use the metal spatula or the back of a spoon to sweep the meringue from the center out to build up a raised rim around the edge of the circle. Make the edge 1¼ to 1½ inches high and about 1 inch wide across the top. Inside this rim the thickness of the center of the meringue is only about ¼ inch. You will have a large meringue shell shaped like a round nest.

Bake the Meringue

✶ Bake for 1 hour and 30 minutes. The meringue feels crisp on top and is lightly colored. Turn off the oven and leave the meringue in the turned-off oven for 30 minutes. Remove from the oven and let it cool thoroughly on the baking sheet, about 1½ hours. Cook the orange sauce while the meringue bakes and cools.

Cook the Sauce

✶ Put the cornstarch and water in a small bowl and stir them together until the cornstarch dissolves. Set aside. Put the egg yolks, sugar, orange juice, and lemon juice in a heavy 2-quart saucepan and whisk them together to blend them. Add the cornstarch mixture and use the whisk to blend it into the mixture. Cook over low-medium heat just until the mixture is hot and the sugar dissolves, whisking slowly but constantly, about 4 minutes. Increase the heat to medium-high and bring to a boil, using a large spoon to stir the mixture constantly. Stir the mixture carefully where the bottom and sides of the pan meet to prevent burning. It will take about 5 minutes to come to the boil. Cook just until the mixture thickens, which is soon after it boils. It will be a thick syrup. Remove the pan from the heat. Pour the orange sauce through a strainer into a medium bowl. Discard any bits in the strainer. Stir the orange zest into the sauce. Press a piece of plastic wrap onto the sauce and poke a few holes in the plastic wrap with the tip of a knife to let the steam escape. Refrigerate the sauce for at least 1½ hours or overnight, until the sauce is cool to the touch. The sauce thickens further as it cools.

Assemble the Cake

✶ Put the cooled meringue shell on a cardboard cake circle or flat serving plate. Drizzle about ½ cup of the cooled orange sauce over the bottom of the meringue shell. Use an ice cream scoop, ice cream spade, or large spoon to gently fill the meringue with round balls or large clumps of ice cream. Any pattern of ice cream looks attractive when the sauce is added. Place the ice cream carefully in the meringue without pressing down hard on the meringue, so as not to break the meringue shell. Spoon the cool orange sauce over the ice cream, letting it drip down between the scoops of ice cream to fill the crevices. Drizzle a few thin lines of sauce over the thick edges of the meringue shell. Freeze the cake about 30 minutes to firm the orange sauce, then cover the cake tightly with plastic wrap and heavy aluminum foil. Label with the date and contents. Freeze at least 5 hours or up to 1 week.

Serve the Cake

✶ Use a large, sharp knife to cut the frozen cake into slices. If your freezer is quite cold (around 0°F.), the ice cream cake needs to soften for about 10 minutes at room temperature, until it is easy to cut. Cover and return any leftover cake to the freezer before melting occurs.

Variations ✧ *The baked meringue shell is a great component to have in the freezer. It can be filled with many combinations of ice cream and sauce. For example, coffee or peppermint ice cream with old-fashioned hot fudge sauce (page 418), or raspberry or strawberry ice cream with the above orange sauce. Or, fill the meringue with berries, strawberries and fresh pineapple, sliced peaches and raspberries, or any fresh seasonal fruit combination. Cover the fruit-filled meringue with sweetened whipped cream (pages 339–40). Once it is filled with fruit, the meringue should be served.*

Mom's Lemon Meringue Pie

L emon meringue pie is our traditional Thanksgiving dessert. My grandmother Sophie always served it, then my mother, and now I carry on the tradition. Although our other Thanksgiving pie choices change from year to year, lemon meringue is always at the top of the list. If you stop and think about it, a refreshing lemon pie makes the perfect ending to a big holiday feast. Those moms and grandmoms knew what was good.

Baking Answers ✧ The piecrust is baked completely before it is filled, then the warm filling and meringue topping are added and the pie bakes for a short time to cook and brown the meringue. The filling should be warm when the meringue topping is spread over it. If the filling is cold when the meringue topping is added, the meringue could slide right off the filling when the slices are cut.

When making the lemon filling, cook the water, egg yolks, sugar, and lemon juice together just to dissolve the sugar. At this point the mixture should not boil, as it could curdle. Once the dissolved cornstarch mixture is added, the starch stabilizes the mixture so it can be brought to the boil and thickened without worrying about curdling.

Remember to grate the lemon zest for the filling from the lemon before squeezing the juice. For the zest, grate only the yellow skin of the lemon. The white pith is bitter and has no lemon flavor.

Using about 1 tablespoon of sugar per egg white for the topping produces a very soft meringue mixture that cooks quickly and remains soft after it bakes. Beat the sugar slowly into the egg whites to allow the sugar time to dissolve.

My mother uses a 9-inch-diameter Pyrex glass pie dish that is just under 2 inches deep for this pie. It is the one that has indentations around the edge for an aid in crimping the crust edge. I prefer using ovenproof glass or ceramic pie dishes when making a pie with an acidic filling such as this one.

Necessities ↝ *One 1-crust recipe Fearless Pie Crust (page 199), unbaked, cold and refrigerated, in a 9-inch ovenproof glass or ceramic pie pan*

1-crust unbaked cold Fearless Piecrust (page 199) in a 9-inch ovenproof glass or ceramic pie pan that is 1¾ to 2 inches deep, and metal pie weights or 2½ cups dried beans

LEMON FILLING	1¾ cups sugar
⅓ cup cornstarch	½ cup fresh lemon juice
1½ cups water	2 teaspoons grated lemon zest
5 large egg yolks	

SOFT MERINGUE TOPPING	½ teaspoon cream of tartar
5 large egg whites	⅓ cup sugar

Bake the Crust

↝ Position a rack in the bottom third of the oven. Preheat the oven to 375°F. Line the prepared crust with heavy aluminum foil or a double layer of standard foil, pressing the aluminum foil gently over the edges of the pie pan. Fill the aluminum foil with about 2½ cups of dried beans or metal pie weights. Check to see that the weights evenly cover the entire bottom of the crust. The weights should make a thick layer over the bottom, but they do not have to come to the top of the pan. Bake the crust for 10 minutes. Protect your hands with potholders and carefully remove the aluminum foil by lifting it and the beans or pie weights from the crust. Set them aside to cool and store for another use. Prick the piecrust in about 6 places with a fork. Bake the uncovered crust for about 12 more minutes until the crust is golden. Remove the crust from the oven and set aside while you prepare the filling. Reduce the oven temperature to 325°F.

Cook the Filling

↝ Stir the cornstarch and ½ cup of the water together in a small bowl until the cornstarch dissolves. Set aside.

Put the egg yolks, sugar, lemon juice, and remaining 1 cup water in a heavy 2-quart saucepan and whisk them together to blend them. Cook over low-medium heat just until the mixture is hot and the sugar dissolves, whisking slowly but constantly. Stir the mixture carefully where the bottom and sides of the pan meet to prevent burning. Do not boil the mixture. Add the cornstarch mixture, increase to medium heat, and bring to a boil, using a large spoon to stir the mixture constantly. It will take about 6 minutes to come to the boil. Boil for up to 1 minute, or until the mixture thickens and looks clear. The mixture thickens soon after the boil is reached. Remove from the heat. Stir in the lemon zest. Set aside while you immediately prepare the meringue topping.

Make the Topping

↶ Put the egg whites and cream of tartar in a clean, large bowl and use an electric mixer with clean, dry beaters on medium speed to beat the egg whites until they are foamy and the cream of tartar is dissolved, about 15 seconds. Increase the speed to high and continue beating the egg whites until they look white, shiny, and smooth, and the movement of the beaters forms lines in the mixture, about 30 seconds. Move the beaters around in the bowl if using a handheld electric mixer. If you stop the mixer and lift up the beaters, the whites should cling to them. Slowly beat in the sugar, 1 tablespoon every 15 seconds, beating for about 30 seconds after the last addition of sugar.

Assemble and Bake the Pie

↶ Pour the warm lemon filling into the baked crust. Use a rubber spatula to scrape the meringue mixture from the bowl and use a thin metal spatula to spread the meringue over the warm filling, mounding it toward the center and spreading it to seal the crust at the edges. Swirl the meringue slightly by dipping the metal spatula gently into the meringue and lifting it to form swirls. Bake for about 20 minutes, until the top is evenly golden. Cool 1 hour at room temperature. Cover loosely with plastic wrap and refrigerate.

Serve the Pie

↶ Serve cold. This pie is best served the day it is baked, but it can be prepared up to 1 day ahead.

Baking
with Chocolate

CHOCOLATE CUPCAKES THICK WITH FUDGE FROSTING, CHOCOLATE CAKE LOADED WITH CHOCOLATE CHIPS, CHOCOLATE-PACKED BROWNIES, AND A SMALLER VERSION OF MY DAUGHTER'S CHOCOLATE WEDDING CAKE ALL DEPEND ON EXTRAVAGANT quantities of chocolate. If you are in need of a chocolate immersion, these are the desserts you want to try. Since all of them include some form of melted chocolate, the emphasis here is on the process of melting chocolate and how to incorporate it smoothly into cakes, frostings, fillings, and brownies.

Melted unsweetened, semisweet, and white chocolate and cocoa powder are used in this chapter, and milk chocolate is included in another chapter in the filling for the Two-for-One Hazelnut Lace Cookie Sandwiches or Stacks (page 359). Deciding whether or not one type of chocolate can be substituted for another is simple. Since unsweetened chocolate contains no sugar, it cannot be substituted for semisweet or bittersweet chocolate. However, the more common semi-sweet chocolate that I use in most of my recipes can be replaced by the less sweet bittersweet chocolate. White or milk chocolate used as chunks or chips can replace dark chocolate in a recipe, but when melted chocolate is specified in a cake or frosting, do not substitute milk or white for dark chocolate.

White and milk chocolate should be stored in the refrigerator or freezer so the milk solids in them do not turn rancid, but dark and unsweetened chocolate are fine stored in a cool, dark place. Chocolate has a great affinity for picking up odors, so be sure to wrap all chocolate well before storing it. I use Dutch process cocoa powder because it has been treated with an alkali that darkens the color and mellows the flavor. If you are unsure about whether chocolate or cocoa powder is fresh, taste it. If it is fresh, it will have a pleasant and definite chocolate taste.

Slow and low is what chocolate likes when it is melting. A low, gentle heat source that melts the chocolate slowly is ideal. When melting chocolate, you want to melt the cocoa butter but not the sugar in the chocolate. Cocoa butter is one of the few fats that is solid at room temperature and will not soften, as butter will, if left at room temperature. At 92°F. cocoa butter, and in turn choco-late, begins to melt. When it reaches body temperature (98.6°F.), the chocolate melts, and it should be completely melted by the time the temperature of the chocolate reaches 113°F. At higher tem-peratures, the sugar in chocolate begins to melt and burn, which in turn causes the chocolate to become grainy and lumpy during the melting process. If this happens and the chocolate becomes grainy, it is necessary to discard the chocolate and begin again. To avoid this, chop the chocolate into small pieces, which will allow it to melt evenly. Otherwise, the outside of a large piece of chocolate could become too hot and turn grainy before the inside even melts. Stirring chocolate and other ingredients together during melting also makes for a smooth, creamy result. Chocolate does not like sudden temperature changes. When melting chocolate over a pan of hot water, you must be sure that the water doesn't boil, so that steam or hot water doesn't splash onto the melting chocolate. Once the chocolate melts remove it from the heat source to stop further heating.

I melt chocolate by two different methods. Both methods use pieces of chopped chocolate so the chocolate melts evenly. When the chocolate is melted without other ingredients, I usually put it in a preheated 175°F. oven. When I melt chocolate with other ingredients and need to keep stirring it to keep everything smooth, I put it in a heatproof container set over, but not touching, a pan of hot or barely simmering water.

To melt chocolate by the oven method, put the chopped chocolate in a heatproof container and put it in a preheated 175°F. oven. Be sure to use a nonreactive stainless-steel, ceramic, or heatproof glass container anytime you melt white chocolate. Pieces of chocolate melt in about 12 to 15 minutes, depending on the quantity of chocolate, but note that the chocolate holds its shape until it is stirred after removing it from the oven. You can poke the chocolate with a spoon to check to see that it is completely melted. Remember that you are not heating or baking the chocolate to 175°F., but allowing it to melt in this warm, dry environment and removing the chocolate from the oven when it melts. My other method of melting the chocolate over a pan of hot water can substitute for this oven method in any of the recipes.

To melt chocolate or chocolate with other ingredients (often butter or shortening) over a pan of hot water, put everything in a heatproof container, such as a small saucepan or the top of a double boiler. Place the container with the chocolate and other ingredients over very hot or barely simmering water and stir them often until the mixture is smoothly melted. Keep the heat at about low-medium and decrease the heat if steam forms or the water boils. Remove the chocolate mixture from over the hot water as soon as it is melted. White chocolate should be melted in a nonreactive container.

When combining warm melted chocolate with other ingredients, it helps to have those other ingredients at room temperature, so specks of hard chocolate do not form from coming in contact with a cold ingredient. When adding melted chocolate to a cake batter, the melted chocolate is normally added after creaming the butter and sugar together and before beating in the eggs. The melted chocolate incorporates easily into this room-temperature mixture, yet the chocolate is not warm enough to melt the butter mixture, nor have any cold eggs been added that could harden the chocolate. If adding melted chocolate to a completed or cool batter such as the Reverse Chocolate Marble Cake (page 293), remove about 1 cup of the batter to another bowl. Use a whisk to blend the melted chocolate into this small quantity of batter. As soon as the chocolate is incorporated smoothly, add it to the original batter and quickly whisk the 2 mixtures to blend them together. This same method is used for incorporating melted chocolate into a cold whipped cream mixture.

Double Fudge Brownies

Rich chocolate taste, dark color, dense texture, and moist all the way through—that's what I look for in my brownies. I personally guarantee that you'll find those qualities in these brownies. They include both unsweetened and semisweet chocolate to produce a powerful chocolate flavor that is capable of satisfying the most desperate chocolate craving. The batter can be mixed in minutes, and the hardest part of making these brownies is to wait for them to finish baking.

Baking Answers ❧ As with most brownie recipes, you want a dense result, so there is no leavening in the form of baking powder or baking soda to lighten them. It is not necessary to beat a lot of air into the batter, so a whisk rather than an electric mixer works fine for mixing the batter. If you use an electric mixer, set it on a low speed.

Melt the 2 types of chocolate and butter over barely simmering water. If the water is boiling, it could overheat the chocolate and turn it grainy. Stir the melting chocolate and butter often so that they melt into a smooth mixture. Cutting both the chocolate and butter into pieces before melting them helps the mixture to melt evenly.

Fudge brownies often stick to the bottom of their baking pan and are difficult to remove. I find that lining the brownie pan with a piece of aluminum foil long enough to hang over the edges of the pan makes for easy removal. After the baked brownies cool, I just lift brownies and foil from the pan. They cut into neat squares and slide easily off the foil. Better still, there is no greasy pan to clean.

These brownies are done when a toothpick inserted in the center comes out with moist crumbs clinging to it.

A Step Ahead ❧ Brownies freeze well. The brownies can be wrapped in plastic wrap, then heavy aluminum foil, and stored in the freezer for up to 3 months. Label them with the date and contents. Defrost the wrapped brownies at room temperature.

MAKES 12 TO 16 BROWNIES

Necessities ❧ *A 9-inch square pan or an 11 x 7-inch rectangular pan, both with 2-inch-high sides, and a double boiler or heatproof container to put over a pan of barely simmering water for melting the chocolate mixture*

6 ounces (1½ sticks) unsalted butter,
 cut into 12 pieces
½ cup (3 ounces) semisweet
 chocolate chips or chopped
 semisweet chocolate
5 ounces unsweetened chocolate,
 chopped

3 large eggs
1½ cups sugar
¼ teaspoon salt
1 teaspoon vanilla extract
1 cup unbleached all-purpose flour

Mix the Brownies

◆ Position an oven rack in the middle of the oven. Preheat the oven to 325°F. Line a 9 x 9 x 2-inch square or an 11 x 7 x 2-inch rectangular baking pan with heavy aluminum foil that extends over 2 ends of the pan. Butter the foil inside the pan.

 Put the butter, semisweet chocolate, and unsweetened chocolate in a large heatproof container set over, but not touching, barely simmering water in a saucepan. Stir the mixture often until the butter and chocolate are melted and smooth. As soon as the chocolate mixture melts, remove it from over the water and set it aside to cool slightly.

 Put the eggs, sugar, and salt in a large bowl and use a whisk to blend them together thoroughly. Use a rubber spatula to scrape all of the warm chocolate mixture into the egg mixture, add the vanilla, and whisk until the chocolate mixture is incorporated and the mixture is smooth. Add the flour and continue whisking just until the flour is incorporated and no white specks remain. Use a rubber spatula to stir any loose flour into the batter, then scrape all of the batter into the prepared pan. Smooth the top.

Bake and Serve the Brownies

◆ Bake for about 40 minutes until a toothpick inserted into the center of the brownies comes out with a few moist crumbs, but not liquid, clinging to it. Cool the brownies in the pan for about 1 hour.

 Use the overhanging ends of aluminum foil to carefully lift the brownies out of the pan. Loosen the foil from the sides of the brownies. Cut into 12 to 16 pieces. Use a wide spatula to slide the brownies off the foil. Wrap the individual cooled brownies in plastic wrap and store at room temperature up to 4 days, or freeze as directed above in "A Step Ahead."

Half-Baked Brownie Ice Cream Pie

I n my dreams—that's where this ice cream pie originated. Vanilla ice cream in a crisp chocolate crumb crust covered with not quite baked soft brownies and thick fudge sauce is my dream combination. Now that I have it written down, it's a scrumptious reality.

The old-fashioned hot fudge sauce (page 279) makes a good "house" fudge sauce for any ice cream occasion. It is a thick fudge sauce made with evaporated milk that produces the flavor I remember from the hot fudge sundaes of my childhood.

Baking Answers ✒ I use a good-quality but not a premium ice cream for this pie. A pie with premium ice cream and brownies and fudge sauce seems excessively rich to me. When preparing this pie, soften the ice cream just until it is easy to scoop and spread. The less the ice cream melts, the better it will taste after it freezes firm again. Cool the fudge sauce slightly before adding it to the pie so the hot sauce does not melt the ice cream. Vanilla ice cream is a natural with chocolate, but peppermint, raspberry, coffee, or cherry vanilla ice creams also make excellent choices.

This pie uses only half of the pan of partially baked Double Fudge Brownies (page 276). You can freeze the remaining brownies for another use, make 2 ice cream pies, or just eat them as brownies. These partially baked brownies are firm enough to cut and eat once they are thoroughly cooled. When frozen in the ice cream pie, the pieces of brownie look and taste like fudge candy.

The hot dish towel method given below for removing the sides of the springform pan from an ice cream pie eliminates loosening ice cream pie from the sides of the pan. The pan sides remove easily and the sides of the unmolded ice cream pie are neat and smooth.

A Step Ahead ✒ Ice cream desserts actually have to be made at least 5 hours ahead so they have time to firm up in the freezer. This ice cream pie can be made up to 10 days ahead. Wrap it tightly with plastic wrap and heavy aluminum foil, label with the date and contents, and put it in the freezer.

The fudge sauce can be prepared up to a week ahead, cooled, covered, and refrigerated. There are two ways to warm the fudge sauce: in a saucepan over low heat, or over a pan of barely simmering water. The brownies can be baked 1 day ahead, wrapped, and stored at room temperature. Or the half-baked and cooled brownies can be wrapped in plastic wrap, then heavy aluminum foil, and stored in the freezer for up to 3 months. Label them with the date and contents. Defrost the wrapped brownies at room temperature.

Necessities ⤙ *One 9-inch springform pan with sides at least 2¾ inches high and a double boiler or heatproof container to put over a pan of barely simmering water for melting the chocolate mixture*

OLD-FASHIONED HOT FUDGE
SAUCE—
MAKES ABOUT 1¼ CUPS

4 ounces unsweetened chocolate, chopped

2 ounces (½ stick) unsalted butter

⅔ cup sugar

One 5-ounce can (⅔ cup plus 2 teaspoons) whole or low-fat evaporated milk

¼ cup light corn syrup

1 teaspoon vanilla extract

1 recipe Double Fudge Brownies (page 276), baked for only 25 minutes at 325°F., cooled thoroughly or overnight

½ gallon good-quality vanilla ice cream, softened until spreadable but not melted

1 chocolate crumb crust (page 103) baked in a 9-inch springform pan, cooled

Make the Sauce

⤙ Put the chocolate, butter, sugar, evaporated milk, and corn syrup in a large heatproof container set over, but not touching, barely simmering water in a saucepan. Cook the mixture over the hot water, stirring often, until the butter and chocolate are melted and smooth, about 8 minutes. Continue cooking for about 5 more minutes, stirring often, until the mixture thickens slightly and becomes shiny. If a spoon is dipped in the chocolate sauce, the sauce will coat the spoon smoothly with no trace of graininess, and it will leave a path on the back of the spoon if you run your finger down the sauce on the spoon. Remove the sauce container from over the water and stir in the vanilla. Set aside for about 15 minutes to cool slightly.

Assemble the Pie

⤙ Use a large, sharp knife to cut half of the brownies into ½- to ¾-inch pieces. The brownies are easy to cut if they are throughly cooled or refrigerated. Save the remaining brownies for another use.

Use an ice cream spade or a large spoon to spread half of the softened ice cream over the crumb crust. Spread the ice cream gently so as not to disturb the crumb crust. Place half of the brownie pieces evenly over the ice cream. Use a teaspoon to drizzle about ½ cup of the cooled fudge sauce over the brownies. Spread the remainder of the ice cream over the fudge sauce. Place the remainder of the brownie pieces evenly over the ice cream. Drizzle about ½ cup of the cooled fudge sauce over the brownies. Leave the remaining fudge sauce in the heatproof container and set aside to serve with the pie, or cover and refrigerate it if you are serving the pie on a later day.

Freeze the Pie

⤙ Freeze the ice cream pie 15 minutes to firm the topping. Wrap the pie tightly with plastic wrap. Then cover with heavy aluminum foil, gently pressing the aluminum foil against the pie. Label with the date and contents. Freeze at least 5 hours or up to 10 days.

Serve the Pie

⤙ Set the reserved fudge sauce in its heatproof container back over, but not touching, barely simmering water in a saucepan. Stir it over the hot water until it is warm, about 5 minutes. If the sauce has been put into a container and refrigerated, it can be put into a small saucepan and heated over low heat for about 5 minutes until it is warm, stirring constantly.

Remove the ice cream pie from the freezer and let it sit at room temperature for about 5 minutes. On a hot summer day, this slight softening before serving may be unnecessary. Remove the sides of the springform pan by dipping a dish towel in hot water and wringing out the water. Hold the hot towel around the sides of the pan for 15 seconds. Release the sides of the springform pan. Either leave the wrapped pie on the springform bottom or slide it onto a serving plate. Use a large, sharp knife to cut the pie into wedges and serve. Pour the warm sauce into a small pitcher and serve with the ice cream pie. Wrap any leftover pie in plastic wrap and heavy aluminum foil and return it to the freezer before it begins to melt.

Chocolate Chip Cookie and Fudge Brownie Pie

I can't believe I went so many years without thinking of layering chocolate chip cookies and brownies together in one pie. As soon as I put the two together, I knew I had a winner. Chocolate chip cookie batter forms the crust, and brownies make the fudgy topping. Our friend Woody Emanuel thinks this pie is so good that the recipe should be patented, but I decided to share it with everyone.

Baking Answers ◦ Cool the partially baked chocolate chip cookie crust before adding the brownie batter; then the layers remain separated after they bake.

This pie tastes even better the day after it is baked. The flavor of each layer is more pronounced.

Please don't be put off by the long ingredient list. Many of the ingredients repeat in both layers, and each layer mixes together quickly.

SERVES 8 TO 10

Necessities ◦ *A 9-inch shiny metal or ovenproof glass pie pan and a double boiler or heatproof container to put over a pan of barely simmering water for melting the chocolate mixture*

CHOCOLATE CHIP COOKIE CRUST
¾ cup unbleached all-purpose flour
½ teaspoon baking soda
¼ teaspoon salt
5 tablespoons soft unsalted butter
⅓ cup packed light brown sugar
3 tablespoons granulated sugar
1 large egg
½ teaspoon vanilla extract
1 cup (6 ounces) semisweet chocolate chips

BROWNIE TOPPING
6 tablespoons (¾ stick) unsalted butter, cut into 8 pieces
3 ounces semisweet chocolate, chopped
1 ounce unsweetened chocolate, chopped
¼ cup unbleached all-purpose flour
¼ teaspoon baking powder
⅛ teaspoon salt
1 large egg
6 tablespoons granulated sugar
1 teaspoon vanilla extract

Mix and Bake the Crust

❧ Position a rack in the middle of the oven. Preheat the oven to 325°F. Butter a 9-inch pie pan.

Sift the flour, baking soda, and salt together onto a piece of wax paper or into a medium bowl and set aside.

Put the butter, brown sugar, and granulated sugar in a large bowl and beat with an electric mixer on medium speed for about 1 minute, until the mixture looks smooth and creamy. Move the beaters around in the bowl if using a handheld electric mixer. Stop the mixer and scrape the mixture from the sides of the bowl and any that becomes caught in the beaters as needed throughout the mixing process. Mix in the egg and vanilla until they are blended in thoroughly. Decrease the speed to low and add the flour mixture, mixing just until it is incorporated and there is no loose flour. Use a large spoon to stir in the chocolate chips. Use a rubber spatula to scrape all of the dough into the pie pan, spreading it evenly over the bottom of the pan. Bake 15 minutes. Cool 30 minutes. The center will sink slightly.

Mix the Topping

❧ Put the butter, semisweet, and unsweetened chocolate in a heatproof container set over, but not touching, barely simmering water in a saucepan. Stir the mixture often over the hot water until the butter and chocolate are melted and smooth. As soon as the chocolate mixture melts, remove the container from over the water and set it aside to cool slightly for about 5 minutes.

Stir the flour, baking powder, and salt together in a small bowl and set aside.

Put the egg, granulated sugar, and vanilla in a large bowl and beat with an electric mixer on medium speed for about 1 minute until the mixture thickens and the color lightens slightly. Move the beaters around in the bowl if using a handheld electric mixer. Decrease the speed to low and mix in the melted chocolate, mixing just to combine it with the other ingredients. Add the flour mixture, mixing just until the flour is incorporated. Use a rubber spatula to scrape all of the batter over the partially cooled chocolate chip cookie layer, spreading it evenly.

Bake and Serve the Pie

❧ Bake for about 20 minutes, until a toothpick inserted in the center of the brownie layer comes out with a few moist crumbs, but not wet batter, clinging to it. Cool the pie thoroughly in the pan.

Serve the pie at room temperature. Leftover pie can be covered with plastic wrap and stored at room temperature up to 3 days. Ice cream and warm old-fashioned hot fudge sauce (page 279) make a good accompaniment.

Chocolate Chip Fudge Cake

This one-pan cake is ready to serve as soon as it is cool enough to be cut. It has so many chocolate chips inside it that there's no need to add any frosting. Without any frosting to melt or become squashed, this cake makes a good choice to take on a picnic or send through the mail. Because the cake batter is thick, the chocolate chips float nicely throughout it, rather than sinking to the bottom.

Baking Answers ∽ Since the chocolate in this cake melts by itself rather than with butter or other ingredients, I use my easy method for melting chocolate in the oven. Preheat the oven to a low 175°F., cut the chocolate into ½- to ¾-inch pieces, and put it in an ovenproof container. Place the container of chocolate in the oven to melt, then remove the chocolate from the oven as soon as it is melted, about 12 minutes for the 3 ounces of chocolate used here. Chocolate melted in the oven holds its shape until it is stirred smooth. Remember that you are not trying to heat the chocolate to 175°F., since you remove the chocolate from the oven as soon as it melts, long before it reaches 175°F. After the chocolate melts, increase the oven temperature to bake the cake.

SERVES 9

Necessities ∽ *A 9-inch square pan or an 11 x 7-inch rectangular pan, both with 2-inch-high sides, and a heatproof container for melting the chocolate in the oven*

3 ounces unsweetened chocolate,
   chopped
1¼ cups unbleached all-purpose
   flour
1 teaspoon baking powder
½ teaspoon baking soda
¼ teaspoon salt
¼ pound (1 stick) soft unsalted
   butter
1 cup plus 2 tablespoons granulated
   sugar

2 large eggs
2 teaspoons vanilla extract
1 cup sour cream
½ cup water
1⅔ cups (10 ounces) semisweet
   chocolate chips
Powdered sugar for dusting the top
   of the cake, optional

Mix the Cake

↪ Position an oven rack in the middle of the oven. Preheat the oven to 175°F. Butter the bottom and sides of a 9 x 9 x 2-inch square baking pan or an 11 x 7 x 2-inch rectangular baking pan.

Put the unsweetened chocolate in a small ovenproof container and place it in the oven to melt. It will take about 12 minutes to melt. As soon as the chocolate melts, remove it from the oven and stir it smooth. Increase the oven temperature to 325°F. Set the chocolate aside to cool slightly while you mix the cake.

Sift the flour, baking powder, baking soda, and salt together onto a piece of wax paper or into a medium bowl and set aside.

Put the butter and granulated sugar in a large bowl and beat with an electric mixer on medium speed until the mixture looks smooth and creamy, and the color lightens, about 2 minutes. Move the beaters around in the bowl if using a handheld electric mixer. Stop the mixer and scrape the mixture from the sides of the bowl and any that becomes caught in the beaters as needed throughout the mixing process. Decrease the speed to low and mix in the melted chocolate, mixing just to combine it with the other ingredients. Increase the speed to medium and add the eggs one at a time, beating for 1 minute after adding each egg. Decrease the speed to low and add the vanilla and sour cream, mixing just until the sour cream is incorporated. Add half of the flour mixture and mix to incorporate the flour. Add the water, mixing to incorporate it. Add the remaining flour mixture, mixing just to incorporate it. Stop the mixer and scrape the sides of the bowl after the last addition of flour. The batter is ready when the final addition of flour is mixed completely into the batter. If any flour is clinging to the sides of the bowl, stir it into the batter. Use a large spoon to stir in the chocolate chips.

Use a rubber spatula to scrape all of the batter into the prepared pan, spreading it evenly.

Bake and Serve the Cake

↪ Bake for about 40 minutes, until the top feels firm and a toothpick inserted in the center of the cake comes out slightly sticky but not coated with liquid. If the toothpick penetrates a chocolate chip, test another spot. Cool the cake thoroughly in its pan, about 1½ hours. Dust with powdered sugar, if desired. Cut into squares to serve. Leave leftover cake in the pan, and cover and store it at room temperature for up to 3 days.

Hot Chocolate Cake

When I was a kid, my mother used to warn me that eating warm cake would make me sick. I could never see how something so good could ever upset anyone, and happily the current popularity of serving chocolate cake hot, barely baked, or even molten and liquid has proved the fans of warm cake right. This Hot Chocolate Cake tastes as if it is made from nothing but chocolate, but it actually calls for a normal quantity of chocolate that would be used for a cake. It supports my opinion that warm, melted chocolate in cake or in any form produces an extremely rich and intense chocolate flavor.

Baking Answers ❧ Melt the chocolates and butter over barely simmering water. If the water is boiling, it could overheat the chocolate and turn it grainy. Stir the melting chocolate and butter often so they melt into a smooth mixture. Cutting the chocolate and butter into pieces helps the mixture melt evenly.

There are 2 options when baking this cake. Bake it for 15 minutes and the center will be thick, but still liquid—similar to a thick but not heavy fudge sauce. There will be a border of moist, but not liquid, cake around the edge. Bake it for 20 minutes and the center will be soft and extremely moist, but not liquid, and the edge will be moist and cake-textured.

The cake bakes in a springform pan, which makes it easy to unmold and serve. It is best served soon after it is baked. If allowed to cool, the cake will firm up and resemble a soft brownie. It is fine, but it is different from a warm, semiliquid cake.

Try serving different flavors of ice cream with the warm cake. Peppermint is refreshing, black raspberry is a good fruit match with chocolate, and coffee makes a comforting mocha combination.

SERVES 10

Necessities ❧ *A double boiler or heatproof container to put over a pan of barely simmering water for melting the chocolate mixture, and one 9-inch-diameter springform pan with sides at least 2 inches high*

¼ pound (1 stick) unsalted butter,
   cut into pieces
6 ounces semisweet chocolate,
   chopped
1 ounce unsweetened chocolate,
   chopped
4 large eggs

¾ cup sugar
1 teaspoon vanilla extract
½ cup unbleached all-purpose
   flour
¼ teaspoon baking powder
Ice cream for serving with the cake,
   optional

Mix the Cake

↬ Position an oven rack in the middle of the oven. Preheat the oven to 375°F. Butter the bottom and sides of a 9-inch springform pan with sides at least 2 inches high.

Put the butter and chocolates in a large heatproof container set over, but not touching, barely simmering water in a saucepan. Stir the mixture often over the hot water until the butter and chocolate are melted and smooth. As soon as the chocolate mixture melts, remove it from over the water and set it aside to cool slightly.

Put the eggs and sugar in a large bowl and beat with an electric mixer on high speed for about 2 minutes until the mixture looks fluffy, thickens, and lightens to a cream color. This is the stage of the mixing that lightens the cake. Move the beaters around in the bowl if using a handheld electric mixer. Mix in the vanilla. Reduce the speed to low and stir in the melted chocolate mixture, mixing until it is blended. Put the flour and baking powder in a flour sifter and sift over the chocolate batter. Stir in the flour mixture just until it is incorporated. Use a rubber spatula to scrape the batter into the prepared pan.

Bake and Serve the Cake

↬ Bake for 15 minutes until the edges look set and the center is soft and just baked enough to hold its shape. A toothpick inserted in the center comes out with batter clinging to it, and one inserted into the edge of the cake comes out with moist crumbs clinging to it.

Cool the cake in the pan for 15 minutes to firm it slightly. Use a small sharp knife to loosen the sides of the cake from the pan. Release the sides of the springform pan and remove them. Use a knife and a large flat spatula to cut and move slices of cake to serving plates. The center of the slices are a thick liquid. Serve with a scoop of ice cream, if desired.

O reo cookies are a great American classic, but imagine a homemade version that sandwiches a soft chocolate buttercream between 2 crisp and buttery chocolate cookies. Then add a striking black-and-white finish by coating half the cookie with powdered sugar. You might call them the super-duper version.

Baking Answers ❧ Rolling and cutting the soft dough for these cookies employs a no-stick method. Roll the freshly prepared soft dough between 2 sheets of wax paper. The butter-rich dough is not stretchy and rolls easily when soft. Then chill the dough between the sheets of paper until it is cold and firm. Remove the top piece of paper and cut out the desired shapes. The cold dough lifts easily off the wax paper.

This dough holds its shape when it bakes and can be cut into stars, hearts, trees, leaves, or other decorative shapes.

The butter for the frosting must be softened so the frosting beats into a creamy mixture.

MAKES ABOUT TWENTY-THREE 1 ¾-INCH COOKIE SANDWICHES

Necessities ❧ *A heatproof container for melting the chocolate, 2 heavyweight baking sheets, a rolling pin, one 1¾-inch-diameter fluted round cookie cutter or other appropriate cookie cutters, and 2 wire racks for cooling the cookies*

CHOCOLATE COOKIES
1 cup plus 2 tablespoons unbleached
   all-purpose flour
2 tablespoons cornstarch
¼ cup unsweetened Dutch process
   cocoa powder, such as Droste or
   Hershey's European

¼ teaspoon salt
6 ounces (1½ sticks) unsalted butter,
   room temperature
¾ cup powdered sugar
1 large egg yolk
1 teaspoon vanilla extract

SIMPLE CHOCOLATE BUTTER CREAM—
MAKES ABOUT 1¼ CUPS

2 ounces unsweetened chocolate, chopped

6 tablespoons (¾ stick) soft unsalted butter

1½ cups powdered sugar, sifted

1 teaspoon vanilla extract

1 tablespoon plus 1½ teaspoons whipping cream

Powdered sugar for decorating the top of the cookies

Mix the Cookies

~ Sift the flour, cornstarch, cocoa powder, and salt together onto a piece of wax paper or into a medium bowl and set aside.

Put the butter and powdered sugar in a large bowl and beat with an electric mixer on medium speed until the mixture looks smooth and the color lightens, about 2 minutes. Move the beaters around in the bowl if using a handheld electric mixer. Stop the mixer and scrape the mixture from the sides of the bowl and any that becomes caught in the beaters as needed. Add the egg yolk and vanilla and mix to incorporate them. Decrease the speed to low and add the flour mixture, mixing just until it is incorporated and a smooth, soft dough forms. Divide the dough into 2 portions and pat each into a 1-inch-thick disk. Cut 4 large pieces of wax paper and place each piece of dough between 2 pieces of wax paper. Roll out each disk of dough between the wax paper pieces to a circle that is ⅛ inch thick or slightly thicker. Refrigerate the dough flat and in its wax paper until it is firm, about 30 minutes or overnight. Stacking the 2 paper-covered sheets of dough on a baking sheet is a good way to ensure that they remain flat in the refrigerator.

Position 2 oven racks in the middle and upper third of the oven. Preheat the oven to 300°F. Line 2 baking sheets with parchment paper.

Remove 1 sheet of dough from the refrigerator. Lift off and discard the top piece of wax paper. Use a 1¾-inch fluted round or smooth round metal cutter to cut out circles. Cut the circles close to each other to cut as many circles as possible. Use a thin metal spatula to lift the cookies off the wax paper and place them ¾ inch apart on a prepared baking sheet. The cookies do not spread much during baking. Wrap the dough scraps in plastic wrap and set aside. Repeat the rolling and cutting with the second sheet of cold dough. Transfer the cookies to a prepared baking sheet. Press all of the dough scraps together to form a smooth disk of dough and place it between 2 clean sheets of wax paper. Repeat the rolling, chilling, and cutting process. Transfer the cookies to the baking sheet and discard any dough scraps remaining. You will have 2 baking sheets filled with cookies.

Bake the Cookies

↝ Bake the 2 pans of cookies for about 20 minutes, until the tops feel firm, reversing the sheets top to bottom and back to front after 12 minutes of baking. Cool the cookies 5 minutes on the baking sheet. Transfer the cookies to a wire rack to cool thoroughly.

Mix the Frosting

↝ Preheat the oven to 175°F. or let the oven cool down if it is still warm from baking the cookies. Put the chocolate in a small heatproof container. Melt the chocolate in the oven, about 12 minutes. Remove the chocolate from the oven as soon as it is melted and stir it smooth. Set the chocolate aside to cool slightly while you prepare the rest of the frosting. Put the butter and powdered sugar in a large bowl and beat with an electric mixer on medium speed for about 2 minutes, until the ingredients are blended. The mixture will have large crumbs of powdered sugar and butter. Add the melted chocolate and vanilla, mixing until the chocolate is incorporated and a thick, smooth mixture forms. Decrease the speed to low and add the whipping cream, mixing until the frosting becomes smooth, soft, and lightens in color, about 1 minute.

Fill the Cookies

↝ Turn half of the cooled cookies bottom side up. Use a thin metal spatula to spread about 1½ teaspoons of frosting evenly over the bottom of these cookies. Press a plain cookie, bottom side down, onto each frosted cookie.

Put 2 tablespoons of powdered sugar in a small strainer. Place a small piece of wax paper or a thin, clean piece of cardboard over half of a filled cookie. Strain powdered sugar over the top of the exposed half of the cookie. Carefully lift off the wax paper. Repeat to decorate all of the cookies, changing to a clean piece of wax paper as needed. Add more powdered sugar to the strainer, if needed. The top of each cookie is half white and half dark chocolate colored.

Serve the Cookies

↝ Serve the cookies at room temperature. The cookies can be carefully covered and stored in a single layer at room temperature for up to 3 days. A metal tin makes a good container for storing them.

Chocolate Cake and Ice Cream Roll

I remember a supermarket store-bought chocolate and ice cream cake roll that my mom used to serve for Sunday dessert. The cake was a bit dry and didn't really have a rich chocolate taste, but this ice cream and chocolate lover loved it anyway. I haven't seen it around in years, but it was that memory that inspired this thin chocolate cake rolled up with ice cream. The miniature chocolate chips included in the cake batter produce a moist cake roll that is filled with soft bits of chocolate and can be rolled with ease.

It takes 2 pints of ice cream to fill the cake roll. Any flavor of ice cream that tastes good with chocolate, which means most flavors to me, can be rolled with the cake. Coffee, vanilla, raspberry, butter pecan, chocolate chip, toffee, and mint flavors are especially good. Peach is about the only ice cream flavor that I can think of that I wouldn't use with the chocolate cake.

Baking Answers ❧ This cake roll achieves its light texture from beating the eggs with sugar to a thick, fluffy mixture. It would be difficult to overbeat this mixture, and a minute or two of additional beating does no harm. The flour mixture and cream are stirred into the batter just enough to blend them into it. This cake is especially fast to mix.

Bottles labeled pure almond extract are made with oil of bitter almond and are preferable to bottles labeled almond extract. The pure version is now available in supermarkets.

The 15½ x 10½ x 1-inch baking pan called for here is also known as a jelly roll pan.

When I am ready to roll up the cake roll and to cool it, I cover a clean dish towel with wax paper, put the warm cake roll on top of the wax paper, place another piece of wax paper on the cake, and roll up the cake. The dish towel helps roll the cake up easily, and the wax paper pieces prevent the roll from sticking to itself and keep the dish towel clean.

The finished cake roll is over 14 inches long. I often cut it in half after filling it and freeze it as 2 cake rolls.

SERVES 14

Necessities ❧ *One 15½ x 10½ x 1-inch baking pan and a baking sheet*

CHOCOLATE CAKE ROLL

¾ cup unbleached all-purpose flour

3 tablespoons unsweetened Dutch
process cocoa powder, such as
Droste or Hershey's European

½ teaspoon baking soda

¼ teaspoon salt

3 large eggs

1 cup granulated sugar

1 teaspoon vanilla extract

¼ teaspoon pure almond extract

¼ cup whipping cream

¾ cup (4½ ounces) miniature
semisweet chocolate chips

2 pints ice cream, such as chocolate
chip, raspberry, or coffee, softened just
until spreadable

Powdered sugar for dusting the cake

1 recipe warm old-fashioned hot
fudge sauce (page 279), for
serving with the cake roll

Mix the Cake

❧ Position a rack in the middle of the oven. Preheat the oven to 350°F. Butter the bottom and sides of a 15½ x 10½ x 1-inch baking pan. Line the bottom of the pan with parchment or wax paper and butter the paper.

Sift the flour, 2 tablespoons of the cocoa powder, baking soda, and salt together onto a piece of wax paper or into a medium bowl and set aside.

Put the eggs in a large bowl and beat with an electric mixer on medium speed just to combine the yolks and whites. Add the granulated sugar and beat on high speed for about 4 minutes until the mixture is fluffy, thickened, and lightened in color. Move the beaters around in the bowl if using a handheld electric mixer. Decrease the speed to low and add the vanilla and almond extract, mixing to incorporate them. Add half of the flour mixture, mixing just until it is incorporated. Add the whipping cream, mixing to blend it into the mixture. Add the remaining flour mixture, mixing until it is incorporated. Use a large spoon to stir in the miniature chocolate chips. Use a rubber spatula to scrape the batter into the prepared pan, spreading it evenly.

Bake the Cake

❧ Bake until a toothpick inserted in the center of the cake comes out clean, about 13 minutes. Use a small, sharp knife to loosen the cake from the edges of the pan. Cool the cake in the pan for 5 minutes. Use a strainer to sift the remaining 1 tablespoon of cocoa powder evenly over the top of the cake. Spread a clean dish towel on the counter and place a large piece of wax paper on the dish towel. With the long side of the cake parallel to the edge of the counter, invert the cake onto the wax paper. Peel off the paper liner by tearing off strips of paper and discard them. Top with a clean piece of wax paper. Using the towel to help roll, roll up the cake in the dish towel and wax paper pieces. Let the rolled cake cool thoroughly, about 1 hour.

Fill the Cake

~ Unroll the cake in its wax paper and dish towel. Place a baking sheet, bottom side down, on top of the wax paper. Using the baking sheet as support to help hold the cake and holding the bottom dish towel against the cake, invert the cake so it is resting on the baking pan. Remove the top dish towel and wax paper. The cake roll will be on a piece of wax paper on top of the baking sheet, and the long side of the cake roll should be parallel to the edge of the counter. Leaving a 1-inch edge bare at the top and bottom of the cake roll, spread the ice cream evenly over the cake. The ice cream will be about ½ inch thick. Using the remaining piece of wax paper to help and leaving the wax paper behind as you roll, roll up the cake with the ice cream. Smooth the edges of the ice cream at the ends of the roll. Turn the roll seam side down. Strain powdered sugar lightly over the top. If desired, cut the cake into 2 rolls. Slide the cake roll off the wax paper and wrap it tightly in plastic wrap. Gently press heavy aluminum foil around the roll. Label with the date and contents. Freeze until firm, at least 5 hours, or up to 1 week.

Serve the Cake

~ Unwrap the frozen ice cream–filled cake roll and put it on a long platter. Cut into 1-inch-thick slices and serve with a pitcher of warm old-fashioned hot fudge sauce (page 279).

Variation ~ *The cake roll can also be filled with whipped cream. Dust the filled cake roll with powdered sugar. Whip 1½ cups whipping cream with 3 tablespoons powdered sugar and 1 teaspoon vanilla. As with the ice cream, leave a 1-inch edge bare at the top and bottom of the cake roll and spread the whipped cream evenly over the cake. Roll up the cake roll with the whipped cream, cover, and refrigerate it for up to 1 day.*

Reverse Chocolate Marble Cake

Traditionally, marble cake is a yellow cake with a few swirls of chocolate. I imagine it is no surprise that my choice for marble cake takes an opposite and chocolate approach. Now the swirls are yellow and the majority of the cake is darkest chocolate.

I add a bit of pure almond extract to the yellow batter and enrich the chocolate batter with both melted chocolate and cocoa powder. With its hint of almond, the light swirls of batter make a noticeable contrast to the predominant chocolate cake.

Baking Answers ⤙ Use a fixed-bottom tube pan for this cake rather than a tube pan that has a removable bottom. The batter can leak out of a tube pan that has a removable bottom. For directions on lining a tube pan with parchment or wax paper, see page 147.

Bottles labeled pure almond extract are made with oil of bitter almond and are preferable to bottles labeled almond extract. The pure version is now available in supermarkets.

Melted chocolate is added to the batter at the end of the mixing process after some of the yellow batter is removed. Melt the chocolate for this cake over hot water and keep it warm over the hot water until you combine it with the cake batter. When the chocolate is warm it combines smoothly into the cake batter. It is easier to keep the chocolate warm over hot water than if it was melted in the oven. The best way to incorporate the warm melted chocolate smoothly into a portion of the completed batter is to remove some batter to a small bowl and quickly whisk the chocolate into it. This small bowl of chocolate batter firms quickly, so it should be immediately whisked into the chocolate portion of the cake batter. Just work quickly and there will be no problem. If there are a few specks of firm chocolate in the batter, they will melt during baking.

There are two options for the top of the cake. The first is to dust the top with powdered sugar, and the second is to drizzle melted dark and white chocolate over the top. The white chocolate for the topping is melted in a nonreactive container. Pyrex glass or stainless steel containers are nonreactive; aluminum is not.

SERVES 12 TO 16

Necessities ⤙ *A 9½- or 10-inch-diameter tube pan with a fixed bottom and at least 3¾-inch-high sides, a double boiler or heatproof container to put over a pan of barely simmering water for melting the chocolate, and 1 wire rack for cooling the cake*

MARBLE CAKE

2 ounces unsweetened chocolate, chopped

2 cups cake flour

1 teaspoon baking powder

1 teaspoon baking soda

½ teaspoon salt

6 ounces (1½ sticks) soft unsalted butter

1¾ cups granulated sugar

3 large eggs

2 teaspoons vanilla extract

1 cup sour cream

1 cup water

½ teaspoon pure almond extract

2 tablespoons unsweetened Dutch process cocoa powder, such as Droste or Hershey's European

TOPPING OPTIONS

2 tablespoons powdered sugar for dusting over the top of the cake

Or,

2 ounces semisweet chocolate, chopped

2 ounces white chocolate, chopped, Callebaut or Lindt preferred

Mix the Cake

✧ Position a rack in the middle of the oven. Preheat the oven to 325°F. Butter the bottom, sides, and center tube of a 9½- or 10-inch-diameter tube pan with at least 3¾-inch-high sides. Line the bottom of the pan with parchment or wax paper and butter the paper.

Put the unsweetened chocolate in a large heatproof container set over, but not touching, barely simmering water in a saucepan. Stir the chocolate often over the hot water until the chocolate is melted and smooth. As soon as the chocolate melts, remove the saucepan from over the heat, but let the chocolate remain over the pan of hot water. Set aside.

Sift the cake flour, baking powder, baking soda, and salt together onto a piece of wax paper or into a medium bowl and set aside.

Put the butter and granulated sugar in a large bowl and beat with an electric mixer on medium speed until the mixture looks fluffy and the color lightens, about 4 minutes. The mixture will look sugary and will have clumps of blended butter and sugar rather than a completely smooth mass. Move the beaters around in the bowl if using a handheld electric mixer. Stop the mixer and scrape the mixture from the sides of the bowl and any that becomes caught in the beaters as needed throughout the mixing process. Add the eggs one at a time, beating for 1 minute after adding each egg. Decrease the speed to low and add the vanilla and sour cream, mixing just until the sour cream is incorporated. In 5 additions (3 flour, 2 water) add the flour mixture and the water alternatively, beginning and ending with the flour mixture. Let each addition of water and flour incorporate before adding another. Stop the mixer and scrape the sides of the bowl after the last addition of flour. The batter is ready when it is smooth and the final addition of flour is mixed completely into the batter. If any flour is clinging to the sides of the bowl, stir it into the batter.

Put 2 cups of batter into a medium bowl and stir in the almond extract. Set aside. Use a large spoon or the electric mixer on low speed to stir the cocoa powder into the plain batter in the large bowl. Remove about 1 cup of this chocolate batter to a small bowl. Use a rubber spatula to scrape the warm melted chocolate over this batter. Use a whisk to blend the melted chocolate into the small bowl of batter. As soon as the chocolate is incorporated, scrape the mixture into the cocoa batter in the original large bowl and whisk the 2 mixtures to blend them thoroughly. You will have a large bowl of chocolate batter and a smaller bowl of yellow batter. Scrape about two thirds of the chocolate batter into the prepared pan, spreading it evenly. Spoon all of the yellow batter evenly over the chocolate batter. Spread the remaining chocolate batter evenly over the yellow batter. There may be some yellow batter showing through. Dip the rubber spatula into the batter in the pan and draw it once around the pan and through the center of the batter to marbleize the batter slightly. This will leave large areas of yellow swirls in the cake. Smooth the top.

Bake the Cake

 Bake for about 55 minutes. To test for doneness, gently press your fingers on the top middle of the cake. It should feel firm. If the cake feels firm, insert a toothpick in the center of the cake. When the toothpick comes out clean, the cake is done. Some of the yellow batter rises to the top so the top looks marbleized.

Cool the cake in its pan for 20 minutes. Use a small, sharp knife to loosen the cake from the sides and the center tube of the pan. Invert the cake onto a cake plate. Carefully remove and discard the paper lining the cake bottom. Place a wire cake rack on the bottom of the cake and invert the cake onto it. The cake is now right side up. Cool the cake thoroughly.

Add the Topping and Serve the Cake

 Put the powdered sugar in a small strainer and sift it over the top of the cake. Or preheat the oven to 175°F. Put the semisweet and white chocolate in separate ovenproof containers, with the white chocolate in a nonreactive container, and melt them in the oven, about 12 minutes. As soon as the chocolates are melted, remove both from the oven and stir them smooth. Dip a small spoon or fork in the semisweet chocolate, and using about three fourths of the chocolate, move the spoon or fork quickly over the top of the cake to drizzle thin lines of chocolate over the top. Use a clean spoon or fork to drizzle all of the white chocolate over the top of the cake. Drizzle the remaining dark chocolate over the top of the cake. Slide the cake onto a cardboard cake circle or serving plate. Use a large knife to cut the cake into slices. Serve at room temperature. Wrap leftover cake with plastic wrap and store at room temperature for up to 3 days.

Dark Chocolate Cupcakes with Fudge Frosting

My daughter Laura knows good chocolate cake. When she told me that she had found a bakery that made a wonderful dark chocolate cupcake topped with lots of creamy fudge frosting, I knew she was on to something good. My next birthday rolled around and Laura arrived with a box of the chocolate cupcakes. They were completely covered with thick swirls of dark chocolate frosting and were worthy of any birthday. Soon after, the bakery suddenly stopped making them, so it was into the kitchen to duplicate the cupcakes and frosting. Now we can have these all-chocolate cupcakes any day, whether it is a birthday or not. It's a nice turnabout when daughters bring the birthday cake for moms.

Try piping the frosting from a pastry bag fitted with a star tip onto the cupcakes. It is fun, surprisingly fast, and makes a sophisticated swirled topping. For a more homespun look, you can spread the frosting with a spatula.

Baking Answers ❖ It is the combination of melted chocolate plus cocoa powder that produces the dark chocolate color and rich chocolate taste in these cupcakes. Although the outside of the chocolate frosting becomes firm as it sits, it remains creamy throughout on the inside.

Since the chocolate for the cupcakes is melted without any other ingredients, I put it in a heatproof container and melt it in a preheated 175°F. oven. Rather than melting the chocolate over hot water, this saves using the additional pot of hot water and eliminates any worry about escaping steam overheating the chocolate. However, you are not trying to heat the chocolate to 175°F., and the chocolate should be removed from the oven as soon as it melts.

The frosting is made by melting butter, sugar, cream, and chocolate together, then mixing the warm mixture with powdered sugar and vanilla. Once the mixture chills to the point that it is cool to the touch, it can be beaten to a smooth frosting.

Use a pastry bag to pipe the frosting over the cupcakes. I tried using a heavy self-sealing plastic bag, but the weight of the frosting burst the bag.

MAKES 12 CUPCAKES

Necessities ❖ *2 muffin tins that hold 6 cupcakes each or 1 muffin tin that holds 12 cupcakes, paper cupcake liners, 1 wire rack for cooling the cupcakes, a heatproof container for melting the chocolate, and a thin metal spatula or pastry bag with a star tip for frosting the cupcakes*

CHOCOLATE CUPCAKES

2 ounces unsweetened chocolate

1 cup unbleached all-purpose flour

⅓ cup unsweetened Dutch process cocoa powder, such as Droste or Hershey's European

½ teaspoon baking soda

¼ teaspoon salt

2 ounces (½ stick) soft unsalted butter

1 cup granulated sugar

1 large egg

1 large egg yolk

1 teaspoon vanilla extract

⅔ cup sour cream

FUDGE FROSTING

1¼ cups powdered sugar

¼ pound (1 stick) unsalted butter

½ cup granulated sugar

½ cup whipping cream

3 ounces semisweet chocolate, chopped

4 ounces unsweetened chocolate, chopped

1 teaspoon vanilla extract

Mix the Cupcakes

❧ Position a rack in the middle of the oven. Preheat the oven to 175°F. Line 12 muffin tin openings with paper cupcake liners.

Put the unsweetened chocolate in a small heatproof container and place it in the oven to melt. It will take about 12 minutes to melt, and it holds its shape until stirred. As soon as the chocolate melts, remove it from the oven and stir it smooth. Increase the oven temperature to 350°F. Set the chocolate aside to cool slightly while you mix the cupcakes.

Sift the flour, cocoa powder, baking soda, and salt together onto a piece of wax paper or into a medium bowl. Set aside.

Put the butter and granulated sugar in a large bowl and beat with an electric mixer on medium speed until the mixture looks smooth and the color lightens, about 2 minutes. The mixture will look sugary. Move the beaters around in the bowl if using a handheld electric mixer. Stop the mixer and scrape the mixture from the sides of the bowl and any that becomes caught in the beaters as needed throughout the mixing process. Decrease the speed to low and mix in the melted chocolate, mixing just to combine it with the other ingredients. Increase the speed to medium and add the egg and egg yolk, beating for 1 minute after adding them. Decrease the speed to low and add the vanilla and sour cream, mixing just until the sour cream is incorporated. Add the flour mixture and stir it in just to incorporate it completely. If any flour is clinging to the sides of the bowl, stir it into the batter. Divide the batter among the 12 lined muffin cups, filling the paper liners to ¼ inch from the top.

Bake the Cupcakes

↝ Bake until the tops feel firm and a toothpick inserted in the center of a cupcake comes out clean, about 25 minutes. The tops will have some small cracks. Cool the cupcakes in their pan for 5 minutes, then transfer them in their paper liners to a wire rack to cool thoroughly.

Mix the Frosting

↝ Sift the powdered sugar into a medium bowl and set aside. Put the butter, granulated sugar, and cream in a medium saucepan over medium heat and cook it until the butter melts and the sugar dissolves, stirring often. Remove the saucepan from the heat and add the chopped semisweet and unsweetened chocolate, stirring until the chocolate melts. Return the saucepan to low heat for about 1 minute, if necessary, to melt the chocolate completely. Pour the hot mixture over the powdered sugar in the bowl. Add the vanilla and use an electric mixer on low speed to mix the ingredients until they are blended together. Press a piece of plastic wrap onto the surface and refrigerate until cool to the touch, about 1 hour. Remove the cooled chocolate mixture from the refrigerator and beat it with an electric mixer on medium speed until the frosting is creamy and lightens slightly in color, about 1 minute.

Frost and Serve the Cupcakes

↝ Use a thin metal spatula to spread the frosting thickly over the top of each cooled cupcake, swirling it gently with the spatula. Or, put a large star tip, narrow tip down, into a large pastry bag (12 to 14 inches long), pressing the tip of the pastry tip through the hole in the bottom of the bag. Fold the bag back from the top 3 to 4 inches to form a collar so that you can fill the bag about half full with the frosting. (If the bag is completely filled, the frosting might squish out of the top when you press on the bag.) Place the bag in a tall glass or 4-cup measuring cup to hold it steady while filling it. Unfold the folded-down collar of the pastry bag and twist the pastry bag against the frosting to press out any air. With one hand around the twisted section, hold the pastry bag with the pastry tip at the bottom of the bag about ½ inch above the top of a cupcake. Using your free hand to gently guide the pastry tip around the top of each cupcake, and using the hand holding the bag around the twisted section to press out the frosting, move the bag slowly around the top of the cupcake to cover it completely with a swirled spiral of frosting. Or, pipe out swirls in any pattern you like. They will all look nice. Continue to frost all of the cupcakes.

Serve the cupcakes at room temperature. Leftover cupcakes can be covered with plastic wrap and stored at room temperature up to 3 days. In hot weather, store them in the refrigerator, but bring them to room temperature to serve them.

Go for the Chocolate Cake

This cake sets a chocolate example. It is filled with miniature chocolate chips that add sensations of solid chocolate throughout and has cocoa powder to produce its dark chocolate color. A chocolate glaze surrounds the whole cake. Go for this chocolate cake—everyone else will.

Baking Answers ⟶ Beating the eggs and sugar to a fluffy mixture is the step that gives the cake its light texture and good structure. If you are unsure as to whether the eggs and sugar are sufficiently beaten, an additional minute or two of beating is fine. Once this fluffy mixture is achieved, the remainder of the mixing process is just a matter of blending ingredients together to incorporate them into the batter.

For directions on lining a tube pan with parchment or wax paper see page 147.

This cake is turned bottom side up for glazing and serving. This gives a smooth top and sharp edge to the finished cake.

SERVES 12 TO 16

Necessities ⟶ *A 9½- or 10-inch-diameter fixed-bottom tube pan with at least 3¾-inch-high sides and a wire rack for cooling the cake*

2¼ cups cake flour

½ cup unsweetened Dutch process
cocoa powder, such as Droste or
Hershey's European

1 teaspoon baking powder

½ teaspoon baking soda

½ teaspoon salt

3 large eggs

2 cups sugar

1 cup canola or corn oil

1 teaspoon vanilla extract

1 teaspoon instant coffee dissolved in
1 teaspoon water

1 cup sour cream

1½ cups (9 ounces) miniature
semisweet chocolate chips

1 recipe very easy chocolate glaze
(pages 191–92), cooled until thick
enough to spread

Mix the Cake

❧ Position an oven rack in the middle of the oven. Preheat the oven to 325°F. Lightly rub oil on the bottom, sides, and center tube of a 9½- or 10-inch-diameter tube pan with at least 3¾-inch-high sides. Line the bottom with parchment or wax paper and oil the paper.

Sift the flour, cocoa powder, baking powder, baking soda, and salt together onto a piece of wax paper or into a medium bowl. Set aside.

Beat the eggs and sugar in a large bowl on medium speed for about 2 minutes, until the mixture is fluffy, thick, and lightened to a cream color. This is the stage of the mixing that lightens the cake. Move the beaters around in the bowl if using a handheld electric mixer. Reduce the speed to low and slowly add the oil, vanilla, and dissolved coffee, mixing to incorporate them. Add the flour mixture, mixing just until it is incorporated. Add the sour cream, mixing it into the batter just until no white streaks remain. Add the chocolate chips, stirring just to distribute them. Use a rubber spatula to scrape all of the batter into the prepared pan.

Bake the Cake

❧ Bake for about 1 hour and 5 minutes until you can gently press your fingers on the top middle of the cake and it feels firm, and a toothpick inserted in the center of the cake comes out slightly sticky but not wet. If the toothpick penetrates chocolate chips, test another spot. Cool the cake in the pan for 15 minutes. Use a small, sharp knife to loosen the cake from the sides and the center tube of the pan. Invert the cake onto a wire rack. Carefully remove and discard the paper lining the cake bottom. Leave the cake bottom side up to cool thoroughly, about 1½ hours, before adding the chocolate glaze.

Glaze the Cake

❧ Spread a piece of wax paper under the wire rack to catch any drips. Gently pour about half of the chocolate glaze over the cooled cake, which stays bottom side up. Use a thin metal spatula to spread the glaze inside the hole in the center and over the top of the cake. Spread a layer of glaze over the sides of the cake. Spread any remaining glaze on the top of the cake. Use a large spatula to slide the cake onto a cardboard cake circle or serving plate. Let the glaze firm at room temperature before serving the cake.

Serve the Cake

↝ Cut the cake into slices and serve at room temperature. Cover leftover cake with plastic wrap and store it in the refrigerator for up to 3 days, but let it sit at room temperature for about 1 hour before serving.

Chocolate Pound Cake with Chocolate Marshmallow Frosting

W hen I called Mary Jane Quattlebaum to thank her for the terrific Lemon-Glazed Lemon Pound Cake recipe (page 180) that she had shared with me, she asked if I had liked the chocolate pound cake. "What chocolate pound cake?" I asked as my chocolate glands started to salivate. "Oh, I must send you that one, too," Mary Jane promised. That was when Mary Jane became my official pound cake expert.

Cocoa powder produces a dark chocolate color, and a combination of butter and oil make the pound cake so moist. Including some melted marshmallows in the frosting adds a special creaminess to it. This large cake reminds me of an old-fashioned chocolate birthday cake and would be good for any birthday celebration, big kid or little one.

Baking Answers ↝ The cake is mixed by an unusual method that works easily. First, the butter and oil are mixed together. The oil combines with the butter, but some lumps remain. After the sugar is added, a thorough beating promotes the light structure of the cake and a smooth batter begins to form. The eggs, flour mixture, and milk mixture are added separately and in alternate portions, rather than the usual process of adding the eggs before the flour and milk. The oven is turned on when you put the cake in the oven, so baking begins gently.

For directions on lining a tube pan with parchment or wax paper see page 147.

The baked cake has a crusty top and a nice thin dark fudge area right below the crisp top. Once the frosting is added, the top softens slightly.

Use miniature marshmallows for the frosting. They melt faster than large marshmallows, but they still take about 5 minutes to melt with the chocolate.

Necessities ❧ *A 9½- or 10-inch-diameter tube pan with a fixed bottom with at least 3¾-inch-high sides, a double boiler or heatproof container to put over a pan of barely simmering water for melting the chocolate mixture, and 2 wire racks for inverting and cooling the cake*

CHOCOLATE POUND CAKE	
3 cups unbleached all-purpose flour	½ pound (2 sticks) soft unsalted butter
½ teaspoon baking powder	½ cup canola or corn oil
½ teaspoon salt	3 cups granulated sugar
¾ cup unsweetened Dutch process cocoa powder, such as Droste or Hershey's European	2 teaspoons vanilla extract
	1 cup whole milk
	5 large eggs

CHOCOLATE MARSHMALLOW FROSTING	
¼ pound (1 stick) unsalted butter, cut into 8 pieces	1 cup miniature marshmallows
	2½ cups powdered sugar
2 ounces unsweetened chocolate, chopped	1 teaspoon vanilla extract
	⅛ teaspoon salt
	4 to 5 tablespoons whipping cream

Mix the Cake

❧ Position a rack in the middle of the oven. Do not preheat the oven. Butter the bottom, sides, and center tube of a 9½- or 10-inch tube pan with at least 3¾-inch-high sides. Line the bottom of the pan with parchment or wax paper and butter the paper.

Sift the flour, baking powder, salt, and cocoa powder together onto a piece of wax paper or into a medium bowl and set aside.

Put the butter and oil in a large bowl and beat with an electric mixer on low speed for about 1 minute to blend them. The mixture is liquid and creamy but has lumps of butter in it. Move the beaters around in the bowl if using a handheld electric mixer. Stop the mixer and scrape the mixture from the sides of the bowl and any that becomes caught in the beaters as needed throughout the mixing process. Increase the speed to medium and add the granulated sugar, beating for 3 minutes until the mixture looks fluffy and creamy. It will also look sugary. Stir the vanilla into the milk. Reduce the speed to low and in 5 additions beginning with the eggs, add the eggs, then the flour mixture, and then the milk mixture alternately. Add the milk in only 4 additions so that the last addition is flour. You will have 5 egg, 5 flour, and 4 milk additions. The milk and flour additions do not have to be divided exactly. Let each addition of egg, flour, or milk incorporate before adding another. The batter will be smooth and thick. Use a rubber spatula to scrape all of the batter into the prepared pan and smooth the top.

Bake the Cake

↝ Put the filled pan in the oven and turn the oven temperature to 300°F. Bake for about 1 hour and 30 minutes, just until a toothpick inserted in the center comes out dry of batter but with a crumb or two of cake clinging to it. The top of the cake may have a few small cracks. Cool the cake in the pan for 30 minutes. Use a small, sharp knife to loosen the cake from the sides and the center tube of the pan. Invert the cake onto a wire rack or serving plate. Carefully remove and discard the paper lining the cake bottom. Place a wire rack on the bottom of the cake and invert the cake onto it. The cake is now right side up on the wire rack. Cool the cake thoroughly, about 2 hours.

Make the Frosting and Frost the Cake

↝ Put the butter, unsweetened chocolate, and marshmallows in a large heatproof container set over, but not touching, barely simmering water in a saucepan. Stir the mixture often over the hot water until the butter, chocolate, and marshmallows melt and the mixture is smooth. The melting process takes about 5 minutes, with the marshmallows the last to melt. Scrape the warm chocolate mixture into a large bowl and add the powdered sugar, vanilla, and salt. Beat with an electric mixer on low speed for about 1 minute to blend them. The mixture looks crumbly, not smooth. Add 4 tablespoons of cream and beat until the frosting is smooth. Add 1 additional tablespoon of cream, if necessary, to make a smooth, spreadable mixture. Since this frosting firms quickly, it should be spread immediately with a thin metal spatula over the top, sides, and center hole of the cake.

Serve the Cake

↝ Cut the cake into slices and serve. The cake can be covered and stored at room temperature up to 3 days.

Chocolate Bride's Cake

As you can imagine, cake decisions are important in our family, but when my daughter Laura chose her wedding cake, she never wavered. It would be chocolate through and through—no wedding white frosting for her. This is a family-size version of the cake that graced the wedding feast. It is a tender-textured cake that is filled with a whipped mixture of creamy ganache and is covered with a thick glaze of fudgelike unwhipped ganache. Ganache is an ultra-smooth mixture of chocolate, cream, and often butter that can be flavored with vanilla, coffee, orange, or various liqueurs. The word "truffle" refers to the same mixture. This ganache has some vanilla to enhance the flavor, but otherwise it concentrates on the idea of pure chocolate. Both the ganache filling and glaze are prepared from the same simple mixture.

I know this recipe looks long and it does take time to prepare, but not as much as it looks from the length of this recipe. The cake layers and coffee syrup can be prepared ahead of time, and the preparation time for making the ganache for the filling and glaze is short. I made this cake for our New Year's Eve millennium celebration. A cake for a wedding and a millennium—now that's an impressive recommendation and worth your time.

Baking Answers ❧ The chocolate cake is mixed by creaming the butter and sugar, mixing in the melted chocolate, then beating in the eggs. The sour cream is mixed into the batter and then the flour and water are added in alternate portions. Thorough beating is important to develop the cake's structure when creaming the butter and the sugar and when adding the eggs to the cake batter. Adding the sour cream, dry ingredients, and water to the batter is only a process of blending them thoroughly into the batter and does not require long beating.

Unsweetened chocolate gives the cake a rich chocolate flavor, and cocoa powder adds some chocolate flavor but mostly adds to the dark rich color.

When melting chocolate without other ingredients, I put the chocolate in a heatproof container and melt it in a preheated 175°F. oven. Rather than melting the chocolate over hot water, this saves using the additional pot of hot water and eliminates any worry about escaping steam overheating the chocolate. However, you are not trying to heat the chocolate to 175°F., and the chocolate should be removed from the oven as soon as it melts.

For the ganache, heat the cream and butter just until they are hot and the butter melts. Chop the chocolate into small pieces so that it melts easily in the hot mixture. To chop chocolate quickly, I seal about eight 1-ounce pieces of semisweet baking chocolate in its paper wrappers in a plastic bag and pound them into small pieces with the edge of a flat meat pounder or with a hammer. Pound them on a hard surface that won't be harmed by the pounding, such as a brick floor or a wooden board. Then remove the paper wrappers, put the chocolate in a bowl, and continue with another batch until all of the chocolate is chopped.

Preparing whipped ganache is simple but there are a few important points to note. The chilled ganache is ready to be whipped when it is cold and thick, but before it hardens throughout. The edges of the ganache in the bowl will be firm. Use a whisk to beat ganache for a short time, just until the color lightens from a dark brown to a medium brown and thickens slightly. The taste changes from fudgelike to creamlike. It is hard to overwhip ganache with a whisk, whereas an electric mixer could overwhip it and turn it grainy. If the ganache is not whipped enough, it still tastes fine but is more like the fudgelike glaze on top of the cake. Use whipped ganache immediately, as it firms up quickly and becomes difficult to spread.

If the unwhipped ganache for the glaze becomes too firm to spread, heat it in a saucepan over low heat, stirring constantly, just until it softens enough to spread.

Both of the 2 cake layers are split horizontally to produce 4 thin layers. I use a long, serrated knife and a sawing motion to split the cake layers evenly. The flat removable bottom of a tart pan is useful for moving and stacking the cake layers.

The coffee syrup adds flavor and additional moisture to the cake, prevents crumbs from adhering to the ganache during spreading, and helps the ganache filling and glaze cling to the cake.

The top or sides of the cake can be decorated with chocolate cutouts (page 49).

A Step Ahead ❦ The cake layers can be baked, cooled, wrapped in plastic wrap and heavy aluminum foil, and frozen for up to 1 month. Defrost the cake layers with the wrapping on at room temperature. Or, the cake layers can be baked a day ahead, cooled, wrapped in plastic wrap, and left at room temperature overnight.

The coffee syrup can be put in a small bowl, covered, and stored in the refrigerator for up to 1 week.

The completed cake can be refrigerated for up to 4 days. Refrigerate the cake, uncovered, to firm the glaze, then cover it with plastic wrap.

SERVES 12 TO 16

Necessities ❦ *Two 9-inch-diameter cake pans with 1¾- to 2-inch-high sides, a heatproof container for melting the chocolate in the oven, 2 wire racks for cooling the cake layers, and a pastry brush*

CHOCOLATE CAKE LAYERS

3 ounces unsweetened chocolate, chopped

2 cups cake flour

2 tablespoons unsweetened Dutch process cocoa powder, such as Droste or Hershey's European

1 teaspoon baking powder

1 teaspoon baking soda

½ teaspoon salt

6 ounces (1½ sticks) soft unsalted butter

1¾ cups sugar

3 large eggs

2 teaspoons vanilla extract

1 cup sour cream

1 cup water

GANACHE FILLING AND GLAZE— MAKES ABOUT 4½ CUPS

2 cups whipping cream

2 ounces (½ stick) unsalted butter, cut into 4 pieces

24 ounces (1½ pounds) semisweet or bittersweet chocolate, chopped into ½-inch or smaller pieces

2 teaspoons vanilla extract

COFFEE SYRUP

¼ cup strong coffee

2 tablespoons sugar

Chocolate cutout hearts or other shapes (page 49) to decorate the cake, optional

Mix the Cake

◦ Position a rack in the middle of the oven. Preheat the oven to 175°F. Butter the inside of two 9-inch-diameter cake pans with 1¾- to 2-inch-high sides. Line the bottom of each pan with parchment or wax paper and butter the paper.

Place the unsweetened chocolate pieces in a heatproof container and melt them in the oven, about 12 minutes. When melted, the chocolate holds its shape until it is stirred. As soon as the chocolate is melted, remove it from the oven and stir it smooth. Increase the oven temperature to 350°F. Set the chocolate aside to cool slightly while you mix the cake.

Sift the cake flour, cocoa powder, baking powder, baking soda, and salt together onto a piece of wax paper or into a medium bowl and set aside.

Put the butter and sugar in a large bowl and beat with an electric mixer on medium speed until the mixture looks fluffy and the color lightens, about 5 minutes. The mixture will look sugary and will have clumps of blended butter and sugar rather than be a completely smooth mass. Move the beaters around in the bowl if using a handheld electric mixer. Stop the mixer and scrape the mixture from the sides of the bowl and any that becomes caught in the beaters as needed throughout the mixing process. Decrease the speed to low and mix in the melted chocolate, mixing just to combine it with the other ingredients. Increase the speed to medium and add the eggs one at a time, beating for 1 minute after adding each egg. Decrease the speed to low and add the vanilla and sour cream, mixing just until the sour cream is incorporated. In 3 additions (3 flour, 2 water) add the flour mixture and the water alternatively, beginning and ending with the flour mixture. Let each addition of water and flour incorporate before adding another. Stop the mixer and scrape the sides of the bowl after the last addition of flour. The batter is ready when it is smooth and the final addition of flour is mixed completely into the batter. If any flour is clinging to the sides of the bowl, stir it into the batter. Use a rubber spatula to scrape all of the batter into the prepared pans, dividing it evenly. Smooth the top.

Bake the Cake

~ Bake for about 40 minutes. To test for doneness, gently press your fingers on the top middle of the cake. It should feel firm. If the cake feels firm, insert a toothpick into the center of the cake. When the toothpick comes out clean, the cake is done. Remember that a toothpick will also come out clean if the cake is dry and overbaked, so begin testing with the toothpick after about 35 minutes.

Cool the cake layers in their baking pans on a wire rack for 10 minutes. Use a small, sharp knife to loosen the sides of the cakes from the pans and invert them onto the wire racks. Carefully remove the paper liners, but let the papers rest on the cakes while they cool. Cool the cakes thoroughly. Discard the paper liners.

Prepare the Filling and Glaze

~ Put the cream and butter in a large saucepan and heat over medium-low heat until the cream is hot and the butter is melted. The hot cream mixture will form tiny bubbles and measure about 175°F. if tested with a food thermometer. Do not let the mixture boil. Remove the pan from the heat. Add the chopped chocolate and let it melt in the hot cream mixture for about 30 seconds to soften. Use a whisk to stir the mixture smooth. If all of the chocolate is not melted, return the mixture to low heat for about 1 minute, stirring the mixture until the chocolate is melted and smooth. Remove the pan from any heat and stir in the vanilla. This is the ganache mixture for the filling and glaze.

Pour 2 cups of ganache, which will be used for the glaze topping, in a small bowl and set aside at room temperature. Pour all of the remaining ganache into a large bowl and press plastic wrap onto the surface. Refrigerate until the mixture is cool to the touch, thick, and just beginning to harden around the edges, about 1 hour. Stir once to ensure the mixture chills throughout. Or, let the mixture sit at room temperature until thickened and firm, about 3 hours depending on the kitchen temperature. The mixture should be firm, but soft enough to mix easily with a whisk.

Prepare the Syrup

🌤 Put the coffee and sugar in a small saucepan and stir them together over low heat until the sugar dissolves. Set the syrup aside to cool.

Fill and Frost the Cake

🌤 Ready the cake layers for the ganache filling. Place a large plate over the bottom of each cake layer, and using the wire rack to hold the cake in place, invert both cakes onto the plates. The top side of each cake layer is now up. Use a large, serrated knife and a sawing motion to cut each cake evenly into 2 horizontal layers. Cut into each cake layer with the serrated knife, turning the cake as you cut through to the middle until you have cut through the cake layer. You now have 4 thin cake layers. To remove the top of each cake layer, slide the removable bottom of a tart pan under the top half and set it aside. Place the bottom of 1 cake layer, cut side up, on a serving plate or cardboard cake circle. If you have a turntable, such as a plastic turntable or cake turntable, put the cake on its plate on the turntable to help frost it evenly. Slide wax paper strips under the cake to protect the plate. Use a pastry brush to lightly brush the top of each cake layer with coffee syrup.

Remove the cooled ganache from the refrigerator and use a whisk to mix it until the color changes from a dark chocolate to a medium chocolate color and it thickens slightly, about 2 minutes. Immediately, use a thin metal spatula to spread about one-third of the whipped ganache cream (a generous ¾ cup) over the cake layer on the plate. Slide the bottom of the tart pan under the top half of the cake layer and carefully place it on the ganache. Spread the top of this layer with half of the remaining whipped ganache. Slide the bottom of the tart pan under the bottom half of the second cake layer and place it on the ganache. Spread the remaining whipped ganache over it. Top with the top of the remaining cake layer. There will be 3 ganache-filled layers topped with a cake layer brushed with coffee syrup. Pour about 1½ cups of the thickened room temperature ganache glaze over the top of the cake. The glaze should be thick enough to cling to the cake, but soft enough to spread easily. Use a thin metal spatula to spread the glaze evenly over the top. Spread the remaining glaze and any glaze that has dripped over the sides onto the sides of the cake, turning the cake on its plate or the turntable to glaze all sides. The entire cake should be covered with a coating of chocolate glaze. Remove the wax paper strips and discard them. Place a border of chocolate hearts or other chocolate shapes around the top or onto the sides of the cake, if desired.

Serve the Cake

🌤 Use a sharp knife to cut the cake into wedges to serve. Or, the cake can be covered and refrigerated up to 4 days. Let the cake chill in the refrigerator until the glaze is firm, then cover the cake with plastic wrap and refrigerate it. For the best chocolate flavor, remove the plastic wrap and let the cold cake sit at room temperature for 1 hour before serving it.

Whipping Cream
for Cakes,
Pies, and Pastries

❧

FROM TOPPING A PUMPKIN PIE WITH CINNAMON WHIPPED CREAM TO FILLING A DEEP-DISH CHOCOLATE CHIP COOKIE CAKE TO HEAPING OVER STRAWBERRIES AND SHORTCAKES, WHIPPED CREAM IS A CHOICE THAT WORKS IN ANY SEASON. SINCE IT TAKES ONLY about 4 minutes to whip 2 cups of whipping cream, I can't think of another filling or frosting that can beat it for speed of preparation. Once whipped, the cream is ready to use—no cooking required and no long list of ingredients to have on hand. And, by whipping spices, cocoa powder, coffee, or a fruit puree with the cream, you can produce countless flavor combinations.

There are 2 types of cream that can be whipped. The cream in cartons labeled light whipping cream or whipping cream has from 30 to 36 percent butterfat. Note, however, that cartons labeled light cream that do not have the word "whipping" are not the same. For my recipes, I use the term whipping cream, and this is the type of cream that I use most often. When the dessert calls for a softly whipped cream, whipping cream is the one to buy. The other type of cream is heavy whipping cream, which contains up to 4 percent more butterfat than whipping cream and these cartons are labeled heavy whipping cream, or heavy cream. I prefer the term "heavy whipping cream," and I use it to make a firm and stable whipped cream frosting for Aunt Elaine's Mocha Whipped Cream Shadow Cake (page 332) or a thick filling for the Zuccotto—Italian Chocolate and Vanilla Cream Cake (page 341). In addition to producing this firmer result, heavy whipping cream normally holds its shape for a longer time than whipping cream.

There is one other type of whipped cream besides these two, the whipped cream that comes in those squirt cans. While you may consider it a timesaver, this is quite different from homemade whipped cream and has considerably less body and richness. Once it is released from the can it melts in minutes and is not a good substitute for homemade whipped cream.

Homemade whipped cream is worth the extra effort, so take your time. I used to whip cream at the highest speed and worry about it overwhipping and becoming grainy. One day my son Peter was whipping cream and using a medium speed to whip it. I noticed that it took a minute or two longer to whip, but the cream held its shape for hours and could be whipped for an additional minute or so without any problem. In fact, at the lower speed it was difficult to overwhip. I think the cream also holds its shape for a longer time because the air is incorporated more slowly than at the high speed. Using this method, a bowl of whipped cream can be whipped at least 2 hours ahead, whipped cream used as a pie topping lasts as long as overnight, and the heavy whipped cream that frosts Aunt Elaine's Mocha Whipped Cream Shadow Cake (page 332) lasts on the cake for up to 3 days. If a bowl of whipped cream does lose some of its volume, beating it for a minute or two with a whisk can restore it.

The usual proportions for sweetening and flavoring a basic whipped cream are 1 tablespoon powdered sugar and ½ teaspoon vanilla extract for each cup of cream. When adding a powdered or liquid flavoring, such as instant coffee, cinnamon, cocoa powder, or a liqueur, to whipped cream, I add it to the cream at the beginning of the process and whip everything together. Such solid ingredients as chocolate chips, grated chocolate, or nuts are folded into the cream after whipping. Adding melted chocolate to whipped cream, however, is a slightly different procedure. To add the melted chocolate so it incorporates smoothly and does not form tiny hard pieces when it is added to the cold whipped cream, whisk a small amount of the whipped cream into the warm melted chocolate to produce a smooth mixture. Immediately fold the remaining whipped cream into the chocolate mixture. The result is a smooth, thick chocolate whipped cream.

Cream whips best if is cold and can remain cold during the whipping, so on a warm day it is a good idea to chill the bowl and beaters that will be used for whipping the cream in the refrigerator or freezer. Cream whips in less time on a cold day in a cold kitchen than in a warm kitchen.

To whip cream, put it and any sweetening or flavorings in a large bowl. Use an electric mixer on medium speed to beat the cream to the desired stage. If you are using a handheld electric mixer, move the beaters around in the bowl so that the cream whips evenly.

Whipping cream or heavy whipping cream can be beaten to a softly whipped or firmly whipped stage. At the softly whipped stage, the movement of the beaters will form smooth lines in the cream, and if you dip a spoon in the cream and lift it out, the cream will form a point that falls over at its tip. Softly whipped cream forms a soft mound on a spoon that falls off the spoon. The texture of the whipped cream is like a thick, fluffy sauce. At the firmly whipped stage, the movement of the beaters of a hand mixer will form wrinkled lines in the cream, and if you dip a spoon in the cream and lift it out, the cream will form a point that stands straight up and remains that way. Firmly whipped cream forms a firm mound on a spoon that holds its shape. The movement of the beaters of a standing countertop mixer is different, and the mixer forms a small teardrop shape when cream is firmly whipped.

Always keep whipped cream and desserts that include whipped cream refrigerated and serve them cold.

Several of these recipes use previously prepared pound cake loaves or chocolate chip cookies. These components can be baked ahead and frozen. With a pound cake or chocolate chip cookies ready to go, you can assemble a Deep-Dish Strawberry Whipped Cream Cake (page 312), Zuccotto—Italian Chocolate and Vanilla Cream Cake (page 341), or Deep-Dish Chocolate Chip Cookie Cake (page 314) in short order.

Deep-Dish Strawberry Whipped Cream Cake

The luxurious combination of cake and whipped cream calls for a lot of whipped cream—I mean the cake should be buried in whipped cream. But trying to pile thick layers of whipped cream between cake layers creates a slippery situation. The top layer of cake could even begin to slide off the bottom one. The solution is to assemble layers of cake, whipped cream, and in this case strawberries, in a large bowl. The bowl holds everything together and allows the addition of as much filling as anyone could want. Although the generous portions look extravagant, serving the cake is as easy as digging into the bowl of cake with a big spoon. A deep-dish cake made with any combination of ingredients is a good choice for a buffet or for a serve-yourself dessert.

Baking Answers ✧ Save the nicest-looking strawberries for topping the cake, and chop the others for the filling.

The cream is beaten to the firmly whipped stage.

Deep-dish cakes look nice served from a glass bowl. Be sure to spread each layer to the edge of the bowl so that the distinct colors show through.

A Step Ahead ✧ Bake the pound cake ahead. Cool the cake, wrap it in plastic wrap and heavy aluminum foil, and freeze it for up to 3 months. Defrost the wrapped cake at room temperature.

The Grand Marnier syrup can be put in a small bowl, covered, and stored in the refrigerator for up to 1 week.

SERVES ABOUT 10

Necessities ✧ *One 3-quart bowl, preferably glass, for holding the cake, a pastry brush, and 1 loaf (½ recipe) of Deep South Pound Cake (page 157), baked and cooled*

GRAND MARNIER SYRUP	¼ cup granulated sugar
¼ cup water	¼ cup Grand Marnier liqueur

STRAWBERRY WHIPPED CREAM FILLING	1 tablespoon granulated sugar
1½ cups fresh strawberries, cleaned and coarsely chopped	3 cups cold whipping cream
	3 tablespoons powdered sugar
	2 teaspoons vanilla extract

| 1 loaf Deep South Pound Cake (page 157), baked and cooled | 15 whole cleaned and stemmed strawberries for topping the cake |

Prepare the Syrup

➤ Put the water and granulated sugar in a small saucepan and stir them over low heat just until the sugar dissolves. Remove the pan from the heat and stir in the Grand Marnier. Set the syrup aside to cool. The syrup can be put in a small bowl, covered, and stored in the refrigerator for up to 1 week.

Mix the Filling

➤ Put the chopped strawberries and granulated sugar in a medium bowl and stir them together. Set aside to marinate for 30 minutes.

Put the cream, powdered sugar, and vanilla in a clean large bowl and beat with an electric mixer on medium speed until the cream is firm enough to hold its shape. Move the beaters around in the bowl if using a handheld electric mixer. If you stop the mixer and lift up the beaters, the cream forms a point that stands straight up when the beaters are removed. The movement of the beaters first forms smooth curving then wrinkled lines in the cream at this stage. Put 4 cups of the whipped cream in a large bowl. Put the remaining whipped cream for the topping in the refrigerator while you assemble the cake.

Drain off and discard any accumulated juice from the chopped strawberries and use a rubber spatula to gently mix them into the 4 cups of whipped cream.

Assemble and Serve the Cake

➤ Trim the ends from the pound cake and discard or eat them. Cut the pound cake into sixteen to eighteen ⅓-inch slices. There may be a piece of pound cake left over for another use.

Line the bottom of a 3-quart glass bowl with slices of pound cake, breaking the cake to fit the bowl, if necessary. Use a pastry brush to brush the cake lightly with the Grand Marnier syrup. Spread about one third of the strawberry and whipped cream mixture evenly over the cake. Repeat this layering of cake, Grand Marnier syrup, and the strawberry and whipped cream mixture for 2 additional layers. Add a fourth layer of cake and brush it lightly with Grand

Marnier syrup. You will have 4 layers of cake filled with 3 layers of the strawberry and whipped cream mixture. Spread the reserved plain whipped cream evenly over the top layer of cake. Arrange the whole strawberries, pointed side up, over the top. The strawberries may sit higher than the top edge of the bowl. Cover carefully with plastic wrap and refrigerate for at least 3 hours or overnight. Resting the cake in the refrigerator for 3 hours lets the flavors blend together. Serve cold. Use a large spoon to serve the cake, digging down to the bottom of the bowl for each serving.

Deep-Dish Chocolate Chip Cookie Cake

Chocolate chip cookies cross the Atlantic! That was my surprised reaction when we were served a cake made from chocolate chip cookies at a London tea party. However, I seemed to be the only guest who noticed this Americanization of English high tea. Our friend Rosemarie Robertson had filled a bowl with layers of whipped cream and chocolate chip cookies to serve as her "tea cake." Granted, she added an English touch by giving the cookies a quick dip in sherry, but that made the whole idea even better. I decided my job was to pack up the idea and bring it back across the pond.

Baking Answers ◦➤ Dip the bottom only of the cookies quickly in the sherry. If left to soak in the sherry, the cookies could become saturated with the liquor and crumble. If you don't have sherry, a quick dip in regular-strength coffee is another option.

The cream is beaten to the firmly whipped stage.

A Step Ahead ◦➤ Bake the chocolate chip cookies ahead. Cool the cookies, wrap them in plastic wrap, place them in a metal or plastic freezer container, and cover tightly. Label with the date and contents and freeze for up to 3 months. Defrost as many of the wrapped cookies as you need at room temperature.

SERVES 8

Necessities ◦➤ *One 2-quart bowl, preferably glass, for holding the cake and 10 Jumbo Chocolate Chip Cookies (page 115)*

2 cups cold whipping cream	½ cup dry sherry
¼ cup powdered sugar	10 Jumbo Chocolate Chip Cookies
2 teaspoons vanilla extract	(page 115)

Whip the Cream

✎ Have ready a 2-quart serving bowl, preferably glass. Put the cream, powdered sugar, and vanilla in a clean large bowl and beat with an electric mixer on medium speed until the cream is firm enough to hold its shape. Move the beaters around in the bowl if using a handheld electric mixer. If you stop the mixer and lift up the beaters, the cream forms a point that stands straight up when the beaters are removed. The movement of the beaters first forms smooth curving then wrinkled lines in the cream at this stage.

Assemble the Cake

✎ Pour the sherry into a shallow dish that can easily accommodate 4- to 5-inch-diameter cookies. Dipping 1 cookie at a time, quickly dip the bottoms of 3 of the cookies in the sherry and arrange them to cover the bottom of the bowl. Break the cookies into smaller pieces, if necessary, to fit the bowl. Use a large spoon to spread about 1 cup of whipped cream over the cookies. Repeat to form 2 more layers, using 3 sherry-dipped cookies for each layer. You may not use all of the sherry. Spread the remaining whipped cream over the top layer of cookies. Use your fingers to crumble the remaining cookie that has not been dipped in sherry into small pieces, about ¼ inch in size or smaller. Sprinkle the cookie crumbs over the whipped cream. Cover and refrigerate at least 1 hour or up to 24 hours.

Serve the Cake

✎ Serve cold. If the cake sits for more than about 24 hours, the cookies tend to become soggy. Use a large spoon to serve the cake, digging down to the bottom of the bowl for each serving.

New England Maple Pumpkin Pie

We can never wait until Thanksgiving for pumpkin pie. As soon as the pumpkins decorate the front doorways and the leaves begin to turn, it is our signal to make this maple syrup–sweetened pumpkin pie topped with cinnamon whipped cream. It's too good to have only once a year.

Baking Answers ❧ The piecrust is partially baked before the filling is added. The cream for the topping is beaten to the firmly whipped stage.

Check to see that the label on the can says pumpkin rather than pumpkin pie filling.

Maple syrup is the only sweetener used for this pie filling. It adds a subtle maple flavor to the pie. Be sure to use the pure maple syrup that comes from the sap of maple trees for a good result. It is usually found in the pancake syrup section of supermarkets or in natural foods stores.

The pie filling is mixed with a whisk, just to blend all of the filling ingredients smoothly. There is no long beating required.

A Step Ahead ❧ Roll the piecrust, put it in its pan, and refrigerate overnight.

SERVES 8

Necessities ❧ *1 unbaked cold Fearless Piecrust in a 9-inch shiny metal or ovenproof glass pie pan and metal pie weights or 2½ cups dried beans*

One 1-crust recipe unbaked cold
Fearless Piecrust (page 199) in a
9-inch pie pan

PUMPKIN FILLING
2 cups canned pumpkin (one 15-
 ounce can)
3 large eggs
¾ cup pure maple syrup
¾ cup whipping cream

2 tablespoons (¼ stick) unsalted
 butter, melted
1 teaspoon ground cinnamon
½ teaspoon ground nutmeg
¼ teaspoon ground cloves
¼ teaspoon salt

CINNAMON WHIPPED CREAM	3 tablespoons powdered sugar
TOPPING	1 teaspoon ground cinnamon
1 cup cold whipping cream	1 teaspoon vanilla extract

Partially Bake the Crust

↝ Position a rack in the bottom third of the oven. Preheat the oven to 375°F. Line the prepared crust with heavy aluminum foil, or a double layer of standard foil, pressing the aluminum foil gently over the edges of the pie pan. Fill the aluminum foil with about 2½ cups of beans or metal pie weights. Check to see that the weights evenly cover the entire bottom of the crust. The weights should make a thick layer over the bottom, but they do not have to come to the top of the pan. Bake the crust for 10 minutes. Protect your hands with potholders and carefully remove the aluminum foil by lifting it and the pie weights from the crust. Set the weights or beans aside to cool and store for another use. Bake the uncovered crust for 5 more minutes to firm it slightly. Remove the crust from the oven and set aside. Reduce the oven temperature to 325° F.

Mix the Filling

↝ Put the pumpkin, eggs, maple syrup, and cream in a large bowl and use a whisk to mix them smooth. Add the melted butter, cinnamon, nutmeg, cloves, and salt and continue whisking until all of the ingredients are blended together smoothly. Use a rubber spatula to scrape all of the batter into the partially baked crust.

Bake the Pie

↝ Bake the pie until the filling looks set in the center, about 1 hour. Check to see that the pie is set by giving it a gentle shake; the center should remain firm. Cool thoroughly at room temperature or cover the cooled pie and refrigerate it overnight.

Whip the Topping

↝ Put the cold cream, powdered sugar, cinnamon, and vanilla in a clean large bowl and beat with an electric mixer on medium speed until the whipped cream is firm enough to hold its shape and to spread. Move the beaters around in the bowl if using a handheld electric mixer. If you stop the mixer and lift up the beaters, the cream forms a point that stands straight up when the beaters are removed. The movement of the beaters forms smooth curving then wrinkled lines in the cream at this stage. Use a rubber spatula to spread the whipped cream over the top of the cooled pie, mounding it slightly to the center.

Serve the Pie

↦ Use a large knife to cut the pie into slices and serve. Or, cover it carefully with plastic wrap and refrigerate overnight. A few toothpicks inserted carefully in the whipped cream prevent the plastic wrap from disturbing the topping. Serve cold.

Strawberry Shortcake

Many a Maine church steeple has been built from strawberries. The Fourth of July is the official opening of strawberry season, and village groups around the state often celebrate with a strawberry festival to raise money for their projects. The best bakers in town bake hundreds of biscuits, volunteers keep the cream whipped, and local farms supply their ripest strawberries. No strawberry festival in your neighborhood? Then slice up several pints of strawberries while your shortcakes bake, whip up a bowl of whipped cream, and heap the strawberries and cream over your own freshly baked shortcakes. The only maxim to follow is to be generous.

Shortcakes are similar to biscuits but are usually made from a richer dough that also has more sugar than standard biscuit dough. Cream enriches this shortcake dough, and an egg adds to its tenderness. I eliminate rolling and cutting out the dough by patting it into a circle and cutting it into wedges.

Baking Answers ↦ The shortcake dough can be mixed with an electric mixer or with a large spoon. It is a soft dough that is easy to handle. The one-step procedure of mixing the dough is to stir the cream and egg into the flour mixture until a soft dough forms.

Six cups of strawberries might sound like a lot of strawberries for 8 shortcakes, but an abundance of strawberries and cream is what makes great shortcakes.

When sliced strawberries sit with some sugar for 30 minutes, or all day in the refrigerator, they give off some juice and soften slightly. Some cooks mash the strawberries with the sugar, but I prefer the firmer sliced version.

I beat cream for shortcakes to a softly whipped stage; soft peaks rather than firm peaks. It forms soft, delicate mounds on the strawberries. It is fine to whip the cream to firm peaks, but I prefer the softer stage for this dessert.

A nice way to serve these shortcakes is to serve each person a split shortcake and then pass bowls of strawberries and whipped cream to spoon over them.

A Step Ahead ⟿ The shortcakes can be baked a day ahead, cooled, covered, and stored at room temperature. Or, shortcakes can be wrapped in plastic wrap, sealed in a plastic freezer bag, and frozen for up to 1 month. Defrost the shortcakes in the plastic bag at room temperature. To freshen the shortcakes, wrap them in aluminum foil and warm them in a preheated 250°F. oven for about 15 minutes.

SERVES 8

Necessities ⟿ *1 heavyweight baking sheet*

SHORTCAKES	*1½ teaspoons baking powder*
1¾ cups unbleached all-purpose	*½ teaspoon salt*
flour	*1 cup cold whipping cream*
¼ cup granulated sugar	*1 large egg*
STRAWBERRY TOPPING	*¼ cup sugar*
6 cups cleaned, stemmed, and sliced	
strawberries (about 4 pints)	
WHIPPED CREAM TOPPING	*3 tablespoons powdered sugar*
3 cups cold whipping cream	*1½ teaspoons vanilla extract*

Mix the Shortcakes

⟿ Position a rack in the middle of the oven. Preheat the oven to 375°F. Butter a baking sheet or line a baking sheet with parchment paper. It is not necessary to butter the paper.

Sift the flour, granulated sugar, baking powder, and salt together into a large bowl. Put the whipping cream and egg in a small bowl and use a fork to stir them until blended together. Pour the cream mixture over the flour mixture. Use a large spoon or an electric mixer on low speed to stir the mixture until a soft dough forms and all of the flour is incorporated into the dough.

Gather the dough together and form it into a round ball. Pat the ball of dough into an 8-inch circle that is about ¾ inch thick. Use a sharp knife to cut the dough into 8 wedges. It is easiest to first cut the dough into quarters then into eighths. Place the wedges 1 inch apart on the prepared baking sheet.

Bake the Shortcakes

↝ Bake about 16 minutes until the bottoms are light brown. The tops will be barely colored. Cool the shortcakes on the baking sheet. Shortcakes should be served the same day, or if covered and stored overnight, warm them wrapped in aluminum foil in a preheated 250°F. oven for about 15 minutes before serving them.

Prepare the Strawberries

↝ Put the strawberries in a large bowl. Sprinkle the sugar over them and stir the strawberries and sugar together. Set aside for 30 minutes, or cover and refrigerate for up to 8 hours. The sugar melts and some sweet strawberry juices form.

Whip the Cream

↝ Put the cream, powdered sugar, and vanilla in a large bowl and beat with an electric mixer on medium speed until the movement of the beaters forms smooth curving lines in the cream. If using a handheld electric mixer, move the beaters around in the bowl. If you stop the mixer and lift up the beaters, the cream forms a point that falls over at its tip. The whipped cream can be covered and refrigerated up to 2 hours.

Serve the Shortcakes

↝ For each serving, cut a shortcake in half horizontally and place the 2 halves on an individual plate, cut side up. Spoon a generous spoonful of whipped cream over each half. Spoon about ¾ cup of strawberries and some of their juice over the cream and top with another spoonful of whipped cream. The red strawberries will be visible under a mound of white whipped cream.

Variations ↝ *Substitute 4 cups of fresh raspberries, omitting the sugar, for the strawberries. Stirring the raspberries with sugar would crush them. Or, use 4 cups sweetened blackberries, blueberries, or 6 cups peeled sliced fresh peaches sweetened with 2 to 3 tablespoons of sugar in place of the strawberries. A mixture of 6 cups of berries sweetened with ¼ cup of sugar is also a good choice. Strawberries and blueberries make a great mixture for the Fourth of July.*

Chocolate Icebox Pie

Chocolate pie has always played an important role in my life. When I was growing up, my birthday "cake" was always a chocolate pie. When I married, I bonded with my new family over their favorite family pie—chocolate icebox.

Chocolate Icebox Pie requires little baking and makes a good choice for summer when the last thing you want to do is turn on your oven. Three simple components make up the pie. There is a crisp chocolate crumb crust (that's the only part that bakes), a creamy mousse-like chocolate filling that is firm enough to slice neatly, and a whipped cream topping. I usually decorate the whipped cream with a large piece of chocolate lace, but grated chocolate or even leaving the whipped cream plain is also fine.

Baking Answers ❧ I use Nabisco Famous Chocolate Wafers for the chocolate crumb crust. To make the crumbs, put about 8 cookies at a time between 2 pieces of wax paper and crush them with a rolling pin into fine crumbs, or process the cookies in 2 batches in a food processor until crumbs form.

Cool the crust thoroughly after baking it. Warm crust could melt the filling.

The cream is beaten to the firmly whipped stage.

If using grated chocolate for the top of the pie, grate it on the large holes of a 4-sided grater. To grate the 1 ounce of chocolate, grate it from a large (about 4 ounces) piece of chocolate so it is easier to grate

A Step Ahead ❧ The crumb crust can be mixed and prebaked a day ahead. Cover the cooled crust with plastic wrap and store at room temperature.

SERVES 8

Necessities ❧ *One 9-inch shiny metal or ovenproof glass pie pan and a double boiler or heatproof container to put over a pan of barely simmering water for melting the chocolate mixture*

CHOCOLATE CRUMB CRUST
1⅓ *cups chocolate wafer cookie crumbs*

2 *ounces (½ stick) unsalted butter, melted*

CHOCOLATE CREAM FILLING

3 ounces unsweetened chocolate,
chopped

⅔ cup whipping cream

3 tablespoons granulated sugar

1 teaspoon instant coffee dissolved in
1 tablespoon water

6 tablespoons (¾ stick) soft unsalted
butter

¾ cup powdered sugar

1 teaspoon vanilla extract

**WHIPPED CREAM FOR FILLING
AND TOPPING**

1½ cups cold whipping cream

1 teaspoon vanilla extract

2 tablespoons powdered sugar

---

1 ounce semisweet chocolate, grated,
or one 5-inch piece chocolate lace
(page 48), optional

Make the Crust

↬ Position an oven rack in the middle of the oven. Preheat the oven to 325°F. Butter a 9-inch pie pan.

Stir the crumbs and melted butter together in a medium bowl, stirring until the crumbs are evenly moistened with the butter. Put the crumb mixture in the prepared pan and use the back of your fingers or the back of a spoon to press the crumb mixture evenly over the bottom and sides of the pan. Bake for 8 minutes. Set aside to cool thoroughly.

Mix the Filling

↬ Put the unsweetened chocolate, cream, and granulated sugar in a large heatproof container set over, but not touching, barely simmering water in a saucepan. Stir the mixture often over the hot water until the chocolate melts and the mixture is smoothly blended. As soon as the chocolate mixture melts, remove it from over the water. Stir in the dissolved coffee and set aside to cool slightly.

Put the butter and powdered sugar in a large bowl and beat with an electric mixer on medium speed until the mixture looks smooth, about 2 minutes. At first the mixture forms crumbs; continue mixing until it becomes smooth. Move the beaters around in the bowl if using a handheld electric mixer. Stop the mixer and scrape the mixture from the sides of the bowl and any that becomes caught in the beaters as needed throughout the mixing process. Mix in the vanilla. Decrease the speed to low and stir in the slightly cooled, but liquid, chocolate mixture. Continue mixing until the mixture is smooth and all of the chocolate mixture is incorporated. Set aside and immediately whip the cream.

Whip the Cream for the Filling and Topping

~ Put the cold cream, vanilla, and the 2 tablespoons powdered sugar in a clean large bowl and beat with an electric mixer on medium speed until the whipped cream is firm enough to hold its shape and to spread. Move the beaters around in the bowl if using a handheld electric mixer. If you stop the mixer and lift up the beaters, the cream forms a point that stands straight up when the beaters are removed. The movement of the beaters first forms smooth curving then wrinkled lines in the cream at this stage. Put 1½ cups of the whipped cream in the bowl of reserved chocolate mixture. Use a rubber spatula to fold the 2 mixtures together by digging down to the bottom of the bowl and bringing the 2 mixtures up and over each other until no white streaks of cream remain.

Fill the Pie and Add the Topping

~ Use the rubber spatula to scrape the chocolate filling into the cooled piecrust and spread it smooth. Use a clean rubber spatula to spread the remaining whipped cream over the filling, mounding it slightly to the center. Sprinkle the top with grated chocolate or gently place the piece of chocolate lace in the center of the pie. If the chocolate lace breaks, break it into pieces and arrange them around the top of the pie. Or, leave the whipped cream plain. Cover the pie carefully with plastic wrap and refrigerate it. Put several toothpicks in the whipped cream topping to keep the plastic wrap from squashing it.

Serve the Pie

~ Use a large knife to cut the pie into slices and serve cold. The covered pie can be refrigerated for up to 1 day.

Deluxe Coconut Cream Pie

White chocolate curls and whipped cream cover the coconut pastry cream filling in this lavish version of coconut cream pie. Toasted coconut and store-bought shortbread cookie crumbs produce a crumb crust with the crunch of coconut. The large white chocolate curls suggest flower petals and make this pie a nice choice for a spring occasion.

Baking Answers ◦ I use store-bought shortbread cookies for this cookie crumb crust. Lorna Doone cookies make a good choice, but any plain shortbread cookie works fine. To make the cookies into crumbs, put about 6 cookies at a time between 2 sheets of wax paper and use a rolling pin to crush them into crumbs, or process the cookies in a food processor until crumbs form.

The cream is beaten to the firmly whipped stage.

The coconut cream filling is made with the same pastry cream that is used in the Cherry Custard Tart with Pouring Crust (page 105). The only difference is that shredded coconut is mixed into the warm pastry cream.

White chocolate is softer than dark chocolate and is easy to scrape into large petal-like curls. These large curls have the same soft curving shape as wood shavings. When making chocolate curls, use a large piece of chocolate that is as thick as you can find. An 8-ounce or larger bar or a thick block of chocolate from a cookshop or gourmet grocery works well. It is easier to hold a large piece of chocolate in your hand, and large pieces have less of a tendency to break as you scrape off curls with a vegetable peeler. Handle the white chocolate curls gently and as little as possible to avoid breaking them. If the white chocolate curls are refrigerated or frozen, they are less likely to break when handled.

A Step Ahead ◦ Make the coconut cream filling a day ahead and refrigerate the covered coconut pastry cream overnight. Add the whipped cream to the filling when you assemble the pie. Make the white chocolate curls ahead and store them in a tightly covered container for up to 3 days in the refrigerator or up to a month in the freezer.

SERVES 8

Necessities ◦ *1 shiny metal or ovenproof glass 9-inch pie pan*

COCONUT CREAM FILLING	1½ cups shredded sweetened coconut
1 recipe warm freshly prepared pastry cream (pages 105–6)	

SHORTBREAD COOKIE CRUMB CRUST	⅔ cup shredded sweetened coconut, toasted (pages 40–41)
1⅓ cups shortbread cookie crumbs (about 5 ounces), such as Lorna Doone	2 ounces (½ stick) unsalted butter, melted

WHIPPED CREAM TOPPING	1 tablespoon powdered sugar
1½ cups cold whipping cream	1 teaspoon vanilla extract

1½ cups (about 3 ounces) white chocolate curls (pages 50–51)

Mix the Filling

↬ Put the warm pastry cream in a medium bowl and stir in the shredded coconut. Press a piece of plastic wrap onto the coconut cream and poke a few holes in the plastic wrap with the tip of a knife to let the steam escape. Refrigerate the custard until it is cold, for a least 3 hours or overnight.

Prepare and Bake the Crust

↬ Position an oven rack in the middle of the oven. Preheat the oven to 325°F. Butter the inside of a 9-inch pie pan.

Put the cookie crumbs and toasted coconut in a medium bowl and stir them together. Stir in the melted butter, stirring until the mixture is evenly moistened with the butter. Put the crumb mixture in the prepared pan and use the back of your fingers or the back of a spoon to press it evenly over the bottom and sides of the pie pan. Bake for 10 minutes. Set aside to cool.

Whip the Cream for the Filling and Topping

↬ Put the cold cream, powdered sugar, and vanilla in a clean large bowl and beat with an electric mixer on medium speed until the whipped cream is firm enough to hold its shape and to spread. Move the beaters around in the bowl if using a handheld electric mixer. If you stop the mixer and lift up the beaters, the cream forms a point that stands straight up when the beaters are removed. The movement of the beaters first forms smooth curving then wrinkled lines in the cream at this stage. Put ¾ cup of the whipped cream topping in the bowl of cold coconut cream. Use a rubber spatula to fold the 2 mixtures together by digging down to the bottom of the bowl and bringing the 2 mixtures up and over each other until no white streaks of whipped cream remain.

Fill the Pie and Add the Topping

❧ Scrape the coconut cream filling into the cooled crumb crust, spreading it evenly. Use a clean rubber spatula to spread the remaining whipped cream over the filling, mounding it slightly to the center.

Add the White Chocolate Curls and Serve

❧ Use a large spoon to place the white chocolate curls gently and evenly over the whipped cream. Use a large knife to cut the pie into slices and serve. Or, cover carefully with plastic wrap and refrigerate up to 2 days. The white chocolate curls protect the whipped cream under the plastic wrap. Serve cold.

Orange-and-White Chocolate Truffle Cake

This cake combines the best of two worlds. It has 2 large American-style yellow cake layers that are filled with a European-style orange-and-white chocolate truffle filling. The filling is easily made by melting white chocolate with hot cream and butter. The white chocolate frosting that covers the cake is a simple whipped combination of cold cream and some of the truffle filling.

Baking Answers ❧ "Truffle" refers to the classic mixture of chocolate or white chocolate, cream, and sometimes butter. The basic mixture can form a thick glaze or filling, but when cool it can be whipped to form a creamy mixture. "Ganache" refers to this same mixture.

Orange zest lends a substantial orange flavor to the cake and truffle. A thick-skinned orange yields about 2 teaspoons grated zest. For the zest, grate only the orange skin of the orange. The white pith is bitter and has no orange flavor.

For the truffle heat the cream and butter just until they are hot and the butter melts. If the cream boils, you must remove any skin that forms on top of it. Chop the chocolate into small pieces so that it melts easily in the hot mixture. White chocolate is softer than dark chocolate and is easily cut into small pieces with a large knife.

Since white chocolate produces a thinner truffle mixture than dark chocolate, I prefer to use heavy whipping cream for the filling and frosting. Heavy whipping cream has a higher butterfat content than whipping cream and makes a thicker mixture for the filling and frosting. Look in the dairy section for cartons that include the word "heavy" on the whipping cream label. The portion of the white chocolate mixture that is whipped with the cream should be cool to the touch and pourable, but not cold and hard. A warm mixture would prevent the cream from whipping firmly, whereas a cold, hard white chocolate mixture would be difficult to whip with the cream. The white chocolate mixture should be melted in a nonreactive container. Pyrex glass or stainless steel containers are nonreactive; aluminum is not.

A Step Ahead ◦ The cake layers can be baked, cooled, wrapped in plastic wrap and heavy aluminum foil, and frozen for up to 1 month. Defrost the cake layers, with the wrapping on, at room temperature. Or, they can be baked a day ahead, wrapped with plastic wrap, and stored at room temperature.

SERVES 12 TO 16

Necessities ◦ *2 baked and cooled 9-inch orange butter cake layers (pages 194–95)*

ORANGE-AND-WHITE CHOCOLATE FILLING	18 ounces chopped white chocolate, Callebaut or Lindt preferred
1 cup heavy whipping cream	2 teaspoons grated orange zest
4 tablespoons (½ stick) unsalted butter	

2 orange butter cake layers (pages 194–95), baked and cooled	

ORANGE-AND-WHITE CHOCOLATE WHIPPED CREAM FROSTING	1 teaspoon grated orange zest
1¾ cups cold heavy whipping cream	1 teaspoon vanilla extract
1 tablespoon Grand Marnier, or other orange-flavored liqueur	Reserved 1 cup truffle mixture

2 ounces chopped white chocolate or 1 cup (about 2 ounces) white chocolate curls (pages 50–51) for topping the cake	

Mix the Filling

↝ Put the cream and butter in a large saucepan and heat over medium-low heat until the cream is hot and the butter is melted. The hot cream mixture will form tiny bubbles and measure about 175°F. if tested with a food thermometer. Do not let the mixture boil. Remove the pan from the heat. Add the chopped white chocolate and let it melt in the hot cream mixture for about 30 seconds to soften. Whisk the mixture smooth. If all of the chocolate is not melted, return the mixture to low heat for about 1 minute, stirring the mixture until the white chocolate is melted and smooth. Remove the pan from any heat and stir in the orange zest. This is the truffle mixture for the filling and frosting.

Pour 1½ cups of the truffle mixture that will be used to fill the cake into a medium bowl. Cover and refrigerate it until it is cold and firm enough to spread, about 45 minutes. Set aside the remaining truffle mixture at room temperature (about 1 cup) until cool to the touch but pourable, about 45 minutes.

Fill the Cake

↝ Using the bottom of a tart pan to help, place 1 cake layer, top side up, on a serving plate. Tuck waxed paper strips just an inch or so under the bottom of the cake all the way around to keep the plate clean. Remove the 1½ cups of truffle filling from the refrigerator and spread it over the top of the cake layer, spreading it to the edges. Place the second layer, top side up, on the truffle-topped layer. If any filling drips onto the sides of the cake, spread it smoothly onto the sides. The whipped frosting will cover the sides. Refrigerate the cake while you make the frosting.

Whip the Frosting

↝ Put the cold cream, Grand Marnier, orange zest, vanilla, and the reserved slightly cooled but pourable 1 cup of truffle mixture in a large bowl and beat with an electric mixer on medium speed until it is firm enough to spread. Move the beaters around in the bowl if using a handheld electric mixer. The mixture thickens quickly and will probably be firmly whipped in about 1 minute. The movement of the beaters forms a distinct pattern of curving lines in the frosting at this stage.

Frost and Serve the Cake

↝ Use a thin metal spatula to spread the frosting over the top and sides of the cake, mounding it slightly on top toward the center. Sprinkle the chopped white chocolate or white chocolate curls over the center of the top of the cake. Gently pull out the wax paper strips, while sliding a knife under the cake to avoid pulling out smears of frosting, and discard them. Cover and refrigerate up to 3 days. Use a large knife to cut the cake into slices and serve cold.

Raspberries and Cream Macaroon Tart

Cool looks are what it takes to attract me to a dessert on a sweltering summer day. This fresh raspberry and almond tart has a topping of whipped cream and white chocolate curls that fulfills the cool and creamy promise. The attractive ridged-edged crust, abundance of fresh raspberries, and classy white chocolate topping put this in the elegant summer party category.

Baking Answers ⋄ The almond filling is quickly made in a food processor. You can grind the almonds for the filling in the food processor, remove them, then process the filling. It is not necessary to wash the work bowl after processing the almonds.

Bottles labeled pure almond extract are made with oil of bitter almond and are preferable to bottles labeled almond extract. The pure version is now available in supermarkets.

The cream for the topping is beaten to the firmly whipped stage.

White chocolate is softer than dark chocolate and is easy to scrape into large petal-like curls. These large curls have the same soft curving shape as wood shavings. When making chocolate curls, use a large piece of chocolate that is as thick as you can find. An 8-ounce or larger bar or a thick block of chocolate from a cookshop or gourmet grocery works well. It is easier to hold a large piece of chocolate in your hand, and large pieces have less of a tendency to break as you scrape off curls with a vegetable peeler. Handle the white chocolate curls gently and as little as possible to avoid breaking them. If the white chocolate curls have been refrigerated or frozen, they are less likely to break when handled.

A Step Ahead ⋄ The crust can be prepared, put in the tart pan, covered, and refrigerated overnight. Or, the crust and filling can be baked together, then covered and set aside overnight refrigerated.

The white chocolate curls can be prepared and frozen for up to 1 month. Seal them tightly in a metal or plastic container, label with the date and contents, and freeze. Use the white chocolate curls frozen.

SERVES 8

Necessities ⋄ *1 cold and unbaked Butter Cookie Tart Crust (page 203) in a 9-inch metal tart pan with a removable bottom and a baking sheet for holding the tart during baking*

ALMOND FILLING
2 large eggs
¼ teaspoon salt
¾ cup granulated sugar
1 teaspoon vanilla extract
¾ teaspoon pure almond extract

2 tablespoons amaretto liqueur (or
   almond-flavored liqueur)
1¼ cups blanched almonds, ground
2 ounces (½ stick) unsalted butter,
   melted

1 recipe unbaked cold Butter Cookie
   Tart Crust (page 203) in a
   9-inch tart pan

2 cups fresh raspberries

WHIPPED CREAM TOPPING
1 cup cold whipping cream
1 tablespoon powdered sugar

1 teaspoon vanilla extract
¼ teaspoon pure almond extract

2 cups (about 4 ounces) white
   chocolate curls (pages 50–51)

Mix the Filling

~ Position a rack in the middle of the oven. Preheat the oven to 400°F.

Put the eggs and salt in a food processor and process a few seconds just to combine the whites and yolks. With the food processor running, add the granulated sugar and process to a smooth fluffy mixture, about 2 minutes. Add the vanilla, almond extract, amaretto, and ground almonds and process for 30 seconds. The mixture is smooth, but you will see tiny pieces of ground almonds. Add the melted butter, processing just to incorporate it into the mixture. Use a rubber spatula to scrape all of the filling into the cold tart crust. Place the filled tart pan on a baking sheet.

Bake the Crust and Filling

~ Bake for 10 minutes. Reduce the oven temperature to 350°F. and bake for about 12 more minutes until the filling feels firm, if touched lightly, and the top is light brown. Cool the crust and filling thoroughly in the pan. Use a small, sharp knife to loosen the sides of the crust from the pan. Set the tart pan on a shallow bowl, such as a soup bowl, and let the rim slide down. Use a thin spatula to loosen the bottom of the crust from the pan and slide the filled crust onto a serving plate.

Add the Raspberries and Whip the Cream

⮞ Arrange the raspberries evenly over the almond filling. The raspberries will be covered with whipped cream, so it is more important to cover the almond filling evenly rather than make a pretty pattern.

Make the Topping

⮞ Put the cold cream, powdered sugar, vanilla, and almond extract in a clean large bowl and beat with an electric mixer on medium speed until the whipped cream is firm enough to hold its shape and to spread. Move the beaters around in the bowl if using a handheld electric mixer. If you stop the mixer and lift up the beaters, the cream forms a point that stands straight up when the beaters are removed. The movement of the beaters forms smooth curving then wrinkled lines in the cream at this stage.

Use a clean rubber spatula to gently spread the whipped cream over the raspberries, mounding it slightly toward the center.

Add the White Chocolate Curls and Serve

⮞ Use a large spoon to place the white chocolate curls gently and evenly over the whipped cream. Use a large knife to cut the tart into slices to serve. Or, cover with plastic wrap and refrigerate the tart for as long as overnight and serve cold.

Variations ⮞ *The white chocolate curls can be omitted and the whipped cream topping left plain, but, if the tart is going to be covered and refrigerated, put several toothpicks in the whipped cream to protect it from being squashed by the plastic wrap.*

Two cups of peeled, pitted, and sliced peaches (page 38)
can be substituted for the raspberries.

Aunt Elaine's Mocha Whipped Cream Shadow Cake

Neighbors and friends all had the same reaction when they tried this cake. "That's the lightest cake I have ever eaten. Is it a chocolate angel food cake?" The cake is actually a cocoa sponge cake that is filled with coffee whipped cream. The unique shadow finish comes from a coating of chocolate that is poured over the whipped cream topping to cover the top and form drizzles down the sides.

My aunt Elaine, whose desserts always come out so neat and beautiful, recently gave me this recipe, which she has been making for many years. I wondered why I had never had it when I was growing up, and then realized that it is a "grown-up" cake that she would have made for the adult crowd.

Baking Answers ⚬ The cake achieves its light texture from egg whites and yolks that are beaten in separate batches with sugar. The sugar stabilizes the whipped yolks and whites so they hold the air that is beaten into them. After the 2 beaten egg mixtures have been folded together, the flour mixture is gently folded into the egg mixture.

Choose cartons labeled heavy whipping cream for this cake. Heavy whipping cream has a higher butterfat content than whipping cream and makes firmly whipped cream that holds its shape even when the chocolate coating is poured over it. Chill the cake thoroughly before adding the chocolate topping.

Putting a chocolate coating on top of a soft whipped cream topping is a fast and fancy-looking technique that works well if the cream is cold and the chocolate topping is liquid and pours easily. Chocolate melted with vegetable oil is the secret to this cake's stunning chocolate finish. This combination forms a thin chocolate mixture that pours and spreads easily over the cold whipped cream topping. As soon as the chocolate cools, it forms a firm coating on the cold whipped cream. The firm coating is best cut with a large, sharp knife. First mark the cut with the knife, then begin at the center of the cake and cut slowly and steadily through the chocolate. Once you cut through the chocolate, the cake is tender and easy to cut. If the chocolate should crack when it is cut, warm the knife under hot water and dry it; it will cut cleanly through the chocolate.

SERVES 12 TO 14

Necessities ⚬ *Two 9-inch-diameter cake pans, both with 1¾- to 2-inch-high sides, 2 wire racks for cooling the cake layers, and a double boiler or heatproof container to put over a pan of barely simmering water for making the chocolate coating*

CHOCOLATE SPONGE CAKE LAYERS	1 teaspoon instant coffee granules
¾ cup plus 2 tablespoons cake flour	6 large eggs, separated
2 tablespoons unsweetened Dutch process cocoa powder	½ teaspoon cream of tartar
	1 cup granulated sugar
½ teaspoon baking soda	1 teaspoon vanilla extract

COFFEE WHIPPED CREAM	1 tablespoon instant coffee granules
2½ cups cold heavy whipping cream	1 teaspoon vanilla extract
½ cup powdered sugar	

CHOCOLATE SHADOW COATING	2 tablespoons plus 2 teaspoons corn or canola oil
1½ cups (9 ounces) semisweet chocolate chips	

Mix the Cake

↝ Position a rack in the middle of the oven. Preheat the oven to 350°F. Butter the inside of two 9-inch-diameter cake pans with 1¾- to 2-inch-high sides. Butter the sides of the pans carefully so the cake layers release easily. Line the bottom of the pans with parchment or wax paper and butter the paper.

Sift the flour, cocoa powder, baking soda, and instant coffee onto a piece of wax paper or into a medium bowl and set aside.

Put the egg whites and cream of tartar in a clean large bowl and use an electric mixer with clean dry beaters on medium speed to beat the egg whites until they are foamy and the cream of tartar is dissolved, about 15 seconds. Increase the speed to high and continue beating the egg whites until they look white, shiny, and smooth, and the movement of the beaters forms lines in the mixture. Move the beaters around in the bowl if using a handheld electric mixer. If you stop the mixer and lift up the beaters, the whites should cling to them. Slowly beat in ½ cup of the granulated sugar, 2 tablespoons every 15 seconds, beating for 1 minute after the last addition of sugar. Set aside while you beat the yolks.

Put the egg yolks, the remaining ½ cup of the granulated sugar, and vanilla in a clean large bowl. Use the electric mixer on high speed (it is not necessary to wash the beaters after beating the egg whites) to beat the yolk mixture until it lightens to a pale yellow and thickens, about 2 minutes. Use a large rubber spatula to fold the egg-white mixture in 2 additions into the egg-yolk mixture. Use the rubber spatula to fold the two mixtures together by digging down to the bottom of the bowl and bringing them up and over each other until no white streaks of egg whites remain. Slowly sprinkle the flour mixture over the egg mixture, folding in the flour mixture until it is completely incorporated and no loose flour remains. Fold quickly and gently so the mixture deflates as little as possible. Use a rubber spatula to scrape all of the batter into the prepared pans, dividing it evenly. Smooth the top.

Bake the Cake

↝ Bake for about 20 minutes. To test for doneness, gently press your fingers on the top middle of each cake. It should feel firm. If the cake feels firm, insert a toothpick into the center of the cake. As soon as the toothpick comes out clean, the cake is done. Cool the cake layers in their baking pans on a wire rack for 10 minutes. Use a small, sharp knife to loosen the sides of the cakes from the pans and invert them onto the wire racks. Carefully remove the paper liners, but let the papers rest on the cakes while they cool. Cool the cakes thoroughly, about 1 hour. Discard the paper liners. A thin shred of the top of the layers may stick to the wire racks when you remove them from the racks; this makes no difference to the finished cake.

Whip the Cream

↝ Put the cream, powdered sugar, instant coffee, and vanilla in a clean large bowl and beat with an electric mixer on medium speed until the whipped cream is firm enough to hold its shape and to spread. Move the beaters around in the bowl if using a handheld electric mixer. If you stop the mixer and lift up the beaters, the cream forms a point that stands straight up when the beaters are removed. The movement of the beaters forms smooth curving then wrinkled lines in the cream at this stage.

Fill and Frost the Cake with the Whipped Cream

↝ Place a large plate over the bottom of each cake layer and using the wire rack to hold the cake in place, invert each cake layer onto the plates. The top side of each cake layer is now facing up. Use a large, serrated knife and a sawing motion to cut each cake evenly into 2 horizontal layers. Cut into each cake layer with the serrated knife, turning the cake as you cut through to the middle until you have cut through the cake layer. Lift off the top half of 1 cake layer and move it to the side. Place the bottom of 1 cake layer, cut side up, on a serving plate or cardboard cake circle. Cooled sponge cake layers are stable and easy to move, but if you prefer, slide the removable bottom of a tart pan under the layers when moving them. If you have a turntable, such as a plastic turntable or cake turntable, put the cake on it. Slide wax paper strips under the cake to protect the plate. Use a thin metal spatula to spread about 1 cup of the whipped cream evenly over the top of the cake on the plate. Lift the top half of that split cake layer onto the whipped cream, centering it evenly on the bottom layer. Spread about 1 cup of the whipped cream evenly over the top of the cake. Repeat with the second split cake layer so that there are 4 cake layers filled with 3 layers of whipped cream. Spread a thin layer of whipped cream over the top and sides of the cake to help crumbs adhere to it. You will see cake through the whipped cream. Then spread the remaining whipped cream over the top and sides of the cake. You will have 4 layers of cake, filled and covered with whipped cream. Refrigerate the uncovered cake for at least 1 hour to firm the whipped cream topping. When you are ready to finish the cake, make the chocolate coating.

Make the Coating and Top the Cake

Put the chocolate chips and oil in a large heatproof container set over, but not touching, barely simmering water in a saucepan. Stir the mixture often over the hot water until the chocolate melts and the mixture is smooth. Remove the chocolate coating from over the water.

Remove the cake from the refrigerator. Use a dish towel to wipe the bottom of the pan that the chocolate coating is in so no moisture drips onto the cake. Pour the chocolate coating slowly over the top of the cake, covering it evenly. Pour the coating back and forth over the center of the cake, leaving about 1 inch around the edges plain. Working quickly, use a thin metal spatula to spread the coating evenly over the top, letting some thin lines of chocolate drip down the sides at about 1- to 1½-inch intervals. The chocolate drips will be thicker at the top and thinner as they drip down the sides of the cake. Use a spoon to drizzle any remaining chocolate where any large spaces without drizzle remain on the sides of the cake. The random effect of the drizzle looks nice, and it is not necessary to make evenly spaced drizzles of chocolate. Gently pull out and discard the wax paper strips. Refrigerate the cake, uncovered, to firm the topping, about 20 minutes. When the chocolate is firm, cover the cake carefully with plastic wrap.

Serve the Cake

Use a large, sharp knife to cut the cake. First, use a back-and-forth motion to mark the chocolate topping and partially cut through the chocolate for each slice. Then slice the cake. If the chocolate topping should break as you cut the cake, dip the knife in hot water, carefully wipe it dry, and cut the cake. The cake can be covered and refrigerated up to 3 days.

Chocolate Whipped Cream Truffle Cake

It's difficult to tell where the cake ends and the chocolate fudge filling begins between these chocolate cake layers. The outside of the cake is covered with whipped cream, so when the cake is cut there is a dramatic combination of dark fudge-filled cake and white whipped cream. It may seem as if the recipe calls for a large amount of chocolate truffle filling, but that's what it takes to make that extravagant ½-inch-thick layer of fudge filling.

Baking Answers ◦∙ "Truffle" refers to the classic mixture of chocolate or white chocolate, cream, and sometimes butter. The basic truffle mixture can form a thick fudge-type glaze or filling. When cool, it can be whipped to form a creamy mixture. "Ganache" refers to this same mixture. In this cake, a cool, but not whipped, chocolate truffle mixture is used to fill the cake.

To chop chocolate quickly, I seal about eight 1-ounce pieces of semisweet baking chocolate in their paper wrappers in a plastic bag and pound them into small pieces with the edge of a flat meat pounder or with a hammer. Pound them on a hard surface that won't be harmed by the pounding, such as a brick floor or a wooden board. Then remove the paper wrappers, put the chocolate in a bowl, and continue with another batch until all of the chocolate is chopped.

For the truffle, heat the cream and butter just until they are hot and the butter melts. If the cream boils, you must remove any skin that forms on top of it.

The cream is beaten to the firmly whipped stage.

The coffee syrup adds flavor and additional moisture to the cake while preventing crumbs from adhering to the filling and topping as it is spread.

A Step Ahead ◦∙ The cake layers can be baked, cooled, wrapped in plastic wrap and heavy aluminum foil, and frozen for up to 1 month. Defrost the cake layers, with their wrapping on, at room temperature.

SERVES 12 TO 16

Necessities ◦∙ *Two 9-inch chocolate cake layers, baked and cooled (pages 306–7), and a pastry brush*

CHOCOLATE TRUFFLE FILLING— MAKES ABOUT 2 CUPS	10 ounces (1⅔ cups) semisweet chocolate chips or semisweet chocolate, chopped
¾ cup whipping cream	
2 tablespoons (¼ stick) unsalted butter, cut in pieces	1 teaspoon vanilla extract

COFFEE SYRUP	2 tablespoons granulated sugar
¼ cup hot strong coffee	¼ teaspoon vanilla extract

WHIPPED CREAM TOPPING	⅔ cup powdered sugar
1½ cups cold whipping cream	1 teaspoon vanilla extract

2 chocolate cake layers (pages
306–7), baked and cooled

Make the Filling

↪ Put the cream and butter in a large saucepan and heat over medium-low heat until the cream is hot and the butter is melted. The hot cream mixture will form tiny bubbles and measure about 175°F. on a food thermometer. Do not let the mixture boil. Remove the pan from the heat. Add the chopped chocolate and let it melt in the hot cream mixture for about 30 seconds to soften. Whisk the mixture smooth. If all of the chocolate is not melted, return the mixture to low heat for about 1 minute, stirring the mixture until the chocolate is melted and smooth. Remove the pan from any heat and stir in the vanilla. Set aside at room temperature until thick enough to spread, about 1 hour. Or refrigerate until thickened but not hard.

Prepare the Syrup

↪ Put the coffee and granulated sugar in a small saucepan and stir them together over low heat until the sugar dissolves. Stir in the vanilla. Set aside to cool slightly.

Fill the Cake

↪ Put one of the cake layers, top side up, on a cake plate. Tuck waxed paper strips just an inch or so under the bottom of the cake all the way around to keep the plate clean.

Use a pastry brush to brush some of the coffee syrup over the top. Spread all of the cooled chocolate truffle filling over the top. Refrigerate the cake layer for 10 minutes to firm the filling while you whip the cream.

Whip the Cream and Frost and Serve the Cake

∽ Put the cream, powdered sugar, and vanilla in a large bowl and beat with an electric mixer on medium speed until the whipped cream is firm enough to hold its shape and to spread. If using a handheld electric mixer, move the beaters around in the bowl. If you stop the mixer and lift up the beaters, the cream forms a point that stands straight up when the beaters are removed. The movement of the beaters first forms smooth curving then wrinkled lines in the cream at this stage. The whipped cream looks smooth, not grainy.

Remove the fudge-topped cake layer from the refrigerator and slide the second layer on top of it, top side up. Brush the remaining coffee syrup over the top and sides of the cake. Use a thin metal spatula to spread the whipped cream over the top and sides of the cake. Gently pull out the wax paper strips, while sliding a knife under the cake to avoid pulling out smears of frosting, and discard them. Cover carefully with plastic wrap and refrigerate up to 2 days. A few toothpicks in the top of the cake keep the plastic wrap from disturbing the whipped cream. Use a large knife to cut the cake into slices and serve cold.

Pecan Meringues Stacked with Whipped Cream and Strawberry Sauce

These individual pecan meringues layered with whipped cream and strawberry sauce let everyone dig into their own personal dessert. Meringues that are doubly crisp from the addition of crunchy pecans and heaped with smooth whipped cream and sauce become stacks of pure indulgence. Frozen strawberries serve as an always-available fruit to use for the sauce.

Baking Answers ∽ Since humidity puts moisture back into crisp meringues and softens them, they should be stored in a dry place. When the weather is humid, I usually wrap the cooled meringues and store them in the freezer until I am ready to use them. On the other hand, I have found that in dry weather the wrapped meringues can be stored at room temperature for as long as 5 days.

I grind the pecans for the meringues in a food processor and process them up to the point that some small pieces of pecans, about ⅛ inch in size, remain among the ground nuts.

Defrost the strawberries for the sauce before pureeing them in a food processor or a blender.

Then press the strawberry puree through a strainer to remove any pulp and make the sauce smooth. A blender also works well for pureeing the strawberries.

The cream is beaten to the firmly whipped stage.

A Step Ahead ↝ The meringues can be baked up to a month ahead and frozen. Put the bottoms of 2 meringues together (this helps prevent breakage) and wrap them in plastic wrap. Put the wrapped meringues in a metal or plastic freezer container, label with the date and contents, seal tightly, and freeze. Defrost the wrapped meringues at room temperature.

The strawberry sauce can be prepared up to 3 days ahead, covered with plastic wrap, and refrigerated.

MAKES 12 MERINGUE CIRCLES TO SERVE 6

Necessities ↝ *1 heavyweight baking sheet*

PECAN MERINGUES	¼ cup powdered sugar
3 large egg whites	1 teaspoon vanilla extract
¼ teaspoon cream of tartar	¾ cup coarsely ground pecans, largest
½ cup granulated sugar	pieces about ⅛ inch
STRAWBERRY SAUCE— **MAKES ABOUT 1¼ CUPS**	2 teaspoons fresh lemon juice
One 16-ounce carton sliced frozen strawberries in syrup, defrosted and not drained	
WHIPPED CREAM	2 tablespoons powdered sugar
1½ cups cold whipping cream	1 teaspoon vanilla extract
6 whole strawberries for garnishing the meringues, optional	

Mix the Meringues

↝ Position an oven rack in the middle of the oven. Preheat the oven to 250°F. Line a baking sheet with parchment paper. Butter the paper lightly and dust it with powdered sugar. With the tip of a dull knife and pressing lightly, mark twelve 3-inch circles 1 inch apart on the parchment paper. A 9-ounce paper cup turned upside down makes a good guide for marking the circles.

Put the egg whites and cream of tartar in a clean large bowl and use an electric mixer with clean dry beaters on medium speed to beat the egg whites until they are foamy and the cream of tartar is dissolved, about 15 seconds. Increase the speed to high and continue beating the egg whites until they look white, shiny, and smooth, and the movement of the beaters forms lines in the mixture, about 30 seconds. Move the beaters around in the bowl if using a handheld electric mixer. If you stop the mixer and lift up the beaters, the whites should cling to them. Slowly beat in the granulated sugar, 1 tablespoon every 15 seconds, beating for another 15 seconds after the last addition of sugar. Beat in the powdered sugar in 2 additions, beating for about 15 seconds after each addition. I time adding the sugar at the beginning so I don't have a tendency to rush it. Stir in the vanilla. The tiny bubbles that were visible before the sugar was added have disappeared and the mixture is silken smooth and soft yet firm in texture. It looks like whipped marshmallow. Use a large spatula to fold in the pecans.

Put a dab of meringue on the baking sheet underneath each corner of the parchment paper to hold the paper in place. Drop large tablespoonfuls of the meringue mixture over each marked circle. Use a thin metal spatula to spread the mixture over each circle, holding the flat side of the spatula on the meringue mixture and sweeping it back and forth in small sweeps to spread the meringue to an even thickness. When you lift the spatula, it makes a little curl on the top of the meringue; this is fine. The meringues will be about ½ inch thick. The meringues do not spread or rise much during baking.

Bake the Meringues

↝ Bake for about 1 hour until the meringues feel crisp on top and are lightly colored. Cool the meringues on the baking sheet until cool to the touch, about 1 hour. Once the meringues cool, they are ready to fill or can be sealed in a metal tin for up to 2 days, or up to 5 days if the weather remains dry. It is better not to bake meringues on a rainy or humid day, but if you must, turn off the oven and leave the meringues in the oven until they are cool, about 2 hours. Then, freeze the cooled meringues as directed above or leave them in the turned-off oven to use later in the day.

Make the Sauce

↝ Put the strawberries and their liquid in a food processor. Process to form a puree. Place a strainer over a small bowl and put the pureed strawberries in the strainer. Press the strawberries against the strainer to strain a smooth puree into the bowl. Discard any pulp in the strainer. Stir the lemon juice into the strawberry sauce. The sauce is ready to use or it can be covered with plastic wrap and stored in the refrigerator for up to 3 days.

Whip the Cream

↝ Put the cream, powdered sugar, and vanilla in a clean large bowl and beat with an electric mixer on medium speed until the cream is softly whipped. The movement of the beaters forms curving lines in the cream at this stage. The whipped cream forms a soft mound when it is spooned onto a plate. The whipped cream can be covered and refrigerated up to 2 hours.

Assemble the Stacks and Serve the Meringues

✑ When you are ready to serve the meringue stacks, have ready 6 dessert plates. Put 1 meringue, bottom side down, on each plate. Spoon about 2 heaping tablespoons of whipped cream over each. Drizzle about 1 tablespoon of strawberry sauce over each. Place a meringue bottom side down gently on top of the strawberry sauce and top with more whipped cream and strawberry sauce. Serve immediately. A whole strawberry makes a nice garnish, if desired.

Zuccotto—Italian Chocolate and Vanilla Cream Cake

I'm glad that you can't see this cake. From its impressive appearance you might think it too difficult to attempt. It is actually a cake made up of simple components that are put together in a clever way. An ordinary round bowl lined with plastic wrap is the mold that gives the cake its perfect round shape, and the plastic wrap liner ensures that the cake comes out of the bowl easily. The bowl is lined with long strips of pound cake and filled with 2 flavors of whipped cream. I divide a batch of whipped cream and add chopped chocolate, toasted almonds, and orange peel to one part of it and melted chocolate to the other. Chill the whole cake before turning it out of the bowl, brush it with melted jam to make it shine, and it is ready. With a pound cake on hand, the whole thing assembles quickly and gives a big fancy payoff for just a little time.

Baking Answers ✑ The rounded shape of a Zuccotto imitates the form of the elongated domes of Italian cathedrals. The shape of the bowl used for the mold determines the final shape of the cake. Deep mixing bowls that the English call pudding basins work well, but any round bowl produces a pleasing shape.

Choose cartons labeled heavy whipping cream for this dessert. Heavy whipping cream has a higher butterfat content than whipping cream and produces the desired firmly whipped filling.

Since there is no reason to turn on the oven, unless you must bake the pound cake, melt the chocolate for the chocolate cream filling in a pan set over hot water. When adding the melted chocolate to the whipped cream, whisk ½ cup of the whipped cream mixture thoroughly into the melted chocolate. Then the remaining whipped cream can be folded smoothly into the chocolate mixture. This is a simple but important mixing technique that will keep the finished chocolate cream mixture smooth by preventing the warm chocolate from hardening when it is combined with the cold whipped cream.

The pound cake and presentation are not affected if there are wrinkles in the plastic wrap that lines the bowl.

The pound cake is cut lengthwise in long strips for this cake, so it should be baked in a loaf pan rather than a tube pan. It is unlikely that any of the pound cake strips will break, but if one does, use it to line the bottom of the bowl or the top of the cake (which becomes the bottom when unmolded).

For the zest, grate only the orange skin of the orange. The white pith is bitter and has no orange flavor.

A Step Ahead ↝ Bake the pound cake (page 157) ahead. Cool the cake, wrap it in plastic wrap and heavy aluminum foil, and freeze it for up to 3 months. Defrost the wrapped cake at room temperature.

The Cointreau syrup can be made up to a week ahead.

SERVES 10 TO 12

Necessities ↝ *1 round bowl with about a 1¾- to 2-quart capacity for assembling the cake, a heatproof container for melting the chocolate, a pastry brush, and 1 loaf (½ recipe) of Deep South Pound Cake (page 157), cooled*

COINTREAU SYRUP	2 tablespoons Cointreau, orange-flavored liqueur, or brandy
2 tablespoons hot water	
1 tablespoon granulated sugar	

1 loaf Deep South Pound Cake, (page 157), baked and cooled or defrosted if frozen

WHIPPED CREAM FILLINGS	2 teaspoons Cointreau, orange-flavored liqueur, or brandy
3 ounces semisweet chocolate, coarsely chopped	¼ cup toasted blanched almonds (page 40), coarsely chopped
2 cups cold heavy whipping cream	3 ounces semisweet chocolate, chopped into ¼-inch pieces
¼ cup plus 2 tablespoons powdered sugar	2 teaspoons grated orange zest
2 teaspoons vanilla extract	

Prepare the Syrup

➤ Put the water and granulated sugar in a small saucepan and stir them over low heat just until the sugar dissolves. Remove the pan from the heat and stir in the Cointreau. Set the syrup aside to cool. The syrup can be put in a small bowl, covered, and stored in the refrigerator for up to 1 week.

Line the Bowl with Cake

➤ Line a round bowl with a 1¾- to 2-quart capacity with plastic wrap, letting the edges extend over the edges of the bowl.

Trim a thin slice from each of the long sides of the pound cake and discard or eat them. Use a large knife to cut 7 lengthwise slices about ¼ inch thick from the cake. You will have long, thin rectangles of pound cake. Cut a small piece of pound cake from one of the slices to fit the bottom of the bowl. Place it in the bottom of the bowl. Cut the remaining long pound cake rectangles in half along a diagonal (from one corner to an opposite corner) to make 2 long triangular-shaped pieces from each slice. Trim each slice to fit the depth of the bowl. If any cake needs trimming, trim it from the narrow, pointed end of the triangle. Save these cake scraps. Arrange the trimmed pound cake slices, narrow end down, around the inside of the bowl. The edges of the cake slices should be touching and the inside of the bowl should be completely covered with pound cake. You will use about 12 of the trimmed triangles, depending on the circumference of the bowl. If you should need more slices, cut them from the remaining pound cake loaf. Brush the liqueur syrup generously over the pound cake lining the bowl.

Whip the Fillings

➤ Put the coarsely chopped semisweet chocolate in a large heatproof container set over, but not touching, barely simmering water in a saucepan. Stir the chocolate often over the hot water until it is melted and smooth. As soon as the chocolate melts, remove it from over the water and set it aside to cool slightly while you whip the cream.

Put the cream, ¼ cup of the powdered sugar, vanilla, and Cointreau in a clean large bowl and beat with an electric mixer on medium speed until the cream is firm enough to hold its shape. It will take about 4 minutes for the heavy cream to beat firm. If you stop the mixer and lift up the beaters, the cream forms a point that stands straight up when the beaters are removed. The movement of the beaters forms smooth curving then wrinkled lines in the cream at this stage. Put 2 cups of the whipped cream in a large bowl and set aside. Use a large spatula to fold the remaining 2 tablespoons of powdered sugar, almonds, chopped chocolate, and orange zest gently into the whipped cream left in the original bowl. Spread this mixture over the bottom and sides of the pound cake lining in the bowl, leaving a cavity in the center. The thick mixture clings to the cake.

Use a rubber spatula to scrape the reserved melted chocolate into a clean, large bowl. Use a whisk to mix about ½ cup of the reserved whipped cream mixture into the chocolate, whisking until the mixture is smooth and the chocolate is incorporated. Immediately use a rubber spatula to fold the remaining whipped cream into the chocolate mixture by digging down to the bottom of the bowl and bringing the 2 mixtures up and over each other until no white streaks of whipped cream remain. Scrape the chocolate cream into the cavity in the center of the cake. Smooth the top. Cover the top of the cake with scraps of pound cake slices. This becomes the bottom of the cake, so it does not show and does not have to look perfect.

Cover and refrigerate at least 4 hours or overnight. The cake firms and the flavors blend as the cake rests in the refrigerator. Place a serving platter on top of the cake and invert the bowl onto the serving platter. Release the cake from the bowl by lifting the bowl from the cake, while pulling down on the edges of the plastic wrap. Remove and discard the plastic wrap if it still clings to the cake.

Glaze the Cake

↦ Heat the apricot preserves in a small pan over low heat just until they melt. Remove the pan from the heat. Use a pastry brush to gently brush the melted preserves over the outside of the cake. Leave any large pieces of preserves in the pan and discard them. Arrange the whole almonds around the top of the cake.

Serve the Cake

↦ Use a large, sharp knife to cut slices of cold cake. Each section of pound cake can define a slice. Leftover cake can be covered and refrigerated for 1 day.

Melting Sugar for Caramel and Praline

I THINK EVEN CARDBOARD WOULD TASTE GOOD IF IT WERE COVERED WITH CARAMEL SAUCE, PRALINE, OR ANY KIND OF CARAMELIZED SUGAR. NO, I'M NOT RECOMMENDING THAT YOU EAT CARAMEL-COVERED CARDBOARD, BUT I AM SUGGESTING THAT YOU TRY caramelizing sugar or making nutty praline. Despite the fact that it looks as if it is some mysterious and challenging task, caramelizing sugar is easy. It is simply a matter of melting sugar and letting it cook and bubble away until it reaches the desired dark golden, amberlike color. When sugar is caramelized, it becomes less sweet than pure sugar and develops a rich flavor. Burning is really the only thing to worry about—burning yourself, or burning the caramel. To prevent burning yourself, just be careful not to splash any on yourself and be aware that when a liquid is added to hot caramel, the mixture bubbles up to at least 4 times its volume. To prevent burning the caramelized sugar, watch it carefully and keep an eagle eye on it as soon as it begins to change its color from clear to golden. Resist any temptation to answer the telephone or leave the bubbling sugar for a minute (voice of experience speaking here), and you too will be comfortable with the process.

The formula for making classic caramel sauce or caramel syrup is simple. Hot cream is added to the caramelized sugar to make caramel sauce, and hot water is added to make caramel syrup. Cooking the sugar with some water helps the sugar dissolve and melt evenly, but the more water that is added in proportion to the sugar, the longer the cooking time required to caramelize the sugar. I have found that nonstick-lined pans, with their slippery surface, work especially well for caramelizing the sugar evenly. To caramelize the sugar, put the sugar and water in a saucepan, cover the pan, and cook the mixture over a low heat to dissolve the sugar. Uncover the pan, raise the heat, and boil the mixture until it thickens and becomes an evenly dark golden color. This happens as the water evaporates and the sugar mixture reaches a temperature of over 320°F. The boiling bubbles change from large bubbles that are about ½ inch in diameter to tiny and fewer in number bubbles. Stir the mixture at this point so it colors evenly. Use a wooden spoon to stir the caramel. It will not retain heat and become uncomfortably hot to hold as a metal spoon could. It takes some time to reach the golden-colored stage, but as soon as the color begins to change, the process goes quickly. Remember, the only way you can ruin caramel is to burn it, so keep your eagle eye on it.

Once the sugar is caramelized, you can add hot water to make caramel syrup or hot cream to make a thick caramel sauce. When either liquid is added to the hot sugar, the mixture bubbles up vigorously and you should take particular care not to burn yourself. Add liquids that are warm or hot rather than cold, so the liquid doesn't solidify the carefully melted caramel. If small, hard pieces of caramel do form when some liquid is added, simply stir the syrup or sauce over low heat until it is smooth and any hard pieces melt. At this point, the caramel sauce or syrup is ready, if it is to be used while warm. The caramel sauce thickens as it cools and thickens further if refrigerated.

Since the sauce and syrup can be stored for up to 1 week in the refrigerator, I pour the warm caramel into a nonreactive heatproof container and have it ready to warm over low heat whenever I need it. Stainless-steel and ceramic pans are nonreactive, aluminum and cast iron are not. I often use a Corning Ware casserole that can go from refrigerator to stove-top burner. The caramel sauce does not bubble up again when it is warmed over low heat.

To make a larger quantity, make a double recipe by doubling the ingredients, but be sure to use a large saucepan that allows for the bubbling when the hot cream or hot water is added.

To make praline, cook the sugar to the caramel stage and then add the nuts to the hot caramelized sugar. The caramelized nuts form an intensely flavored nut brittle that can be ground to a powder or crushed into small pieces to add to a dessert. Almonds and hazelnuts are commonly used, but pecans, pine nuts, walnuts, pistachios, or any nut can be mixed with the caramelized sugar. Each nut produces a new flavor of praline, with a pecan praline tasting quite different from a hazelnut praline. I melt the sugar for praline in a heavy nonstick frying pan and then continue the cooking until it becomes a dark, golden liquid caramel. Since the sugar for praline cooks by itself, without the addition of water, it melts into a clear, smooth caramel and does not bubble as it cooks. If any hard lumps of sugar should form, they melt as the sugar caramelizes. It is different from caramel sauce or syrup because there is no cream or water added to the caramelized sugar after the sugar caramelizes, and no bubbling up out of the pan to concern you. However, the caramelized sugar is very hot, and care should be taken not to let any spill on you. Producing a super-sophisticated nut praline is even easier than making caramel sauce or syrup.

Some other ways to add a caramel flavor to a dessert are to boil brown sugar with cream, as in the caramel frosting for the Pear and Almond Cake with Caramel Frosting (page 370) or to cook condensed milk with butter to a caramel, as for the Banoffee Pie (page 373). An alternative to the classic praline preparation is to bake brown sugar–coated nuts until they are caramel-like and crunchy and use them as a topping for a Pumpkin Pecan Praline Cheesecake (page 363).

Cranberry Caramel Buckle

Traditionally a buckle is a moist fruit-filled cake topped with crumbs. To enrich the tradition, I've mixed the cranberries in this buckle with caramel sauce and drizzled additional caramel sauce over the crumbs to create a topping that is both sticky and crunchy. The tart and colorful cranberries complement the sweet cake and crumb topping.

The buckle can be cut into squares to carry on a picnic or dressed up by serving it warm and topped with scoops of vanilla ice cream. Or, try the extravaganza presentation by doubling the recipe for the caramel sauce (using a 4-quart saucepan to cook it) and spooning warm sauce over the ice cream and buckle.

Baking Answers ✦ I find the easiest way to caramelize sugar for caramel sauce is to dissolve the sugar in some water by cooking the mixture over a low-medium heat to melt the sugar, then raising the heat and boiling it until it turns an evenly dark golden color. Cooking the sugar with some water helps the sugar to melt evenly. The sugar caramelizes as the water evaporates and the sugar mixture reaches a temperature above 320°F. As the sugar mixture boils and becomes hotter, the boiling bubbles change from large bubbles to tiny bubbles and the number of bubbles decreases. The change in the bubbles signals the sugar is about to reach the caramel stage. It takes about 10 minutes to reach this dark golden-colored stage, but as soon as the color begins to change, the process goes quickly, so watch it constantly. The higher the heat that the burner is set at, the faster the sugar cooks and the faster the color change of the sugar to the dark golden caramel color. It is a good idea to be very patient and cook the sugar on a burner set at the lower end of medium-high heat, until you have made caramel sauce several times and feel comfortable with it. If you should see a tiny wisp of smoke from the still cooking but caramelized sugar mixture, remove the caramelized sugar from the heat immediately. A wisp of smoke signals the caramel is ready, and if it cooks any longer it can burn. You can drop a bit of caramel on a light-colored plate to test the color, then remove the caramel from the heat as soon as the color you want is reached. Remember, the only way you can ruin caramel is to burn it. Any hard sugar crystals that form as the mixture cooks will dissolve in the hot caramel at the end of the cooking process.

Once the sugar caramelizes, remove the pan from the heat and slowly add warm cream to the hot caramel. This produces caramel sauce or a caramel filling; the more cream that is added, the thinner the finished sauce. When the warm cream is added to the hot caramelized sugar, the mixture bubbles up, so be careful that it does not splash on you. That is why you want to add the cream slowly and use a large saucepan to cook caramelized sugar that will have a warm liquid added to it.

Use a wooden spoon to stir the caramel. It will not retain heat and become too hot to handle as a metal spoon can.

For a double recipe of the caramel sauce, double the ingredients and cook the sugar to a caramel in a 4-quart saucepan. A double recipe of the mixture will take longer for the sugar to dissolve and turn to a caramel than a single recipe does. To clean the saucepan easily, fill it with hot water and let it soak until the caramelized sugar dissolves.

Bottles labeled pure almond extract are made with oil of bitter almond and are preferable to bottles labeled almond extract. The pure version is now available in supermarkets.

A Step Ahead ⟿ The caramel sauce can be prepared up to a week ahead, cooled, poured into a heatproof container, covered, and refrigerated. When you are ready to use it, heat the caramel sauce in a small saucepan over low heat until it softens.

SERVES 9

Necessities ⟿ *One 9-inch square baking pan or an 11 x 7-inch baking pan, both with 2-inch-high sides, a 3-quart saucepan for cooking the caramel mixture, and a small 2-cup saucepan for heating the cream*

CARAMEL SAUCE—	½ cup water
MAKES ABOUT ¾ CUP	⅔ cup granulated sugar
½ cup whipping cream	

CRUMB TOPPING	½ cup packed light brown sugar
3 ounces (¾ stick) soft unsalted	1 teaspoon ground cinnamon
butter	¾ cup unbleached all-purpose flour

CRANBERRY CAKE	3 ounces (¾ stick) soft unsalted
2 cups unsweetened cranberries, fresh	butter
or frozen and defrosted	⅔ cup granulated sugar
¼ cup reserved caramel sauce (see	2 large eggs
above)	1 teaspoon vanilla extract
2 cups unbleached all-purpose flour	½ teaspoon pure almond extract
1½ teaspoons baking powder	½ cup whole milk
¼ teaspoon salt	

Cook the Sauce

⟿ Put the cream in a small saucepan and heat it over low heat. When the cream is added to the hot caramelized sugar, it should be hot, about 150°F. if measured with a food thermometer. Do not boil the cream. If the cream should boil and a skin forms on top, use a spoon to lift out the skin and discard it. Keep the cream hot over low heat while you cook the water and sugar to a caramel. Adjust the heat or remove the cream from the heat to keep it hot, but not at the boil.

Put the water and granulated sugar in a heavy-bottomed saucepan that has at least a 3-quart capacity. Cover and cook over low-medium heat until the sugar dissolves, about 6 minutes. Stir the mixture occasionally to help the sugar dissolve. Do not worry if a few sugar crystals form on the side of the pan. Remove the cover, increase the heat to medium-high, and bring the mixture to a boil. Boil the mixture until the sugar begins to change color, then caramelizes and turns a dark golden color, about 10 minutes. As the sugar reaches the caramel stage, the bubbles become tiny, and as the water evaporates, the mixture thickens to a thick syrup. You can quickly dip the spoon in the caramel and drop a drop on a light-colored plate to see the color. As soon as the mixture begins to turn golden, stir it with a wooden spoon once or twice to ensure the sugar cooks evenly and all of the sugar caramelizes. Once the caramel begins to change color, it reaches the dark golden stage quickly, so watch it constantly and remove it from the heat immediately. If you see a wisp of smoke, remove it from the heat immediately.

Slowly and carefully pour the hot cream into the hot caramelized sugar. The mixture will bubble up, so be careful. Once the caramel sauce stops bubbling, you can return the pan to low heat if the caramel is sticking to the bottom of the pan or is not completely smooth. If the pan is put back on the heat when the caramel sauce is still bubbling, it could bubble up and out of the pan, so be sure to wait for the bubbles to subside. You will feel any caramel that sticks to the bottom of the pan as you stir it, or if the pan is tilted slightly, you will see caramel sticking to the bottom. If the caramel sauce needs to be returned to low heat, stir continuously with the wooden spoon over the heat for 1 or 2 minutes until the caramel is completely dissolved and the mixture is smooth. Set the sauce aside to cool slightly while you mix the crumbs and cake. Or, pour it into a heatproof container, cool, cover, and refrigerate it for up to 1 week. Caramel sauce thickens as it cools.

Mix the Topping

↜ Put the butter, brown sugar, and cinnamon in a medium bowl and beat with an electric mixer on medium speed until it is smooth and blended together, about 1 minute. Move the beaters around in the bowl if using a handheld electric mixer. Reduce the speed to low and add the flour, mixing just until the mixture forms crumbs and all of the flour is incorporated, about 15 seconds. Set aside.

Mix the Cake

↜ Preheat the oven to 325°F. Line a 9 x 9 x 2-inch baking pan or an 11 x 7 x 2-inch baking pan with heavy aluminum foil that extends over 2 ends of the pan. Butter the inside of the foil.

Put the cranberries in a small bowl and add ¼ cup of the caramel sauce, stirring to coat the cranberries with sauce.

Sift the flour, baking powder, and salt together onto a piece of wax paper or into a medium bowl and set aside.

Put the butter and granulated sugar in a large bowl and beat with an electric mixer on medium speed until it is smooth, about 1 minute. The mixture forms large clumps of butter and sugar, then forms a smooth mass. Move the beaters around in the bowl if using a handheld electric mixer. Stop the mixer and scrape the mixture from the sides of the bowl and any that becomes caught in the beaters as needed throughout the mixing process. Add the eggs, then beat for 2 minutes. Add the vanilla and almond extract, mixing just to incorporate them. Decrease the speed to low and add half of the flour mixture, mixing to incorporate it. Add the milk, mixing just until it is blended into the mixture. The mixture may look slightly curdled. Add the remaining flour mixture, mixing just until it is mixed completely into the batter and the batter looks smooth. If any flour is clinging to the sides of the bowl, stir it into the batter. Use a large spoon to stir the caramel-coated cranberries into the cake batter.

Use a rubber spatula to scrape the batter from the bowl and spread the batter evenly in the pan. Leaving a ½-inch edge bare, use a spoon to drizzle the remaining caramel sauce, about ½ cup, evenly over the batter. Sprinkle the reserved crumb topping evenly over the caramel sauce.

Bake and Serve the Cake

↬ Bake about 50 minutes, until a toothpick inserted into the center of the cake comes out clean. Reverse the pan in the oven after 30 minutes of baking. Cool the cake thoroughly in the pan at room temperature, about 2 hours. Some indentations in the top of the cake may form as the cake cools and the caramel sauce sinks into it; this is fine. Carefully lift the aluminum foil liner with the cake from the baking pan. Use a small knife to loosen the liner from the sides of the cake.

Use a wide spatula to slide the cake off the foil liner. Cut into squares and serve with vanilla ice cream, if desired. Cover the cake and store it at room temperature up to 3 days.

Variation ↬ *Double all of the ingredients for the caramel sauce and use a 4-quart saucepan to cook the sugar and water. You will have about ¾ cup of caramel sauce remaining after making the cake. Warm this caramel sauce over low heat in a small saucepan. Serve the cake topped with vanilla ice cream and pass a pitcher of warm caramel sauce to pour over the ice cream.*

Fantasy Bars

Some people play golf when they retire, some take up sailing, and then there is my uncle Howard, who travels the world looking for new desserts to reproduce when he returns home. Happily, he sends me the day-by-day results of his frequent experiments. When he was trying to reproduce his memory of these bars, our e-mails flew back and forth for days as he perfected the recipe. With these bars, which have a layer of caramel, white chocolate, and walnuts baked between chocolate chip cookie dough, my uncle fulfilled his fantasy—and that of anyone who tries them.

Baking Answers ⋅◦ The caramel filling is drizzled on the bottom layer of cookie dough, then put in the refrigerator to firm so when the top cookie dough layer is added it spreads easily over the firm filling.

Lining the pan with aluminum foil prevents the bars from sticking to the pan in case any caramel has bubbled onto the sides or bottom of the pan. Let the foil lining extend over the edges of the pan so it is easy to lift the foil and bars from the pan.

White chocolate chips can be substituted for the chopped white chocolate, but I prefer the larger and more irregular chunks of chopped white chocolate. If using white chocolate chips, check to see that the ingredient list on the package includes cocoa butter.

It takes about 8 hours for these bars to cool enough for the chocolate to become firm, but eating them while the chocolate is soft is definitely fine. Refrigerating the partially cooled bars firms them in a couple of hours.

These rich bars should be cut into 35 small squares.

A Step Ahead ⋅◦ The caramel sauce can be prepared up to a week ahead, cooled, covered, and refrigerated. Soften the sauce by warming it slightly over low heat before using it.

MAKES 35 BARS

Necessities ⋅◦ *One 9-inch square baking pan or an 11 x 7-inch baking pan, both with 2-inch-high sides*

COOKIE DOUGH

2½ cups unbleached all-purpose
flour
1 teaspoon baking soda
¼ teaspoon salt
½ pound (2 sticks) soft unsalted
butter

¾ cup packed light brown sugar
½ cup granulated sugar
1 large egg
2 teaspoons vanilla extract
2 cups (12 ounces) semisweet
chocolate chips

FILLING

¾ cup coarsely chopped walnuts
1 cup (about 6 ounces) white chocolate,
chopped in about ½-inch pieces,
Callebaut or Lindt preferred

1 recipe caramel sauce (¾ cup),
cooled until warm to the touch,
about 30 minutes (page 349, for
Cranberry Caramel Buckle)

Mix the Dough

↪ Position an oven rack in the middle of the oven. Preheat the oven to 350°F. Line a 9 x 9 x 2-inch or 11 x 7 x 2-inch pan with heavy aluminum foil that extends over 2 ends of the pan. Butter the inside of the foil in the pan.

Sift the flour, baking soda, and salt together into a medium bowl or onto a piece of wax paper and set aside.

Put the butter, brown sugar, and granulated sugar in a large bowl and beat with an electric mixer on medium speed until the mixture looks blended together thoroughly, about 1 minute. Move the beaters around in the bowl if using a handheld electric mixer. Stop the mixer and scrape the mixture from the sides of the bowl and any that becomes caught in the beaters as needed throughout the mixing process. Mix in the egg and vanilla until they are blended in and the mixture is smooth and creamy, about 1 minute. Decrease the speed to low and add the flour mixture, mixing just until it is incorporated and there is no loose flour. Use a large spoon to stir in the chocolate chips. Spoon half of the cookie dough in large clumps evenly over the bottom of the lined pan. Use your fingers or a thin metal spatula to smooth the dough into an even layer that covers the pan bottom. Set the remaining dough aside.

Make the Filling

↪ Spoon the walnuts and white chocolate pieces evenly over the cookie dough. Leaving about a ½-inch edge bare, drizzle the caramel sauce evenly over the walnuts and white chocolate. Some of the caramel will spread to the edge. Refrigerate the pan until the caramel sauce is firm, about 20 minutes. Remove the pan from the refrigerator and drop pieces of the reserved cookie dough evenly over the firm filling. Spread the dough evenly over the filling to cover it completely.

Bake the Bars

~ Bake the bars for about 35 minutes, until the top feels firm and is lightly browned. Testing with a toothpick does not work, as the thick filling makes the toothpick come out wet with filling. Cool the bars for about 3 hours at room temperature. The chocolate will still be soft, but this is fine for serving or cutting. The chocolate becomes firm after about 8 hours or overnight. To firm the bars more quickly, cool them for 1 hour at room temperature, then refrigerate them for 2 hours.

Serve the Bars

~ Carefully lift the aluminum foil liner with the bars from the baking pan. Use a small knife to loosen the liner from the sides of the bars. Cut the bars into 35 pieces, cutting 5 rows lengthwise and 7 rows across. The bars will be slightly smaller than 1½ inches square. Use a wide spatula to slide the bars off the foil liner. Serve at room temperature. Vanilla, chocolate, or caramel ice cream, if it is available, makes a good accompaniment, if desired. Leftover bars can be covered and stored at room temperature for up to 3 days.

Caramel Milky Way Ice Cream Pie

Children of all ages will go for this ice cream pie topped with pieces of frozen Milky Way candy bars and caramel sauce. The generous covering of candy and sauce coupled with ice cream and a graham cracker crumb crust, just may produce an ice cream pie that is better than going to the circus. I use vanilla ice cream, but butter pecan, chocolate, or caramel are other good choices.

Baking Answers ~ When the caramel sauce is added to the ice cream pie, it should be cool to the touch, but easy to pour, so the ice cream does not melt. The portion of caramel sauce that is served with the pie should be warmed in a small saucepan over low heat.

This pie is made up of a nice combination of store-bought and previously prepared components.

A Step Ahead ⌁ A double recipe of the caramel sauce on page 349 can be prepared up to a week ahead, cooled, covered, and refrigerated. Warm the sauce for each step of the pie when you are ready to use it.

Ice cream desserts actually have to be made at least 5 hours ahead so they have time to firm up in the freezer, but if this ice cream pie is wrapped well, as directed below, it can be made up to 10 days ahead.

SERVES 8

Necessities ⌁ *1 graham cracker crumb crust (page 97) baked in a shiny metal or ovenproof glass 9-inch pie pan*

1 recipe caramel sauce (¾ cup), cooled about 30 minutes until cool to the touch but pourable (page 349, for Cranberry Caramel Buckle)
1 graham cracker crumb crust baked in a 9-inch pie pan and cooled (page 97, for Glazed Fresh Raspberry Pie)

2 pints vanilla ice cream, softened just until spreadable
1 cup (two 2.05-ounce) Milky Way bars cut into about ½-inch pieces
1 recipe caramel sauce (¾ cup), warmed over low heat for serving with the pie (page 349, for Cranberry Caramel Buckle)

Make the Pie

⌁ Drizzle ¼ cup of cooled caramel sauce over the crust. Use a large spoon or ice cream spade to spread the softened ice cream in the crumb crust. Sprinkle the candy pieces over the ice cream. Drizzle the remaining ½ cup of cooled caramel sauce over the top. Freeze the pie, uncovered, for about 30 minutes to firm the caramel sauce. Wrap the pie tightly with plastic wrap. Then cover with heavy aluminum foil, gently pressing the aluminum foil against the pie. Label with the date and contents. Freeze at least 5 hours or up to 10 days.

Serve the Pie

⌁ Remove the ice cream pie from the freezer and let it sit at room temperature for about 10 minutes. On a hot summer day, this slight softening before serving may be unnecessary. Use a large, sharp knife to cut the pie into wedges and serve. Pour the warm caramel sauce into a small pitcher and serve with the ice cream pie. Cover any leftover pie carefully with plastic wrap and heavy aluminum foil and return it to the freezer before it begins to melt.

Caramel Pecan Cookie Sandwich Hearts

Two hearts beat as one in these brown sugar and pecan cookie sandwiches filled with caramel and pecans. I cut the cookies into 3-inch dessert-size hearts, but smaller or other versions cut into hearts, stars, or rounds are equally good choices. The caramel filling used for these cookies is a slightly thicker mixture than caramel sauce.

Baking Answers ⟶ I grind the pecans for the cookies in a food processor and process them up to the point that some small pieces of pecans, about ⅛ inch in size, remain among the ground nuts.

Rolling the dough between 2 pieces of wax paper prevents the dough from sticking to the rolling surface and makes it easy to cut and transfer the cookies to the baking sheet. By using the wax paper, the dough can be re-rolled several times without additional chilling.

I find the easiest way to caramelize sugar is to dissolve the sugar in some water by cooking the mixture over a low heat to melt the sugar, then raising the heat and boiling it until it turns an evenly dark golden color. Cooking the sugar with some water helps the sugar melt evenly. The sugar caramelizes as the water evaporates and the sugar mixture reaches a temperature of over 320°F. As the sugar mixture boils and becomes hotter, the boiling bubbles change from large bubbles to tiny bubbles, to almost none or a very few bubbles. The change in the bubbles signals the sugar is about to reach the caramel stage. It takes about 10 minutes to reach this dark golden–colored stage, but as soon as the color begins to change, the process goes quickly, so watch it constantly. You can drop a bit of caramel on a light-colored plate to test the color, then remove the caramel from the heat as soon as the color you want is reached. Remember, the only way you can ruin caramel is to burn it. Any hard sugar crystals that form as the mixture cooks will dissolve in the hot caramel at the end of the cooking process.

Once the sugar caramelizes, remove the pan from the heat and slowly add warm cream to the hot caramel. This produces caramel sauce or a caramel filling. The more cream that is added, the thinner the finished sauce. When the warm cream is added to the hot caramelized sugar, the mixture bubbles up, so be careful that it does not splash on you. That is why you want to add the cream slowly and use a large saucepan to cook caramelized sugar that will have a warm liquid added to it.

Use a wooden spoon to stir the caramel. It will not retain heat and become too hot to handle as a metal spoon can.

Necessities ✧ *1 heavyweight baking sheet, a rolling pin, 1 wire rack for cooling the cookies, a heart-shaped cookie cutter that is about 3 inches long, or cookie cutters of your choice, and a heavy 3-quart saucepan*

PECAN COOKIES

¾ cup plus 2 tablespoons unbleached all-purpose flour

2 tablespoons cornstarch

¼ teaspoon salt

½ teaspoon ground cinnamon

¼ pound (1 stick) soft unsalted butter

⅓ cup packed light brown sugar

1 teaspoon vanilla extract

½ cup coarsely ground pecans, largest pieces about ⅛ inch

3 tablespoons finely chopped pecans, about ¼ inch in size

CARAMEL FILLING

⅓ cup whipping cream

¼ cup water

½ cup granulated sugar

¼ cup finely chopped pecans

Powdered sugar for dusting the top of the cookie sandwiches

Mix the Dough

✧ Position the oven rack in the middle of the oven. Preheat the oven to 325°F. Line a baking sheet with parchment paper.

Sift the flour, cornstarch, salt, and cinnamon together onto a piece of wax paper or into a medium bowl and set aside.

Put the butter, brown sugar, and vanilla in a large bowl and beat with an electric mixer on medium speed for about 1 minute until the mixture looks smooth. Move the beaters around in the bowl if using a handheld electric mixer. Stop the mixer and scrape the mixture from the sides of the bowl and any that becomes caught in the beaters as needed throughout the mixing process. Decrease the speed to low and mix in the ground pecans. Add the flour mixture, mixing just until no loose flour shows and the dough holds together in large clumps and pulls away from the sides of the bowl. Gather the dough into a ball, then press it into a disk about 6 inches in diameter. Wrap the dough in plastic wrap and chill it in the refrigerator for about 40 minutes until it is cool and firm, but soft enough to roll. The chilled dough should not be so hard that you can't press your finger into it. The dough can chill overnight, but it will need to soften at room temperature for at least 1 hour to become soft enough to roll.

Put the dough between 2 large pieces of wax paper. Roll the dough from the center out to about a 12-inch circle that is ⅛ inch thick. Carefully peel off the top piece of wax paper. Use a 3-

inch-long heart-shaped cookie cutter to cut out cookie hearts. Use a thin metal spatula to loosen the cookies from the wax paper and slide them onto the prepared baking sheet, placing them 1 inch apart. Press all of the dough scraps together to form a smooth ball of dough and repeat the rolling and cutting process between pieces of wax paper. If you still have a lot of scraps of dough, press them together and repeat the rolling and cutting for a third time. Each rolling produces a smaller circle of rolled dough and fewer cookies. Leaving about a ¼-inch edge bare, sprinkle a generous teaspoon of chopped pecans onto the center of half of the cookies. Press them gently into the dough.

Bake the Cookies

✎ Bake the cookies for about 18 minutes until the tops have colored slightly, reversing the baking sheets after 10 minutes front to back and top to bottom to ensure that the cookies bake evenly. Gently touch a cookie and it will feel crusty on the outside. Be careful not to burn yourself. The cookie bottoms will be evenly golden. Cool the cookies for 5 minutes on the baking sheet. Use an offset metal spatula or wide spatula to transfer the cookies to a wire cake rack to cool thoroughly. The cookies become crisp as they cool.

Cook the Filling

✎ Put the cream in a small saucepan and heat it over low heat. The cream should be hot, about 150°F. if measured with a food thermometer when it is added to the hot sugar mixture. Do not boil the cream. If the cream should boil and a skin forms on top, use a spoon to lift out the skin and discard it. Cook the water and granulated sugar to a caramel while keeping the cream hot over low heat.

Put the water and granulated sugar in a heavy-bottomed saucepan that has at least a 3-quart capacity. Cover and cook over low heat until the sugar dissolves, about 5 minutes. Stir the mixture occasionally to help the sugar dissolve. Remove the cover, increase the heat to medium-high, and bring to a boil. Do not worry if a few sugar crystals form on the side of the pan. Boil the mixture until the sugar melts, caramelizes, and turns a dark golden color, about 10 minutes. As the sugar reaches the caramel stage, the bubbles subside and become small. You can dip the spoon in the caramel and drop a drop on a light-colored plate to see the color. As soon as the mixture begins to turn golden, stir it with a wooden spoon once or twice to ensure that the sugar cooks evenly and that all of the sugar caramelizes. Once the caramel begins to change color, it reaches the dark golden stage quickly, so watch it constantly.

Remove the caramel from the heat. Slowly and carefully add the hot cream to the hot sugar. The mixture will bubble up, so be careful. Once the bubbles subside, if the caramel is sticking to the bottom or is not completely smooth, return the saucepan to low heat. Cook the caramel, stirring continuously with the wooden spoon, for 1 or 2 minutes until the caramel is completely dissolved and the mixture is smooth. Remove the pan from the heat and stir in the finely chopped pecans. Cool the caramel filling for about 1½ hours, until it is thick enough to spoon onto the cookies without running off them. The caramel filling can be cooled for about 15 minutes, poured into a heatproof container (a Pyrex-type measuring cup works well), and refrigerated for about 40 minutes to thicken.

Fill and Serve the Cookies

↬ Turn the cookies without the pecan topping bottom side up. Leaving a ¼-inch edge bare, spread about 1 tablespoon of cooled caramel filling over these cookie bottoms. Press the remaining cookies, pecan side up, gently onto the caramel filling. Dust with powdered sugar and serve. The 3-inch cookie hearts can be served as individual desserts. The cookies can be covered and stored either at room temperature or in the refrigerator for up to 4 days. Serve cold or at room temperature.

Two-for-One Hazelnut Lace Cookie Sandwiches or Stacks

D elicate and elegant, lace cookies may look as if they're a challenge to produce, but happily the opposite is true. Named for the lace-like holes that form as they bake, these cookies have both the flavor of caramel and the crispness of praline. It will probably surprise you that they are one-pot (no bowl needed) drop cookies, and once the batter cooks briefly in a saucepan and several ingredients are added, teaspoonfuls of the batter can be quickly dropped onto a baking sheet. The oven does the rest as the sugar in the cookies caramelizes during baking and the cookies become brittle and praline-like as they cool. They are all-crunch cookies as they shatter with each bite.

Versatile lace cookies can be filled with chocolate, formed into cookie cups or curves when still warm, or thickly filled with whipped cream and berries. These two possibilities are to fill cookie sandwiches with a milk chocolate truffle filling or to make the cookies into a party dessert by stacking pairs of cookies with a thick filling of whipped cream and fresh raspberries.

Baking Answers ↬ The process for making lace cookies is to cook butter, sugar, and corn syrup until the sugar dissolves and then bring the mixture to a boil. The butter and corn syrup that cook with the sugar prevent the mixture from developing any hard sugar crystals and keep it smooth. After the mixture boils, remove the pan from the heat and stir in the flour, nuts, and flavoring. Drop teaspoonfuls of the warm liquid at least 2½ inches apart to allow for spreading and bake the cookies. Since the batter thickens if it cools, it is easiest to drop the batter onto the baking sheets when it is warm.

It is important to line the baking sheets for lace cookies so the cookies do not stick to the baking sheet and cleanup is easy. Although heavy aluminum foil can be used, I find parchment paper or a nonstick liner works best for lining the baking sheets for these cookies; then the cookies spread smoothly and evenly. There are 2 types of nonstick liners. Thin nonstick liners that can be cut to fit baking sheets or the more expensive, thick Silpat nonstick liners can be used. Silpat liners are bought in one of two finished sizes that fit most baking sheets. Both types of nonstick liners are available from King Arthur Flour's Baker's Catalogue, and Silpat liners are available from Bridge Kitchenware and Williams-Sonoma. These companies are listed in Mail-Order Sources on page 384. If baked on the nonstick liner, the cookies spread a bit thinner than if baked on parchment paper, but the difference is minimal.

MAKES ABOUT TWENTY 3½-INCH ROUND COOKIES FOR 10
SANDWICHES OR STACKS

Necessities ❧ *2 heavyweight baking sheets, 2 wire racks for cooling the cookies, and a heavy 1½- to 2-quart saucepan*

HAZELNUT LACE COOKIES
2 ounces (½ stick) unsalted butter
⅓ cup granulated sugar
2 tablespoons light corn syrup
¼ cup unbleached all-purpose flour
1 teaspoon vanilla extract

½ cup peeled toasted hazelnuts (page 40), ground
½ cup peeled toasted hazelnuts, (page 40), coarsely chopped (¼ to ⅜ inch)

MILK CHOCOLATE TRUFFLE FILLING FOR COOKIE SANDWICHES— MAKES ABOUT ¾ CUP
⅓ cup whipping cream

1 ounce (¼ stick) unsalted butter
4 ounces milk chocolate (Lindt or Callebaut preferred), in ½-inch or smaller pieces

WHIPPED CREAM FILLING AND RASPBERRIES FOR COOKIE STACKS
1 cup cold whipping cream

2 tablespoons powdered sugar
1 teaspoon vanilla extract
2½ cups fresh raspberries

Powdered sugar for dusting the cookie stacks

Make the Cookie Mixture

↝ Position the oven racks in the middle and upper third of the oven. Preheat the oven to 325°F. Line 2 baking sheets with parchment paper, nonstick liners, or heavy aluminum foil. Do not butter the baking liners. If you have only 1 nonstick liner, use it on 1 baking sheet and line the second baking sheet with parchment paper or foil.

Put the butter, granulated sugar, and corn syrup in a medium saucepan and cook it over low heat until the butter melts and the sugar dissolves, stirring often. Increase the heat to medium-high and bring the mixture to a boil, stirring constantly. The mixture will be smooth and syrupy. Remove the pan from the heat and add the flour, stirring until it is incorporated. Add the vanilla, ground hazelnuts, and chopped hazelnuts, stirring to mix them into the mixture. Use a small spoon to drop rounded teaspoons of batter 3 inches apart on the baking sheets to form 1¼-inch mounds.

Bake the Cookies

↝ Bake the cookies about 12 minutes, until they have spread flat and are evenly light brown. Some of the cookies will be lighter in the center than at the edges. Reverse the baking sheets after 7 minutes front to back and top to bottom to ensure that the cookies bake evenly. Remove the cookies from the oven and immediately use a sharp knife to separate any cookies that might have spread together by pushing a bit of the warm cookie edge toward the center. Cool the cookies on the baking sheet for 5 minutes until they are firm enough to move without breaking. Use a wide spatula to transfer the cookies to a wire rack to cool completely. The cooled cookies can be stored tightly covered in a metal tin, stacked between layers of wax paper, for up to 3 days.

Make the Truffle Filling

↝ Put the cream and butter in a large saucepan and heat over medium-low heat until the cream is hot and the butter is melted. The hot cream mixture will form tiny bubbles and measure about 175°F. if tested with a food thermometer. Do not let the mixture boil. Remove the pan from the heat. Add the chopped milk chocolate and let it melt in the hot cream mixture for about 30 seconds to soften. Use a large spoon or a whisk to stir the mixture smooth. If all of the chocolate is not melted, return the mixture to low heat for about 1 minute, stirring the mixture until the chocolate is melted and smooth. Remove the pan from the heat. Use a rubber spatula to scrape the mixture into a small bowl, and let the milk chocolate truffle sit until it is thick enough to spread on the cookies without running off them.

Fill and Serve the Cookie Sandwiches

↝ Arrange the cookies in pairs of similar size. Turn half of the cookies bottom side up. Leaving a ¼-inch edge bare, carefully spread about 2 teaspoons of the milk chocolate truffle filling over the bottom of half of the cookies. Gently place the remaining cookies bottom side down on the milk chocolate truffle filling to form sandwiches. Put the cookies on a serving plate and serve them or cover them and refrigerate them. Or, layer them between sheets of wax paper in a metal tin and refrigerate them until the filling is firm. Serve the cookie sandwiches cold or at room temperature, but store the cookies, covered, in the refrigerator. The filled cookies can be stored up to 3 days.

Make the Whipped Cream Filling

When you are ready to serve the cookie stacks, put the cream, powdered sugar, and vanilla in a large bowl and beat with an electric mixer on medium speed until the movement of the beaters forms smooth curving lines in the cream. If using a handheld electric mixer, move the beaters around in the bowl. If you stop the mixer and lift up the beaters, the softly whipped cream forms a point that falls over at its tip.

Fill and Serve the Cookie Stacks

Arrange the cookies in pairs of similar size. Put half of the cookies top side up on individual serving plates. Spoon about ⅓ cup of the whipped cream over each of these cookies. Scatter about ¼ cup of raspberries over the cream, letting some spill onto the plate. Place a cookie top side up on top of the whipped cream and raspberry filling. Dust with powdered sugar and serve immediately. To make 5 cookie stacks rather than 10, use half of the cookies and prepare half of the quantity of whipped cream and raspberry filling.

Pumpkin Pecan Praline Cheesecake

Pumpkin cheesecake, with its warm, golden pumpkin color and a crunchy topping of butter and brown sugar–coated pecans, can take a new approach to the traditional Thanksgiving dessert. Not that you have to wait until Thanksgiving to try this cheesecake, because it is appropriate for any fall or winter occasion.

Rather than the classic praline of caramelized sugar and nuts, this "American style" praline is made from a combination of pecans mixed with butter and brown sugar that bakes in the oven.

Baking Answers
The crust is made from store-bought gingersnap cookies crushed into crumbs. To make the crumbs, put half of the gingersnap cookies between 2 sheets of wax paper and use a rolling pin to crush them into crumbs. There will be some tiny pieces of cookie. Repeat with the remaining cookies. Or, process the cookies in a food processor until crumbs form.

For guidelines on preparing cheesecake see the Vanilla Cheesecake on page 99.

Check to see that the label on the can of pumpkin says pumpkin rather than pumpkin pie filling, which would have spices added.

A Step Ahead
The cooled cheesecake can be covered and stored in the refrigerator for up to 1 week. Add the pecan topping when you are ready to serve the cheesecake so it remains crisp.

The cooled pecan praline can be sealed in a clean metal tin and left at room temperature for up to 1 week. Or, freeze the pecan praline in a tightly sealed clean metal tin or plastic container for up to 1 month. Defrost the pecan praline at room temperature in the covered container.

SERVES 12 TO 16

Necessities ❧ *A baking sheet, a 9-inch springform pan with sides at least 2¾ inches high, a large baking pan with at least 2-inch-high sides large enough to hold the foil-wrapped springform pan, and heavy aluminum foil for wrapping the pan*

PECAN TOPPING	6 tablespoons packed light brown sugar
3 tablespoons unsalted butter	¾ cup pecans, coarsely chopped

GINGERSNAP CRUST

2 cups gingersnap cookie crumbs
(made from about 9 ounces of
gingersnap cookies)

1 teaspoon ground cinnamon
3 ounces (¾ stick) unsalted butter,
melted

PUMPKIN FILLING

Four 8-ounce packages cream cheese,
softened 3 to 4 hours at room
temperature
1½ cups granulated sugar
3 tablespoons unbleached all-purpose
flour

4 large eggs, room temperature
1½ teaspoons ground cinnamon
¾ teaspoon ground ginger
1 teaspoon vanilla extract
3 tablespoons bourbon
1½ cups canned solid pack pumpkin

Make the Topping

↝ Position an oven rack in the middle of the oven. Preheat the oven to 350°F. Line a baking sheet with heavy aluminum foil and butter the foil lightly.

Put the butter and brown sugar in a medium saucepan and cook it over medium heat until the butter melts, stirring constantly. Increase the heat to medium-high and bring the mixture to a boil, stirring until the mixture boils. Boil for 1 minute without stirring. Remove the pan from the heat and stir in the chopped pecans, coating them evenly with the butter and brown sugar mixture. Spread the pecan praline mixture evenly on the prepared baking sheet. It will not cover the baking sheet. Bake for 10 to 12 minutes, stirring after 6 minutes, until the mixture is bubbling vigorously. Remove from the oven and cool the pecan praline on the baking sheet, stirring several times to separate the nuts as they cool. The cooled nuts can be made up to 1 week ahead or frozen for up to 1 month as directed above. Decrease the oven temperature to 325°F.

Prepare the Crust

↝ Butter a 9-inch springform pan with sides at least 2¾ inches high. Wrap the outside of the pan with a large piece of heavy aluminum foil. Have ready a large baking pan with at least 2-inch-high sides that is large enough to hold the foil-wrapped pan.

Stir the gingersnap crumbs and cinnamon together in a medium bowl. Add the melted butter, stirring until the crumbs are evenly moistened with the butter. Put the crumb mixture in the prepared pan and use the back of your fingers or the back of a spoon to press the crumb mixture evenly over the bottom and 1 inch up the sides of the pan. Be careful not to make the crust too thick at the bottom of the pan where the sides and the edges of the pan meet at an angle. Bake for 8 minutes. Set aside.

Prepare the Filling

➤ Put the cream cheese and granulated sugar in a large bowl and beat with an electric mixer on low speed until the mixture looks smooth. If using a handheld electric mixer, move the beaters around in the bowl. Mix in the flour to incorporate it. Put the eggs in a small bowl and stir them vigorously with a fork to blend the yolks and whites. Add the eggs in 2 additions, mixing just to blend them into the mixture. Stop the mixer and scrape any thick batter from the sides of the bowl and any batter that becomes caught in the beaters as needed. Add the cinnamon, ginger, vanilla, and bourbon, beating just until they are incorporated and the batter is smooth. Add the pumpkin, mixing just to blend it in smoothly. Pour the batter into the baked crust in the wrapped springform pan.

Bake and Serve the Cheesecake

➤ Put the cheesecake in its wrapped pan in a large baking pan with at least 2-inch-high sides and place it in the preheated oven. Pour hot water in the large pan to reach 1 inch up the sides of the springform pan.

Bake about 1 hour and 20 minutes or until you give the cheesecake a gentle shake and the top looks firm. When done, the cheesecake looks set and may have a few tiny cracks around the edge. These cracks close up as the cheesecake cools.

Cool the cheesecake, covered loosely with paper towels, in the water bath for 1 hour. Carefully remove the cheesecake from the water bath. Remove the paper towels and foil wrapping and cool 1 hour more. The cheesecake should feel cool to the touch. Cover with plastic wrap and chill thoroughly in the refrigerator for at least 6 hours or overnight. The cheesecake becomes firm when cool.

When you are ready to serve the cheesecake, remove it from the refrigerator and leaving a 1-inch plain border, spoon the pecan praline over the top. Use a small knife to loosen the cheesecake from the sides of the pan and remove the sides. Let the cheesecake sit at room temperature for 1 hour before serving. Use a large, sharp knife to cut the cheesecake, wiping the knife clean after cutting each slice. A clean knife makes a neat slice. Once the pecan praline is added, any leftover cheesecake can be covered with plastic wrap and stored in the refrigerator for up to 3 days.

➤

Double-Decker Raspberry and Almond Praline Cheesecake

Almond praline flavors the butter crumb crust, separates the 2 raspberry cheesecake layers, and tops this made-for-an-elegant-party cheesecake. A raspberry puree flavors the smooth cheesecake on the bottom layer, and whole raspberries dot the top cheesecake layer.

Baking Answers ✴ Praline is a mixture of sugar that is cooked to the caramel stage and has nuts mixed into the hot caramelized sugar. The caramelized nuts form a brittle that can be ground to a powder or crushed into small pieces. For this cheesecake, the almond praline is ground to a powder in a food processor. Any nut can be used for the praline, but almonds and hazelnuts are the classic ones most commonly used.

The process for cooking praline is to melt sugar in a heavy frying pan to a dark golden color, stir in nuts to coat them evenly with the caramelized sugar, and pour the caramelized nuts onto an oiled baking sheet to cool. When the praline cools, it is brittle and can be crushed into small pieces or ground to a powder. Using a pan with a nonstick interior is preferable, as the sugar slides around the pan easily and caramelizes evenly, but a heavy frying pan without a nonstick finish will work. Hot liquid is not added to this sugar mixture, so a deep saucepan is not required as in caramel sauce, which bubbles up.

The freshly caramelized sugar is very hot, so be careful not to touch it or to splash any on yourself. Since the sugar is cooked to over 320°F., any sugar crystals that form melt from the high temperature, so there is no worry about sugar crystallizing and becoming grainy. When the sugar begins to turn golden, watch it carefully, as it will darken and caramelize quickly.

You will use 1½ cups of almond praline powder and have about ½ cup of the praline remaining for another use.

Blanched (peeled) slivered or sliced almonds stir easily into the caramelized sugar.

The crust is made from a crumb mixture that is pressed into the springform pan.

Bottles labeled pure almond extract are made with oil of bitter almond and are preferable to bottles labeled almond extract. The pure version is now available in supermarkets.

For guidelines on preparing cheesecake see the Vanilla Cheesecake on page 99.

A Step Ahead ✴ Any nut praline can be made up to 3 months ahead and frozen and makes a handy mixture to have ready in the freezer. To freeze praline, put the crushed or ground praline in a plastic freezer container and press plastic wrap onto the praline. Cover the container tightly and freeze. The praline can be used directly from the freezer. Spoon out the amount needed and return any remaining praline to the freezer.

Necessities ❧ *A heavy 2-quart frying pan, preferably with a nonstick finish, one 9-inch springform pan with sides at least 2¾ inches high, a baking pan with at least 2-inch-high sides large enough to hold the foil-wrapped springform pan, and heavy aluminum foil for wrapping the pan*

ALMOND PRALINE— MAKES ABOUT 2 CUPS ALMOND PRALINE POWDER	¾ cup sugar 1 cup (about 4 ounces) blanched (page 40) slivered or sliced almonds
ALMOND PRALINE CRUST 1 cup unbleached all-purpose flour ½ cup almond praline powder	¼ pound (1 stick) cold unsalted butter, cut into ½-inch pieces
RASPBERRY CHEESECAKE FILLINGS 2 cups fresh or frozen and defrosted unsweetened raspberries 2 pounds cream cheese, softened 3 to 4 hours at room temperature 1⅓ cups sugar	2 tablespoons unbleached all-purpose flour 4 large eggs, room temperature 2 teaspoons vanilla extract ¾ teaspoon pure almond extract 2 tablespoons whipping cream ½ cup almond praline powder
½ cup almond praline powder for topping cheesecake	1 cup fresh raspberries for topping the cheesecake, optional

Make the Praline

❧ Lightly oil a metal baking sheet.

Put the sugar in a heavy 2-quart frying pan, preferably with a nonstick bottom, and cook over medium heat, stirring occasionally with a wooden spoon until the sugar begins to melt, about 2 minutes. When the sugar begins to melt and turn golden, begin stirring the sugar constantly until it turns evenly dark golden in color, about 6 minutes. Small lumps of hard sugar will form that melt as the sugar caramelizes completely. Add the almonds, stirring with the wooden spoon to coat them completely with the caramelized sugar for about 1 minute. The mixture will turn a slightly darker golden color. Immediately pour the almond praline onto the baking sheet, spreading it with the wooden spoon. The mixture is thick and spreads to a thick layer. Be careful, as the mixture is very hot. Cool the praline until it hardens and is cool to the touch, about 25 minutes.

Break the praline into 1- to 2-inch pieces. Wrap pieces of praline in heavy aluminum foil and use a clean mallet, rolling pin, or meat pounder to crush the praline into approximately ¼- to ½-inch pieces. You will have crushed praline that can be sprinkled over ice cream or desserts. To prepare praline powder, transfer the crushed praline to a food processor fitted with a metal blade and process for about 30 seconds, just until the praline forms a powder. Overprocessing can turn the praline into a paste, but this actually takes some time and is not likely to happen. Use the praline the same day or freeze it for up to 3 months as directed above in "A Step Ahead."

Prepare and Bake the Crust

↬ Position a rack in the middle of the oven. Preheat the oven to 350°F. Butter a 9-inch springform pan with sides at least 2¾ inches high. Wrap the outside of the pan with a large piece of heavy aluminum foil. Have ready a large baking pan with at least 2-inch-high sides that is large enough to hold the foil-wrapped pan.

Put the flour and praline powder in a medium bowl and stir them together. Add the butter pieces. Rub the butter pieces and flour mixture between your thumb and fingertips or use a pastry blender to cut the butter into the flour until fine crumbs form that are about ¼ inch in size. A few odd larger crumbs remain. Put the crumb mixture in the prepared pan and use the back of your fingers or the back of a spoon to press the crumb mixture evenly over the bottom and 1 inch up the sides of the pan. Bake for 20 minutes. The crust will be light golden. Set aside to cool slightly while you mix the filling. Reduce the oven temperature to 325°F.

Mix the Fillings

↬ Put 1 cup of the fresh or frozen and defrosted raspberries in a strainer and place it over a small bowl. Use a spoon to press on the raspberries to strain raspberry puree into the bowl. You will have about ⅓ cup of puree. Discard the seeds and pulp left in the strainer. Set aside the raspberry puree and remaining raspberries.

Put the cream cheese and sugar in a large bowl and beat with an electric mixer on low speed until the mixture looks smooth. If using a handheld electric mixer, move the beaters around in the bowl. Mix in the flour to incorporate it. Put the eggs in a small bowl and use a fork to stir them vigorously to blend the yolks and whites. Add the eggs in 2 additions, mixing just to blend them into the mixture. Stop the mixer and scrape any thick batter from the sides of the bowl or any batter that becomes caught in the beaters as needed. Add the vanilla, almond extract, and cream, mixing to incorporate them. Put 2½ cups of the batter in a medium bowl and gently stir in the remaining 1 cup of fresh or frozen and defrosted raspberries. The mixture will be thick. Set aside.

This will be for the top vanilla layer that has whole raspberries. Mix the reserved raspberry puree into the batter in the large bowl, stirring just until the mixture is evenly pink. Pour the pink raspberry batter into the crust in the prepared pan.

Bake and Cool the Cheesecake

෴ Put the cheesecake in its wrapped pan in a large baking pan with at least 2-inch-high sides and place it in the preheated oven. Pour hot water into the large pan to reach 1 inch up the sides of the springform pan.

Bake 40 minutes. Carefully slide the oven rack out several inches. Sprinkle ½ cup of the praline powder over the raspberry layer. Carefully spoon the reserved raspberry and vanilla batter evenly over the praline powder. Bake about an additional 25 minutes or until the cheesecake looks set if you give it a gentle shake. It may have a few tiny cracks around the edge. These cracks close up as the cheesecake cools.

Cool the cheesecake, covered loosely with paper towels, in the water bath for 1 hour. Carefully remove the cheesecake from the water bath. Remove the paper towels and foil wrapping and cool 1 hour more. The cheesecake should feel cool to the touch. Cover with plastic wrap and chill thoroughly in the refrigerator for at least 6 hours or overnight. The cheesecake firms when cool.

Serve the Cheesecake

෴ When you are ready to serve the cheesecake, sprinkle ½ cup of praline powder evenly over the top. Use a small knife to loosen the cheesecake from the sides of the pan and remove the sides. Let the cheesecake sit at room temperature for 1 hour before serving. Use a large, sharp knife to cut the cheesecake into slices, wiping the knife clean after cutting each slice. Spoon fresh raspberries over each slice, if desired A clean knife makes a neat slice. Once the almond praline powder topping is added, any leftover cheesecake can be covered with plastic wrap and stored in the refrigerator for up to 3 days.

Pear and Almond Cake with Caramel Frosting

I t is no secret that pear and caramel are a made-for-each-other combination, but this cake does reveal some baking secrets. The secret to the moist texture of the cake is to puree pears and ground almonds with the batter, and the secret to mixing this cake quickly is to mix it in a food processor. The caramel for the frosting is made from a guaranteed-easy method that cooks cream and brown sugar together. That's it; all secrets revealed.

The top of this square cake also has a clever design of diagonal sections of toasted almonds dusted with powdered sugar.

Baking Answers ↔ The major part of this cake is mixed in a food processor. After the flour, baking powder, baking soda, and salt for the cake are sifted into a large bowl, the remaining ingredients are processed in a food processor until smooth. This now liquid batter is stirred into the flour mixture and the cake batter is ready to bake.

Bottles labeled pure almond extract are made with oil of bitter almond and are preferable to bottles labeled almond extract. The pure version is now available in supermarkets.

The caramel for this frosting is made by cooking a mixture of brown sugar, cream, and corn syrup together. The corn syrup contributes to the smooth texture of this caramel frosting. The brown sugar mixture is cooled to the point that it will not melt the butter and powdered-sugar mixture when the two are combined.

A Step Ahead ↔ Bake the cake, cool it, and remove from its pan, then wrap it in plastic wrap and store it overnight at room temperature.

SERVES 9

Necessities ↔ *One 9-inch square baking pan or an 11 x 7-inch baking pan, both with 2-inch-high sides, and 1 wire rack for cooling the cake*

PEAR AND ALMOND CAKE

2 cups cake flour

¾ teaspoon baking powder

¾ teaspoon baking soda

¼ teaspoon salt

6 canned pear halves (one 15-ounce can) in light syrup preferred, drained

¾ cup chopped blanched almonds

¾ cup buttermilk (nonfat is fine)

2 large eggs

¼ pound (1 stick) soft unsalted butter

¾ cup granulated sugar

½ cup packed light brown sugar

1 teaspoon vanilla extract

¾ teaspoon pure almond extract

CARAMEL FROSTING

½ cup whipping cream

¾ cup packed dark brown sugar

1 tablespoon light corn syrup

¼ pound (1 stick) soft unsalted butter

1 cup powdered sugar, sifted

1 teaspoon vanilla extract

1 cup slivered almonds, toasted (page 40)

Powdered sugar for dusting the cake topping

Mix the Cake

❧ Position a rack in the middle of the oven. Preheat the oven to 350°F. Butter the bottom and sides of a 9 x 9 x 2-inch or 11 x 7 x 2- inch pan. Line the bottom of the pan with parchment or wax paper and butter the paper.

Sift the cake flour, baking powder, baking soda, and salt together into a large bowl and set aside.

Put the drained pear halves and almonds in the work bowl of a food processor and process to a thick puree for about 30 seconds. Add the buttermilk, eggs, butter, granulated sugar, brown sugar, vanilla, and almond extract. Process until the mixture becomes blended and smooth, about 30 seconds. The mixture may look curdled. Use a rubber spatula to scrape the pear mixture into the reserved flour mixture, then mix them together, stirring just until the flour is evenly moistened. Use the rubber spatula to scrape the batter into the prepared pan and smooth the top.

Bake the Cake

❧ Bake the cake for about 30 minutes, until a toothpick inserted into the center of the cake comes out clean. Cool the cake in the pan for 10 minutes. Use a small sharp knife to loosen the cake from the sides of the pan. Invert the cake onto a flat serving plate. Carefully remove and discard the paper lining the cake bottom. Place a wire rack on the bottom of the cake and invert the cake onto it. The cake is now right side up. Cool the cake thoroughly, about 2 hours. The cake can be prepared 1 day ahead, wrapped tightly, and stored at room temperature.

Cook the Frosting

↬ Put the cream, brown sugar, and corn syrup in a medium saucepan and cook over medium heat until the sugar dissolves, stirring often. Increase the heat to medium-high and bring the mixture to a boil. Boil for 2 minutes, stirring occasionally. Pour the mixture into a medium bowl and refrigerate it, uncovered, until it is cool to the touch, about 1 hour. The brown sugar caramel should still be soft when it has cooled enough to mix with the butter and powdered sugar mixture. It will measure about 90°F on a food thermometer.

Put the butter and powdered sugar in a large bowl and beat with an electric mixer on medium speed until the mixture is smooth, about 1 minute. Move the beaters around in the bowl if using a handheld electric mixer. Stop the mixer and scrape the mixture from the sides of the bowl and any that becomes caught in the beaters as needed throughout the mixing process. Add the cooled brown sugar caramel mixture and the vanilla, continuing to beat for about 1 minute or less, until the frosting is smooth and the color lightens from brown to light brown.

Frost the Cake

↬ Slide the cake onto a cake plate. Tuck waxed paper strips just an inch or so under the bottom of the cake all the way around to keep the plate clean. Use a thin metal spatula to spread the frosting over the top and sides of the cake. Cut 3 strips of parchment or wax paper that are at least 12 inches long and 1 inch wide. Lay the paper strips 1 inch apart and diagonally over the top of the cake, leaving the corners of the cake uncovered. Spoon the toasted almonds evenly on the exposed frosting. Dust the almonds lightly with powdered sugar. Carefully lift the paper strips from the top of the cake and discard them. You will have a pattern on the cake frosting of diagonal strips of almonds dusted with powdered sugar alternating with strips of plain frosting. Gently pull out the wax paper strips, while sliding a knife under the cake to avoid pulling out smears of frosting, and discard them.

Serve the Cake

↬ Use a large knife to cut the cake into squares, or cover the cake carefully with plastic wrap and refrigerate it. The covered cake can be refrigerated for up to 2 days, but let it sit at room temperature for 1 hour before serving it.

Banoffee Pie

I think that every restaurant and tea shop in England must have its own version of this banana and toffee caramel pie. Banoffee Pie is the grown-up version of those comforting English nursery puddings. The pie has a graham cracker crumb crust filled with bananas that are surrounded by soft, chewy caramel and covered with whipped cream—that is certainly a memory to cherish.

The caramel for this pie is made by cooking condensed milk and butter together until they turn a light toffee color. The color and texture resemble a soft caramel candy.

Baking Answers ❧ The condensed milk mixture for the caramel must be stirred constantly as it cooks. The condensed milk is quite sweet and the sugar in it would burn if not stirred constantly. It takes a bit of patience, but is not at all difficult. The rest of the preparation is the now familiar making of a simple graham cracker crumb crust and whipping some cream to the firmly whipped stage.

Tossing bananas with citrus juices, such as lemon juice, helps them to keep their white color.

SERVES 8

Necessities ❧ *A heavy 3-quart saucepan and one graham cracker crumb crust (page 93) baked in a 9-inch pie pan*

CARAMEL TOFFEE FILLING— MAKES 1½ CUPS

6 ounces (1½ sticks) unsalted butter

One 14-ounce can sweetened condensed milk

4 medium to large bananas, sliced in rounds about ¼-inch thick

1 tablespoon fresh lemon juice

1 graham cracker crumb crust in a 9-inch pie pan, baked and cooled (page 93, for Lemon Icebox Pie)

WHIPPED CREAM TOPPING

1 cup cold whipping cream

1 tablespoon powdered sugar

1 teaspoon vanilla extract

Cook the Filling

➤ Put the butter in a heavy-bottomed saucepan that has a 3-quart capacity. Cook over low heat until the butter melts. Add the condensed milk and use a whisk to stir the butter and condensed milk together to blend them. Increase the heat to medium-high and bring the mixture to a gentle boil, whisking slowly but constantly. As soon as the boil is reached, decrease the heat to low and continue cooking the mixture at a gentle boil, whisking slowly but constantly for about 15 minutes, until it thickens and turns a light brown camel color. It is the color of light toffee candy. Some brown flecks may appear, but they disappear as the mixture cooks. At the gentle boil, the mixture has 3 to 5 bubbles gently bursting at a time. Remove the caramel mixture from the heat, and let it cool slightly for about 10 minutes before pouring it into the crust.

Fill the Pie

➤ Put the sliced bananas in a medium bowl. Add the lemon juice, stirring to coat the bananas. Use a spoon to put about 1 cup of the slightly cooled caramel mixture into the prepared crumb crust. Spoon it into the crust evenly so it covers the bottom. Spread the banana mixture in an even layer over the caramel. Drop spoonfuls of the remaining caramel evenly over the bananas, using the back of the spoon to spread it over the bananas. The bananas will not be completely covered. Refrigerate the pie while you whip the cream.

Whip the Topping

➤ Put the cold cream, powdered sugar, and vanilla in a clean large bowl and beat with an electric mixer on medium speed until the whipped cream is firm enough to hold its shape and to spread. Move the beaters around in the bowl if using a handheld electric mixer. If you stop the mixer and lift up the beaters, the cream forms a point that stands straight up when the beaters are removed. The movement of the beaters first forms smooth curving then wrinkled lines in the cream at this stage. The whipped cream looks smooth. Use a rubber spatula to spread the whipped cream over the top of the pie, mounding it slightly to the center.

Serve the Pie

➤ Refrigerate the pie at least 2 hours and serve cold. Leftover pie can be covered carefully with plastic wrap and refrigerated for up to 2 days. A few toothpicks inserted carefully in the whipped cream prevent the plastic wrap from disturbing the topping.

Caramel Cream Pie

I t only takes 2 nouns to describe this pie—caramel upon caramel and cream upon cream. Caramel sauce soaks into the graham cracker crumb crust and caramel flavors the pastry cream filling, then whipped cream blankets the caramel cream filling.

This pie is made from a combination of components from previous recipes listed in this book that combine to make this completely new result.

Baking Answers ⤖ The filling for this pie is soft and creamy. When the slices are cut, the filling spreads slightly rather than holding a firm shape.

Chilling the pie before it is served firms both the filling and the whipped cream topping.

A Step Ahead ⤖ The caramel sauce can be prepared up to a week ahead, cooled, covered, and refrigerated. When you are ready to use the sauce, heat it over low heat just until it is soft and pourable.

SERVES 8

Necessities ⤖ *1 graham cracker crumb crust (page 93) baked in a shiny metal or ovenproof glass 9-inch pie pan*

1 recipe caramel sauce (¾ cup) that is warm to the touch and pourable (page 349, for Cranberry Caramel Buckle)

1 recipe warm freshly prepared pastry cream (page 106, for Cherry Custard Tart with Pouring Crust)

1 graham cracker crumb crust baked in a 9-inch pie pan, cooled (page 93, for Lemon Icebox Pie)

1 recipe whipped cream topping (pages 373–74, for Banoffee Pie), firmly whipped

Assemble the Pie

⤖ Add ½ cup of the warm caramel sauce to the warm pastry cream, stirring to blend it into the pastry cream. Pour the caramel pastry cream into a medium bowl, press a piece of plastic wrap onto the sauce, and poke a few holes in the plastic wrap with the tip of a knife to let the steam escape. Refrigerate the caramel pastry cream for at least 3 hours or overnight until it is cold and thickened.

Drizzle the remaining caramel sauce over the graham cracker crumb crust.

Use a rubber spatula to scrape the cold caramel pastry cream into the caramel-topped crumb crust.

Use a clean rubber spatula to spread the firmly whipped cream over the filling, mounding it slightly toward the center.

Serve the Pie

⤖ Refrigerate the pie at least 2 hours and serve cold. Use a large knife to cut the pie into slices. Leftover pie can be covered carefully with plastic wrap and refrigerated for 1 day. A few toothpicks inserted carefully in the whipped cream topping prevent the plastic wrap from disturbing the topping.

Blaze of Glory Chocolate Cake

You may well ask what the musical *Rent* has to do with chocolate cake. When I saw the play and heard the song about contributing one blaze of glory during your life, I knew the last recipe in my book had to be a spectacular Blaze of Glory Chocolate Cake. Of course, I didn't know what that cake would be, and I discarded idea after idea as not worthy. Finally my husband hit on the perfect solution. The cake would unite some of the techniques and components that I had used throughout the book.

The cake starts with a chocolate, chocolate chip cake layer. This cake layer is split into 2 layers and the cake is assembled in a springform pan that acts as a mold to hold the several fillings. Half of the split cake layer goes into the bottom of the pan. First a layer of caramel sauce goes on top of the cake, next a 1-inch-thick layer of milk chocolate and hazelnut praline whipped cream, then the remaining top half of the cake layer is added and is spread with more caramel sauce. After the cake chills and is unmolded, the whole cake is covered with whipped cream and decorated with chocolate flames of glory. It is gorgeous.

Baking Answers ⤖ The chocolate cake layer is a half recipe of the chocolate cake that is used in the Chocolate Bride's Cake on page 304, but it has chocolate chips added to the batter. The caramel sauce is a double recipe of the caramel sauce from the Cranberry Caramel Buckle on page 349. The filling is milk chocolate truffle that is whipped with cream and uses the same technique found in the Orange-and-White Chocolate Truffle Cake on page 326. Hazelnut praline is added to the whipped cream filling and is made by the same method as the almond praline in the Double Decker Raspberry and Almond Praline Cheesecake (page 366). This all adds up to a very fancy cake that can be prepared ahead in several stages using some familiar components.

The chocolate chips sink to the bottom half of the chocolate cake layer, making it easier to split the cake layer in half horizontally. If you prefer chocolate chips throughout the cake layer, use miniature chocolate chips. I prefer the more pronounced texture and taste of the large chocolate chips and don't mind that they end up in only half of the cake, since they are present in every bite of cake.

The 9-inch-diameter springform pan is used to bake the cake, then washed and used as a mold to assemble the cake. If you prefer, the cake layer can bake in a 9 x 2-inch round cake pan. The necessities list may look long, but all of the equipment has been used in previous recipes.

A Step Ahead ◦ Although this recipe looks long, this cake lends itself to being prepared in stages, and some components can be prepared a week or more ahead. Before the whipped cream is added, the cake must be assembled and refrigerated in the springform pan at least 6 hours ahead, but it can remain in the refrigerator for up to 2 days. On serving day, unmold the cake, cover it with whipped cream, and add the chocolate decorations. The caramel sauce can be prepared up to a week ahead, cooled, poured into a heatproof container, covered, and refrigerated for up to 1 week. When you are ready to use it, heat the caramel sauce in a small saucepan over low heat until it softens.

The cake layer can be baked, cooled, wrapped in plastic wrap and heavy aluminum foil, and frozen for up to 1 month. Defrost the cake layer with its wrapping on at room temperature.

The hazelnut praline can be made up to 3 months ahead and frozen. To freeze the praline, put the crushed or ground praline in a plastic freezer container and press plastic wrap onto it. Cover the container tightly and freeze. The praline can be used directly from the freezer. Spoon out the amount needed and return any remaining praline to the freezer.

The chocolate decorations can be prepared, covered, and refrigerated up to 5 days. Or, they can be wrapped carefully and frozen in a metal or rigid plastic container for up to 3 months. Use the decorations cold or frozen.

SERVES 12 TO 16

Necessities ◦ *One 9-inch springform pan with sides at least 2¾ inches high, 1 wire rack for cooling the cake layer, a heatproof container for melting the chocolate in the oven, a heavy 2-quart frying pan (preferably with a nonstick finish), 1 baking sheet for holding the chocolate decorations*

CHOCOLATE AND CHOCOLATE CHIP CAKE LAYER

1½ ounces unsweetened chocolate, chopped
1 cup cake flour
1 tablespoon unsweetened Dutch process cocoa powder, such as Droste or Hershey's European
½ teaspoon baking powder
½ teaspoon baking soda
¼ teaspoon salt
3 ounces (¾ stick) soft unsalted butter
¾ cup plus 2 tablespoons sugar
1 large egg
1 large egg yolk
1 teaspoon vanilla extract
1½ cups sour cream
¼ cup water
1 cup (6 ounces) semisweet chocolate chips

HAZELNUT PRALINE POWDER— MAKES ABOUT 2 CUPS

¾ cup sugar
1 cup (about 4 ounces) peeled hazelnuts (page 40), toasted at 350°F. for about 15 minutes until golden

MILK CHOCOLATE PRALINE WHIPPED CREAM FILLING

1 cup whipping cream
2 tablespoons (¼ stick) unsalted butter
12 ounces chopped milk chocolate, Callebaut or Lindt preferred
1¼ cups cold whipping cream
1 teaspoon vanilla extract
¾ cup hazelnut praline powder (see above recipe)

2 recipes caramel sauce (1½ cups), cooked in a 4-quart saucepan and cooled until warm to the touch and pourable, about 30 minutes (page 349, for Cranberry Caramel Buckle)

WHIPPED CREAM TOPPING

1½ cups cold whipping cream
2 tablespoons powdered sugar
1 teaspoon vanilla extract

*Chocolate flame decorations for
garnish, optional, about 20 pieces
chocolate rectangles (4 inches long
and about 1½ inches wide) with
1 ragged (flamelike) edge on a
narrow end (pages 49–50)*

Mix the Cake

❧ Position a rack in the middle of the oven. Preheat the oven to 175°F. Butter the inside of a 9-inch-diameter springform pan with sides at least 2¾ inches high. Line the bottom of the pan with parchment or wax paper and butter the paper.

Place the unsweetened chocolate pieces in a heatproof container and melt them in the oven, about 12 minutes. As soon as the chocolate is melted, remove it from the oven and stir it smooth. Increase the oven temperature to 350°F. Set the chocolate aside to cool slightly while you mix the cake.

Sift the cake flour, cocoa powder, baking powder, baking soda, and salt onto a piece of wax paper or into a medium bowl and set aside.

Put the butter and sugar in a large bowl and beat with an electric mixer on medium speed until the mixture looks fluffy and the color lightens, about 3 minutes. The mixture looks sugary and has clumps of blended butter and sugar rather than a completely smooth mass. Move the beaters around in the bowl if using a handheld electric mixer. Stop the mixer and scrape the mixture from the sides of the bowl and any that becomes caught in the beaters as needed throughout the mixing process. Decrease the speed to low and mix in the melted chocolate, mixing just to combine it with the butter mixture. Increase the speed to medium and add the egg and egg yolk, beating for 1 minute after adding them. Decrease the speed to low and add the vanilla and sour cream, mixing just until the sour cream is incorporated. Add half of the flour mixture, mixing to incorporate it. Add the water, mixing to incorporate it. Add the remaining flour mixture, mixing just until all of the flour is completely incorporated into the batter. Stop the mixer and scrape the sides of the bowl after the last addition of flour. Use a large spoon to stir the chocolate chips into the batter. Use a rubber spatula to scrape all of the batter into the prepared pan. Smooth the top.

Bake the Cake

❧ Bake in the preheated oven for about 40 minutes. To test for doneness, gently press your fingers on the top middle of the cake. It should feel firm. If the cake feels firm, insert a toothpick into the center of the cake. When the toothpick comes out clean, the cake is done. If the toothpick penetrates a chocolate chip, test another spot.

Cool the cake layer in its baking pan on a wire rack for 15 minutes. Use a small, sharp knife to loosen the sides of the cake from the pan and release the sides. Invert the cake onto the wire rack. Lift off the bottom of the pan and carefully remove the paper liner, but let the paper rest on the cake while it cools. If any chocolate chips stick to the paper, replace them on the bottom of the cake. Cool the cake thoroughly and discard the paper liner. Wash and dry the springform pan so it is ready to use to assemble the cake.

Make the Praline Powder

◦ Lightly oil a metal baking sheet.

Put the sugar in a heavy 2-quart frying pan, preferably with a nonstick interior, and cook over medium heat, stirring occasionally with a wooden spoon, until the sugar begins to melt, about 2 minutes. When the sugar begins to melt and turn golden, stir the sugar constantly until it turns an evenly dark golden color, about 6 minutes. Small lumps of hard sugar will form that melt as the sugar caramelizes completely. Add the nuts, stirring them for about 1 minute with the wooden spoon to coat them completely with the caramelized sugar. The mixture will turn a slightly darker golden color. Immediately pour the hazelnut praline onto the baking sheet, spreading it with the wooden spoon. The mixture is thick and spreads to a thick layer. Be careful as the mixture is very hot. Cool the praline until it hardens and is cool to the touch, about 25 minutes.

Break the praline into 1- to 2-inch pieces. Wrap pieces of praline in heavy aluminum foil and use a clean mallet, rolling pin, or meat pounder to crush the praline into approximately ¼- to ½-inch pieces. To prepare the praline powder, transfer the crushed praline to a food processor fitted with a metal blade and process for about 30 seconds, just until the praline forms a powder. Overprocessing can turn the praline into a paste, but this actually takes some time and is not likely to happen.

Make the Milk Chocolate Truffle for the Whipped Cream Filling

◦ Put the 1 cup cream and the butter in a large saucepan and heat over medium-low heat until the cream is hot and the butter is melted. The hot cream mixture will form tiny bubbles and measure about 175°F. if tested with a food thermometer. Do not let the mixture boil. Remove the pan from the heat. Add the chopped milk chocolate and let it melt in the hot cream mixture for about 30 seconds to soften. Whisk the mixture smooth. If all of the chocolate is not melted, return the mixture to low heat for about 1 minute, stirring the mixture until the milk chocolate is melted and smooth. Remove the pan from any heat.

Set the milk chocolate mixture aside at room temperature until it is cool to the touch (about 87°F. if tested with a food thermometer), about 10 minutes. The mixture cools quickly. If your kitchen is warm, you can refrigerate it for 5 to 10 minutes to cool it, but the mixture should remain pourable.

Whip the Cream Filling

↝ Put the 1¼ cups cold cream, the vanilla, and the slightly cooled milk chocolate mixture in a large bowl and beat with an electric mixer on medium-high speed until it thickens, about 2 minutes. Move the beaters around in the bowl if using a handheld electric mixer. The movement of the beaters forms a distinct pattern of curving lines in the filling at this stage. The mixture firms as it chills with the cake, but if the milk chocolate mixture was too warm and the cream does not thicken, refrigerate it for about 20 minutes or until it is cold and beat it again with the electric mixer for about 30 seconds until it thickens. Use a rubber spatula to stir in the hazelnut praline powder. It is not necessary to defrost the praline powder if it is frozen. Set the filling aside in the refrigerator while you begin to assemble the cake.

Assemble the Cake

↝ The cake should be top side down on the wire rack. Use a large, serrated knife and a sawing motion to cut the cooled cake layer evenly into 2 horizontal layers. Cut into the cake layer with the serrated knife, turning the cake as you cut through to the middle until you have cut through the cake layer. To remove the top half of the cake layer, slide the removable bottom of a tart pan between the 2 layers and move the top piece to the side. Carefully slide the bottom of the spring-form pan under the remaining cake layer, centering it to cover the pan bottom. Replace the sides of the springform pan. The cake may not quite come to the edge of the pan. Pour half of the caramel sauce evenly over the cake in the pan. Use a rubber spatula to scrape all of the milk chocolate whipped cream over the caramel and smooth the top. Carefully slide the reserved cake layer onto the chocolate cream. Pour the remaining caramel sauce evenly over the cake. Insert several toothpicks in the cake to protect the caramel from sticking to the plastic wrap. Cover the cake with plastic wrap and refrigerate for at least 6 hours or up to 2 days.

Whip the Cream and Frost the Cake

↝ Put the 1½ cups cream and the powdered sugar and vanilla in a large bowl and beat with an electric mixer on medium speed until the whipped cream is firm enough to hold its shape and to spread. If using a handheld electric mixer, move the beaters around in the bowl. If you stop the mixer and lift up the beaters, the cream forms a point that stands straight up when the beaters are removed. The movement of the beaters first forms smooth curving then wrinkled lines in the cream at this stage. The whipped cream looks smooth and is firmly whipped.

Remove the cold cake from the refrigerator and uncover it. Release and remove the sides of the springform pan. Remove any toothpicks. Either leave the cake on the springform bottom or preferably, slide a large sharp knife under the cake to loosen it from the bottom of the pan. Slide the removable bottom of a tart pan under the cake and slide the cake onto a serving plate. Wipe any crumbs off the plate. Use a thin metal spatula to spread the whipped cream over the top and sides of the cake.

Add the Flames, If Desired

⤚ Carefully press the chocolate flame rectangles, ragged side up, onto the sides of the cake, overlapping them slightly. It will take about 18 rectangles to cover the sides, but make additional ones to allow for breakage. The rectangles should rise over the top edge of the cake.

Serve or cover carefully with plastic wrap and refrigerate up to 2 days. Inserting several toothpicks into the top of the cake keeps the plastic wrap from disturbing the whipped cream. Use a large sharp knife to cut the cake into slices and serve cold. A sharp knife cuts easily through the chocolate decoration. Leftover cake can be covered carefully with plastic wrap and stored in the refrigerator for up to 2 days.

Epilogue

I gave a big sigh when I finished writing this book, but it was not a sigh of relief. It was a nostalgic sigh that it was over, for now anyway. Whether I realized it or not, I have spent most of my life preparing to write this book. It began the first time I climbed up on a chair in my mother's kitchen to help her bake some of the thousands of cookies she made during my childhood. Mom and I never hiked a mountain together or traveled to exotic cities; we shared our fun times by baking together. We talked, we mixed, we rolled, we baked, and we filled the house with our laughter and the scent of chocolate melting, butter browning, and brown sugar bubbling.

That was my mother's legacy to me. It is the one I am passing on to my children and that they will pass on someday to their offspring. I hope with this book that I can extend the legacy to you, so wherever you are, your home can be filled with buttery cookies, chocolate cakes, and apple pies. Baking is great fun—pass it on.

Mail-Order Sources

BRIDGE KITCHENWARE

214 East 52nd Street
New York, NY 10022
(800) 274-3435 or (212) 838-1901
Fax: (212) 758-5387
www.bridgekitchenware.com

Large selection of kitchen equipment that includes nonstick liners, parchment paper, and heavy baking sheets. They stock many imported kitchen utensils.

BUCHANAN HOLLOW NUT COMPANY

6510 Minturn Road
LeGrand, CA 95933
(800) 532-1500
Fax: (209) 389-4321
www.bhnc.com

High-quality nuts, organic raisins, and dried fruit.

HADLEY FRUIT ORCHARDS

P.O. Box 495
Cabazon, CA 92230
(800) 854-5655
Fax: (909) 849-8580
www.hadleyfruitorchards.com

Good selection of quality nuts and dried fruits, including pears and cherries.

KING ARTHUR FLOUR'S BAKER'S CATALOGUE

P.O. Box 876
Norwich, VT 05055
(800) 827-6836
Fax: (800) 343-3002
www.kingarthurflour.com

Equipment and baking ingredients, including unbleached all-purpose flour, Callebaut chocolate, peeled hazelnuts, almond paste, parchment paper, and nonstick liners.

NEW YORK CAKE AND BAKING CENTER

56 West 22nd Street
New York, NY 10010
(212) 675-2253
Fax: (212) 675-7099
www.nycakesupplies.com

Large assortment of baking equipment and decorating supplies, including edible royal icing flowers, many colors and sizes of glitter, sprinkles, dragees, and other decorations, paper baking cups in many sizes and colors.

PENZEYS SPICES

P.O. Box 933
W19362 Apollo Drive
Muskego, WI 53150
(800) 741-7787
Fax: (262) 679-7878
www.penzeys.com

Complete selection of fresh spices and dried herbs. Source for high-quality extra-fancy Vietnamese cassia cinnamon.

WILLIAMS-SONOMA

P.O. Box 379900
Las Vegas, NV 89137
(800) 541-2233
Fax: (405) 717-6077
www.williams-sonoma.com

Baking equipment and ingredients.

ZINGERMAN'S

422 Detroit Street
Ann Arbor, MI 48104
(888) 636-8162
Fax: (734) 769-1260
www.zingermans.com

Callebaut chocolate; ships for 2-day delivery.

Bibliography

Anderson, Kenneth N. and Lois E. *The International Dictionary of Food and Nutrition.* New York: John Wiley and Sons, 1993.

Bloom, Carole. *The International Dictionary of Desserts, Pastries, and Confections.* New York: Hearst Books, 1995.

Cunningham, Marion. *The Fannie Farmer Baking Book.* New York: Wings Books, 1984.

Herbst, Sharon Tyler. *Food Lover's Companion.* New York: Barron's, 3d edition, 2001.

Labensky, Steven, Gaye G. Ingram, and Shara R. Labensky. *Webster's New World Dictionary of Culinary Arts.* Englewood Cliffs, NJ: Prentice Hall, 1997.

McGee, Harold. *On Food and Cooking.* New York: Macmillan, 1984.

Whitman, Joan, and Dolores Simon. *Recipes into Type.* New York: HarperCollins, 1993.

Index

GAYLORD M